OS
ESTADOS UNIDOS
DO
BRAZIL

THE CONQUEST OF BRAZIL *by* ROY NASH

WITH EIGHT MAPS AND SEVENTY-SEVEN ILLUSTRATIONS

BIBLO and TANNEN
NEW YORK
1 9 6 8

Printed in U.S.A. by
NOBLE OFFSET PRINTERS, INC.
NEW YORK 3, N. Y.

SAUDAÇÃO

BRAZIL—immense; fantastic; green, and brown, and sear.
Forests of deadly silence. Prairies, and pack trains, and the
sound of a guitar. Gay cities robed in the sparkle of modernity, cities becoming strident with the cry of the machine. Dugouts gliding down sluggish rivers and coffee in straight rows to
the far horizon. Gold in the gravels, gold on the cacao stems,
the golden crown of the *ipé*. Mud and melancholy. And the
march of human hosts against the embattled forces of nature.

When Cabral touched her shore in 1500 it was all a great
wilderness; and two-thirds of Brazil is still *sertão*, as they call
the large wild. But in the traversing of these four centuries,
Man has set his mark upon the wilderness. His canoe has ventured down unimagined rivers. The footprints of his steed
have made a path across the prairie. His herds have spread
over pampa and plateau, cropping the sweet grass. His pick
and shovel and pan have separated golden dust and diamonds
from the gravels accumulated by the ages. The fires of his
cultivation are everywhere eating into the margins of the forest.
No man may say where civilization ceases and the sertão begins. As you approach and try to define a boundary, it eludes
like the details of a dream. But the progress of its retreat and
the process by which man is conquering the Brazilian wilderness are not difficult to portray.

That is my story, a narrative of the interaction of land and
people. Too much land and too few people. The marks
made by mankind upon the land, and the impress of plain and
plateau and mountain upon mankind. This is not a book of
travel; although in its preparation I have traveled in every
state of Brazil except Piauhy and Goyaz, and visited Portugal

to question the old mother of the greatest of South American republics. Nor does *The Conquest of Brazil* make pretense either of photographic accuracy or of exhaustiveness; in order to bring the activities of four centuries upon a continental stage within one field of view, I have tried to look at a vast array of facts through a reducing glass so powerful that all insignificant details will be reduced below the limit of vision, leaving facts of social significance standing out boldly from a stark background. An impressionistic sketch, yet one based upon the best science of my time.

In the days of the eclipse of one of the world's greatest empires, Brazil inherited from her doddering parent one of the two or three finest landed properties in the world, an estate larger than the United States. How has the heir handled his property? Has he developed it? has he planted and cultivated it? or has he spent his patrimony in riotous living? Are his tenants happy, healthy, schooled, and productive? or does he squeeze them pretty hard, perhaps to his own detriment?

The landlords and city dwellers who govern Brazil number not over five millions; the men and women next the soil are twenty-five million strong. My field glasses are focussed upon the man on the land. I am interested in Nature only as she has modified that man. I deal with climate, and forests, and the shape of the earth's crust only because they condition that man's development in Brazil. With other prepossessions of science this book has no concern. Belles-lettres and the pursuit of beauty by the classes I omit to make room for a discussion of such topics as the burdens of hookworm and illiteracy borne by the masses. All the world knows of the brilliant folk who dwell on the shores of Guanabára Bay; knows Rio the gorgeous and São Paulo the industrious. He who reads herein will learn something, too, of the man who dwells in the mud hut: of the *gaucho* who rides herd over the cattle on the pampas of Rio Grande do Sul, the *matuto* who makes his clearing in the edge of the jungle, the *sertanejo* produced by the droughts and famines of the arid northeast, the *seringueiro* who gathers rubber in the wet, wet waste of Amazonas.

If an astronomer wants to know where a comet is going and when it is likely to get there, he plots its path through a bit of the heavens and sees where the curve leads. If a farmer wants to know where his neighbor's creaking oxcart is going, he saunters down to the bars and asks the driver as the cart goes by. Brazil is neither a comet nor an oxcart, but by roughly plotting her course for the four centuries during which she has been on the map, and by asking the present drivers of her destiny whither they are bound, one may arrive at a rational idea of the direction and rate of her evolution.

ROY NASH.

6 April, 1926.

ACKNOWLEDGMENT

THE criticism of manuscript-in-the-making is as thankless a task as dressing a buck that somebody else has shot. I feel heavily indebted to those who read parts of mine: Dr. Clark Wissler, Curator of Anthropology in the American Museum of Natural History; Dr. W. E. B. Du Bois, America's foremost authority on the Negro; Dr. Isaiah Bowman, Director of the American Geographical Society; Dr. Lewis Wendell Hackett, for six years Regional Director for Brazil of the International Health Board; Mr. Murdo Mackenzie, formerly managing director of the Brazilian Land, Cattle, and Packing Company; Dr. Wilson Popenoe, Agricultural Explorer, Bureau of Plant Industry, United States Department of Agriculture; and two of my former colleagues of the Philippine Forest Service who have made themselves equally masters of the Brazilian bush, Dr. H. N. Whitford, Professor of Tropical Forestry in the Yale Forest School and Chief of the Crude Rubber Survey, United States Department of Commerce, and Mr. Hugh Curran, recently resident manager of Colonia do Gongogy in the State of Bahia. That I have endeavored to burnish my tale on the emery wheels of their special knowledge should not be construed as an attempt to cloak my heresies with the mantle of their approval. They have afforded me sanctuary within the portals of their kindliness; I alone am responsible for the crime.

CONTENTS

Book I

THE PEOPLING OF THE LANDS

CONTENTS

Book II

THE ESSENTIAL FACTS OF HUMAN GEOGRAPHY

Book III

SOME ESSENTIALS OF HUMAN HAPPINESS

CONTENTS

Book IV

LOOKING AHEAD

LIST OF MAPS AND ILLUSTRATIONS

MAPS

ILLUSTRATIONS

xiv

Book I

THE PEOPLING OF THE LANDS

CHAPTER I

ANNO DOMINI 1500

IT was glorious to be Pope on New Year's Day, in the year of our Lord 1500. Although Copernicus was then gazing at the stars, he had not yet vetoed the edicts which declared Our World the center of the universe, and reduced us to the contemptible position of a satellite of the sun. The monk, Luther, was pacing the floor and plotting treason but not yet offering disputation. Although the great Crusades were over, the crusading spirit was by no means dead. The Holy Inquisition was working splendidly; and over in Spain an imaginative boy of eight was growing up to carry the Cross to Indians and Asiatics whose very existence was as yet undreamed, St. Ignatius of Loyola.

It was very splendid to be a king on New Year's Day in the year 1500, and the two who ruled over the Iberian Peninsula had every reason to be pleased with their jobs. The King of Spain had recently received the continent of North America as a present from an Italian mariner named Columbus; and only three months before, one Vasco da Gama had returned from Calicut with Africa and India as a souvenir for the King of Portugal. Over on the next peninsula, a clever Florentine named Machiavelli was busy gathering material for handbooks designed to improve the kingly technique of profiting by such opportunities; Leonardo da Vinci, Raphael, and Michelangelo were adorning the civilization of the day; and although the Swiss Confederation had just gone frankly republican, it was such a diminutive oasis in the desert of absolute monarchy that a king could don his raiment of divine right and ride forth to greet the best of all possible worlds.

3

Particularly the King of Portugal, with the new title which he was trying on that morning for the first time—"LORD OF THE CONQUEST, NAVIGATION AND COMMERCE OF ETHIOPIA, ARABIA, PERSIA, AND INDIA." One of his trusty skippers, Pedro Alvares Cabral, was even then loading his ships with hardtack and port wine and gunpowder, preparatory to discovering Brazil on his way out to assume for the Crown of Portugal the monopoly of the greatest commercial prize in the known world—the trade of Asia. Lisbon was about to become as preëminent in the commerce of the sixteenth century as London in the nineteenth or New York in the twentieth, and the King of Portugal the Croesus of his generation.

Down in the middle latitudes along the west coast of Africa, New Year's Day, 1500, did not dawn so bright. Half a century before, as the blacks were setting fire to the bush in preparation for the big annual hunt, eight birds with snow white wings had appeared floating upon the western water. The blacks flocked to the shore to gaze in wonder. The wings were folded, and men came from beneath them to the shore, strange men, men who wore clothes, men with white skins. And these white men had taken two hundred of the tribe away on the white-winged monsters, into the Unknown. The blacks of West Africa did not fully understand that they were needed to work for the Pope, on the domains of the Order of Christ, in the Algarves, in Portugal. All they knew was that of the two hundred, not one came back. And these visits had become ever more frequent since that fatal day. White hands, in whose clutches naked black bodies writhed powerless, reached out of the North, reached up from the sea, and grasped their daughters and sons, their chiefs, and their priests, and their most stalwart warriors. Into the Unknown they went, in chains. Not one came back. Calamity brooded above the blacks of West Africa on New Year's Day, in the year of our Lord 1500.

But across the blue water to the west, other gentle savages reclined in their hammocks along the Amazon, naked brown tobacco-smokers unconcerned about the morrow, for they still had three months to rehearse for the ceremony of being discovered and there was probably not one among those Hopeless Heretycks who would have offered a Brazil nut for all the blessings Christianity had to confer. The simple souls did not even know that 1500, the Year of their Doom, had dawned.

Portuguese, Negroes, Indians.

These are to play the leading parts in the drama we are about to witness. As they all speak different languages and none of them speak English, perhaps a word of introduction before they come upon the stage may make the action more clear.

CHAPTER II

THE SEED

§ 1. THE INDIAN IN BRAZIL

SOME knowledge of the Indian is more essential to an understanding of Brazil than of the United States. We eliminated him from our civilization so far as we were able, and isolated him upon reservations where he participates in our daily life to about the same extent as the inmates of a pesthouse. In Brazil, the Indian's adaptation to the environment was preserved and absorbed to a great extent; and today Indian elements are quite as important constituents, of both the blood and the culture of the republic, as are Portuguese.

It is just as well to confess at the outset that less is known about the Indians of Brazil than about the aborigines of any other region in the two Americas. Indeed, there still exist tribes in the Amazon forest which are experiencing their first contact with white men in the twentieth century. What we do know about the Indian, fortunately for the general reader, has recently been brought together by Dr. Clark Wissler in a splendid work which gives for the first time within the covers of one book the outstanding results of the specialized research in both continents.[1]

Anthropologists no longer doubt the Asiatic origin of the American Indian. For a long time Science fastened upon him the status of a foundling, wandering over the two Americas with uncertain relations to the rest of the human race, speaking a perfect babel of languages belonging to one hundred and sixty-nine distinct *stocks,* no one of which has so far been identified with any Asiatic or European tongue. Today, the

[1] Clark Wissler, *The American Indian* (2nd ed.; New York, 1922).

prints of his moccasins have been traced back until his tracks
become indistinguishable in those of the Mongoloid-red horde
from which Mongolians are likewise descended; and living
relatives in Asia have been found to mitigate the loneliness of
these, his swiftly declining years. He paraded across the
Alaskan corridor with the rest of the mammals, following the
old track beaten by the primates which preceded him, and probably driven by the same urge.[2]

At just what period in the development of the race the
American Indian branched off from the Mongoloid-red stream
of humanity, we cannot yet say. Positive evidence of his presence in America before the last shrinkage of the polar ice-
cap is so far lacking. Yet the profound dissimilarity of culture
and language between America and Asia argues for a very
early and long-continued separation. So distinguished an anthropologist as Franz Boas holds that man reached North
America during an interglacial period; and to Wissler, too, it
seems reasonable to assume that man drifted over into America at about the same time that he entered Europe in numbers,
the return of the ice dividing the American from the paternal
stock and forcing him to go his separate way. Here, however,
we are on controversial ground.

There is no longer controversy about his foreign origin,
about his relatives in Asia, or about his crossing from Siberia
to Alaska, drifting down through the northern continent, and
finally crossing by way of the Isthmus of Panama and the
Antilles into the continent which is our present concern. That
does not deny the possibility of stray canoes coming now and
then to our western shore from Polynesia, but it does negate
the theory that man originally came to America by way of the
islands of the Pacific.

Neither is there any longer reason to doubt the essential
homogeneity of physical type of the great bulk of the Indians
of both continents. The hair of the original American was

[2] William B. Scott, *A History of Land Mammals in the Western Hemisphere*, p. 588.

straight, black, and scant on the body. The eyes were dark brown. The skin color ranged from yellowish to chocolate tones. The face was markedly broad in proportion to the width of head. And more than ninety out of every one hundred Indians had incisor teeth which were distinctly shovel-shaped, concave, a characteristic rare in Europeans or Negroes.

Within that type, in Brazil as in the United States, there were many superb physiques. There was much truth in the first sentence ever written about the Indian in Brazil. It is found in the letter dated 1 May, 1500, from Pero Vaz de Caminha to his King, D. Manoel, "the fortunate" (Cabral nodding approval over the shoulder of his scribe as he wrote):

"These people are good, simple folk, and can be moulded to any form we elect. And since the Lord has given them good bodies and good faces—the bodies and faces of good men—I think He did it for some good purpose."

We know less about the Indians of the Plateau or the Pampas before civilization set its mark upon them; but we are on eminently safe ground in affirming that a large proportion of the Indians in the Amazon Basin and south along the coast, in the days before the coming of the Portuguese, were very fine types of men and women physically.[3]

Although I am far from convinced of the importance many anthropologists attach to cranial measurements, it should perhaps be noted that among American Indians are found some of the highest cephalic indices exhibited by the human race; i.e., such tribes were evolved later than either the Nordic or Mediterranean types in Europe, according to that school of anthropology.[4]

Besides a fine physique, what other equipment for a man's job did the Indian bring with him when he ran away from his home in Asia and struck out for himself in the Americas?

---

[3] Alfred Russel Wallace, *Travels on the Amazon and Rio Negro* (London, 1853), p. 478. See also Prince Adalbert of Prussia, *Travels on the Xingú*, II, 251.

[4] See Griffith Taylor, "The Evolution and Distribution of Race, Culture, and Language," *Geog. Rev.* (New York), Jan., 1921.

When a weapon like the bow is found in every nook and corner from Patagonia and Pernambuco to Greenland and Alaska, it hints strongly at an early introduction. Among the traits of culture which likewise have such a wide distribution as to convince anthropologists of their early arrival, are the dog, the spear-thrower, the lip plug, the fire drill, coil basketry, string-twisting, stone-chipping, and the lean-to shelter. Cereals, cattle, the wheel, the plow—those four traits which express so much of the culture of Asia—not one came over. The existence of primitive hunters in Patagonia makes it permissible to picture the first man who gazed upon the Gulf of Darien as entering South America with no more than some such simple bag of tricks upon his bronzed back.

Before man, however, there was Manioc!

And manioc was destined to play such a tremendous part in the history of Brazil that emperors and conquerors, priests and politicians, shrink into insignificance in contrast. In the Tupi language, *mandi* means bread and *óca* the house, and *"mandioca"* they named it. A plant which grows without cultivation or fertilization, from a cutting stuck into the unprepared earth of any clearing in the forest; a sort of elder brother of the potato whose great tubers two or three feet long ripen in from five to nine months but which will patiently await harvesting for a year or more thereafter!

The products, in palatable forms upon which alone life can be supported, are as numerous as the varieties of the plant. The non-poisonous varieties can be eaten raw if the fire should fail; hogs, cattle, horses, relish it as they do corn. Boil the root and you have something not unlike a sweet potato. Soak the roots in water until they are soft enough to be broken by hand, roast the fragments, and the product, "water flour," contains practically the whole ingredient. Shred the pulp of other varieties, squeeze out the poisonous juice, roast the beautiful white flakes, and you have a flour of the consistency of coarse cornmeal, which has lost some of the starch along with the juice but which is endowed in a superlative degree with those two greatest qualities that a staple food can possess—keeping quality and compactness for transport. Manioc meal will keep at least two or three weeks even in the hot, moist lowlands of Amazonas. When sealed in five-gallon kerosene tins, agricultural explorers from our Bureau of Plant Industry found it would keep several years.[5] It is ever ready to eat without further preparation.

Earth never bestowed upon her favorite child a finer gift. In the Indian legend, from the sorrows of Atiolo, the Parecis maiden who was buried alive that her body might serve her people, Manioc was born. Like an ever-willing handmaid she accompanied Man in all his wandering and his waiting in Brazil until he came to the fringe of the forest and saw herds of guanaco grazing upon the pampas. And when he was hungry, she provisioned the board out of the abundance of her being. Northward through the whole sweep of the Antilles she became the staff upon which he leaned; as after the discovery of America she crossed the wide waters to minister to the daily need of all the black peoples of Africa.[6] She who had been scorned in life became very great in death —the greatest of many gifts the southern continent held in store for the man we left standing beside the Gulf of Darien.

Any detailed description of his dispersal throughout the continent from that point would be pure conjecture, nor is it important. Obviously, three lines of least resistance led away from Panama. The first was along the seashore to the east. The second followed the longitudinal valleys and plateaus of the Andes, a way free from impenetrable forest growth, temperate in the main, inviting to men in whose protoplasm still lingered memories of northern homes. This Continental Corridor lead-ing to the grassy plains of the La Plata drainage and the Far South became the highroad beside which arose the only civilization that developed in South America, that of the Inca of Peru. The third line of dispersal is the most extensive

---

[5] Wilson Popenoe, U.S. Dept. of Agriculture, in a personal letter.
[6] Jean Brunhes, *Human Geography*, p. 274.

network of inland waterways in the world, more than forty thousand miles of navigable rivers which head in the high Andes and lead everywhere throughout the great plains of Venezuela, Colombia, Brazil, Paraguay, Uruguay, and Argentina. Whether man first dived into this watery kingdom from the Andes or from the Antilles, we cannot say. All that concerns us here is that the Indian was dispersed throughout every part of South America long, long before the year 1500, where I have chosen to stand for a moment and look about, before the curtain rises upon the modern Brazilian drama.

It is not easy to picture a people. It is doubly difficult to picture a people who have passed. And I suppose it is about as impossible for a civilized mind to enter sympathetically into the mind of a naked forest Indian as it is for a rich man to enter the Kingdom of Heaven. There are certain things which we can say about all Brazilian Indians which suggest the living realities, crudely, as those scratches in the caves of Altamira and Alter do Chão suggest the mammoth shapes those artists of the Reindeer Age had in mind.

Yet how am I, with almost illegible pen scratches, to make you understand these things, you whose ear is attuned to the metallic rhythm of industrial civilization? The note of the anvil bird in the cool depth of the forest is so different from the clang of the anvil in the heat of the factory. The howling of monkeys in the jungle vibrates a deeper chord within us than the periods of the politician or the evensong of a prima donna. And a naked forest Indian is something so much more vital than a catalogue of characteristics! It will be plainer if we look first into three characteristic Indian homes. If you have the stomach for it, leave all behind except those remnants of the savage which linger deep within the most civilized of us, and journey with me back along the years.

We take canoe at Belém, where the Amazon greets the sea, and fight its current until we come to where the black waters of the Rio Negro enter from the north. We pole, and paddle, and pull along the banks of the Rio Negro into the heart of this green inferno of stinging pests, so far beyond the edge of the world that we abandon all hope of escaping the narrowing jaws of this overwhelmingly fecund monster, jaws which close upon us the more crushingly as we enter the Rio Uaupés up in the extreme northwest corner of Brazil. And when two thousand miles of winding water bordered by four thousand miles of monotonous green has made its mark upon our souls, we leave the too great publicity of this desolate highway and enter the still greater solitude of a canoe-path, above which the entangled crowns of the forest completely close. Suddenly a huge form looms in the rain that is drenching the jungle. It is a *maloca,* a long house of the forest Indians; and we have come to our journey's end.

The chief comes to the water's edge and greets us with quiet dignity as friends from afar whom he has no cause to fear. From the height of our superior culture we gaze at the crude structure over which he presides, as some caliph of Moorish Spain might have gazed upon the dwellings of the lords of medieval Europe, "chimneyless, windowless, and with a hole in the roof for the smoke to escape, like the wigwams of certain Indians." [7] But not so fast! A closer inspection will reveal much to admire. The uprights are selected from among the most durable timbers that grow. The beams and rafters are straight, beautiful pieces of wood, proportioned to the stress of their loads, and bound together with withes of split rattan as neatly as any sailor rigs a spar. The eaves are low and the pitch of the roof steep; no rain, however torrential, will enter. And these walls of fan-shaped palm leaves are so cunningly and compactly thatched that neither arrow nor old-fashioned bullet will penetrate.

We are shown into the apartment of the chief and given space to hang our hammocks. The afternoon is drawing to a close, and it takes a moment for our eyes to grow accustomed to the gloom and the smoke that hangs under the soot-darkened

[7] John W. Draper, *The Intellectual Development of Europe* (revised ed.; New York, 1875), II, 31.

eaves; but an agreeable warmth and the sense of triumph
over the impotent rain driving against the thatch pervades our
being, even before we begin to differentiate the plan of the
interior. We find ourselves in a hall over a hundred feet long
by seventy-five wide and thirty high at the ridge. A partition
shoulder-high, of palm thatch, shuts off rather more than the
semicircular end for the chief and his four wives and their
children. Down the center runs an open passageway twenty
feet broad, lined by columns of upright posts which support
the roof, opened out in the center of the house to form a
dancing floor. Extending from this common passage to the
side walls are rows of more slender pillars filled in with a
screen of palm-thatch so as to form ten or a dozen separate
apartments, each of which serves for an entire family. The
resemblance of interior arrangement to certain twentieth-cen-
tury cafés puts you at your ease immediately. But no midnight cabaret of either Manhattan or Montmartre holds the
sensations that were commonplaces along the Amazon at such
annual festivals as the feast of the fruits, or the plucking of
the hair from the heads of the children, or the puberty rites
of the virgins.[8]

In each family apartment are pans, stools carved from solid
blocks of beautiful hardwood, cleverly woven baskets, water
pots of decorated pottery, blowguns eight feet long, bows and
arrows of cunning craftsmanship,—some tipped with poison so
deadly that the merest prick will start one on a journey to
the happy hunting grounds,—mats of rushes, a fireplace, and
the hammocks which are both beds and chairs. Not the cheap
cotton things that satisfy the standards of civilized North
America, but hammocks six feet wide woven of the fibers of
the *tucum* palm, as soft as the finest Panama hat, with strong
black patterns woven into the straw-colored body—objects of
great beauty, which make one of the two finest beds for the
hot tropics that mankind has devised. These things, and the
multiplicity of gay macaws, parrots, curassow birds, and mon-

[8] H. W. Bates, *The Naturalist on the Amazons.*

keys which swing and balance on each partition, constitute the private property of the inmates. Everything else is owned and used in common. The ovens for roasting manioc meal, the press for expressing the juice, pans and pottery jars for the beer, these are arranged in a communal kitchen which any one may use.

When we enter, there are not more than a dozen women puttering about their fires. A few old men: one weaving a basket, another repairing a fish net, the rest either squatting on their haunches or reclining in their hammocks. The women are quite naked except for the tightly laced garter they have worn from childhood to distend the calf, the body-hair and eyebrows carefully plucked, the hair of the head "bobbed" moderately short. Ornamentation was a masculine monopoly on the Uaupés. The black hair of the men is carefully parted in the middle, slicked back above the ears, and bound in a cue by a cord of monkey hair which hangs almost to their hips. Each wears an ornate comb of palm spines and toucan feathers, and a bit of straw keeps open the aperture pierced in the ear. Between their legs is passed a narrow piece of some soft inner bark secured at either end to a cord about the waist, and all wear garters. Other raiment have they none. When the Indian came out of the North and plunged into the tropics, he took off his clothes, like the sensible man he was.

With the body covered by their battle shields, it is easy to understand how such effeminate-looking warriors were mistaken for Amazons by the early explorers.

As night draws near, the women come home from the manioc patch in the forest, bearing baskets of roots to be made into bread on the morrow. The men return from their fishing. One brings a monkey he has shot. It disappears with the fish into the "pepper-pot," that widespread device of the tropics for camouflaging unsavory morsels of meat. We count a hundred human beings of all ages in the maloca when the great door is dropped for the night: a happy enough crowd, though taciturn, except for the girl of twelve whining up there

Typical forest Indian.

Left. Indian girls wearing the characteristic ear and lip plugs. Note the "bobbed" hair. *Right*. An Indian mother and child.

An Indian family group, showing the blowgun and flute.

in the smoky loft, on manioc and water, and little of that for a month, in preparation for the ceremonial beating that will proclaim her entrance into the full joys and privileges of womanhood; and for the three or four who shiver and moan beside their fire in the clutch of fever.

At dawn, as reveille rolls off the lips of the pan-pipes, every last man, woman, and child rushes out for the morning plunge —a forest Indian would no more think of missing his morning bath than would an English gentleman.

There is no rush to work after breakfast, yet these folk are far from being idlers. The women have their plantations to look after: crops of potatoes, yams, pineapples, maize, peppers, various fruits for which there are no names in English, plants for cordage and dyes, and tobacco—besides manioc. They have bread to bake every day upon the Uaupés. They have poisons to distill for tipping arrows and poisoning fish, an extrahazardous industry in which the mortality among the women was often higher than among the men who used them in war. There was generally a hungry youngster pulling at their breasts. No, the women of the forest Indians were not altogether idlers. In fact, a good woman was about the most valuable possession a man could acquire; if he had two or three, he counted himself rich.

Now the fact that these men were not entirely independent economically should not prejudice the modern mind against them. They cut down the timber in the forest when a plantation was to be made; and felling the hardwoods of the Amazon forest, by hacking with a stone ax and wedging, was no summer picnic. They made dugout canoes as large as fifty feet long by four wide, well fitted for dragging over the rocks of the rapids. They made beautiful weapons: the blowgun is a better arm for bringing down a bird from the lofty roof of the Amazon forest than a rifle. If the whole weight of agricultural labor devolved upon the women, the men assumed the functions of fishermen, hunters, and warriors. Their technique of getting fish with hooks of palm spines, ring nets, fish traps, elaborate weirs, baskets braced in the waterfalls to catch those carried over the brim, and by poison—to say nothing of diving and grasping them with bare hands in their native element—not many modern sportsmen can teach them any tricks. They knew the sand bars where the turtles bury their eggs and the trees where the bees secrete their honey; both bees and turtles were in their daily employ, if not on their pay roll.

But today no one is engaged in such mundane pursuits, for tonight is to be heard the music of the Juruparí. Every one is primping for the dance. It shall last so long as the *caxirí,* so let the great jars be filled unto their generous brims. Bring the wine of the *baccába* palm, the *patawá,* and the *assaí!* Bring the fermented excellence of corn, of sweet potatoes, of yams, of manioc! For tonight caxirí shall flow like water, and the children of the forest shall be gay! But what is that villainous smell? and what that mess charring in the oven? It is nothing villainous, O stranger from another world. It is the body of the strong man buried a month ago beneath the floor of clay on which we shall dance the night. In these charred fragments, which shall be burnt to powder and mingled with our wine even as you mingle sugar and spice with your red claret, lie the excellences of a departed friend.

Nightfall is come and toilettes have been made. Every canoe-path has disgorged its welcome load of guests. Four hundred men and women are gathered under the roof of the maloca, an assemblage with elements of beauty and raiment rare that no ballroom of ancient Babylon surpassed. Some twenty men are on the dance floor, each with hand on the shoulder next in crescent, splendid brown fellows standing five feet eight or ten. On their heads a coronet of red and yellow feathers, colored in the life by inoculating a macaw with the milky secretion from the skin of a toad. In their hair, combs from which droop the white plumes of the *garça real,* the egrets of the modern milliner; some even have the under tail-coverts of the harpy eagle. Cords of monkey hair hanging down the back terminate in feathery jewels that a Tiffany or Cartier might envy. In their ear lobes, one wears a gay feather, another a bundle of tiny arrows; and from the lower lip of a third hang three strings of some light seed. About the neck, suspended from a black chain, hangs a polished cylinder of translucent quartz. A simple ornament. Yet that one upon the breast of the Tushaúa, eight inches long and pierced from end to end, represents the labor of two lifetimes of titrating with sand and water and the leaf shoot of the wild plaintain, truly a regal ornament. About the waist of these valiant hunters the prized girdles of panthers' teeth. Upon the forehead a circlet of snowy, rose-tinged pendants that smile like mother-of-pearl, the "fish-eyes" of the *pescada*. About their ankles, chains of polished seed which rattle in the rhythm of the dance.

The women are more simply arrayed, as befits their sex. All have the garters, and like the men are painted in blacks and reds and yellows arranged in regular patterns; and those who enter the dance wear dainty aprons of beads or beaten bark, pretty nothings six inches square which are taken off and put away as soon as the dance is over.

Suddenly the women disappear in a panic of unfeigned terror. The dancing stops. All ears listen. Upon the silence of dusk breaks the music of pan-pipes and trumpets. Nearer it comes and more poignant grows its wail, the music of the Juruparí. For a female to look upon these sacred instruments, by design or accident, is to look upon certain death, by poison generally; and willingly a father yields his daughter or a husband his wife if she so deeply sin. Nor may these nervous young men begin to enter into the mystery of Juruparí until after the ceremonial beating which accompanies the puberty rites.

If you would see them, or the many mad things that are done when wine and rhythmic motion and terrific stimulants have done their work, you must go back to the many books about the Indian; or, better still, go to the Amazon before it is too late. For he who will penetrate far enough into the wilds of Amazonas can still see strange rites enough, although the day is probably not far off when they will linger only as dim tribal memories.

All I have tried to do here is to suggest a people who long since mastered the technique of abundantly supplying themselves with food and a comfortable place to sleep, and who went on to the making of beautiful things and clever adaptations of life to its environment; with surplus energy and wealth for no end of music and dancing, wine and women, enjoyed in their own savage way.

We leave them to peep in upon another family living in a rude skin tent upon the pampas of Rio Grande do Sul, at the extreme southern end of Brazil. This is the home of a primitive hunter, as the maloca of the Amazon was the home of agriculturists. Neither frost nor snow is unknown upon the pampas, and this Indian wears rude wraps against the cold, as his descendants today wear the poncho; nevertheless, when he went into battle he stripped down to the simplicity of his brothers under the equator. His whole culture is built about the herds of guanaco and the flocks of *emas* (the South American ostrich) that roam the grassy plains, even as the Indians of the Great Plains of the United States built theirs about the buffalo. His cleverness consists in whirling the bolas, those three rawhide-covered balls which swish through the air like an extended chicken track and wrap about whatever the thongs encounter, tripping the long-legged bird as it threw the forebear of the llama.

These are the ancestors of the Gaucho, the most picturesque man in modern Brazil; but they were destined to undergo such a complete revolution in culture as soon as horses and cattle put in an appearance upon the pampas that I defer my tribute to them until those animals arrive from Europe.

Until such time as the Brazilian Government completes an ethnological survey of existing Indian tribes, these two culture areas, the Amazon and the guanaco, are the only ones that stand out with any degree of clearness. The one occupied the riverine forest plains of the Amazon and Orinoco; the other prevailed not only in Rio Grande do Sul, but also in Uruguay, Paraguay, the pampas of Argentina, the Chaco, and must have included the extension of the grassy plains into Matto Grosso.

Yet the plateau of eastern Brazil is so different from either of those regions that it is obvious the plateau culture must have differed in many respects, particularly in the region that begins with the rolling prairies and bare mountains of Minas Geraes and sweeps northeast through Bahia and Pernambuco to Maranhão and Ceará. One is out of the evergreen forest in the southern part of the belt, and in its northern extension there is only that scrub growth known in Brazil as *caatinga*. Instead of the torrential rains of Amazonas, one gets periodic droughts which drive all animal life out of great sections. A canoe culture could not exist because there are comparatively few navigable streams. It is north of the range of the guanaco; so the staple food had to be something else. From the viewpoint of a man equipped with primitive technique, it is the least attractive region in Brazil.

We have hints of what their lives were like. The Tapuya language stock was distributed all over this region; and many who spoke Tapuyan tongues were apparently primitive hunters leading very nomadic careers, planting little if anything, and building no permanent shelters. One sixteenth-century writer says they did not know how to swim, but would go leagues up a river hunting for a ford in order to reach the other side.[9] The Botocudos, some of whom still exist in southern Bahia and northern Espirito Santo, have always wandered as small nomadic hordes living entirely on game and fruit. A learned priest of the early nineteenth century says the tribes in the dry sertão north of the Rio São Francisco were ignorant of any

[9] Gabriel Soares de Souza, quoted by Faith Hunter Dodge, "Brazil's Coastal Aborigines in Colonial Times," *The Brazilian-American*, July 8, 1922.

kind of agriculture, and not very nice about the way they prepared their game.[10]   John Mawe, too, was disgusted at the sight of an Indian woman gnawing at a half-roasted parrot which was spiked on a stick, with the feathers scarcely burnt off, and the entrails hanging out.   Polygamy, an institution which is popular where there is an abundance of food, was unknown.

It seems reasonably established that the dry highlands served as a refuge for a culture which differed from that of the Amazon in essential respects.   The one was primarily agricultural; the other, hunting.   The Amazon Indian never got far from a canoe; the wanderer of the desert could not make one and had few rivers to float it if he did.   The one was almost amphibious; the other could not swim.   The Amazons were good cooks, whereas the plateau Indians ate their parrots unpeeled.   Indeed there is no evidence as yet that either pottery vessels or water-tight baskets were known in parts of the plateau; they had little if any weaving; and it does not appear that they even worked stone!

I stress the point, because the higher Amazon type of culture extended not only along the river margins of the Amazon lowlands, but southward along the coast as far as canoe would carry it, and was the culture which the early Portuguese first encountered everywhere.   The Tupian language stock went with this culture for four thousand miles, from the mouth of the Madeira to Pará, and then south along the seacoast to northern Rio Grande do Sul; and Tupi became the *Lingoa Geral*.   Perhaps nine out of ten of the crosses between Portuguese and Indian were with the hard-working women of this splendid agricultural stock.

Space will not permit going further into the interesting traits of Indian culture.   If the reader will remember merely that the farmers and fishermen of the wet woods were very different from either the highland hordes or the guanaco hunters of the

[10] James Henderson, *A History of Brazil* (London, 1821), which is based on the Portuguese of Padre Manoel Ayres de Cazal.

pampas, there can be no confusion in going on to the things which we can say about all Brazilian Indians.

At the coming of the Portuguese in 1500, they were still in the Stone Age. With the possible exception of the peoples in contact with the fringe of the Inca civilization of Peru, the working of metals was unknown. Sculpture or stone carving was exceedingly rare, nor is there evidence of stone quarrying in South America outside of the Andes. Writing was unknown —not even the Inca could write. Animal transport was nowhere in vogue in Brazil. Everybody either walked or canoed, and the footpath represented the height of the Indian's development as a road-builder. The Indian did not exist on either continent who knew what a chimney was; although everybody smoked, cigars in the Amazon Basin, pipes for the rest. It seems strange that a man who smoked an elbow pipe all day could not invent a chimney! The prevailing fashion in clothes followed the chaste styles of the Garden of Eden. They shepherded no herds, and the only domesticated animal was the dog brought from Asia. Neither intoxicating drink nor narcotics held any mysteries for the savages of Brazil, and as a class we have got to call them hard drinkers, as were our forebears in the forests of northern Europe. As the hordes inhabiting the arid regions were not agriculturists, of course irrigation, an art developed on a magnificent scale by the Inca, was completely absent in Brazil—a point of significance today when great reclamation systems are building in Ceará.

One very fundamental trait which characterized the social concepts of the Indians of both Americas, the agricultural as well as the hunting peoples, Inca and forest Indian alike, a trait which even today leads to constant misunderstanding along the frontier, was the communistic conception of land ownership. There was personal property in weapons, animals, ornaments, crops sometimes; but private property in land was unknown. That should never be forgotten by those who have to deal with "squatters." Many of the Amazon Indians lived in communal dwellings of the type we have seen, not all by any means; yet the maloca existed as an institution from Colombia in the northwest to São Paulo and Rio de Janeiro in the southeast, and to Paraguay in the southwest. In some tribes the huntsmen serving in rotation maintained a storehouse from which any one could draw if the stuff were there to draw upon. They were rather thoroughgoing communists.

As throughout the Americas, there were myriad mutually unintelligible languages; yet four chief stocks embrace the languages of a very large part of Brazil: Tupi, Tapuya, Arawak, and Carib.

Whether the marriage relation was monogamous or polygamous with these people seems to have depended more upon the state of the larder than upon any deep-seated social usage —not altogether different from modern actuality in many civilized countries. Most men contented themselves with one wife; chiefs and medicine men usually had several; and there was no objection to a man contracting an alliance with as many women as he could persuade to work for him. Polyandry, that by-product of primitive poverty, was nowhere known in Brazil. Chastity before marriage was not insisted upon, but it was not a live issue, inasmuch as the average girl married as soon as she matured. Her coming-out party at the age of puberty was a barbarous performance in many tribes. After a month on manioc and water, the friends of the family assembled with pieces of flexible rattan; and her naked body received such a terrible beating, repeated four times at intervals of six hours, that she generally fell senseless and not infrequently died.[11]

Indeed, the life of the Brazilian woman was one long agony of service. Customs differ widely, of course, but it may be generalized in some such terms as these: During childhood she was kept on a more limited diet than the boys. After the ordeal of a ceremonial whipping, she married, at the age of ten or twelve, a youth of from fifteen to eighteen, whose slave she proudly became. When the tribe unfurled its sails

11 Wallace, *Travels on the Amazon and Rio Negro*, p. 345.

and ran before the wind, she carried his luggage. When he shot a monkey or a peccary in the forest, he trained her in the part of retriever. Upon signs of pregnancy, the man withdrew; and she was put upon a strict diet from which all meat was excluded. When the moment of birth approached, she went alone into the forest, tore or bit the navel string in two, went to the stream to wash herself and the infant, and then went about her work—while the husband took to his hammock and was nursed until the cord of the infant had dried away, for Brazil is one of the many lands of the couvade, the union between father and child being regarded as so intimate that the utmost care must be taken of him lest the child suffer. If she looked upon the ceremonial masks or the pan-pipes of the Jurupari, she was put to death. If she committed adultery, a club or a knife slash; while the other party was considered quite innocent. When she was not weaving a hammock, there was the manioc patch. And at twenty-five, a hag with pendent breasts and ugly visage, it became her privilege to wait upon the younger bride who displaced her in her husband's affections. Polygyny would be deemed a welcome division of such dubious honors. I can see no single redeeming feature in the social status of the primitive Indian woman. The monkeys and parrots of the establishment fared better.[12]

The shaman, or *pagé,* as he was called, was as characteristic of Brazil as of the United States. He commonly combined the functions of priest and medicine man, and it was one of the best paying jobs in the tribe. No croupier ever raked in the chips with an easier grace than he. Deriving his powers from some extrahuman source, able to converse with animals or birds and assume the form of a jaguar at will, to suck out the cause of disease through a hollow reed and perform with a calabash rattle miracles worthy of a Catholic saint, to divine the enemy responsible for the death of one's wife or brother, to make the fish leave the river—he was consulted by every one in difficulty or sorrow, you may be sure. His ability to

[12] Spix and Martius, *Travels,* etc. (Eng. trans.), II, 246.

point the finger and fan the flame of suspicion was an essential link in the sequence of murders by poisoning and blood feuds which followed perfectly normal death up and down the Amazon. Priests have never exercised such power without making it pay at every turn of the wheel.

The Indians both of the Amazon and of the Plateau are accused of being notorious cannibals. Some tribes kept the heads of enemies killed in the fray so beautifully smoked that the trophy was a perfect miniature of the original; and there are accounts by reliable scientists of smoke-drying human meat for future consumption. The idea is so attractive to a subway mind that such matters always get undeserved prominence in the story. Human meat could not have been more than an insignificant item on the menu of an agricultural folk who raised manioc, potatoes, lima beans, peanuts, squash, corn, and cacao. It was more a matter of ceremony, superstition, like the drinking of the ashes of the departed to absorb their strength. It seems to me very significant that General Rondon, who has had more contact with existing primitive tribes in Brazil than any other man living, states that he has never yet run into any sign of cannibalism in the course of his work in Matto Grosso, although he has been constantly on the watch.[13]

As to the number of Indians in Brazil in 1500, we cannot make even an intelligent guess. The density of population was probably so slight that an airplane observer flying over Brazil at a thousand feet would have seen no marks of man upon the surface of the earth beyond tiny clearings in the forest and the smokes of scattered fires. (However, in stating that the Indians of the Amazon type of culture existed as the merest fringe along the banks of the rivers and the seashore, we should not lose sight of the fact that there is far more river bank to Amazonas than top to a turnip.) The population of any primitive hunting society like that of the

[13] Candido Mariano da Silva Rondon, *Ethnographia.*

guanaco area is always sparse. The northeast is subject to
periodic droughts which drive out the modern population and
devastate the whole region from the São Francisco north.
Many other considerations besides food tended to keep the
population from increasing rapidly: birth control by abortion
had the sanction in some tribes for women up to the age of
thirty; Indian mothers nursed their offspring sometimes four
and five years; in parts of the Amazon region it was the
custom to bury the baby with a mother who died in childbirth,
unless some other woman volunteered to take the infant.
Infant mortality is always high among primitive people. Cannibalism was a fact although not an important one, and inter-
tribal wars a normal state of existence. The Indian certainly
lacked the tremendous fertility of the Negro.

He seems to have lacked another thing that the Negro possessed, and it is a prime essential to the building of any great
structure out of human beings—the ability to coöperate with
his fellows. Consciousness of kind in the Indian was reduced
to microscopic proportions. His sense of social solidarity extended no farther than his own tribe, and his tribe was small.
Often on the same river there were half a dozen hordes of
Indians, no one of which could communicate with the others,
each regarding the rest with the cordiality of Frenchmen and
Germans. Certain it is that in 1500 the Indians of Brazil were
to the uttermost pole removed from that sense of a common
world-wide humanity toward which the most enlightened peoples are now approaching.

An appraisal of Indian character would have even less meaning than an estimate of the population of Brazil in 1500. Scientifically minded men are no longer given to characterizing
the traits of races in the offhand manner of a generation or
two ago. The difference between primitive and civilized man
we are finding to be so slight that one cannot throw stones
at the savage without danger of hitting the savant.

Bates lived among the Indians on the Amazon from 1848

to 1859, and came to the conclusion that the race was rather phlegmatic, and gloomy, and not very imaginative.

Professor Orton says:

Laziness is the prominent characteristic. A gentleman offered an Indian passing his door twenty-five cents if he would bring him a pitcher of water from the river, only a few rods distant. He declined. "But I will give you fifty cents." Whereupon the half-clothed, penniless aboriginal replied: "I will give you a dollar to bring me some." Darwin met a similar specimen in Banda Oriental: "I asked two men why they did not work. One gravely said the days were too long; the other that he was too poor." [14]

Now that sort of stuff passed until recently as characterization of the mental traits of a race, millions strong, by our foremost scientists. Bates, to judge from his writings, after eleven years in the Amazon forest, saw the whole world through a mist of melancholy. In the other two cases, Indians with a delightful sense of humor were plainly amusing themselves at the expense of the long-bearded wise men.

There is one important point, however, where Bates's opinion should again be heard:

I have already remarked on the different way in which the climate of this equatorial region affects Indians and Negroes. No one could live long amongst the Indians of the upper Amazons, without being struck with their constitutional dislike to the heat. Europeans certainly withstand the high temperatures better than the original inhabitants of the country; I always found I could myself bear exposure to the sun or unusually hot weather quite as well as the Indians, although not well fitted by nature for a hot climate. Their skin is always hot to the touch, and they perspire little. . . . They bathe many times a day, but do not plunge in the water, taking merely a *sitz-bath*, as dogs may be seen doing in hot climates, to cool the lower parts of the body. . . .They are restless and discontented in fine dry weather, but cheerful in cool days, when the rain is pouring down on their naked backs. . . . How different all

[14] James Orton, *The Andes and the Amazon*, p. 243.

this is with the Negro, the true child of tropical climes! The impression gradually forced itself on my mind that the red Indian lives as a stranger or immigrant in these hot regions, and that his constitution was not originally adapted, and has not since become perfectly adapted, to the climate.

An immigrant and a stranger in a strange land he was! And the Indian in Brazil made so little progress in the conquest of a brutal wilderness within the Allotted Time, that when the clock struck 1500, the Lord lost patience and decided to turn it over to a man who thought he could do the job.

Before the conqueror comes, let us look in upon the "true child of tropical climes."

§ 2. THE NEGRO IN AFRICA

If it is difficult for a civilized mind to enter sympathetically into the mind of a naked forest Indian, it is well-nigh impossible to contemplate the Negro except through a veil of prepossession and prejudice which distorts the image and warps the most patent fact. Yet the day is not distant when all men will be forced by the logic of events and the siftings of science to recognize the simple truth, that one species, *Homo sapiens,* embraces the totality of human beings upon this earth, and that there is no widespread type of mankind but has vital contributions to make to any civilization intelligent enough to avail itself thereof.

When the curtain rises upon the Brazilian drama, we are going to witness the conscription of an African Army of Labor and its hurried transport across the Atlantic for the relief of the forces battling against Nature along a front far flung from Pará to Montevideo, comparable in import to, and of vastly greater dimensions than, the conscription of American man-power and its hurried dispatch across the "middle passage" in the opposite direction in the second decade of the twentieth century, for the relief of the forces intrenched between the Channel and the Alps. The recruiting ground in the one case extended from Halifax to Hawaii and from Hudson Bay to the Gulf of Mexico; the recruiting ground of the African Expeditionary Force was equally extensive. From Angola they were summoned and the Congo; from Dahomé, Lagos, Old Calabar, and the Bonny River; from the Central Niger and Hausaland; from Portuguese Guinea and the Gaboon. Far above Stanley Pool the arm of the Portuguese recruiting sergeant reached; even to Mozambique and the region south of the Kunene River on the east coast. Upon the tribes of the Yoruba, Egba, Jekri, and Sobo they called for contingents. Upon Mandingoes and the Bateke peoples, upon Hottentots and Bushmen as upon the forest dwellers, levies were made. Both Muhammadan and pagan were listed in Class 1-A of the draft boards that opened offices in Wydah and embarked the cohorts for Brazil.[1]

For him who would understand these black folk in the light of modern science, Dr. W. E. B. Du Bois has performed much the same service that Dr. Wissler has for those interested in the American Indian.[2] The outline of the story is this:

When our forefathers struck out from the old home in Central Asia, the taciturn, straight-haired boy went northeast; and the curly-haired lad with the incorrigible good humor, southwest. He burnt his feet on the sands of Arabia, cooled them in the Red Sea, and plodded on until he came to the banks of a river flowing northward, "like some grave, mighty thought, threading a dream." The Nile led him southward and revealed to him her secret, those Great Lakes hidden in Africa's highland heart. The open park lands beckoned beyond to that plateau which is still the sportsman's paradise. The pulse of a distant ocean drew him irresistibly along the desert's golden brim until he saw the sun enter the portals of descent and sink into the western water. And then he sat him down to rest from his wandering in the cool depth of the Congo forest.

[1] Sir Harry H. Johnston, *The Negro in the New World.*
[2] Du Bois, *The Negro* (New York, 1915).

"A goodly land!" he said. "I will stay." From a hollow tree he fashioned a drum, and the word boomed back: "A Continent for the Negro!"

From the host that followed and the progeny of their fertile loins, Africa became peopled with as dense a population as North America supports in these early years of the twentieth century. Behind the reddish dwarfs who were crowded back into the more inaccessible fastnesses of the forest, and the Negroes with clear yellow skins like the Bushmen and Hottentots of the southwest, came (or developed, it matters not which) the tall, black Nilotic Negro of the eastern Sudan and the powerfully built Forest Negro who took unto himself the west coast from the Gambia to the Congo, as well as the dense forests of the Congo Basin and the Niger Delta. There was no ice sheet to shut the door to Asia behind the Negro, as it probably did behind the American Indian. The Mediterranean type of humanity, the Iberian race, flowed in behind him and occupied the lands to the north of the Sahara. Negroland then became all that part of Africa lying south of the great barrier of sand. From the mingling of the blood of the Nilotic Negro and the Iberian sprang the Egyptian (Du Bois); and from the mingling of Iberians and Forest Negroes, such hybrid stocks as the Songhai, Mandingo, Fula, and Nyamnyam (Johnston). At a later date, other representatives of this Mediterranean type began to establish contacts with Negroland. The Semitic-speaking Assyrians, Phoenicians, Arabs, Carthaginians, and after them the Aryan-speaking Greeks and Romans, all had trade relations with the Negro; and all took from his culture, even as they contributed to it.

What was the culture of Negroland? It is an important question. John Stuart Mill laid down a pretty square rule for measuring men when he said: "The principle of the modern movement in morals and politics is that conduct, and conduct alone, entitles to respect: that not what men are, but what they do, constitutes their claim to deference." What is the Negro's claim?

About both the Sahara and the Kalahari are pasture lands, the two regions connected by the grassy highlands which center in the Great Lakes country. Into these pastures the Negro turned cattle, and he became one of the world's greatest herdsmen. Among the tribes of the eastern Sudan and the Bantus to the south, villages with ten or twelve thousand head were not uncommon. The Kafirs have always been noted breeders. Stall fattening was practiced about Kilimanjaro. And even in the Congo Basin sheep, goats, and cattle were common. Indeed, it is hard to find any place in Africa where sheep, goats, and chickens were not a part of the domestic regimen.

If a good herdsman, he was a better farmer. It was Friedrich Ratzel who said that "among all the great groups of the 'natural' races, the Negroes are the best and keenest tillers of the ground."[3] With them, as with the Indians, agricultural work was chiefly in the hands of the women; many regions in Africa, however, were so completely agricultural that the whole life of the tribe centered in the field. Fertilization and irrigation were, in places, regular features of their technique.

As a craftsman, the Negro had highly developed the arts of basketry, weaving, and dyeing. As far back as the eleventh century he was known as a manufacturer of cotton goods. The Negro's canoes were as good as those of the Brazilian Indian. His houses, of thatch and mud characteristically, were fully as comfortable as those of the peasants of medieval Europe. Of clothes he had small need, yet there were tribes which fabricated beautiful garments. He tanned leather as well as any European and manufactured the product into cloaks, shields, sandals, and vessels for water and oil.

Nor had the Negro failed to make a beginning in the fine arts. His carving of ivory and hippopotamus teeth (Lower Guinea) must be so ranked. He invented many musical instru-

[3] *History of Mankind,* II, 380.

ments. The Ashanti of the Gold Coast embroidered rugs and carpets and set gold and precious stones. Not only were there wood carvings in the temples of Yoruba, but these people worked quartz and granite; they made terra cotta images that are a delight to the critical eye; they manufactured glass!

Where admiration begins to turn to amazement, however, is in contemplating the Negro's work in metals. Nothing but archeological finds yet to be made can wrest from the Negro his claim to be the inventor of the smelting of iron, the very keystone of modern industrial civilization, a gift to the race that ranks with fire or written speech. Pittsburghers ought to make pilgrimage to the heart of the Dark Continent as Muhammadans do to Mecca. Out of his iron, the Negro fashioned axes, hoes, knives, scythes, and other implements cunningly fabricated. At the time of the People's Crusade he was an exporter of these commodities to India. He was equally clever in his handling of copper, silver, and gold. Benin and Yoruba, at least, knew bronze and brass casting. The Kafirs and Zulus drew wire from copper.

Although even in the Congo, before the Arabian and European invasion, there were towns of twenty or thirty thousand people,[4] characteristically the culture of Negroland was that of the family, village, and small tribe. A most interesting development of division of labor between village groups occurred in the Lower Congo, all the members of one village fishing, another village specializing on palm wine, a third trading for the whole group. Indeed, communism was as basic a conception in Africa as in America, particularly the common ownership of land.

Religion was a fetishism, not unlike that of aboriginal Brazil. Tracing of relationship through the mother was all but universal; polygamy was common; and cannibalism held just about the same place in the life of the forest Negro that it did in the life of the forest Indian. Of all his social traits, however, the one most important for Brazil is the fact that in

[4] Frobenius, *The Voice of Africa,* I, 14-15.

ability to combine, coöperate, and form large political units, the Negro had attained a position at the dawn of written history to which the Brazilian Indian never attained.

The dawn of written history. How simple and beautiful was the geography of those days: "On the north there was the delicious country of the Hyperboreans, beyond the reach of winter; in the west the garden of the Hesperides, in which grew apples of gold; in the east the groves and dancing-ground of the sun; in the south the country of the blameless Ethiopians, whither the gods were wont to resort."

Both the blood and the cultural beginnings of these blameless Ethiopians were mingled generously in the civilization of ancient Egypt. During the middle empire, in the lands south of the second cataract, arose the more purely Negro civilization of Ethiopia. Something like 2,700 years ago this black kingdom was strong enough to conquer Egypt and rule over it for a century as the Twenty-fifth Dynasty.[5] The only written language produced by Africa arose in these two centers of civilization, and from them of course the Negroes fringing the Sudan received much. Also, they gave.

From beyond the desert at a later time, traders brought shreds and shadows of Christianity, too; as they had brought back news of Carthage, and Greece, and Rome in the days before Christ. Then, in the seventh century, the dim outline of the Cross was totally obscured, as the brilliant Crescent rose above the northern horizon. Entered the knife that severed Europe from Negroland for a thousand years. Entered the sharp wedge of a militant faith that put the Negro beyond Islam, beyond the pale of the Christian conscience.

When Arab armies crossed the west end of the Sahara and came to Negroland in the tenth century, they first came into touch with a kingdom called Ghana which traces back to about the time Pharaoh Necho of the Twenty-sixth Dynasty sent out the Phoenician expedition which circumnavigated Africa. The Mandingo Negroes acted as liaison officers in

[5] See Wells, The Outline of History, I, 200.

these earliest contacts between the indigenous Negro culture of
Benin and Yoruba and that of the Moorish invaders. As in
Spain and Portugal, the Muhammadan civilization was a tremendously vitalizing influence; and from the fertile mating of
the two arose several great Negro states, the first of which
was the Mandingan kingdom of the Mellestine (1235)—the
birthplace of many a future Bahian.

The seat of empire in the Sudan passed to Songhai, the
largest and most famous of the black empires, in the beginning
of the sixteenth century. This empire, centering in the great
bend of the Niger, was likewise the home of many Brazilians-
to-be. It endured, all told, for a thousand years. Under
Muhammad Askia, who was reigning when Cabral discovered
Brazil, it extended from the Atlantic to Lake Chad and from
the salt mines of Tegazza in the north to about 10° north
latitude in the south. The University of Sankore, in touch
with Egyptian and North African centers of learning, taught
law, literature, grammar, geography, and surgery to a swarm
of black Sudanese students.

Thus Arabic became the written tongue of the Sudan and
Muhammadanism the dominant religion everywhere in Africa
north of the tenth parallel, and strong for another five degrees
to the south. Thus it was that when Vasco da Gama, by following the shore, reached Melinde on the east coast, he found
Muhammadan Negro pilots to show him the way across the
open Indian Ocean to Calicut. So also it happens that in the
twentieth century we encounter both Arabic and Muhammadanism in Bahia, in far-off Brazil.

Such, in barest outline, is the history and culture of the
Negro in Africa. I have had to sketch the contours of the
centuries too rapidly to draw a convincing picture, but no fair-
minded man who will take the time to survey the literature
and view the collections in several European museums (we
have no adequate African exhibit in the United States), can
escape the conclusion of Franz Boas:

The traits of African culture as observed in the aboriginal home of the Negro are those of a healthy primitive people, with a considerable degree of personal initiative, with a talent for organization, and with imaginative power, with technical skill and thrift. Neither is a warlike spirit absent in the race, as is proved by the mighty conquerors who overthrew states and founded new empires, and by the courage of the armies that follow the bidding of their leaders. There is nothing to prove that licentiousness, shiftless laziness, lack of initiative, are fundamental characteristics of the race.[6]

§ 3. THE PORTUGUESE IN EUROPE

So much for the black and the brown. Now for the white man who was to give to both a new language and an old civilization. Who, then, were the Portuguese who discovered and settled Brazil?

A historical accident. A by-product of that same tendency to separatism which, like a burst of shrapnel, divided Latin-America into a whole flock of republics. Until the late date of 1140, when the sons of two French adventurers of the gay crusading days decided by the toss of a coin, so to speak,—the tourney of Valdevez,—that the Count of Portugal should no longer be a feudatory of Galicia, the history of the south-western provinces is in no essential distinct from that of the rest of the Iberian Peninsula. And racially today, according to Ripley, the Iberian Peninsula is more homogeneous than any other equal area of Europe, although that is not saying much. Difference of language has nothing to do with difference of racial type, but even in language it is easier for a Castilian peasant to understand Portuguese than Catalan.[1]

The primitive Iberians from whom all three are descended, back in the days when a polished stone hatchet represented what a broadcasting set does today, were distributed not only throughout the Iberian Peninsula, but also over England Ireland, France, and everywhere about the Mediterranean; with certain tracks which anthropologists are now following

---

[6] Boas, *The Mind of Primitive Man* (New York, 1922), p. 271.
[1] W. Z. Ripley, *The Races of Europe,* p. 19.

seeming to lead far afield from the Mediterranean area. Their descendants with whom we are concerned are people of a rather small human type, light of frame, slender, agile; very dark of hair and eye, almost black; with skins of a beautiful olive-white. The perfect brunet. The type prevails today everywhere south of the Pyrenees, along the shores of southern France and southern Italy including Sicily and Sardinia, and, according to Ripley, is allied in all important anthropological respects with the peoples inhabiting Africa north of the Sahara, from the Red Sea to the Atlantic.

From its position, the Iberian Peninsula has been the western highway between Europe and Africa, and as such was overrun and conquered by wave after wave of mankind-on-the-march. One of the earliest of which we have knowledge was a wave of Keltic-speaking people who came from the north. They probably never formed more than a dominant aristocracy.

By sea, at a much later period, came the Greeks, who established trading posts at the mouths of the Tagus, Douro, and Minho, and gave the Portuguese the priceless gift of their alphabet. The Carthaginians had colonies and trading posts all over the Iberian Peninsula, but never exerted much influence over the more barbarous western provinces. The Romans took the Peninsula away from the Carthaginians after the second Punic War and held it for six hundred years, from 201 B.C. until the beginning of the fifth century. That was long enough for the Iberian folk to become thoroughly Latinized in language and governmental institutions, and Roman Catholic in religion. These three invaders, the Greek, the Carthaginian, and the Roman, were of the same Mediterranean type as the inhabitants of the Iberian Peninsula; none of them was numerous; so they could not have modified deeply anything except culture and language. A new and important ethnic element was introduced, however, when the Emperor Hadrian (117 A.D.) transplanted fifty thousand Jewish families into Spain.

The next wave of conquerors was of the Nordic type, blond, blue of eye, and flaxen-haired. About 425 or so the Visigoths came drifting over the Pyrenees on the heels of the Vandals, as snowbirds appear in the midst of a winter storm. They settled in the Peninsula as the Vandals moved on into North Africa, conquering the land in a physical sense, ousting the Roman overlords, promoting themselves to the jobs of the petty kinglets and the landed aristocracy; themselves conquered absolutely by the language and culture of the Roman civilization rooted in the soil. Roderic, the last of the Gothic Kings, was drowned in the Guadalquivir in endeavoring to stop the Moors who crossed from Africa to Gibraltar in A.D. 711.

These warm winds of the desert that blew over the Peninsula from the south were vastly different from the cold blasts that brought the Barbarians out of the north. The nomads of Arabia who spread from the Ganges to the Loire on the prancing steeds of militant Muhammadanism, came with gifts in their hands—learning, tolerance, science, sanitation.

For nearly three hundred years Portugal enjoyed under its Asiatic rulers greater prosperity than under either Roman or Visigothic overlords. Then for upward of two hundred years more, until 1250 or thereabouts, the most profitable occupation for Christian gentlemen became the game of looting Moorish strongholds and the seizure of Moorish lands. There are towns in Portugal which must have changed hands a dozen times; and common folk found a strict neutrality much to their interest, not knowing whether Christian or Saracen knight would be in the castle when they got up in the morning.

How much did the Moors modify the physical type of Spain and Portugal? The only physical traits which distinguished the invader from the native son were a deeper pigmentation and perhaps an occasional curly lock. He had lived under the more fiercely blazing sun of the Arabian desert and north Africa and had crossed to some extent with Negroid strains. Ripley says the Moors were so similar in type to the natives

that it is impossible to identify their descendants; that inter-
mixture would not have modified stature or head form in
any degree.

From the period of Moorish dominance in Portuguese history three things are worth stressing as bearing directly upon
twentieth century Brazil, and the first has to do with just
that subtle difference between brown and brunet. Many
North Americans profess horror at the intermarriage of white
and colored types which is so common in South America.
Mark well, then, that the first contact of the Portuguese and
Spanish with a darker-skinned people was the contact of the
conquered with their brown-skinned conquerors. And the
darker man was the more cultured, more learned, more artistic. He lived in the castles and occupied the towns. He was
the rich man, and the Portuguese became serfs upon his land.
Under such conditions, it would be deemed an honor for the
white to marry or mate with the governing class, the brown
man, instead of the reverse. Nor was it only the Portuguese
peasantry whose blood mingled with the Moors: Alfonso VI,
who united Castile, Leon, and Galicia in 1073, to cite but one
of many instances of marriages between Christian and Arab
nobles, chose a Moorish princess, the daughter of the Emir
of Seville, to be the mother of his son Sancho.

Secondly, in the game of wrestling with the Moor originated
one of the crying evils of Brazil's system of land tenure.
When a feudal lord got in a tight place with the infidel, he
summoned the chivalry of Europe; and he paid the adventurers who answered his call by enormous grants of land from
territory they helped wrest from the Moor. It cost the giver
nothing, and it became decidedly to the interest of the new
feudatory to defend his frontier against the brown-skinned
gentlemen across the river.

Thirdly, the Crusades in the Peninsula resulted in the in-
jection of strains of every people of northern Europe into the
blood of Portugal. After the Pope decreed that crusading in
the Peninsula should count equally in the sight of God with

harrying the Holy Land, it became the custom for those knights of England and Flanders, Denmark and Normandy, who went by sea, to put in at Porto or Lisbon and have a go at the infidel by way of exercising their horses and breaking the monotonous voyage.

The net result of this process is the Portuguese stock which settled Brazil, in whose veins mingled the blood of Iberian, Kelt, Greek, Phoenician, Roman, Visigoth, Jew, Arab, French, English, Flemish, and Spanish. Which brings me to an important digression.

Wells, after pointing out how varieties of *Homo sapiens* differentiated all over the world in an age when everything tended to isolate groups of men for long periods of time, went on to say something which is as significant as true:

At the present age, man is probably no longer undergoing differentiation at all. Mankind from the view of a biologist is an animal species in a state of arrested differentiation and possible readmixture. Men mingle more and more. Readmixture is now a far stronger force than differentiation.[2]

When, to the strains mingled by the migrations of man to and fro across the Iberian Peninsula, you add the blood of the American Indian (first cousin of the Asiatic Mongolian) and the African Negro, you are going to get a type that is more nearly an average and a synthesis of the totality of humanity than anything that has existed upon this planet since differentiation began. From the biologic angle, the Brazilian drama develops a theme of tremendous import for the race.

Now to continue. We must distinguish three social classes in Portugal. At the top was a non-working, hard-fighting, land-holding ruling class. It included the higher clergy but is best typified by the nobleman, the *fidalgo*. Since the fidalgo was above soiling his hands with commerce and found it easier to get money with the sword than with the shovel, he let economic power gravitate more and more into the hands of the

[2] *The Outline of History,* I, 140.

numerous descendants of those fifty thousand Jews Hadrian planted in the Peninsula. These, up to a few years before the discovery of Brazil, formed a rich and efficient middle class of business men and shopkeepers. Staggering along under them both as a coolie shuffles under the weight of his balanced baskets of vegetables, was the working mass of the population, a sturdy peasantry gifted with delicacy and intelligence, in spite of its colossal ignorance and lack of letters.

The fidalgos of Portugal it was who organized and dominated the great commercial empire of the sixteenth century. The discovery of India reveals in this governing class the ability to organize scientific research and dogged persistence in applying results in the field, comparable to the systematic search for oil now being carried on in South America by geologists in the pay of the oil companies. If you would understand one of the splendid qualities that went into the making of Brazilians, take a map of Africa and Asia and watch the disciples of Henry the Navigator carry the ball irresistibly down the field from the discovery of Madeira in 1419 until Vasco da Gama shoved a squadron over for a touchdown at Calicut in India in 1498, with a touchback at Nova Zembla in proving the northern route impracticable. That the mastery of the water route to India was achieved just eighty years after Prince Henry settled down at the jumping-off place of Europe (Sagres) for that express and announced purpose, is much more significant than if it had been achieved at once. Nor did exploration cease when that goal had been won.

As soon as Vasco da Gama got back to Lisbon, Pedro Alvares Cabral was dispatched to India with a squadron of thirteen ships and orders to bring back the goods and arrange matters so that the wealth of Asia should continue to flow back to the old home town. Blown far west of their course by the breath of Destiny, in April, in the year of our Lord 1500, the prows of Portugal grounded on the shore of Brazil.

CHAPTER III

THE SOIL

IF a pine seed be planted in the shadow of its fathers in the deep soil of some sheltered cove where mist lingers through the morning and moisture settles through the night, men of the hereafter will gaze with delight upon a tall, straight trunk bearing aloft the symmetrical crown of a dominant king of the forest. If a seedling from the same pine cone become rooted in thin soil upon a seaside crag, far from its fellows, where the winds of a northern ocean beat, and swirl, and tear, the tree will be a puny thing, a gnarled thing, a wry thing with distorted crown and knotty limbs stretching in the direction of the force that most fiercely distorts. Quite unrecognizable as blood brothers to the casual eye. Soil and site account for the difference.

The environment in which human societies are planted produces effects equally profound. It is not enough to know the quality of the seed. In what soil that seed was planted is equally important. All life moves nervously across a contact zone between a thin slice of rock or water at the surface of the earth and a light blanket of air at the bottom of the atmosphere, and man among the rest. But whether the Pride of the Primates moves easily across the whirling periphery of swift-swinging earth, well fed and warm, or only because of canny preparations and heroic efforts, depends upon topography, and climate, and the cover of the lands, and the lesser life upon which man preys. In Brazil these factors represent controls so tremendous that there is no understanding either the past or the future of man there without focusing attention for a moment upon these major determinants of destiny.

I approach the task of picturing nature in Brazil with much the same feeling with which men of the Stone Age must have approached the task of skinning a mammoth. Less is known about the southern half of the western hemisphere than of any other major division of our terraqueous globe. Science has cast but a flickering light upon the domain between the Andes and Atlantic. Where the face of earth is man-tamed and tabulated it is sufficiently difficult to bound natural regions: there is rarely a sharp line where the mountains break into the plateau or where the plateau merges into the plain. It is impossible to set even approximately accurate boundaries to some of the natural regions of Brazil or to the areas of forest and grassland, because the essential field studies have not yet been made. Enormous areas are still unexplored and the maps thereof merely misleading examples of imaginative draughtsmanship.

With such tools we have to work upon a piece of the earth's hide larger than the United States. Of the 57.5 millions of square miles which protrude above the surface of the seas, the two Americas embrace 16.2 millions.[1] Of this, the Portuguese who followed Cabral were to stake out as their claim no less than 3.3 millions of square miles, an area larger than the territory between Canada and Mexico by a quarter of a million. Of that part of the western hemisphere south of the equator, well over half was soon to swear fealty to the government at Lisbon. Canada, China, Australia, Soviet Russia, the United States—these are the only land masses constituting political entities which are comparable quantities.

Now everybody knows that Brazil is vast; yet the average North American, for whom I am writing, will not take the next step and realize that vastness implies diversity.

"How is the climate down there?" is a question frequently asked by people who know perfectly well that the climates of Maine and Florida are extremely different, that deserts ex-

[1] Brunhes, *Human Geography,* p. 70. Salisbury, *Physiography,* p. 6, gives the land area as 54,000,000 sq. mi.

ist between the heavy rains of Oregon and the moderate rainfall of Illinois.

"What kind of wood do they grow in Brazil?" they ask of a forest that produces over two thousand tree species of commercial size.

"Any good fishing in Brazil?" sportsmen inquire of a network of rivers wherein swim more different kinds of fish than in the whole Atlantic Ocean.

It is only the ignorance of such questioners that gives me the courage to attempt to indicate the major physical forces conditioning the life that swarmed upon our vast, green-curtained stage on that gay morning in 1500 when Cabral bumped into Brazil. No one, however, could be more conscious than I of the limit of error which I permit myself in the survey that follows.

§ 1. TOPOGRAPHY

Mountains, plateaus, and plains are the strongly marked features of the earth's crust which give character to the continents. I shall deal with nothing but these relief features of the second order. Six are the well marked physiographic provinces to be kept in mind: the Guiana Highlands, the Amazon Lowland, the Atlantic Coastal Plain, the Plains of the Upper Paraguay, the Maritime Mountains, and the Central Plateau. The approximate relations of these are shown on the map of physiographic regions.

The Guiana Highlands

The east-and-west boundary between Brazil and the Guianas is the watershed between the rivers flowing into the Atlantic and those flowing into the Amazon. The ridges west of the headwaters of the River Courantyne are called the Serra Acaray; and those to the east, the Serra de Tumucumaque. Dr. Farabee, who recently explored the British Guiana boundary, says the north side is very steep while on the south the

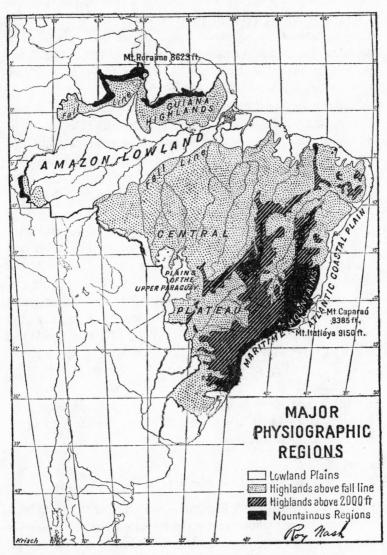

A Rough Approximation Based on Insufficient Data.

slope is more gentle. The highest mountain on the trail was only two thousand feet; and the elevation of the divide between the Courantyne and Amazon waters above the canoe stations on either side is not more than one hundred feet.[1] Most points on this watershed will probably lie below the 400-meter contour (1,300 feet).

Farther west, the boundary between Brazil and Venezuela is more truly mountainous. Roraima rears its head to an elevation of 8,600 feet; Masiati is almost as proud a peak; and between them run the rough ranges of the Serra Pacaraima. The ridges thrust southeast from Masiati, called the Serra Parima, upon whose western flanks the Orinoco is born, are likewise of mountainous dimensions and form.

If you descend any of the Brazilian rivers which drain the southern slopes of these mountains and watersheds, after portaging around numerous falls and running many miles of rapids, you come to a fall line where they finally tumble into the trough of the Amazon Lowland and become sedate streams whereon steamboats may ply without danger of any catastrophe worse than hanging up on a sandbar. That part of Brazil north of this fall line, between the Rio Oiapoc on the east and Colombia on the west, constitutes the Guiana Highlands, a physiographic province without importance in our story. It is still a howling wilderness; much of it, outside the river bottoms, unexplored, the refuge of naked Indian hordes and the descendants of fugitive slaves.

The Amazon Lowland

South of the Guiana Highlands lies the Amazon Lowland, a trough placed under the eaves to catch the drip and the drench of the Andes, Guiana Highlands, and Central Plateau. In sailing from the Atlantic to Tabatinga, where Brazil and Peru meet, you rise less than three hundred feet above sea

[1] William Curtis Farabee, "A Pioneer in Amazonia," *Bulletin* of Geog. Soc. of Philadelphia, XV (1917), 84, 95.

level and pass neither fall nor rapid; although the two points are fourteen hundred miles apart, as the crow flies. But ascend the Tocantins, Xingú, Madeira and affluents like the Roosevelt and Gy-Paraná, and you come to falls where steamers perforce stop. This fall line constitutes the southern margin of the Amazon Lowland. Thus definitely limited, the Amazon Lowland is seen to be a funnel-shaped trough eighteen hundred miles long extending from the Atlantic Ocean to the foothills of the Andes in the Territory of Acre, as low and flat a plain as is to be found anywhere on the earth's surface. It is almost as flat as the ocean, and, indeed, much of it was under water in recent geologic times. For reasons which will appear shortly, the Amazon Lowland plays but a minor rôle in the first four hundred years of Brazil's history. With the future of the region I shall deal toward the close of the book.

The Central Plateau

South of the Amazon Lowland lies the great topographic fact determining the destiny of Brazil: a plateau extending seventeen hundred miles from north to south and two thousand miles from east to west in its most extensive cross-sections. In area it embraces nearly one-half of Brazil. In temperate countries like Europe and the United States, the works of man become fewer the higher the altitude; the dense populations tend to congregate upon lowland plains. In warm latitudes, however, the elevated plateau has advantages of climate and drainage which may pull people out of the lowlands. In Abyssinia the populated zone is almost entirely above six thousand feet. The high plateaus have always been exceedingly attractive to the populations of Mexico and the Andes. And as the story develops, we shall see the Central Plateau of Brazil irresistibly pulling men away from the Atlantic Coast until gold finally shifts the center of population there, there in Minas and São Paulo to remain until the present.

Its margin is readily defined for the traveler who ascends

any of the large rivers which originate upon the plateau. On the São Francisco, for example, steamers may ascend from the Atlantic to the noble falls of Paulo Affonso: that drop of two hundred and sixty feet obviously marks the margin of the plateau.   Ascend the Paraná from Buenos Aires and the steamer encounters no difficulties until it approaches the Sete Quedas, the falls of Guaira, in latitude 24° south.   Above these falls, upon the plateau, river steamers again ply freely over several hundred miles of smooth water.   Where the affluents of both these mighty rivers head in Goyaz and Minas, however, is over three thousand feet above sea level; and the upper courses are full of quick water.   With these two rivers the big leap is over the margin of the plateau.

With the Roosevelt, the Tapajós, the Xingú, and the Tocantins the last leap is not the most imposing.   Roosevelt describes the Salta Bello with a drop of forty or fifty yards, and the falls of Utiarity—twice as high—right up at the very source of the Tapajós; and all the worst rapids encountered by the Rondon-Roosevelt expedition were south of the eleventh parallel.   But it is surely an error to define the margin of the plateau as the foot of these upper rapids?   The ultimate northern fall line on all these southern tributaries of the Amazon would seem to be fully as definite a physiographic boundary as the line between the Piedmont Plateau and the Atlantic Coastal Plain of the United States, for instance.

The eastern margin of the plateau from the city of São Paulo to northern Rio Grande do Sul is an even more definite boundary than that formed by the fall line.   In traveling from west to east anywhere south of Capricorn, you mount higher and higher until at the passes of the Serra do Mar you see the ocean lying almost at your feet, three thousand feet below. While south of the valley of the Rio Jacuhy in Rio Grande do Sul the ridges (*coxilhas*) facing the Atlantic are low and unimposing in comparison with the sheer scarp of the Serra do Mar, they nevertheless do form a distinct boundary between highland and plain to the Uruguayan frontier and beyond.

Likewise the western margin of the Central Plateau from Paraguay to the falls of the Rio Madeira is unmistakable, in many places a sheer scarp. I have seen it only where the railroad quits the plateau and descends into the Plains of the Upper Paraguay. There, near Aquidauana station, the plateau margin is easily traceable as far north and south as the eye can reach. About the headwaters of the Rio Paraguay the margin is a steep and deeply indented escarpment which rises something over two thousand feet above the plains to what is variously called the Parecis Plateau or the Serra dos Parecis. This highland fronts the Guaporé branch of the Rio Madeira along its entire course, gradually breaking down until its outliers appear at the falls of the Madeira and disappear into the Amazon Lowland immediately beyond.[2]

It is not so easy to define the northeastern margin of the plateau nor those portions which abut against the mountains from São Paulo north. Until we have accurate contour maps of these parts, setting a limit to physiographic divisions is little better than a guess. But even with this admission, there are sufficient definite points defining the margin of the plateau to indicate clearly its major dimensions.

Obviously, so vast an expanse of land surface is going to show considerable diversity in its features of minor relief, and one whose theme was topography and not man would be forced to take cognizance of many minor provinces of which I shall make no mention. But the Central Plateau exhibits no such diversity as one would gather from most of the current maps of Brazil. Literally hundreds of "serras" are shown as mountain chains breaking up this surface in every conceivable direction. Most of these are the products of erosion, presenting one sheer face and one gently sloping away into the general level of the terrain; many are flat-topped mesas of considerable extent. The majority were put on the old maps

[2] See Church, "South America: An Outline of Its Physical Geography," *Geog. Journal,* London, April, 1901, p. 371; Orville Derby, "Physical and Geological Features of Brazil," *The Brazilian Yearbook,* 1909; Reclus, *Estados Unidos do Brazil,* chapter on Matto Grosso.

simply by assuming that every divide between two rivers is a mountain range.[3]

The Maritime Mountains

Aside from those along the northern frontier, the real mountains of Brazil are distributed along a northeast-southwest axis very close to the Atlantic seaboard. Approaching Brazil by sea anywhere between Rio de Janeiro and northern Rio Grande do Sul, the eastern scarp of the plateau appears as a forbidding mountain range parallel with the shore. In places it rises sheer from the water's edge; in others there is a narrow shelf at its foot rarely more than a score of miles broad. Although from the plateau itself there appears only a line of rather insignificant hills, from the sea side the deeply eroded scarp of the central *massif* justifies the name Serra do Mar. The mean elevation of the crest is about five thousand feet, with peaks rising another thousand or two above this level and the passes lying some two thousand feet lower as a rule.[4]

South of Santos the Serra do Mar is really, then, a formation that falls sheer in one direction and fades imperceptibly in the other. North of Santos, however, the deep valleys of the Rio Parahyba and the Rio Doce bestow two equally sheer faces upon the Serra do Mar. On the Minas boundary in 20° 30′ south latitude, this eastern range of the Maritime Mountains attains the considerable height of 9,385 feet in the Pico da Bandeira on Mt. Caparaó, the highest point in South America east of the Andes.[5]

North of the city of São Paulo, and separated from the Serra

[3] The sheets of the International Millionth Map issued by the Brazilian Government in connection with the Centenary Celebration, 1922, are better than government maps previously published. While there are not in existence adequate data to justify the contours there shown, the refusal to guess at elevations above 900 meters is a step in the direction of scientific accuracy. The 2,000-foot contour on my map of physiographic regions is taken from these sheets.

[4] Derby, "Phys. Features of Brazil," *Braz. Yearbook* (1909), p. 11.

[5] See Nash, "On the Roof of Brazil—The Ascent of Mount Caparaó," *The Brazilian American*, Dec. 17, 1921.

do Mar by the valley of the Parahyba, the main ridge in the western element of the Maritime Mountains is called the Serra da Mantiqueira. The mean elevation of its crests is about sixty-five hundred feet. Its highest point, Mt. Itatiáya, where the states of Rio de Janeiro, São Paulo, and Minas Geraes meet, is only a couple of hundred feet lower than Caparaó and until a few years ago was considered the highest point in Brazil. Near Barbacena, in Minas Geraes, the main western element in this complex mountain system takes a northerly course and forms the divide between the waters of the Rio das Velhas and the Rio Doce.

Still farther north, under the name Serra do Espinhaço, it forms the eastern margin of the São Francisco basin. That great river has cut a wide valley square across the range. Most of the mountains north of the São Francisco are in-significant in comparison with the Mantiqueira and Serra do Mar; but when almost within sight of the ocean again they gather themselves together for a last laugh at the lowlands, and in the Serra Grande on the Ceará-Piauhy boundary once more pull themselves up above three thousand feet.

To thus single out three or four ranges by name gives no clear picture of the Maritime Mountain province north of São Paulo. The region is a mass of rocks of the oldest geologic formations, folded and eroded into a most complex mountain mass. Eastern Minas Geraes, most of the State of Rio de Janeiro, and western Espirito Santo show range after range running in all directions. While the summits are not lofty judged by Andean standards, the gradients are very steep, and the inhabitant is never in any doubt that he dwells in a mountainous region.

The Plains of the Upper Paraguay

West of the Central Plateau in the state of Matto Grosso lie the Plains of the Upper Paraguay, the northern extension of the plains of Argentina and the Gran Chaco. How flat is

the gradient of the great river which forms the western boundary of Brazil north of Paraguay may be gathered from the
fact that Corumbá, on the 19th parallel, is only five hundred
feet above the level of the sea where these waters meet the
salt in the estuary of La Plata, over a thousand miles farther
south. The eastern margin of these plains at Aquidauana is
only eighty-six feet higher; and São Luiz de Caceres, well
toward the northern extremity of this physiographic province,
has an elevation of only five hundred and ninety feet. Land
does not get much flatter than that. The reason is that this
was part of the bed of the Pampean Sea which covered these
flats as recently as the last glacial epoch.

The Atlantic Coastal Plain

Continuous with the Amazon Lowland and extending south
to Rio de Janeiro with but two or three slight breaks, is a
plain of varying width extending from the seashore to the
edge of the Plateau or to the foothills of the Maritime Mountains. South of Rio it becomes almost nonexistent where the
Serra do Mar rises sheer from the sea, and is nowhere more
than a score or two miles wide until Porto Alegre is reached.

The deep harbors from Bahia south were formed by a subsiding of the coast with reference to sea level. This was
followed by a more recent uplift amounting to about ten feet;
so that in most places there is at least a narrow strip of
alluvium bordering the harbors, however sheer the mountains
rise behind.

Sand dunes characterize the seaward margin of this plain
in Rio Grande do Sul. Inside the line of dunes lies a chain
of great fresh-water lagoons. Dunes are frequent, too, along
the northeast coast from Sergipe to Ceará.

Coral reefs begin to appear at the Abrolhos Islands in
18° south and are encountered off and on up to the mouth of
the Amazon. The volume of fresh water poured into the

ocean by both the Rio São Francisco and the Amazon precludes coral growth in these neighborhoods. Above northern Espirito Santo likewise appear numerous stone reefs formed by the consolidation of beaches. The economic importance of these will appear in the section on the ports of Brazil.

Such are the six major physiographic provinces—essentially a highland with a mountain core, surrounded by a sea of lowlands. The highland and the Atlantic plain are the important parts. If the other lowlands had been under water these four hundred years, the history of Brazil would have been substantially the same.

Some things we may say of Brazil as a whole. While there is ample evidence of glaciation in Permian times of the region from São Paulo south, no part of Brazil was touched by the glaciers of the Pleistocene.[6] (Louis Agassiz went all wrong on this proposition, as the work of later geologists clearly proves.) There is therefore nowhere in Brazil any great lake region such as that for which glaciation is responsible in northeastern United States and southern Canada. There is no active volcano anywhere in Brazil; nor have volcanoes been of importance in the formation of Brazilian mountains, according to Branner.[7] And Brazil is perhaps less disturbed by earthquakes than any other portion of the globe of equal area. Mankind has always shown a predilection for roughly level expanses of soil. Viewed as a whole, the great highland heart of Brazil is anything but level. It is deeply eroded, and nowhere upon the plateau can there be found flat lands of enormous extent such as are encountered in interior United States.

So much for the bones of this monster and the wrinkled hide which covers them. Now let winds blow upon them and waters flow.

[6] J. B. Woodworth, "Geological Expedition to Brazil and Chili," *Bulletin* of the Museum of Comparative Zoölogy, Harvard University, 1912.
[7] John C. Branner, *Geologia Elementar*, Rio, 1915.

§ 2. Climate

Three Titanic forces impinge upon Brazil with a constancy
only equaled by their kindliness: the Equatorial Current, the
Trade Winds, and an Overhead Sun. From the coast of
Africa the equatorial current drifts across the broad belly of
the earth, leisurely, warm, dependable. Upon the easternmost
point of Brazil it breaks and divides. One branch creeps down
along the coast to greet the west wind and hear the gossip
of the pampas; the other wanders northwest to view the won-
ders of the Antilles and add its warmth to the Stream that
keeps old England from freezing to death. The surface temperature of the equatorial current is about eighty degrees (F.).
It is the same in January and in June, by day as by night;
its diurnal range amounts to only two or three degrees; even
fifteen hundred miles north or south of the equator the mean
annual range of the surface of old ocean is a mere six or seven
degrees. A thermostat which determines temperature in every
dwelling along the whole coast of Brazil. Upon the bosom of
the equatorial current the ships of Cabral rode to their great
discovery in 1500, and we shall see it as one of the two factors
separating the government of Maranhão and Pará from that of
the southern captaincies in colonial times.

A zenith sun looks down upon every point between the
Venezuelan and the Paraguayan frontiers of Brazil twice in
each twelvemonth. From that follows approximate equality
of day and night throughout the year; the day is never less
than ten and a half hours between Cancer and Capricorn.
An overhead sun also implies heat. But it does not imply,
as some uncritical Northerners imagine, that Brazilian temperatures rival those of Hades. Because of the unequal distribution of land and water in the northern and southern hemi-
spheres, the thermal equator and geographic equator do not
coincide; in South America, the heat equator is well north
of the northernmost point of Brazil. The world's highest
temperatures are never encountered in the belts of heavy rain-

fall. Aridity is the intimate comrade of fierce heat. As we shall see directly, Brazil is exceedingly well watered and is cursed with no area of extensive desert with terrific temperatures such as characterize the Sahara, parts of India, and northern Australia. Neither does Brazil know such heat as many extensive areas of the United States experience every summer. The elevation of the maritime mountains and of a great portion of the central plateau is sufficient to mitigate temperatures perceptibly. And along the coast, the trade winds make the heat much less sensible than if the air were unmoving.

While the equatorial current breaks on the Brazilian shore and divides, two other gently moving forces converge and continue over the lands. Brazil derives much of its climatic character from the breaths which blow above the middle latitudes of earth with such unfaltering constancy that mariners have named them the Winds of Trade—gossiping women coming from the well with water jars balanced upon level heads. The Wells of Cancer, where drink the Northeast Trades, are as deep as the North Atlantic. Stretched by some mischievous god just high enough to trip shuffling feet, the shore line of South America from Cape São Roque to northern Colombia extends square across their path. Much precious water spills on the coast between the Amazon and Orinoco. Others stumble upon the mountains west of Roraima and spill a deluge upon their seaward flanks. At the sight of the formidable ramparts and bastions which bar the way to the high Andes, the last of them drop their loads in disgust. Bone-dry they arrive at their homes behind the hills where the sun goes down. Without water, but gossiping still. The wells where the Southeast Trades gather moisture lie between 30° and 35° South. Much of the shore line between Recife and Porto Alegre is neck-high and nasty to negotiate. Water is ever streaming down the seaward face of the Serra do Mar and the Mantiqueira. The highlands of Goyaz and Matto Grosso and the unslaked thirst of the insatiable Andes wring from them the rest. Nowhere else in the world is there a sprinkling system comparable. Of all great land masses, Brazil is the best watered.[1]

A glance at the map of water, however, will reveal much inequality of precipitation. At the top is a region dry enough to terminate the evergreen forest and call twenty-five or thirty thousand square miles of grassland into being. Farabee says the rainfall in the eastern part of the savanna country is about sixty inches, while in the western part it is only forty-two.[2] The rainy season is that of the northern hemisphere, from May to August, the opposite of the Amazon rhythm.

Upon quitting this comparatively dry region of the Guiana Highlands and dropping down into the Amazon Lowland, the American from north of the Rio Grande finds it necessary to revamp his definition of rainfall. Aside from a small district on the west coast of Washington which receives one hundred and twenty inches, the music of the rainfall map of the United States crashes in a fortissimo over the motif "sixty to seventy inches." The Gulf Coast in Mississippi and Alabama, the extreme tip of Florida, an area in the heart of the Appalachians, and the Pacific Coast in Oregon and Washington, are so stressed in deepest black. These very wet parts of the United States, however, would take rank as the driest parts of the Amazon plain. Along the great river this comparatively dry zone extends from above Manáos to somewhere below Óbidos, the bulk of the rainfall falling from December to May.

As you descend the Amazon from Óbidos toward the Atlan-

---

[1] Temperature and rainfall are the only two climatic factors which I shall touch. No large number of meteorological stations were established previous to 1908; then their distribution was such as to furnish but scant information about much of the interior. The weather service was reorganized by the Federal Government in 1921 and stations redistributed. In another decade the picture will be fairly complete. The earlier data have been ably brought together by C. M. Delgado de Carvalho (*Météorologie du Brésil;* London, 1917). Temperatures I have taken from that work. My rainfall map follows a recent work of Carvalho's in the arid northeast, *Dados pluviometricos relativos ao nordéste do Brasil* (1922); for the rest of Brazil, Henrique Morize, *Contribuição ao estudo do clima do Brasil* (1922). See *The Geog. Rev.* (New York), Jan., 1924, pp. 127-135.

[2] *Bul.* of Geog. Soc. of Philadelphia, XV (1917), 63.

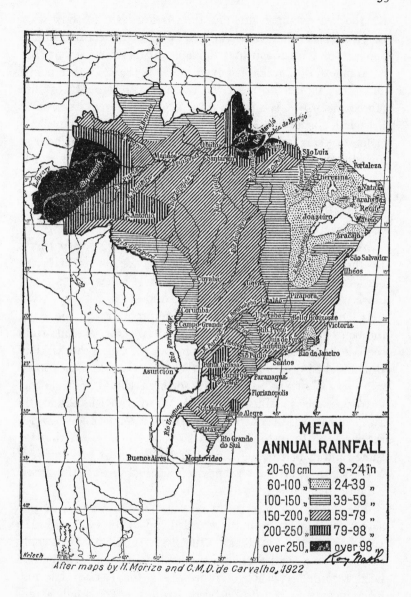

MEAN
ANNUAL RAINFALL

20-60 cm		8-24 in
60-100 „		24-39 „
100-150 „		39-59 „
150-200 „		59-79 „
200-250 „		79-98 „
over 250 „		over 98 „

After maps by H. Morize and C.M.D. de Carvalho, 1922

tic, the heavens open up; and the tropics begin to show what they really can do. Belém receives over eight feet of rainfall. January to May constitutes the heart of the rainy season, but in no month do Paraenses have to pray for rain. Other points about the mouth of the river receive over ten feet of rain (three meters). We know from a long series of records in French Guiana that Cayenne also receives more than three meters a year; so it is safe to conclude that the whole coast in between is deluged by over one hundred inches of water. There is a delightful regularity about the daily rains in Pará. During many months appointments are made for "after the rain" with as much assurance as New Yorkers say, "I'll see you right after lunch."

Westward of Manáos the heavens are likewise very leaky. By the time Coary is reached (63° W.) we are again in the black belt, with more than one hundred inches a year, and black it stays from that point to the Andes.

If Dr. Morize is right in the interpretation of the data, the belt of sixty to eighty inches (150-200 cm.) extends from the middle reaches of the Amazon south through the heart of Brazil and embraces practically the whole coast and the mountain belts from São Salvador to northern Rio Grande do Sul.

West of this in Matto Grosso, south of it in Rio Grande do Sul, and eastward toward the semi-arid region, are areas which receive from forty to sixty inches (100-150 cm.). Within the same rainfall belt in the United States lies most of Louisiana, Mississippi, Alabama, Tennessee, Kentucky, and the whole Atlantic seaboard from Florida to Maine.

The crest of the Serra do Mar in the State of São Paulo shows the highest rainfall recorded anywhere in Brazil. In comparison Manáos is an arid desert, Belém seems only slightly damp, and even the tremendous maxima which have been recorded (perhaps erroneously?) for Recife sink into insignificance. At Alto da Serra it *rains!* The English railway between Santos and São Paulo has kept records since 1870. Where the incline ends and the rails bend over the edge of the plateau, their records show an average annual rainfall of 3,696 millimeters—say twelve feet; with a special effort in 1872 amounting to 5,562 millimeters. If we consider ten feet of rain on the Pacific Coast a prodigious amount of water, what shall we say of eighteen feet and over?

He who complains of the dreadful monotony of intertropical climates should take a boat and make the jump from the twelve feet of rainfall behind Santos to the aridity of Ceará at the height of a *secca*, a "dryness." Instead of the luxuriant foliage of the rain forest, his eyes will be seared by the leaflessness of a thorny scrub and the brittleness of withered grass. Instead of the aroma of ferny glades and forest mold, his nostrils will be assailed by the stench of carrion—cattle, and goats, and horses rotting upon the plain. Instead of men holding umbrellas above them as they hurry to tiffin, he will see thousands of human skeletons dragging their hungry bellies toward the coast.

Upon the map of rainfall the Northeast looks like a pockmarked face with an acid burn across the cheek. Burned and marked by a dread disease it is, a disease that seems to come and go with the cyclones on the surface of the sun. The reason is not plain from the map. We consider twenty inches of rain enough in the United States for dry farming. Most of northeast Brazil has a mean annual rainfall of more than twenty inches; there are times in Ceará when the rivers will rise twenty feet in a single night! But there are other times, recurring through the centuries with a rhythm like the breathing of a troubled god, when the rains fail utterly for one, two, and sometimes three successive years. Then descends a terrible sadness upon the kingdom of the drought, a blazing blasphemy which the downpour upon that waste of Amazon waters does but mock.

Temperature contrasts in Brazil are not so striking. Yet they are great. Between a winter day in Curityba when the thermometer descends to 16° and a summer afternoon in

Uruguayana, on the Argentine boundary, when it runs up to 107.6°—the highest maximum recorded in Brazil—there is room for all reasonable human activities. The Far South with a mean annual temperature of from 60° to 68° differs profoundly from the North, where it hangs around 80°. The miner in the high mountains of Minas Geraes who shivers through a June night and gets up in the morning to find ice on his water bucket is experiencing very different sensations from the rubber gatherer along the Amazon. A south wind blowing over the pampas of Rio Grande do Sul at times bites with the keen-cutting slash of a vicious dog, but the east winds blowing over Rio Grande do Norte ever caress like the hands of a gentle woman. Particularly should those who think of Brazil only as a tropical country realize that, in addition to the greatest of tropical empires, Brazil includes a temperate region as large as France and the United Kingdom combined.

Which makes it necessary to define what we mean by temperate and tropical regions. The tropics have been variously defined as the belt between Cancer and Capricorn; as the region between the polar extension of the trade winds; and as the region between the mean annual isotherms of 20° Centigrade (68° F.), which closely coincides with the habitat of palms. The last best fits the facts. By that definition the whitest area on my map of mean annual temperature is *temperate*—as temperate as the United States south of the Mason and Dixon Line. It includes the mountains of southern Minas Geraes, Rio de Janeiro, eastern São Paulo; and all of Paraná, Santa Catharina, and Rio Grande do Sul. Altitude carries its northern margin to within nineteen degrees of the equator, well north of Capricorn. And in eastern Pernambuco, the highlands carry a chill into the very heart of the tropics, to within eight degrees of the equator.

In the very heart of Brazil, near the Federal District which has been set aside as a future national capital, Catalão, in Goyaz, at an elevation of twenty-seven hundred feet, shows a mean temperature of only 69°, with 91° and 48° as the

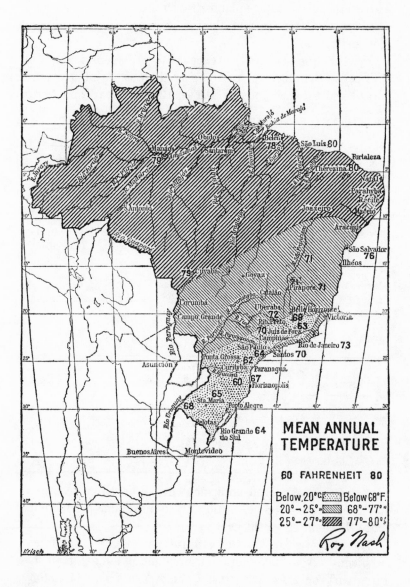

MEAN ANNUAL
TEMPERATURE

60 FAHRENHEIT 80

Below 20°C. ▦ Below 68°F.
20°–25° ▨ 68°–77° "
25°–27° ▥ 77°–80° "

Roy Nash

extremes. The whole upland district forming the watershed between the Amazon and Paraná drainage is similarly cool and delightful.

Few are the scientists, except Ellsworth Huntington, who will argue that there is anything in the *climate* of temperate Brazil and the highlands of Minas, Bahia, Goyaz, and Matto

BRAZILIAN TEMPERATURES (Fahrenheit) IN THE MARITIME MOUNTAINS

METEOROLOGIC STATION	LATITUDE SOUTH	ALTITUDE FEET	MEAN ANNUAL	ABSOLUTE Maxima	Minima
* Petropolis, Rio	22° 31'	2,676	65	89	38
* Alto do Itatiaya, Rio ...	22° 27'	7,245	52	70	23
Nova Friburgo, Rio	22° 17'	2,775	63	91	33
Caxambú, Minas	22° 12'	2,968	64	91	25
Juiz de Fora, Minas	21° 45'	2,230	67	101	35
Barbacena, Minas	21° 15'	3,575	63	88	33
* Ouro Preto, Minas	20° 23'	3,667	64	88	36
Montes Claros, Minas ...	16° 43'	2,017	71	102	35
Caetité, Bahia	14° 03'	2,952	17	95	50
Morro do Chapéo, Bahia..	11° 33'	3,542	68	92	49
* Garanhuns, Pernambuco.	8° 57'	2,788	69	94	58

Figures for the year 1920 *only.*

TEMPERATURES (Fahrenheit) IN TORRID BRAZIL

METEOROLOGIC STATION	Annual	MEAN Hottest Month	Coldest Month	ABSOLUTE Maxima	Minima
Manáos, Amazonas	79	November 81	April 78	99	66
Quixadá, Ceará	80	December and January 84	June 77	97	69
Cuyabá, Matto Grosso....	79	October 81	June 74	100	45

Grosso to prevent even unpigmented Nordics from maintaining generation after generation their maximum productivity and self-admitted excellence.

The black belt of my temperature map presents a different problem. Over that enormous area mean annual temperatures vary only four degrees, from 77° to 80°. Monotony is reality here, a sameness in the march of the seasons that can hardly fail to impress itself upon the spirit of man. The data are almost the same for places as widely distant as Manáos in the super-humid Amazon, Quixadá in the semi-arid Northeast, and Cuyabá in the Plains of the Upper Paraguay. The coldest month is within eight degrees of the hottest. While the temperature never rises above 100°, yet it never falls below 45° in Cuyabá and 66° in Manáos.

A peculiar factor which mitigates this annual monotony should be stressed, however. Night is winter along the Line. At many points under the equator the whole annual range of temperature is experienced within twenty-four hours. And it is probably a literal fact that with a given number of people, there is more shivering of nights among the naked savages of the Amazon forest than in the igloos of the Eskimos of Alaska.

With these qualifications, we must admit that most of Brazil is warm and that most of Brazil is moist. But that the bulk of the population during the first four centuries has congregated in the dryer and cooler portions is by no means due alone to heat and humidity *per se*. Equally it is due to the fact that a by-product of heat and humidity—the evergreen hardwood forest—has always proved a devilish hard nut for the primitive agriculturist to crack.

§ 3. FORESTS [1]

Whatever be their effects upon man, warmth and humidity are certainly the proud parents of the most vigorous offspring of the vegetable world, the evergreen hardwood forest. The conquest of Brazil at every step has been a battle with the exuberant infant. In the half of Brazil where Europeans during four hundred years have made scarcely a mark, the self-renewing armies under their green battle flags are as unconquered today as in 1500. Are they unconquerable? Let

[1] In preparing this section I have enjoyed the unusual courtesy of seeing in manuscript *The Forests of Brazil*, soon to be published by Dr. H. N. Whitford, Professor of Tropical Forestry in the Yale Forest School, and Chief of the Crude Rubber Survey, U.S. Dept. of Commerce.

us penetrate within the lines of these massed forces, these coherent organic entities which in 1500 defended the coast with scarcely a break from São Roque to Rio Grande do Sul and from São Luiz to the Guianas.

Many things the tropical forest has meant to as many men. To the Indian, abundant home. To the convict turned adrift by the early Portuguese, abominable hell. To Hudson these tangles of verdure were "Green Mansions" of inexpressible delight. For Roosevelt it came near being a grave. For two immortals, the high evergreen forest of Brazil was the birthplace of one of the most prolific ideas which illumined thought during the nineteenth century. One originator of the doctrine of natural selection, Alfred Russel Wallace, spent four years in the Amazon forest. "Struggle!" a million voices chanted daily. "It is the Law." And the nicely attuned ear of his attentive intelligence heard and interpreted. Darwin, too, be it remembered, had his first glimpse of the vigor of nature in the tropics in the outskirts of old São Salvador; and in Brazil, after those portentous years in the Pacific, he gazed his last upon the teeming life of the evergreen forest before he propounded the theory that Struggle for Existence is the Law of Life.

To the forester, the forest shows another side than to either savage, settler, artist, hunter, or naturalist. He is often nearer the naturalists of the old school than most overspecialized scientists of today. The ways of the furred and feathered are less mysterious to him than the ways of man; he sometimes kills as part of the day's work, but he never forgets they are his special wards. Upon a canvas of a thousand square leagues he dares design patterns of beauty and utility which require centuries to work out in detail. Upon occasion his medium masters him and he reverts to savagery. But above all and before all, the forester is a scientist with a social viewpoint. Man's need, not of today alone, but down the rippling centuries, is the scale wherein he weighs all values.

Upon entering a new region, the forester's first endeavor is

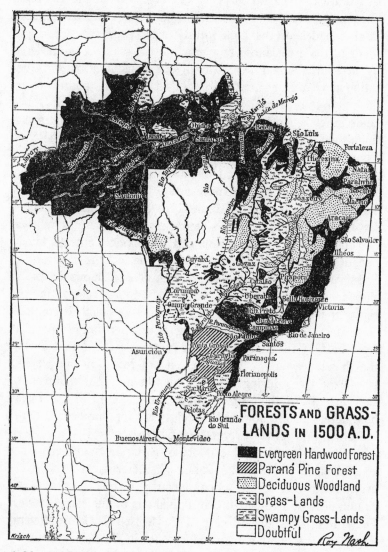

FORESTS AND GRASS-
LANDS IN 1500 A.D.

■ Evergreen Hardwood Forest
▨ Paraná Pine Forest
▦ Deciduous Woodland
▤ Grass-Lands
▨ Swampy Grass-Lands
☐ Doubtful

Roy Nash

A Map Which Detailed Studies Will Modify.

to picture the vegetal carpet as a whole. What are the main lineaments, the large masses? Where has Nature splashed in the shades of the high forest? where and why the highlights of the grasslands? how much of the seashore is bordered by decorative mangrove swamp? A consideration of vegetation now existing and an appraisal of man's modifications during four centuries yields the map of Forests and Grasslands in 1500 A.D.[2] Only three types of forest are there distinguished, the Evergreen Hardwood Forest, the Paraná Pine Forest, and Deciduous Woodlands.

The evergreen hardwood forest is the child of wet weather. In its most luxuriant manifestation it covers the Amazon Valley and the Maritime Mountains where the rainfall is over sixty inches. That portion which clothes the Amazon plain and the margins of the Guiana Highlands and Central Plateau constitutes, with the possible exception of the conifers in Russia and Siberia, the greatest area of continuous forest on the face of the globe. As its name implies, at no time of the year is this forest destitute of leaves, although it contains some deciduous species. In these two super-humid areas, at least half of the full leafy canopy adorns the forest during the driest season. (There are certain parts of the plateau where the trees during the drier months may not retain more than a tenth of their full canopy; the make-up of the forest here differs also somewhat in species; but for simplicity I lump evergreen and partly evergreen types together.)

As simplicity is the chief glory of a stand of southern pine, so complexity is the outstanding characteristic of the evergreen hardwood forest. Look about. Rarely does the eye simultaneously light upon two individuals of the same species. Dr. Huber, one-time director of the Museu Goeldi in Belém, estimated the number of woody plants in the Amazon forest at ten thousand species, of which twenty-five hundred are trees. Dr. Whitford believes that if the smaller trees of the

[2] Based on the *Mappa Florestal*, Serviço Geologico e Mineralogico do Brazil, 1911.

The evergreen hardwood forest, on the Rio Doce, Espirito Santo.

Woodland pastures of eastern Matto Grosso. This type of vegetation alternates with stretches of open prairie. (See pages 74-75.)

The rolling prairies of Rio Grande do Sul, one of the finest cattle ranges in the world. (See page 73.)

under story be included, the number of species of trees in the Amazon is not less than eight thousand—ten times the number so classified in the entire United States. Add to this a profusion of lianas, showy parasites, air plants, bamboos, and palms, and the average northerner is bewildered by the multiplicity of unfamiliar forms. "What charming chaos!" he is apt to say.

A lumberman from the United States or Canada enters this tropical evergreen forest. He is used to logging practically pure stands of pine, or spruce, or Douglas fir. Impatiently he snatches an ax from one of the porters and deals the nearest bole a blow. The ax resounds and rebounds. "The damned stuff is like iron!" he curses. He looks about. "And there aren't two logs of the same kind alike in the whole jungle anyway." He returns to the northland in disgust.

Not so fast, sir! There is a valid historical reason why the man in the street should regard the evergreen hardwood forest as exclusively the home of woods for which general commerce has small need, but there is no reason why any well informed lumberman should continue to cling to the same superstition. Softness, lightness, and ease of working, the great world chiefly demands. The first tropical woods which found their way into European markets possessed the opposite of these qualities. Long before the Portuguese found the route to India, the Arabs possessed a powerful fleet. Teak was used in its construction. Sandalwood, satinwood, ebony, and blackwood formed part of the cargoes which these teak ships started for the markets of the Mediterranean. Such were further singled out as "royal trees" by princelings who desired a monopoly of the lucrative commerce.[3] The other seven thousand nine hundred and ninety species they labeled "jungle." Came the English to dominate India. Teak for the British Navy was the cry that turned the eyes of England toward the tropical hardwood forest. So teak became the royal tree of the English; the rest they, too, labeled "jungle-brush." Thus Europe,

[3] E. P. Stebbing, *The Forests of India,* I, 34.

and later America, came to think of the tropical forest as producing just three kinds of timber: teak; stuff like quebracho and lignum vitae which somewhat resembles iron; and cabinet woods like rosewood and sandalwood which are as rare as gold nuggets. And this misconception persisted long after the German foresters who organized the Indian Forest Service had begun to make manifest the real nature of the evergreen hardwood forest.

American foresters are a product of the present generation; no American forester ever saw a tropical forest until we went into the Philippines. There, during the first decade of the twentieth century, they dealt the superstition another blow. They saw that the despised "jungle-brush" of Burma and the Malay Peninsula, while including many species, showed an essential homogeneity—nearly seventy-five per cent of the stands in the Philippines proved to be related species, mainly of the Dipterocarps, which were sufficiently soft and possessed other physical properties enabling them to compete in the world markets with the conifers which still constitute the bulk of construction timbers.

There is one American boast which even our enemies concede is well founded. As butchers of the bush, North American lumbermen are about ten times as efficient as any other breed whose business it is to disfigure the face of the earth. They are not notoriously sentimental. Foresters in the Philippines induced lumbermen from the Pacific Coast to put in donkey engines and modern sawmills that can handle anything thrown at them, to test out their ideas. Such men invested their hard dollars, weighed the commonest woods of the Philippines in the even scales of international trade, and demonstrated that the evergreen hardwood forest contains a majority of trees for which the world has daily need in quantity. In the output of Philippine sawmills the excessively hard woods and cabinet woods are the merest drop in the bucket.

What have the forests of the Philippines, North Borneo,

and the Straits Settlements to do with Brazil? This: British
and Americans in that part of the world have proved out the
tropical forest. Two of the most competent American foresters who made their mark in the Philippines, Mr. Hugh
Curran and Dr. H. N. Whitford, are the two North Americans
who know best the forests of Brazil. Both hold the generalization as valid in the Amazon and maritime forests of Brazil
as in Malaysia—the evergreen hardwood forest of the tropics
contains in quantity the kind and quality of wood for which
the world most loudly calls.

In the United States of this first quarter of the twentieth
century, the bulk of our hardwood cut consists of oaks and
red gum; beech, birch, and maple; ash and hickory; yellow
poplar and basswood. Brazil has substitutes for every one
of these. In the maritime forests of Bahia back of Ilhéos,
for instance, where I wandered for many months, Mr. Curran
found that ten species compose the bulk of the stand, forty
per cent of which is soft stuff corresponding to yellow poplar
in physical characteristics; thirty per cent about like maple,
ash, and oak; and not more than thirty per cent harder than
white oak. Similar conditions prevail in the bulk of the great
Amazon forest.[4] This is not a wild guess but a deliberate
judgment arrived at by competent foresters after years of
study in the field, mechanical tests at the Yale Forest School
laboratory and at the Forest Products Laboratory in Wis-
consin, and fabrication tests by the Wood-Turners' Association, by the Motor Wheel Company in Michigan, and by
flooring manufacturers in·Memphis. I stress the point because
upon it hinges the practicability of the forest policy which
I shall suggest in Book IV, and because I believe that the
whole question of the ultimate conquest of the Amazon is
bound up with it intimately.

In addition to every conceivable quality of timber, the evergreen hardwood forest contains a bewildering wealth of minor

[4] Zon and Sparhawk, *Forest Resources of the World,* II, 717.

forest products: Brazil nuts, and paradise nuts, and calabashes to carry them home in; palm nuts that yield oil for salad or soap; half a dozen trees and vines that yield rubber to the hand that wounds them; fibers galore for everything from a Panama hat or a tucum hammock to the brushes of a rotary street-cleaner; tanning materials; withes and rattan; vanilla, tonka beans, copal gum, vegetable wax; firewood and wood for charcoal; to say nothing of *ipecacuanha,* and *guaraná,* and *ucuhuhu.* The evergreen hardwood forest is as rich as Sahara is poor; as fundamentally hospitable toward all life as Greenland is hostile; as full of promise as a watermelon of seeds. To primitive man it has yielded such wealth as to relieve him of the necessity of exercising his brain; to the man of science it will yield abundance undreamed. No storehouse outside the Arabian Nights contains treasures comparable.

A very different type of forest clothes the high plateau of Paraná and Santa Catharina, the so-called Paraná pine. (Botanically it is not a pine but an araucaria.) Here the northerner feels much more at home than in the evergreen hardwood forest. The lower story is just such a thicket of bushes and hardwoods as in northeastern United States. Towering above to heights of from a hundred to a hundred and sixty feet, the straight, clean boles of the araucaria lift their very striking crowns in benediction above the lesser denizens of the forest. Justly proud are they of being the only commercial conifer in Brazil. When growing in nearly pure stands, as Paraná pine sometimes does, or where standing as isolated islands of lofty verdure in a sea of grass, these trees form a rarely beautiful type of forest—Asiatic umbrellas opened high above the hills. The type extends into southern São Paulo and northern Rio Grande do Sul; and from the eastern edge of the plateau to the Rio Paraná, where it seems abruptly to end. The leaves of one of the small trees of the under story are marketed as Brazilian tea (*Herva mate*) and consumed morning, noon, and night by all the folk of southern Brazil, Uruguay, Paraguay, and northern Argentina.

The only other type of forest which I have shown on the map is the deciduous woodlands of the semi-arid regions, the *caatingas* and *charravascal* of the Brazilians. Its nearest relative in the United States is the chaparral of our Southwest. As the evergreen forest is the child of wet weather, so are deciduous woodlands the children of the drought. All the wonderful devices which Nature has invented for conserving moisture are evident in the bristle-pointed leaves, the spines, and pores of gnarled and stunted trees which must learn the trick of going without a drink for a couple of years, or perish. Round-headed they are, and commonly not over twenty-five or thirty feet high, like the wry apple trees encountered in the pastures of New England. During the pronounced dry seasons of these regions and the years when rainfall fails entirely, these woodlands are as bare of leaves as New England in midwinter. The Brazilian caatingas furnish inferior fuel and some tanbark, but their prime economic function is as pasture for cattle and goats. From southern Matto Grosso this type alternates with open grasslands all through the region of which the Rio São Francisco is the heart and the coast of Ceará the northern margin.

Athwart these three great types determined chiefly by temperature and rainfall cross all the variations upon these themes played by such factors as scanty soil, too much water, the pulsing of tidal waters, and what not. The moisture of the river bottoms carried threads and ribbons of evergreen forest far into the withered heart of the enemy's country. I have sailed down parts of the Rio São Francisco and Rio Paracatú in northern Minas where, from the forest along the shores, one would have imagined himself in the heart of the Amazon jungle; inland half a mile, however, one enters the caatingas [5] which proclaim the aridity of the region. These minor types,

---

[5] Sir Richard Burton says the word is from the Tupy *Caa,* forest, bush, leaf, grass; and *tinga,* white.

including mangrove swamps, while of vast importance locally, cannot be shown on a small-scale map.[6]

The careful estimate made by the Brazilian Geologic Service in 1911 of the probable area of forest at the time the Portuguese began to modify the landscape, shows fifty-nine per cent of the country originally under forest, some 1,235,172,000 acres. That estimate included under "forests" only my two classes of evergreen forests and Paraná pine; it does *not* include the caatingas.

No statement of acreage running into ten figures, nor of

BRAZILIAN FORESTS AND GRASSLANDS IN 1500 A.D.

(From the Mappa Florestal, Serviço
Geologico e Mineralogico do Brazil, 1911)

STATE	AREA	FORESTS OF EVERGREEN HARDWOOD AND PARANÁ PINE ONLY	GRASSLANDS, DECIDUOUS WOODLAND, AND OTHER FORMATIONS
	Square Miles	Per cent.	
Territorio do Acre	74,100	100	..
Amazonas	707,400	92	8
Pará	470,900	76	24
Maranhão	131,350	43	57
Ceará	60,850	43	57
Piauhy	89,200	27	73
Rio Grande do Norte	21,700	25	75
Parahyba	20,150	37	63
Pernambuco	36,750	34	66
Alagoâs	11,750	28	72
Sergipe	8,400	41	59
Bahia	226,750	37	63
Goyaz	247,250	28	72
Matto Grosso	599,900	39	61
Minas Geraes	234,650	46	54
Rio Grande do Sul........	109,350	31	69
Espirito Santo	15,100	77	23
Rio de Janeiro	17,100	81	19
São Paulo	96,500	65	35
Paraná	69,600	83	17
Santa Catharina	42,500	79	21
TOTAL	3,291,300	58.6	41.4

[6] Any one interested further should consult Dr. Whitford's book when it appears; it is the first adequate description of Brazilian forests that any competent forester has attempted.

board feet five thousand times that figure, however, gives
any concept of the vastness of Brazil's original forests. If
one could drift over the Amazon in a balloon he would get
something of it. Immensity would impress itself upon him
as does a crossing of the ocean. And only thus would one
glory of this vegetable world be revealed, for the flowery
surfaces of the great trees generally face the sun. Nothing
except long residence within the Great Silence, however, would
convey any idea of the vigor of the crashing images of life
and death which succeed one another with astounding swiftness; nor of a fecundity which makes of each veteran who
emerges triumphant from the struggle for light and air—a
struggle as brutal as that in the Black Hole of Calcutta—a
conservatory, a hortus, a botanical garden of air plants and
parasites battening upon his lordly strength.

§ 4. Native Pastures

As the evergreen forest is somber and gloomy, so are Brazilian pastures sunny and gay. In the jungle one can reach
out and touch the horizon. Move where he will, the vertical
bars of his prison ever interpose between him and the sun.
But the open grasslands invite the eye away and away to where
earth curves off toward the level rice-paddies of China; or the
yellow sands of Africa; or the snapping, snow-capped poles.
Here one may bask in the sun and desiccate the dampness
of "the steaming stillness." Here in due season the green
of the Inferno of Monotony gives way to gold, and all the
hillsides deck themselves in brown. I am impatient to call
forth upon them the low-moaning of the kine and the swiftness of the steeds that shall crunch the sweet grass when the
Conquerors have come. The poetry of the first four hundred
years was written in the *campos* of Brazil. About the camp-
fires of the *vaqueiros* is the *violão* most often heard. Swiftly,
then, let me picture the pasture lands.

Upon my map of vegetative types everything which is not

forest has been pictured as "grasslands." This may appear as more optimistic than scientific, yet I know no area in Brazil except bald mountain tops and the sands of the seashore which does not receive sufficient moisture to call some form of vegetation into being: no areas of sandy desert like north Africa, no areas as scantily clad as Arizona and Nevada, no areas even in the dryest caatingas which do not produce enough grass to pasture goats at some season of the year. The worst of this is very poor pasture indeed, as I shall presently point out; but it is nevertheless pasture and serviceable to nomadic neatherds and shepherds. We must distinguish, however, between the swamp pastures, the open grasslands of the plateau, and several varieties of woodland pasture.

At certain seasons of the year the swampy grasslands of Brazil (*pantanaes*) can probably support as many cattle to the square mile as any extensive native pastures in the world. They are flood plains which are in large measure covered with standing water at the height of the rainy season. Their largest extension clothes the Plains of the Upper Paraguay. Those plains once formed part of the bed of the ancient Pampean Sea, they are but slightly elevated above the sluggish streams which drain them, and their soil consists of alluvial deposits of very recent times. At the season of flood the Paraguay River rises from twelve to twenty feet above low-water level, and tributary streams proportionally. Immense areas are converted into shallow lakes. Here lie both the strength and the weakness of these pastures. For at flood it is obvious the grazing grounds are enormously reduced. Islands of higher land (*capoes*) dot the whole plain; but upon these the moisture calls forth not grass but trees; and these islands are for the most part covered with a dense semi-evergreen forest, entirely too dense to afford decent forage. Only about their margins is good grass; and here, between the devil and the deep sea, the cattle must find solid footing and worry through as best they may.

THE
UNITED STATES
OF
BRAZIL

1 RIO GRANDE DO NORTE
2 PARAHYBA DO NORTE
3 ALAGÔAS
4 SERGIPE
5 ESPIRITO SANTO
6 RIO DE JANEIRO
7 DISTRICTO FEDERAL
8 FUTURA CAPITAL FEDERAL

Photograph by São Paulo Geographic and Geologic Commission.

Some of the big constrictors that inhabit the waters and woods of Brazil. These are from the Rio Grande in São Paulo.

The results of a good day's shooting in the forest: a tapir; the great rodent, *capivara;* a monkey; and a *mutum,* a bird, as toothsome as wild turkey.

Another view of the evergreen hardwood forest, on the Rio Doce.

Photograph by São Paulo Geographic and Geologic Commission.

The rugged shore characteristic of the coast between Victoria and Santa Catharina.

The lovely little land-locked harbor of Victoria.

The most extensive swamp pasture in Brazil lies along the main Paraguay River and 'its affluents, the São Lourenço, Cuyabá, Pequiry, Taquary, Negro, and Aquidauana. There is very little pantanal below the twentieth parallel. A second great area of swamp pasture extends along the Rio Guaporé and its affluents, the Cautario, Cautarinho, São Miguel, São Simão, Rio Branco do São Simão, and Colorado do Mequens. Considerable pasture of this type borders the Rio Paraná and the Araguaya. The delta of the Rio Doce, in Espirito Santo, is pantanal. About half the Island of Marajó at the mouth of the Amazon (an island as large as the State of New York) is swamp pasture. And along the Lower Amazon, behind the narrow fringe of forest which deceives the traveler on the river, there are great ribbons of this swamp pasture covering the flood plain. Much of the grassland in the heart of the Amazon forest, such as the great Campos de Puciary north of Santo Antonio on the Madeira, the Campos Tyrene near the mouth of the Rio Acre, and the Campos Esperança in the Territorio do Acre, is flooded at high water.

The open grasslands of the plateau are pastures of a type with which we are thoroughly familiar in the United States. The prairies of Rio Grande do Sul are the counterpart of southern Illinois and Missouri, better to the extent that they are warmer. In the eastern part of the state the terrain is much more rolling than Illinois; west of Santa Maria it begins to flatten out until down in the southwest corner, beyond Alegrete, the land is almost as flat as the pampas of Argentina. Wonderfully watered,—far better than the region west, of La Plata,—with no severe winters to fight, and clothed with luxuriant natural grasses, Rio Grande do Sul is one of the finest cattle-growing regions in the world.

Aside from this region it is difficult to point out any part of Brazil where large extensions of open, high, and dry pasture exist. While the aggregate of good clean pasture (*campo limpo*) encountered within the Paraná pine forest region and beyond the forest in Minas, Matto Grosso, Goyaz, and Bahia, is enormous; yet, aside from Rio Grande do Sul, there is no vast *continuous* pasture free from tree growth such as the Great Plains of the United States or the pampas of Argentina. Characteristically, the campos of Brazil show scattered woody vegetation. Open grasslands are interlarded between various types of woodland pasture in a way impossible to indicate on a small-scale map, even if we possessed the detailed information.

The various names used to designate different qualities of woodland pasture in Brazil (*Campos cerrados, campos agrestes,* etc.) have no very precise meaning. The easiest way to picture them is to think of a series at one end of which are the open pampas, at the other *carrascos* where the vegetation is even more dwarfed and stunted than in the caatingas, ranging between three and six feet, dense and indecent as chaparral. Between them lie the caatingas, where dwarfed trees form an inferior forest; then pastures with very scattered trees lead back to the open lands again. In all these woodland pastures the cover is so open that the sun easily penetrates to the soil and grass grows between the trees. At the magic touch of the rains the caatingas burst into prodigious bloom; tender, succulent grasses spring up with extraordinary luxuriance. The rancher who enters then easily imagines himself in a herdsman's paradise. But in the dry season, much of the caatinga country does not show a vestige of herbaceous vegetation. Bare red soil and beds of gravel. The grass has simply disappeared. It isn't. A single evergreen tree, the *joazeiro,* the grotesque forms of giant cacti, and bushes along the watercourses are the only green things that relieve the grays and the brown of a parching horror.

As the grass fails in certain swamp pastures during the floods, so it fails in the woodland pastures of Piauhy, Ceará, Parahyba, Rio Grande do Norte, Pernambuco, and northern Bahia during the droughts. Between these two extremes, on the plateau of southern Bahia. northern Minas, Goyaz, and

Matto Grosso, woodland pastures alternate with open campos and can be counted on to sustain flocks and herds three hundred and sixty-five days in the year, though the hills get pretty brown at the end of the dry season.

The last great pasture region of Brazil is north of the Amazon in the Guiana Highlands, particularly on the upper Rio Branco. Its precise boundaries cannot be laid down in the present state of our knowledge; such information as we have seems to indicate that an open type of woodland pasture predominates.

With the carrying capacity of these lands I shall deal in a later chapter on Brazilian herds. Obviously it varies widely. Much of Brazilian pasture is as good as the best; much of the semi-arid northeast is almost worthless. The total grass-producing area is so enormous, however, that it is obvious Brazil possessed, at the time of Portuguese discovery, adequate native pastures to feed as vast herds and flocks as the United States ever maintained.

§ 5. POWER

For an agricultural and pastoral civilization, no more is needed than fertile soil, fair weather, forests, and grazing lands. For an industrial civilization, add iron and power. In the chapter on mineral exploitation it will appear that Brazil has fine reserves of high-grade iron ore. Here let me point out that she is not noticeably deficient in power.

Industrial civilization now depends chiefly upon two sources for power: coal and falling water. Of the former, the Brazilian beds so far discovered are not of high grade. Recent hydro-electric developments, however, with the proven possibility of transmitting for distances of five hundred miles or more, have brought about an industrial revolution in countries like California, Switzerland, and Norway, which have no coal resources. Hydro-electric power is the king of the future, and of the falling waters upon which it depends, Brazil possesses an abundance.[1]

The estimates of available hydraulic power quoted by Lindeman give the United States 54,000,000 horsepower,[2] Brazil 50,000,000 horsepower, and Canada 26,000,000. Obviously much less is known about the falls of Brazil than of the northern countries, and it is probable that Brazil possesses more potential hydraulic power than any other country in the world. This results from the enormous extent of the Central Plateau and the Guiana Highlands—the rivers cannot get into the plains without jumping off. Those flowing from the lesser elevation of the Guiana Highlands descend over only moderate falls, like those on the Rio Negro where the equator cuts it and the Rio Branco on the second parallel north, yet all the lesser affluents of the Amazon from the north are capable of developing some power.

It is the mighty rivers of the Central Plateau that produce the stuff about which so much of modern civilization is built. On the Argentine frontier where the Iguassú takes a leap of 225 feet more or less (70 m.), engineers have figured a possible 7,000,000 horsepower on the Brazilian side. Continuing up the Rio Paraná to the corner of Paraguay brings us to the roar of the Sete Quedas, with a possible 8,000,000 H.P. Affluents of the Paraguay like the Cuyabá and Sepotuba, and all the eastern tributaries of the Guaporé, fall off the plateau; but the edge of the plateau is too near their headwaters for them to develop much volume. The falls that interrupt steam navigation on the Madeira for two hundred miles above Santo Antonio could develop prodigious power; and every river that flows towards the Amazon between the Madeira and Tocantins leaves the plateau with a powerful rush; the Gy-Paraná, Roosevelt, Tapajós, Xingú, Tocantins,

[1] The figures which follow are taken from "Hydro-Electric Power in Brazil," by F. Lindeman, *The Brazilian-American*, Anniversary Number, 1920; and "Hydraulic Power in the State of São Paulo," *The Brazilian-American*, April 8, 1922.

[2] Huntington and Cushing, *Human Geography*, p. 202, says 100,000,000 H.P.

and all their lesser sisters are mad streams in many places. Down the Atlantic side, there is no great fall between the Tocantins and the São Francisco. Paulo Affonso, however, makes up for the lapse when you do get there. Its leap is 260 feet (80 m.), and it is rated at 3,000,000 horsepower. Every stream coming out of the highlands from São Salvador to Rio de Janeiro is a power producer: the Rio Paraguassú; the Rio das Contas; the Salto Grande of the Jequitinhonha, with a height of about 150 feet (44 m.); three falls on the Rio Doce; others on all the rivers to the south.

While the three most formidable falls in Brazil—Iguassú, Sete Quedas, and Paulo Affonso—are included in that marginal tour, we have made the merest beginning in the enumeration of great powers. For practically every considerable stream of the plateau descends over a whole series of falls at varying distances inland from the margin. He who wants a vivid idea of the structure of the southern affluents of the Amazon should go *Through the Brazilian Wilderness* with Roosevelt.

After six hours' march we came to the crossing of the Rio Sacre at the beautiful waterfall appropriately called the Salto Bello. . . . There is a sheer drop of forty or fifty yards, with a breadth two or three times as great; and the volume of water is large. . . . It was only two hours' march across to the Papagaio at the Falls of Utiarity. . . . Lovely though we had found Salto Bello, these falls were far superior in beauty and majesty. They are twice as high and twice as broad. . . . I doubt whether, excepting, of course, Niagara, there is a waterfall in North America which outranks this, if both volume and beauty are considered.

Now the point is that these two great falls are at the very sources of the Tapajós! Between Utiarity and the last falls where the Tapajós drops into the Amazon plain between the fourth and fifth parallels, there are dozens of falls, each spelling "Power." The series of falls and rapids on the Rio Roosevelt which came so near wrecking the Roosevelt-Rondon expedition is characteristic of all the big rivers coming off the plateau.

In the State of São Paulo alone there are about one hundred waterfalls, each capable of developing more than ten thousand horsepower. The Cachoeira do Maribondo on the Rio Grande is rated at near 600,000 H.P. The Salto dos Patos (Leap of the Ducks) close by can produce 120,000 more.

It must be patent to whoever ponders the structure of Brazil and its heavy rainfall, that the estimate which puts the possible hydraulic power of the country as equal to the possible hydraulic power of the United States, is founded on abundant fact.

§ 6. FAUNA

Mechanical power is of small consequence to pioneers during the first centuries of their attempts at conquest. But from the moment the prows of their boats ground upon the alien shore, they have a lively interest in fish and game which may be transferred from waters and woods to their pots and spits; in carnivorous beasts and poisonous snakes which may be lurking round the corner; and in the insects that shall pester their slumbers until one, more virulent than the rest, injects the germ which rings down the final curtain.

Let me dispose of the perils first. There is no subject about which the imagination of the stay-at-home Northerner luxuriates so profusely. Let a New Yorker announce that he has a ticket to Borneo, Central Africa, or the Amazon, and immediately family and friends begin to picture him wrenching himself free from the coils of mammoth constrictors, in nightly peril from the man-eating carnivora which prowl about his camp, or caught in the jaws of the crocodile which has overturned his canoe. A primitive mind picturing the perils of crossing Broadway could not invent a tale that is further from the facts. So in reading what follows it is well to bear in mind that the drug which in concentration is poison, in dilution may be but a gentle stimulant. The hazards to human life which here are concentrated in a few paragraphs, in nature are diluted by three million square miles of space.

Wild animals in Brazil are no menace to man whatsoever. The jaguar (*Felis onca*) is the only beast which by any stretch of language could be called a man-killer. The big cat has enough courage to attack and pull down bulls on the Matto Grosso ranges, and there are a few authenticated instances of jaguars padding into camp and nipping a sleeping man.[1] But these instances are so rare that I venture to say there are more Brazilians gored by cattle in a year than are attacked by unwounded jaguars in a century. The naked Indian armed only with a spear and a forked stick pulled its teeth to make him a necklace and stretched its mottled hide to make him a bed. None of the other carnivora are man-killers, except as any animal may become when fighting for life at close quarters.

Nor are the big snakes which, ever since man was driven from the Garden of Eden, have struck terror to the human heart, a lively menace. The Brazilian anaconda, a water serpent, seems to attain the healthiest dimensions of any snake in the world: Bates credits tales of forty-two feet. From that they run up to "The Spirit of the Waters" of the Amazon Indians, a sea-serpent of legendary proportions. Anacondas above twenty feet long and two feet in girth about the middle are in fact common. Neither does the constrictor with a preference for land appear to suffer from malnutrition. But it is significant that in eleven years of constant collecting in the Amazon forest, Bates encountered only two of these big fellows, and narrates a single instance that came under his observation of an anaconda attacking a child bathing. The constrictors are encountered by man so rarely as to constitute no menace at all, although the thought of them sometimes mars the pleasure of a plunge in turbid waters.

Poisonous snakes constitute the liveliest violent peril to

[1] See Roosevelt, *Through the Brazilian Wilderness*, p. 31.

man in Brazil. It is real to whoever has much business in the bush. The pit-vipers are represented by a dozen deadly species, including the giant bush master, the dread fer-de-lance (*jararáca*) whose bite was the equivalent of a sentence to the electric chair until modern science brought forth its serums, and rattlesnakes. All these vipers are armed with fangs as sharp as a hypodermic needle and stiff enough to penetrate anything less than sole leather. Barefooted men have learned to become close students of mottled coils. The poisonous colubrine snakes have small fangs but are fully as deadly. The time to tread lightly is when clearing land: a friend for whose veracity I can vouch killed and counted twenty-six poisonous snakes while stripping the grass and brush from about four acres of land on the Rio Gongogy, in the evergreen forest of southern Bahia. This hazard to man and to domestic animals is not to be minimized; yet it should be noted that it is a peril which practically disappears with the cultivation of land, and that there are large areas of Brazil where poisonous snakes are no menace whatever.

When swimming or fording the rivers of tropical Brazil, there are two or three minor perils to guard against, just as one watches the movements of traffic when crossing Fifth Avenue. The piranha is a small fish with exceeding sharp teeth and a taste for flesh. He hunts in schools and attacks both beast and man, particularly those with open wounds. In certain waters a species of sting-ray is common. Its weapon is a blade about three inches long with jagged edges, growing from the side of a long fleshy tail. The sting-ray does not kill but it nearly paralyzes, and strong men have been lamed for many months by a single wallop.[2] Alligators inspire very little respect; neither do they merit full confidence. Large alligators have a habit during the dry season of taking station in man's favorite bathing pools, where they squint with a disgusting leer along the water in the hope that dog, sheep, pig, child, or drunken native may relax vigilance and furnish refreshment.

[2] H. H. Smith, *The Amazons and the Coast,* p. 304.

A part of the Falls of Iguassú, on the Brazilian-Argentine Boundary. (See page 77.)

Left. A mica pit, Santa Luzia do Carangola, Minas. (See page 283.) *Upper Right.* A manganese mine in Minas Geraes. (See page 283.) *Lower Right.* A modern diamond mine, Minas.

The presence of piranhas or alligator never deters anybody from bathing, however. It is no uncommon sight to see reptile, man, and carnivorous fish in the same pool playing a game of catch-as-catch-can, the bathers scampering ashore with merry peals of laughter when the big fellow gets under way or when somebody gets nipped. Rarely does any one pay the extreme penalty.

In short, in the whole vast array of Brazilian wild life embraced in the orders of reptiles, fishes, birds, and mammals, the only enemies of man worthy of more than momentary consideration are the poisonous snakes. These are no worse than can be found in dozens of canebrakes and swamps from Texas to Carolina.

As headquarters for the insect world, however, primacy must probably be conceded to the tropics. Jaguars, snakes, alligators, sting-rays, and piranhas lumped together sink into insignificance as enemies of man when contrasted with insect pests. Indeed, I consider insect enemies of man, man's crops, and man's herds as the chief obstacle to the conquest of the wet tropics. No one escapes. During the centuries before the mosquito net and today with the millions of super-simple folk who are unprovided, the hours when man courts oblivion in sleep are a sleepless horror, many of his hours of daylight activity a stinging torment.

The exuberance of insect life in the evergreen forest is unbelievable. In all Europe, for instance, there are something like three hundred and twenty-one species of butterflies; Bates collected seven hundred and seventy different species about the city of Belém alone! The same richness prevails throughout the less beautiful orders. Within the species the strength of numbers may be surmised from a sight which is common along Amazon rivers at certain seasons, a line an inch or two in height and breadth continuing without interruption for miles along the water's edge, which inspection shows to consist of the bodies of fire ants caught on the wing by a gust of wind and drowned.

Now the word "ant" will probably suggest nothing formidable to a North American reading this book by an apple-wood hearth fire, but I do aver that the bush master and anaconda are house pets in comparison. When fire ants attack, whole villages suspend themselves, their clothing, and all eatables from the rafters, and defend all approaches with *copauba* balsam and tin cans.[3] Life on such conditions may be sweet to some people; personally, if I must be suspended in mid-air, I should prefer a rope connecting my neck to a strong limb. The only good thing one can say about fire ants is that their habitat is restricted, and that another year they may have gone to some other village. Other pests have an even narrower range. The same naturalist describes a brown fly of the Tabanidae family with a proboscis half an inch long and sharper than the finest needle. It can strike right through ordinary clothing and make a man howl with pain; but he encountered it along half a mile of a certain forest trail and nowhere else in the Amazon.

The habitat of others, again, is wide. Wherever there are muddy shores along the whole Upper Amazon, there is the *piúm*, a minute fly which at sunrise relieves the mosquito with military precision. One sees a canoe with a trail of smoke behind it. Yet there is no engine. The canoemen are covered with myriad disgusting specks, which fill their bellies with good red blood and move slowly off. No pain is felt while their snouts are in the trough, but as soon as they leave it begins to itch. A circular raised spot appears on the skin as a fairly enduring memento. By pressing out the blood that remains in the wound, the sore can be avoided; but so to treat the several hundred daily punctures is an avocation to be indulged in by none but the idle rich.

The *motúca* is another daylight pest with a wide range, found both within and without the forest, a fly with a proboscis so effective that blood trickles in streams from the gash it makes. Mrs. Agassiz pinned the blue ribbon on still another:

[3] Bates, *The Naturalist on the Amazons*.

"Mosquitoes are annoying, piúms are vexatious, but for concentrated misery commend me to the *Mocuim.*" This is a
minute scarlet acarus which infests the bushes and weeds about
the clearings, transfers to your clothes as you brush past, and
sets up an abominable itching.

Most of the pests above mentioned are confined to certain
regions of the Amazon. It must not be inferred, however,
that the rest of Brazil is free from insect pests. Go for a walk
in the bush in almost any of the drier parts of Brazil during
certain seasons and you return swarming with ticks (*cara-
pátos*). Man can spend a rather pleasant half-hour at the
close of day picking them off and rubbing the sores with
tobacco juice or *cachaça;* but the beasts of the field have
no alternative to letting the ugly insects drink their fill, swell
up, and fall off—and fester after they are gone. Fleas are
ubiquitous, the one that burrows under the nails to deposit its
eggs (*Pulex penetrans*) leaving a particularly nasty sore if
the egg-case be not removed with dexterity and the hole dis-
infected.

Black as this picture is, all the chief insect enemies of man
remain to be mentioned! For, after all, such insects as I have
described merely torture the flesh; the mosquitoes which carry
yellow fever and malaria, the *barbeiro* that carries Chagas's
disease, and the fleas which carry the plague, convert the sweet
flesh into carrion, even as a host of leaf-devouring insects
make of man's efforts at agriculture a mockery in many places.
With these I shall deal in the chapters on public health and
agriculture further along. Perhaps I have here said enough
to suggest that insect pests are a real problem?

"Much too much!" a Brazilian critic writes. "I think you
exaggerate a great deal, by accumulating all possibilities in a
much smaller range than they would naturally occupy and
making all of them actual realities in the same space and at
the same time." Wherefore I advised above that these paragraphs on natural perils be diluted by three million square
miles of space before swallowing.

The reader who is unacquainted with the tropics should not read more into those remarks than is there, nor let imagination fill in further details too bountifully. The bad things as well as the good of most environments are seasonal and not constant; few localities are cursed by a concert of pests; and on the plateau south of the Amazon forest they are no more of a problem than in the southern half of the United States. North Americans do not need to leave their own country to find plenty of ticks, fleas, and malarial mosquitoes; and I doubt if the tropics can exhibit worse torments than the black flies and mosquitoes which in the month of June drive every last Indian and Frenchman out of certain regions of Quebec.

The compensation lies in the fact that the same forces which call into being abominable pests, likewise give birth to forms of life serviceable to man in like abundance. Where you have so many insects, you have an equal richness of bird life feeding on insects. So varied and brilliant is it that Hudson somewhere calls South America "the bird continent." Among their myriad gay forms are as toothsome roasts, fries, and stews as the best stocked barnyard yields. The lagoons of Rio Grande do Sul, the marshes of Matto Grosso, the swampy grasslands throughout Brazil swarm with ducks and other aquatic bird life—a veritable sportsman's paradise. Quail and various species of prairie hen abound in all the upland pastures; the *mutúm* is as fine a prize as a wild turkey. This is the phase of the matter which appeals to the pioneer.

Although in comparison with Africa, Brazil appears to be very poorly stocked with the larger mammals,—the tapir, standing about three and a half feet high, is the largest animal in Brazil,—yet there is plenty of small game. What is more delicious than certain wild pig? or paca (*Agouti paca*)? The deer of the grasslands are small but yield good venison. And there are many animals, such as monkeys and the larger cats, which a hungry man finds entirely acceptable, although their meat has never been listed on fashionable menus. Hunting is rather difficult in the dense forest, yet a good shot will never starve either there or on the open plains.

Returns on energy invested at the quiet end of a fish pole, however, are so great that a hungry man rarely has to rely upon his gun. With edible fishes the coast abounds and the rivers teem and swarm. Fish, to the scientist, suggest Louis Agassiz as inevitably as a monkey suggests Darwin. At the close of his year in Amazon waters during our Civil War, Agassiz wrote a brief summary of results to the Emperor of Brazil which contained these suggestive sentences:

I will not return to the surprising variety of species of fishes contained in this basin, though it is very difficult for me to familiarize myself with the idea that the Amazons nourishes nearly twice as many species as the Mediterranean, and a larger number than the Atlantic, taken from one pole to the other. I can no longer say, however, with precision, what is the exact number of species which we have procured from the Amazons. . . . However, I estimate the total number of species which I actually possess at eighteen hundred, and it may be two thousand. . . . Another side of this subject, still more curious perhaps, is the intensity with which life is manifested in these waters. All the rivers of Europe united, from the Tagus to the Volga, do not nourish one hundred and fifty species of fresh-water fishes; and yet, in a little lake near Manáos, called Lago Hyanuary, the surface of which covers hardly four or five hundred square yards, we have discovered more than two hundred distinct species, the greater part of which have not been observed elsewhere.[4]

Although he carried back to Harvard over eighty thousand specimens, it is needless to say that his party did not exhaust Amazon resources in one year; the rest of Brazil he scarcely scratched.

While Agassiz found that the aquatic fauna differed radically in its make-up from place to place and from season to season, other species were encountered everywhere. One such is the giant pirarucú (*Arapaima gigas*): for those who dwell on the banks of Amazon waters its flesh is what beef is to

[4] Prof. and Mrs. Louis Agassiz, *A Journey in Brazil*, p. 383.

all central and southern Brazil.   Another Amazon staple is
turtle meat and turtles' eggs.   A well-stocked turtle tank is
as regular a feature of Amazon establishments as a cattle corral
on the pampas.

So it comes about that the environment which breeds the
worst of the insects that pester man evens up by making it
unnecessary for man to do much except fight flies.

The stage is set.   Its width is half a continent.   Upon it
shines a zenith sun.   In the foreground flows the equatorial
current.   Over it blow the trade winds bearing abundant rain.
Chiefly a highland where drainage is of the best, yet broad
are the lowland plains, and above the plateau tower mountains whose summits are no strangers to white snow.   Forests
of surpassing luxuriance, pastures illimitable, fields of peren-
nial fertility, a fecundity of life, a plethora of power, a wealth
of minerals,—since he first taught his Favorite Form to walk
erect, God never entrusted to a people more excellent materials
or more colossal forces with which to build a worthy home for
Man.

CHAPTER IV

THE SOWING

§ 1. THE FIRST CENTURY

So much for the seed and the soil. Now for the sowing!

Easy roads to wealth were as popular in the sixteenth century as in the twentieth, and the prevailing Portuguese opinion regarding Brazil for the first quarter-century after discovery can readily be imagined. If one had started for California in the gold rush of '49, he would not willingly have been diverted to Death Valley because of its superior charm. The reports of the first explorers listed land, jungle, naked savages; no cities to sack, no gold to loot; whereas every ship from India described cities there in the groves and dancing-ground of the sun full of the accumulated treasures of the ages, a flourishing trade to be wrested from the Infidel for the glory of God—nobody with any real sense of values would dream of going to Brazil. It was like offering a diplomat the choice between the Court of St. James's and Siam.

A few left the shores of Portugal to whom no choice of destination was vouchsafed; just as England later dumped convicts and "sturdy vagabonds" upon Maryland, Virginia, and Carolina to be rid of the burden of supporting them. When the Portuguese were in doubt about the friendliness of the inhabitants of any newly discovered shore, they landed a *degredado*, a man banished for one reason or another. If he were kindly received, a foothold gained and an interpreter-in-preparation; if roasted over a slow fire, one degredado less. For a quarter of a century about all Portugal did was to send out a couple of ships a year to dump a few of these outcasts, and pick up a cargo of brazil, together with parrots, monkeys, and Indians as curiosities and slaves.[1]

Exploring expeditions soon made familiar the whole coast from the La Plata north, and even penetrated to the plateau. One sent out by Spain in 1527 to explore the Rio de la Plata, met the Chief Hydrographer of Spain—the same Sebastian Cabot every American schoolboy knows—coming down the river from Paraguay with a little gold and silver.[2] We have only to recall how North Americans stampeded to California and Alaska in the nineteenth century to imagine the insatiable thirst of the first discoverers for the precious metals. The Spaniards hunted for nothing else; they looked with disdain upon Florida because no mines were found there. Not to become tillers of the soil had they left their happy homes, nor because their own fair land was incapable of supporting them. As the rumor of Cabot's find spread throughout Europe, apathy vanished like mist in the effulgence of the sun.

Portugal very shortly was made to realize that the French were paying more attention to the coast of Brazil than were the owners, and that Master William Hawkins of Plymouth (the father of Sir John) knew the taste of manioc. Hawkins was only one of many adventurers from all over Europe who, from about 1530, began to prowl along the shore of equatorial America dreaming of El Dorado. The Spanish with Cortez had uncovered fabulous gold in Mexico; Cabot came back from Paraguay with dust—why not they in Brazil? Portugal saw that if Brazil was to be held against these freebooters, who cared not a Continental that Pope Alexander VI had divided the undiscovered parts of the world between the Church's two favorite sons, colonies must be planted at once. Her hands were more than full in Asia. In its extremity, the Crown fell back upon the feudal system of *seismarias* from which it had once shaken itself free with so much difficulty, and in 1532

[1] Robert Southey, *History of Brazil*, I, 38. Andrew Grant, *History of Brazil* (London, 1809), pp. 3, 4. H. Morse Stephens, *Portugal* (New York, 1891), p. 224.
[2] Southey, I, 55.

divided the whole coast of Brazil among thirteen court favorites, conferred upon them hereditary titles and sovereign powers, and advised them to lose no time in defending their new concessions from the corsairs of the French. These original Captaincies in Brazil differed from the Proprietary Colonies granted by England to court favorites—Maryland, Carolina, New Jersey, Pennsylvania, and New York after its conquest from the Dutch—solely in that the North American proprietor was limited by the provision that he must make laws "by and with the consent of the freemen," [3] and that the Brazilian Captaincies were just one hundred years older.

Where were the Portuguese Captains to turn for labor? Little Portugal had a population of less than three millions, and Asia was bleeding her white. She had no surplus free labor, and the whole gang of fidalgos and holy men were wedded to the idea of slave labor anyway. The organized slave trade was the only place where a Portuguese capitalist could turn for labor in such an emergency. So when sugar cane, destined to be the first great source of Brazilian wealth, was brought to Santos (São Vicente) from Madeira in 1532, Negroes were brought from the Guinea Coast at the same time to cultivate it; [4] the whole system of large-scale agriculture and Negro slavery as developed on the great estates of the Order of Christ and other religious and military organizations in Algarves, Alemtejo, and the Islands, was transferred to Brazil at the very beginning of colonization. In view of the widespread misapprehension in English literature on this subject, it is worth stressing that this was *before* any really serious attempt by competent and properly armed men had been made to enslave the Indian in Brazil. Beautiful, untamed Brazil was born a slave because her old father in Europe was a slave. When the first blacks were sold in Virginia in 1619, the heavy chains of chattel slavery for nearly a century had hung about

[3] John Spencer Bassett, *A Short History of the United States* (New York, 1919), p. 82.

[4] João Ribeiro, *Historia do Brazil* (9th ed.; Rio, 1920), p. 70.

the neck of the gentle daughter of Portugal growing up toward freedom south of the Amazon.

The fidalgo of course required helpers to work his slaves, and for this purpose ambitious young men of the peasant class with good physiques and without domestic ties were in demand, as they were in demand as soldiers to defend the new settlements. The need of capital and executive ability was solved simultaneously by that bigoted monarch bent upon the utter ruination of his country who, in 1536, introduced the Inquisition into Portugal and began persecuting the ablest business men in the Empire. Many of these rich and influential Jewish families, driven by the rapid approach of persecution and drawn by the prospect of new wealth, closed out at a loss and removed to Brazil, where they were soon joined by friends who had been exiled by Manoel.

So the Portuguese fidalgo, the Portuguese peasant, the Jew, and the Negro, all invaded the home of the American at about the same moment in history. The Jesuits did not make their appearance until the first Governor-General came out and asserted the power of the Crown over the independent captaincies in 1549, with six vessels

on board of which were three hundred and twenty persons in the king's pay, four hundred *degredados,* or banished men, and colonists who make up the whole number a thousand. . . . Another fleet came out the third year, on board of which the Queen sent out many female orphans of noble family, who had been educated in the Convent of Orphans; they were to be given in marriage to the officers, and portioned with Negroes, kine, and brood mares from the royal property. Orphan boys also came out to be educated by the Jesuits; and ships followed every year with like supplies.[5]

In 1570 another Ship of the Orphans brought out a number of girls whose parents had died of the plague; and it was not until Portugal began to go under, during the imbecile government of Cardinal Henrique, that the annual fleets bringing out young and healthy settlers were discontinued; and the

[5] Southey, I, 213, 216, 311.

mother country, having entered the "Sixty Years' Captivity," lost interest in the fate of these colonies.

Thus were the seeds of a great nation sown upon the soil of a fertile land just one century before England succeeded in planting her seed upon a much less fertile coast (Jamestown, 1607; the *Mayflower* at Plymouth in 1620; Massachusetts Bay, 1630; Maryland, 1634). As age is reckoned in this very young thing we call the New World, Santos, Rio de Janeiro, Victoria, São Salvador, and Recife were old towns before Jamestown, New York, or Boston was dreamed of.

Plainly foreseeing the difficulties in the way of commerce, the ruination of social cohesion, and the diminution of allegiance which would result if the colonists established themselves in the interior, the government, in these early years, did everything in its power to restrict settlement to the Coast,[6] and in the main was aided in this by economic interest for two hundred years; but, as I shall show directly, Portugal had sown some seeds which could no more be told where to take root than can the winged seeds of the birch or maple in a high wind.

As to the numbers involved, an official mission in 1614 asserted that "Brazil could not be said to be unoccupied, for it had above three thousand Portuguese inhabitants."[7] Whatever the exact figure, it was insignificant. What was significant of the first century was that every white man who entered Brazil, except the Jesuit, was met on the beach by *The System* and administered *The Parasite's Pledge:*

I solemnly swear I will perform no manual labor so long as I can get a single slave to work for me, so help me God and the King of Portugal!

Under that system there must have been at least ten Negro and Indian slaves for every white man, and for many halfbreeds, at the close of the first century after Brazil's entrance into the arena of world politics; and the picture of an insignificant Portuguese master class driving slaves to the number

<hr>

[6] Southey, II, 300.
[7] Southey, I, 423.

of twenty-five, and more probably fifty, thousand, is not far from reality.

§ 2. THE DUTCH CONTINGENT

Some such proportion of slave and free is indicated by the wealth which the Dutch found when they began to raid the Brazilian settlements in the first quarter of the seventeenth century. (I pass over the abortive attempts of French Huguenots to get a foothold in Brazil as unimportant from the viewpoint of population—the Dutch had the only Protestant organization hard enough to make a dent in this Catholic Coast.) When Brazil became a Spanish possession in 1581, she became fair game for all Spain's enemies; and Spain had the choicest collection of enemies in Europe. For by taking over the Portuguese Empire, Spain put herself in possession of just about everything the other maritime powers, England, Holland, and France, wanted. There is more than a suspicion that Spain was willing to see the Portuguese weakened in every way possible. Brazil as a possession of Portugal, the friend of England, had been tabu; but Brazil as an undefended item in the empire of the hated Castilian was a shorn lamb in the fury of the storm; and it was not many years before the wolves began to prowl about the young and tender morsel. Drake, Cavendish, and James Lancaster (Pernambuco, 1595) left the marks of their teeth upon various settlements; the French founded São Luiz in 1612; and the Dutch were already established north of the Amazon when Belém was founded in 1615, even as Henry Hudson was making a reconnaissance of New York for them in 1609. Although he was on the false scent of El Dorado, the baying of the leader of the pack, Raleigh, was loud enough to draw off the English to the Guiana shore; the French were evicted; but for a long time it looked as though the Dutch had come to stay in Pernambuco as in New York.

In 1594 Philip II of Spain closed the port of Lisbon to

the Dutch, and the fight was on. The Lowlanders could lick anything of their weight with one hand tied behind their back in those years: they ousted the Portuguese from command of the trade of Asia, and as soon as that was accomplished took on Brazil. For this, and other purposes, the Dutch West India Company was founded in 1621. As far as its activities in Brazil are concerned, here was honest, organized piracy in its most perfect form; the Corporation made not the slightest pretense of colonization; the Dutch were straightforward, hard-working men as frankly associated for purposes of plunder as any gang of bootleggers or war profiteers of the twentieth century. I would unhesitatingly hand them the blue ribbon for honesty, if they had not spoilt the picture by the same sickening prating about the salvation of souls and the introduction of a pure religion into South America as characterized the Catholic prostitution of Christianity to avarice and ambition.

The sacking of São Salvador enabled the Directors to declare a handsome dividend, and from 1626 to 1637 (years when the Colonies from Virginia north were in their swaddling clothes) plunder was dutifully brought home every year and distributed to the stockholders. With Recife as general headquarters, they extended their dominion over the whole northeast coast from Sergipe to Maranhão. The dividend was never below twenty per cent, and often rose to fifty.[1]

The Dutch were rather tolerant heretics and disturbed the religious practices of the Portuguese in Brazil as little as possible; but when in 1645 it was discovered that the confessors employed by the Dutch Catholics and by French in the Dutch service had refused absolution for warring against the Christians, as they called the Portuguese, just thirty days was given for the members of every monastic order to quit the Dutch possessions and round up on the Island of Itamaracá, where the Dutch stripped them of their habits and then turned them ashore at remote places along the Spanish Main in nothing

[1] Andrew Grant, *History of Brazil* (London, 1809), pp. 52, 60.

but their shirts and drawers.[2]   That act, however, was less cruel than turning twenty-five Portuguese over to cannibals in Ceará and shipping fifty to Barbados to be sold to the English as slaves. (The English restored them to liberty.)

There were diverting as well as tragic incidents—I find very amusing the spectacle of Maurice of Nassau and Montalvan, the Viceroy of Brazil, engaged in a solemn Conference for the Limitation of Armaments up there in that God-forsaken country in a Godless age—but on the whole the Dutch incident in Brazilian history represents what the measles does in infancy, a temporary setback to Portuguese imperialism without serious issue. The point of chief interest to Brazil is that Dutch blood—excellent stuff—was the only considerable intrusion into that of the three basic stocks prior to the immigration of the nineteenth century. Engineers on the reclamation work in the sertão of Ceará and Pernambuco pointed out to me tow-headed youngsters with blue eyes and unmistakable Dutch features, living mementos of their swashbuckling fathers who exacted tribute from the northern captaincies in the seventeenth century.

A century of strange relations, with Recife serving as a base for attacks upon Chili on the west coast of South America and upon Angola on the west coast of Africa. A thought-provoking century, the one that witnessed the spectacle of two hundred Brazilian Indians fighting against Negroes in Africa to determine whether the Portuguese or the Dutch should have the right to enslave them both!

The greed of the Directors of the Dutch West India Company, after Maurice of Nassau retired, drove the Pernambucans to fight for their liberty and finally wrecked the enterprise; although such distant happenings as a warlike gesture against the Dutch by Cromwell and the gain by the Dutch of far-off Ceylon had not a little to do with their withdrawal from Brazil.

Portugal did not get these northern Brazilian settlements

[2] Southey, II, 65.

back from the Dutch until twenty years after she regained
her much mutilated sovereignty from Spain, and by the treaty
of 1661 she paid Holland four millions of *cruzados* (say
£400,000) for them. So the Dutch were partly driven, partly
bought off, from Brazil as a few years later (1664) they were
ousted from New York; and the destiny of the greatest colonies in the two Americas was definitely entrusted to the Portuguese and the English. In 1661 the Portuguese flag floated
from French Guiana to the Rio de la Plata; four years later,
the English flag floated from Florida to Maine. From that
time until the Napoleonic Wars the flow of Portuguese blood
from the mother country to the embryo developing in the
womb of tropical America was uninterrupted.

§ 3. Contacts of Civilization and Savagery

The Metamorphosis of the Guanaco Hunter

This thin stream of Portuguese and Dutch humanity, however, was discharging into a pond already peopled by several
(no one can say how few or many) millions of human beings.
Let us inquire what was happening in the contact zone between civilization and savagery and trace this thread through
to some conclusion before we spend any more time along the
Atlantic shore watching the white-winged ships disgorge their
cargoes of Europeans and Africans.

As the southward march of the gray goose announces the
approach of winter in the United States, so domestic fowl
announced to the Indian that the White Man was not far
behind. The chickens and ducks of the Portuguese spread
from tribe to tribe far ahead of actual European contact, and
were a part of the domestic regimen of the mass of Brazilian
Indians within fifty years of their introduction by the first
colonists.

A more striking portent appeared upon the southern plains.
I indicated in Chapter III that the area now included in Rio

Grande do Sul, Uruguay, the pampas of Argentina, Gran
Chaco, Paraguay, and southern Matto Grosso constitutes perhaps the finest natural pasture in the world. Into this pasture
the Spaniards turned Andalusian horses in 1534.[1] Recognizing that the mobility of their cavalry was fully as important
as firearms in maintaining military supremacy over the Indians, and foreseeing trouble if the savages should become
horsemen, the government forbade the sale of a horse to an
Indian on pain of death. No legislation, however, can prevent a stallion from hurdling a makeshift fence and whinnying
to his mares to follow. Once free, the world was theirs; and
the golden age of the horse began in South America exactly
as on the Great Plains of the United States. Horses ran wild,
they mated, they covered the plains with their spirited progeny.
A hundred years or so later Falkner, an English Jesuit, tells
us that on one of his journeys he was surrounded by bands
of horses during a fortnight, droves thousands strong passing
him at speed for two or three hours together, so that he and
his companions feared they should be trampled. Horses became so valueless that many were killed merely for their fat,
when some one wanted to soften a deerskin; and brood mares
were lamed by severing a nerve in the hind leg to prevent their
joining the wild bands that ever neighed and whinnied to their
kindred of the corrals.

Cattle were introduced into Brazil at Santos at the same
time horses appeared on the banks of La Plata. Dr. Zeballos
says the basis of the pampa herd was the seven cows and a
bull driven from Santa Catharina to Paraguay by the Portuguese brothers Goes in 1553.[2] I doubt very much if it were
so late. Be that as it may, they wandered at will, became
wild, and increased so that by 1580 the first cargo of hides
was shipped from Buenos Aires to Spain; and in the first
decade of the seventeenth century a million cattle, it is said,

---

[1] Southey, I, 58.
[2] *Anales de la Sociedad Argentina,* Vol. XXXV, quoted by Alvin
Sanders, *The Story of the Herefords,* p. 972.

were driven from about Santa Fe into Peru. This increase was going on in Rio Grande do Sul and the Banda Oriental as rapidly as on the plains of La Plata and Tucuman. Everywhere there were hundreds of wild cattle to one in semi-domestication.

Aside from Englishmen out for exercise, there are few people in the world who will walk when offered a ride. The pedestrian Indian who for ten thousand years had been trying to sneak up on his fugitive quarry, gazed upon the equestrian European and forthwith unfurled the red flag—Revolution was rampant upon the pampas! Upon discovering that a stolen horse would carry a guanaco hunter as well as a white man, whole tribes became equestrian. The Indian's enthusiasm over the horse was as great as the present-day North American's enthusiasm over the automobile. He ate horse; he drank melted horse-fat; he shampooed his head with the blood of the horse in the idea of its strengthening him. He twisted horsehair into ropes. The skin of the foreleg he transferred to his own as a puttee. Of the hide he made his couch, clothing, tent, saddle, and boots. The sinews of the horse became his thread. And when an Indian died, his horses were decked with copper bells, glass beads, and rhea feathers, led solemnly in procession round and around the tent of the deceased, finally sacrificed and staked to his grave with lances from which fluttered brightly colored pennants.[3]

Horsemanship became synonymous with everything that is manly, an art to be learned as soon as a child could walk. Stirrups were not in general use among them: standing on the right, one hand on the bridle, the left grasping his long wooden lance, the Indian vaulted into the saddle at a bound—then woe to rhea, deer, or wild boar! For the equestrian Indian had become as fleet as the wild creatures on which he preyed; no wonder "Horse" and "God" became synonymous in Rio Grande do Sul.

Cattle exercised an influence upon the life of the Indian

[3] Dobrizhoffer, *An Account of the Abipones* (London, 1822), I, 131-33.

of the plains second only to that exercised by the horse. To men who had previously won a precarious living by hunting the wary guanaco and the fleet rhea, a herd of wild cattle was so much meat already in the larder and the killing of it a pleasure deferred. As these primitive hunters were metamorphosed into herdsmen, they became as nearly carnivorous as frugivorous man has ever become. The metamorphosis of the Indian thrown in contact with the fringe of the white man's herds was revolutionary; complete, swift, beneficent. The same cannot be said for all the changes which took place when the Indian came into intimate contact with the man who had introduced those beneficent herds into South America.

Which Was the Savage?

When the white man finds himself in a dark-skinned community in a position of hopeless numerical inferiority, he makes one of the best neighbors in the world; and it is a safe assumption that the first settlers who were dumped on the coast of Brazil made themselves as agreeable to the Indians who gathered round them as they possibly could. One of my colleagues in the Philippine Forest Service one day was walking alone ahead of his party in the forest of Mindoro, when unexpectedly he came upon two Negrito boar-hunters. Instantly two arrows were drawn to the head, a reflex to their surprise and fear. My friend is an unusually agreeable chap; but probably never in his life did he try to please the other fellow as he did those two Negritos, talking at them in two languages neither of which they could understand, smiling, gesticulating, putting himself and all his possessions so obviously and entirely at the disposal of the militant majority that within ten minutes he had swapped what tobacco was in his pouch for the two arrows, which had been intended for him from the first, anyway. From the issue, we may conclude that many of the men who were thrown in contact with savagery in Brazil during the first quarter of the sixteenth century were equally agreeable.

The truth is that, unless he be frightened, your bloodthirsty savage is a thing much more common in fiction than in fact. Time after time we read of degredados, shipwrecked mariners, and destitute Portuguese settlers who were welcomed into Indian tribes, given wives, and elevated to positions of leadership. The original assumption on the part of the Indian was that the Portuguese colonist was as beneficent a commodity as the Portuguese cow, and the evidence is overwhelming that nine-tenths of the trouble was started by the Portuguese against neighbors who amply demonstrated their simple trust and kindliness. As Squanto taught the Pilgrims at Plymouth how to raise Indian corn and to fertilize their fields with fish, so the Indians taught Portuguese men the culture and preparation of manioc, which to this day is the staple food of Brazil; and taught Dutch and Portuguese women how to bring up their babies. At first not one in three survived; but when the stupid European mothers learned from the savages to throw aside European swaddling clothes and accustom the baby to air and water, the curve of infant mortality took a sudden drop. An Indian wet-nurse was as much a matter of course in Portuguese families of the foretime as candy in an army canteen, and the mother tongue (i.e., the tongue learned at the breast) was more often one of the Indian dialects than the language of Camões. Since the earliest days this neighborly attitude has illumined the contacts of civilization and savagery in Brazil —as moonlight illumines the blanching bones of a battlefield.

For another type of relationship also began to develop as soon as the fidalgos came to assume command of their captainships in 1532. The fidalgos who were to exploit Brazil arrived with their Negro slaves, but so many of these Africans died on the middle passage that quotations on "Indian pieces" CIF Brazil were very high. The bush was full of husky Indians.

"Bring them in and put them to work!" ordered the fidalgos.

Whereupon brave men armed with nothing but guns, pistols, swords, bucklers, and daggers attacked naked men, women, and children whose weapons were the blowgun and the bow and arrow. They brought in captives by hundreds, not because of any racial superiority, but because of the superiority of their weapons; just as a German with a well placed machine gun is superior to a hundred French, British, or American riflemen. The captains wanted agricultural laborers to cultivate cane, tobacco, and manioc; but the Portuguese could not get it through their heads that women, not men, were the agricultural laborers among the Indians; it was a superstition with the aborigines that seeds planted by men would not grow. "Father," one of them explained to Padre Gumilla when he remonstrated against making field-work women's work, "you do not understand our custom, and that is the reason why you do not like it. Women know how to bring forth, which is a thing that we do not know. When they sow and plant, the stalk of maize produces two or three heads, the root of manioc two or three basketfulls, and everything multiplies in like manner from their hands. Why? . . . because women know how to bring forth, and to make the seeds and roots bring forth also." But the Portuguese wanted the women in their kitchens and bedrooms and insisted on sending the men to the fields, with the result that they had to skin the hide off their backs to make them work. If four thousand tons of rubber on the Putumayo cost thirty thousand lives, how many Indians did it take to sweeten a thousand tons of brown sugar?

As field labor meant the spilling of a torrent of masculine Indian blood, so concubinage meant the absorption of an equal stream. For a long while Portuguese immigration to Brazil was preponderantly masculine, like recent Greek immigration into the United States. For fifty years those male adventurers, soldiers, and sailors entered a land where there was not the slightest pretense of government or religion. They landed on the shore where, as I pointed out in the second chapter, the finest type of Brazilian Indian lived, naked women who were used to polygamy and who entertained no false notions about chastity. The result was a polygamy that differed from Indian polygamy in that the savage had as many women as consented to become his wives, while the civilized man took as many as he could enslave, nor hesitated to sell at dawn the woman who had lain in his arms through the night, if a good bargain offered. Not all came unwillingly by any means; many women of the conquered always consider it an honor to mate with their conquerors. Miserable as was the lot of these kitchen-and-bed slaves of the Portuguese, it was generally more of a sinecure than marriage in savagery. As a sample of what was going on, we read of a border skirmish in 1536 where the white victor in his articles of capitulation demanded six stags and seven girls for himself, and to each of his soldiers, two women. The plaint of the priest is suggestive: "On the fear of hostile aggression, soldiers are sometimes sent from the city for the defense of a new colony; but we dreaded the coming of the soldiers, more than that of the savages. For the former by their licentiousness do more harm to the women, than the savages could do to the colony with all their weapons." As soon as priests became fairly plentiful in Brazil, some of the colonists thought to wipe out their sins by having their Indian women baptized. Thereupon arose a poser for the Casuists: to set these women at liberty and let them return to their heathen hordes would be an offense against the sacrament of baptism; if they remained, both parties were in a state of mortal sin. They remained—and bore many fine, brown Brazilian babies.

From this union of Portuguese men with the finest and fairest maidens of the agricultural Indians sprang a new race of men possessed of a constitutional and indefatigable activity, fierce, and cruel, and hard, but physically adapted to the stubborn environment in which they were to function. In spite of all the early prohibitions of Portugal seeking to restrict settlement to the coast, as soon as some one penetrated to the lovely plateau of Piratininga and saw that region high above the malaria of the coastal plain, without communication with other towns, beyond the reach of the arm of Portugal but possessed of every natural advantage, adventurers, deserters, and fugitives from justice flocked to found the city of São Paulo. Their half-breed progeny became the arch-persecutors of their mothers' people. Before them lay a Continent claimed only by a type of social organization so loose that it was a temptation to their mettle; on every side called the Unknown to men in whose blood lingered vestiges of the migratory instincts of Visigoth and Moor. Lured by the hope of finding the precious metals and assured of profits from the slave trade in any case, as the horses were lured by the endless pasturage of the pampas, from the infant city on the plateau there very soon began to bud off exploring and slave-raiding bands (*bandeiras*) that for scale and scope quite eclipse the efforts of the Coast. Exactly the same thing happened to them that happened to the horses and cattle on the pampas—domesticated man went wild. Some natural leader, a glossy, arch-necked, prancing stallion of a man, would put himself at the head of a hundred or two kindred spirits and penetrate into the unknown. They called themselves by that poetic term, "*Mamalucos*"—Minions of the Melting. Portuguese-Indian half-breed men were the backbone of these bandeiras; but they usually included some women and always a large number of cattle, horses, and swine.

Their term, *Mamaluco*, soon came to be applied by the Portuguese to the Indian cross as the term Mulatto is applied to the Portuguese-Negro cross.

Life with the *bandeirantes* was one long picnic that lasted for months and often for years. As soon as the small supplies of food with which they started began to give out, they turned their attention to nature. If the forest yielded little and they encountered no plantations of the Indians, perforce they settled for a few months, grew a crop of corn while they explored the region, and then went on. There was no hurry: they had left nothing behind to which they were anxious to return, and probably not even the administrators of the law missed them very much. The initial shortage of women was remedied as soon as the bandeira established contact with a horde of Indians; thenceforth, with slaves to provision their board and women to croon before their fire in the gloaming while some one strummed a violão, with slave girls to share their bed as the coals dimmed to a glow, they asked nothing more of life.

That white men of European stock are amply able to expend the energy necessary to support man in luxury in such a climate as that of the plateau, is proved by the prodigious fatigues and labor expended by them upon these slave raids. Sometimes they returned to São Paulo with but a few hundred slaves; not infrequently they brought back thousands. This was particularly true after the Jesuits established their "reductions" in what is now western Paraná. By beneficent means which I shall describe in the next section, the Jesuit Fathers persuaded whole tribes of Indians to give up their savage way of life and settle down under the tutelage of those high-minded priests.

"So much the easier for us!" said the bandeirantes. "Drive the arrow-shooting cattle into the corral and dehorn them!"

And in 1629 they began their attacks upon the Christian missions. To the supplications of the Jesuits, these case-hardened brigands replied that the Indians had been baptized and were now sure of going to heaven. Worse, they set afoot that poisonous thing, rumor, that the Jesuits had rounded up these forest cattle in order that the slavers might drive them to the killing pens the more easily.

So famous did the Paulista Mamalucos become as bush masters and slave hunters that other captaincies called them in when there was any particularly rough work to be done. In 1670, a distinguished citizen of Bahia was killed by the Guerens Indians, and the Paulistas under João Amaro were summoned. He started to pacify everything to the São Francisco River, and so many Indians were sent back to the capital that the price of slaves fell to around twenty shillings. He terrorized the sertão of Bahia so thoroughly that nothing was heard of savages for half a century; then settled down to become the lord, founder, and patron saint of the city of Santo Amaro.[4]

The range of the Paulista bandeirantes was incredible. When Piauhy was first opened up from the Pernambuco side in 1673, there were the Paulistas already on the ground. We find one party penetrating to Quito, on the plateau of Ecuador, a journey through an absolutely pathless wilderness of, say, three thousand miles. In 1696 we encounter them on the headwaters of the Rio Paraguay in far western Matto Grosso with fifteen hundred slaves in their possession, where they are badly manhandled by a tribe of equestrian Indians. How was this possible? Because of the smallness of the Indian tribes and lack of social solidarity: the aborigines lacked cohesion; one tribe would not coöperate with another. The bandeirantes, like the Bolsheviki, formed a militant minority which could.

If you would visualize the barbarities that accompanied this game of Indian-taming and women-stealing in Brazil, I must refer you to *The Devil's Paradise*.[5] They used to bring home strings of human ears from Goyaz as proud exhibits of their prowess in exterminating the Goya Indians; [6] and there are grounds for the belief that the scene on the Putumayo which shocked the first decade of the twentieth century, was but a glimpse of a process that has been continuous in Brazil for four hundred years, originally practiced on a nation-wide scale with the solid approval of public opinion, in the nineteenth and twentieth centuries become "atrocities" which can be carried on safely only in the dismal, dripping depths of the Amazon forest with the connivance of petty officialdom.

Thus both the Indian and the Portuguese began in the

---

[4] Southey, II, 565.

[5] W. E. Hardenburg, *The Putumayo, the Devil's Paradise* (London, 1913), edited by C. Reginald Enock, F.R.G.S. Contains an extract of Consul-General Casement's Report.

[6] Southey, III, 835.

early sixteenth century to disappear as separate races by the dual process of killing off Indian males in war and slavery, and fusion through the mating of selected Indian females with Portuguese males in informal polygamy. This point of sexual selection should be emphasized. There was a vast plurality of women for the Portuguese adventurers to choose from, and that they did make some distinctions between the agricultural tribes and the primitive hunters of the plateau is evident: "The Indians in Goyaz are looked upon as so inferior a race, that none of those marriages take place there." [7]

It seems incredible how devoted to the ideal of having some one else do all your daily work, originally strong, energetic, able-bodied men could become. Pope Urban VIII in 1639 denounced the severest censures of the Church against any one who enslaved an Indian, converted or not. When the Bull of Excommunication was read in Rio de Janeiro, the people broke open the gates of the Jesuit college and would have murdered some Paraguay Fathers if the Governor had not intervened; in Santos they pulled down the Vicar General who was publishing the Bull and trampled upon both him and it; in São Paulo they rose and expelled the Jesuits from the city.[8] When a devoted Catholic community thus hurls open defiance at the Pope, one may be sure its pocketbook emotions have been deeply touched.

The Jesuits, Defenders of the Faith

Why this violent animosity against the Jesuits?

Because they took themselves and their job seriously.

In the same magnificent manner that one Pope had given the two kings of the Iberian Peninsula the whole of the undiscovered world, so another Pope handed over the natives of Asia and the two Americas to the Jesuits as flocks for their shepherding. Negro slavery was already too flourishing

---

[7] Southey, III, 675.

[8] Southey, II, 326.

a business to make it economically politic for the Pope to
include Africans in his catalogue of potential Christians; but
at the time Loyola organized his devoted band of class-conscious internationalists, America-Indian slavers did not have
much political influence in Lisbon, Madrid, and Rome. So
the battle began between the Brazilian slave-hunters who
wanted the Indian's body, and the Jesuits who wanted his
soul, in which the aboriginal American was destined to lose
both.

The Company of Jesus was founded in 1539. Ten years
later, six Jesuits came to Brazil with the first Governor-General; Father Manoel de Nobrega, a Portuguese of noble family,
as chief of the mission. "There is no individual to whose
talents Brazil is so greatly and permanently indebted," Southey
wrote a hundred years ago, "and he must be regarded as the
founder of that system so successfully pursued by the Jesuits
in Paraguay." What was that system?

Its cornerstone was education: the Jesuits were first, last,
and all the time highly educated, and many of them intellectual,
men. And they were intensely practical men, too. The portico
through which you entered their structure was a magnificent
faith. These men believed! When they renounced the world
their renunciation meant something; they were so convinced
of the worth of their mission to mankind that they were prepared to die for it; nay, they were eager for martyrdom. The
soldier who goes into battle determined to die is very likely
to inflict a lot of damage before death overtakes him. The
Jesuits were soldiers of the Cross who were ever ready to
spend themselves in their battle for the souls of naked Indians.
Such men always achieve, and are clothed in a certain mag-
nificence of spirit, no matter how deluded their desire; whereas,
many of the desires and acts of the Jesuits were among the
most sublime to which Catholic Christians have attained.

Their first act was the establishment of a school in São
Salvador, the old capital of Brazil. Their second, to rush to
the outskirts of the village where the Indians were preparing

a noisy cannibal feast. Into the arena they strode just when the prisoner had been tapped on the head and the women were dragging his body off toward the kettles; they had rescued the meat and carried away the dinner before the astonished Indians could realize what it all meant; and they had the corpse blest and buried before the savages took the warpath. The Governor-General had to call out the whole military force of the little capital on the edge of the jungle to save it from the wrath of the cheated banqueters. That was where the colonists declared war on the Jesuits.

"These fanatics will get us all murdered!" they said, and not without some reason in those early days.

Undeterred, the Jesuits went right back among the Indians, establishing friendly contacts by gestures before they had the power of communicating by speech. They began by winning the affections of the children with a store of trifling presents, from them picked up a few words of Tupi as the children picked up Portuguese, and soon were able to use these youngsters as interpreters. From that they went on to a complete mastery of the Indian languages, and one of these, the Tupi (already widespread, as I pointed out), they chose to be the *Lingoa Geral,* the general language; they wrote grammars, perfected it, made a catechism in the Tupi tongue, translated prayers into it, and made it the language of their missions from the Amazon to the Plata; so that the *Lingoa Geral* for the first two hundred years was more spoken than Portuguese.

Able to converse with the Indians fluently in their own tongue, we see Aspilcueta going among them and adopting the technique of the Indian *pagés,* singing out the mysteries of the Romish faith, running round his auditors, stamping his feet, clapping his hands, making the easy substitution of Hell for *Anhangá,* copying the very tones and gestures of the medicine men by whom they were wont to be affected. But the Jesuit had an elaborate ritual with which the Indian *pagé* could not compete. At Nobrega's school in São Salvador he taught the Mamaluco children not only reading, writing, and arithmetic, but also how to sing and to assist at mass.

Music. What a wonderful weapon for the conquest of a soul! I shall never forget the haunting beauty that greeted my ear one morning as I walked from the forest into a village in the Philippines where a score or more of well trained, childish voices led by a Spanish priest were harmonized in a noble old Gregorian chant to which Tagalog words had been adapted. Pagan that I am, I was entirely ready to worship the God of these songsters. So, too, the heathen Indians were entranced.

When Nobrega went forth to convert them, he always took four or five of these singing half-breeds with him; and when they approached an inhabited place, one child carried the crucifix on before while the rest began singing the Litany. The very snakes of the forest knew that these black-gowned, unarmed men were of a different breed from the slave-raiders.

Of the many difficult problems the Jesuits had to solve in Brazil, none required nicer handling than cannibalism. One Father succeeded in abolishing it among certain hordes by going through them and flogging himself until he was covered with blood; elsewhere they considered themselves fortunate if they could instruct the intended victim in the Catholic faith and baptize him before he was knocked on the head and served up. When some hypersensitive savage took a notion that the baptismal sauce spoiled the taste of the meat, these daring and devoted missionaries managed to secrete a wet handkerchief as a card sharp secretes a fifth ace, or to moisten the sleeve of their habit and in the confusion of the preliminary drinking orgy, to squeeze upon the victim's head the number of drops necessary to insure salvation.[9] But the very importance which the Jesuits placed upon the ceremony of baptism led the Indians to regard it with suspicion.

"Have you noticed," asked the *pagé* whose lucrative professional practice was being ruined by these European medi-

[9] Southey, I, 254.

cine men, "that when the sinister gentlemen in black sprinkle
that poisoned water upon our newborn babies, they generally
die?" (The Jesuits had indeed been particularly eager to
baptize newborn infants who were not expected to live.)
"They are carriers of the pestilence!"

And we have the pathetic spectacle of such frightened hordes
abandoning their homes at the approach of the men of God,
burning pepper as a fumigation against the malignant and
admitted power of the Cross upon which the gentle Jesus
died, meeting His missionaries on the trail and beseeching
them to pass on. Sometimes, rarely, the Father did not succeed in conveying his message to his audience and paid for
his failure with his life—a new glory for this band so devoted
that no Indian tribe could withstand them for long.

Then the idea began to gain and, like the poultry of the
colonists, even to fly ahead of the Fathers; so that on establishing contact with one far-interior tribe they found all the
members tattooed on the forehead with the magic Cross of
the white man, and another horde whose chief had renamed
all the men Jesus and all the women Mary. When the Indians accepted Catholicism, they accepted it not as individuals but as a tribe. A Jesuit might find himself a shepherd
without a flock one day and the next have a thousand men,
women, and children descend upon him and say: "We're
Christians! What are you going to do about it?"

Nobrega's answer was most nobly conceived, yet it was a
solution tragic in the working out. The Jesuit led them to
a piece of rich, unoccupied land, of which Brazil had a super-
fluity. He had them build a church, a school, and houses;
and he had them plant abundant crops. "Your wandering
days are over," he said; "here we are going to stay." He
taught them to read and write, "Ye shall be as gods, knowing good and evil!" and he found the Indians eager to attain
this marvelous power. If you want my conception of nobility
of soul, I point you the picture of Anchieta in the sixteenth
century shivering up there in his mud hut in São Paulo, sit-

ting up far into the night to write out a lesson on a separate leaf for each of his Indian and Mamaluco pupils because there were no books, in a language of which he had just composed the first grammar and vocabulary. Not only Latin and prayers in the native dialect were taught, but also the manual arts; they attacked the problem of introducing the Indian to civilization much as Tuskegee has attacked the problem of educating colored boys and girls in our South. They made carpenters of them, weavers of cloth, blacksmiths, everything that was necessary for an independent, self-supporting community with European standards. In order to instruct their charges, the Jesuit priests made themselves skilled in all these arts and crafts. "I serve as physician and barber," wrote Anchieta the indefatigable. "Besides these employments, I have learned to make *alpargatas* [hemp shoes]; I am now a good workman at this, and have made many for the brethren, for it is not possible to travel with leathern shoes among these wilds."

And how these sincere men wrestled and suffered in their attempts to solve unsolvable problems that conflicted with their faith. It is wrong to shed blood, said that faith; yet often they had to act the part of doctors, and bloodletting was then a chief part of the physician's technique.

"Charity extendeth to all things," said Loyola the practical, and solved that doubt for them.

Plural wives offered a more difficult knot to unravel. There could be but one wife in the Catholic view—which one of these many women, all of whom had borne children to this chief, was his wife in the eyes of God?

"The first woman with whom he lay is his wife," one argued.

"Then none of these is his wife," protested the second.

"Give him his choice," advised a third.

But they were never violent in making such settlements and tolerated what they could not correct until a new generation had been born which could be molded nearer to their hearts' desire. Very gentle taskmasters were the Jesuits, allowing ample leisure for men who had never before been accustomed to regular hours of work, and permitting excursions into the wilds where the Indian's soul continued to return even more frequently than his body.

The approval of Government was early conferred upon the "reductions" of the Jesuits, as their settlements were called, and the disapproval of the slave-minded colonists.

"The American Indian shall not be enslaved!" decreed the Kings of Portugal and Spain in law upon law.

"To hell with your sentimental Law!" replied the Paulista bandeirantes. "We are the Law in the sertão of Brazil."

"Who then will fetch us a pail of water and prepare the manioc meal? Negroes are so expensive!" whined the white settlers of the coast.

There is scarcely a phase in the fluctuating battle between avarice and decency where the Indian did not lose, from his friends as well as from his foes. Antonio Raposo is about to attack one of the "reductions." The Jesuit Mola foresees the attack and immediately prepares to receive it—by baptizing all those about to be butchered, baptizing for seven hours until he could no longer raise his arm, and then continuing with some one lifting it for him. Antonio Raposo with his bandeirantes attacks, sacks the "reduction," butchers all who resist, and drives over two thousand Indians away into slavery.

The Portuguese prevailed upon their Kings to let them enslave those prisoners of "just wars" and those "ransomed from the cord," i.e., snatched from the hands of cannibals before the feast had commenced. Then they proceeded to interpret those laws exactly as white citizens of the southern United States interpret literacy tests and grandfather clauses regarding the enfranchisement of Negroes. Cord-Indians, the rarest of rare phenomena, suddenly became as common in Pará as mangos and Brazil nuts, when the solemn tribunals sat to determine the legal status of Indian slaves. When the settlers were not warring upon their Indian neighbors, they were inciting one tribe to wipe out another. And in all these acts they were encouraged and fortified by the philosophy of the other Catholic priests who abominated the Defenders of the Faith—the Jesuits, men so loathsome as to say mass and perform all the ceremonies of religion gratuitously!

One of Man's salient characteristics is the ease with which he rationalizes and justifies whatsoever he desires, particularly whatsoever profits his pocketbook.

If [wrote Manoel Guedes Aranha in the seventeenth century] the nobles in civilized countries are held in high esteem, with greater reason should white men be esteemed in a land of heathens, because they have been brought up with the milk of the Church and of the Christian faith. Moreover, men are fit for different things; we are fit to introduce religion among them, and they are fit to serve us, to hunt for us, fish for us, and work for us.[10]

So Indian flesh continued to be cut into strips by the tapir-hide lashes of those who had been suckled with the milk of the Church. By the beginning of the seventeenth century those "who were introducing religion among them" had cleared the coast so that they had to go far into the interior to find men "fit to serve" them. As Frenchmen and Englishmen were fed into the maw of the Marne, so Indians were fed into the maw of the merciless system of the seventeenth century; and in slavery they withered as young men wither in modern battle. In the "reductions" (fatal word) of the Jesuits, the Indian population was melting no less rapidly under the withering breath of disease.

Epidemics, like an electric current, require contacts. While living in little isolated tribes, disease had difficulty in attaining epidemic proportions among the Indians; and through thousands of years they had built up a resistance against the common maladies of their environment. The European introduced a whole new set of diseases against which the aborigines had built up no resistance; then their best friends, the Jesuits,

[10] Southey, II, 637.

insisted upon hanging wet and dirty clothes on bodies that for thousands of years had been accustomed to the kiss of wind and weather, and gathered them together in villages of thousands where before had been free-wandering hordes of hundreds, so that smallpox and measles—both fatal with them —tuberculosis, and the rest of our favorite ills could melt them down like snow before a driving April rain.

And here, as exhibiting the whole process of the attrition of the Indian by his friends, I willingly yield the pen to Martin Dobrizhoffer, a Jesuit from Gratz, in Styria, who went on mission among the Indians in the middle of the eighteenth century and whose three-volume *Account of the Abipones* (translated from the Latin by Sara Coleridge) is the greatest work extant on the equestrian Indians of the southern plains. Some Spaniards gathering maté came upon signs of savages and, becoming terrified, asked the Jesuits to "reduce" them and bring them to their settlement.

I applied myself to the task without shrinking, and on the day of St. John the Evangelist commenced my travels, accompanied by forty Indians. . . . discovering at length, on the third day, a human footstep, we traced it to a little dwelling, where an old woman with her son and daughter, a youth and maiden of twenty and fifteen years of age, had lived many years. . . . all the rest, who had occupied this neighbourhood, had died long ago of the smallpox. . . . I exhorted the old mother to migrate as fast as possible to my town, promising that both she and her children should be more comfortably situated. . . . To show how scanty their household furniture was, mention must be made of their clothes. The youth wore a cloak of the thread of the caraquatà, reaching from his shoulders to his knees, his middle being girded with little cords, from which hung a gourd full of the tobacco dust which he chewed. A net of coarser thread [i.e., a hammock] was the mother's bed by night and her only garment by day. The girl in like manner wore a short net by day in which she slept at night. This appearing to me too transparent, I gave her a cotton towel to cover her more effectually. The girl folding up the linen cloth into many folds, placed it on her head to defend her from the heat of the sun, but at the desire of the Indians wrapped it round her. I made the youth, too, wear some linen wrappers, which in my journey I had worn round my head as a defence against the gnats. Before this, he had climbed the highest trees like a monkey to pluck from thence food for his pigs, but his bandages impeded him like fetters, so that he could scarcely move a step. In such extreme need, in such penury I found them, experiencing the rigours of ancient anchorites, without discontent, vexation, or disease.

. . . The mother and son were tall and well-looking, but the daughter had so fair and elegant a countenance that a poet would have taken her for one of the nymphs or dryads, and any European might safely call her beautiful. She united a becoming cheerfulness with great courtesy, and did not seem at all alarmed at our arrival, but the rather enlivened. . . . The girl had seen no woman but her mother nor any man but her brother, her father having been torn to pieces by a tiger before she was born. To gather the fruits that grew on the ground or on the trees, and wood for fuel, the dexterous girl ran over the forest tangled as it was with underwood, reeds, and brambles, by which she had her feet wretchedly scratched. Not to go unattended, she commonly had a little parrot on her shoulder, and a small monkey on her arm, unterrified by the tigers that haunt that neighbourhood. The new proselytes were quickly clothed in the town, and served with the daily allowance of food before the rest. I also took care they should take frequent excursions to the neighbouring woods, to enjoy the shade and pleasant freshness of the trees, to which they had been accustomed. For we found by experience that savages removed to towns often waste away from the change of food and air, and from the heat of the sun, which powerfully affects their frames, accustomed, as they have been from infancy, to moist, cool, shady groves. The same was the fate of the mother, son, and daughter in our town. A few weeks after their arrival they were afflicted with a universal heaviness and rheum, to which succeeded a pain in the eyes and ears, and, not long after, deafness. Lowness of spirits, and disgust to food at length wasted their strength to such a degree that an incurable consumption followed. After languishing some months, the old mother, who had been properly instructed in the Christian religion and baptized, delivered up her spirit, with a mind so calm, so acquiescent with the divine will, that I cannot doubt but that she entered into a blessed immortality. The girl, who had entered the town full of health and beauty, soon lost all resemblance to herself. Enfeebled, withering by degrees like a flower, her bones hardly holding together, she at length followed her mother to the grave, and, if I be not much deceived, to Heaven. Her brother still surviving was attacked by the same malady that proved fatal to his mother and sister, but being of a stronger constitution overcame it. The measles, which made great havoc in the town, left him so confirmed in health that there seemed nothing to be feared in regard to him. He was of a cheerful disposition, went to church regularly, learnt the doctrines of Christianity with diligence, was gentle and compliant to all, and in every thing discovered marks of future excellence. Nevertheless, to put his perseverance to the proof, I thought it best to delay his baptism a little. At this time an Indian Christian, a good man and rich in land, who, at my orders, had received this catechumen into his house, came to me and said, "My father, our wood Indian is in perfect health of body, but seems to have gone a little astray in mind: he makes no complaints, but says that sleep has deserted him, his mother and sister appearing to him every night in a vision, saying, in a friendly tone, 'Suffer thyself, I pray thee, to be baptized. We shall return to take thee away, when thou dost not expect it.' This vision, he says, takes away his sleep." "Tell him," answered I, "to be of good heart, for that the melancholy remembrance of his mother and sister, with whom he has lived all his life, is the probable cause of these dreams, and that they, as I think, are gone to Heaven, and have nothing more to do with this world." A few days after, the same Indian returns, giving the same account as before, and with confirmed suspicions respecting the fearful delirium of our new Christian. Suspecting there was something in it, I immediately hastened to his house, and found him sitting. On my enquiring how he felt himself, "Well," he replied, smiling, "and entirely free from pain"; but added, that he got no sleep at night owing to the appearance of his mother and sister, admonishing him to hasten his baptism, and threatening to take him away unexpectedly. He told me over and over again, with his usual unreservedness, that this prevented him from getting any rest. I thought it probable that this was a mere dream, and worthy, on that account, of neglect. Mindful, however, that dreams have often been divine admonitions and the oracles of God, as appears from Holy Writ, it seemed advisable, in a matter of such moment, to consult both the security and tranquillity of the catechumen. Being assured of his constancy, and of his acquaintance with the chief heads of religion by previous interrogatories, I soon after baptized him with the name of Lewis. This I did on the 23d of June, the eve of St. John, about the hour of ten in the morning. On the evening of the same day, without a symptom of disease or apoplexy, he quietly expired.

This event, a fact well known to the whole town, and which I

am ready to attest on oath, astonished every one. I leave my reader
to form his own opinion; but in my mind I could never deem the
circumstance merely accidental. To the exceeding compassion of
the Almighty I attribute it that these three Indians were discovered
by me in the unknown recesses of the woods; that they so promptly
complied with my exhortations to enter my town, and embrace
Christianity; and that they closed their lives after receiving baptism.
The remembrance of my expedition to the river Empalado, though
attended with so many hardships and dangers, is still most grateful
to my heart, inasmuch as it proved highly fortunate to the three
wood Indians and advantageous to the Spaniards. These last, having been certified by me, that, upon the immense tracts of woodland here mentioned, not a vestige of the savages remained, collected, during the three years they stayed, many hundred thousand
pounds of the herb of Paraguay, from which they derived an amaz-
ing profit.[11]

Taunts were used to pry such Indians loose from their
shepherds by the slave-raiders. "Cowardice," whispered some
half-breed into the ear of his mother's people, "has induced
you to take shelter in the shadow of the Church! Afraid to
meet your enemies in battle, you have put yourselves in the
power of this set of vagabonds turned out of their mother
country!" And stung by such taunts, valiant men came out
with their bows to be enslaved by cowardly men with guns.

Deceit was used to win men whom taunts could not move.
Portuguese decoys and stool-pigeons dressed as Jesuits would
go among the Indians, gain their confidence, and lead a whole
tribe—into slavery.

Sophistry was used to justify men's selling themselves into
slavery. Smallpox at one time wiped out three-fourths of
the Indians about the old capital of Bahia, and the pestilence
was followed by famine. Now against such emergencies the
conscientious Portuguese had erected in Lisbon a tribunal
called the Board of Conscience (*Tribunal da Mesa da Consciencia*) just as we have Boards of Censors and Vice Commis-
sions to guard our morals in New York in the twentieth century. "Can these starving Indians about Bahia sell themselves

[11] Dobrizhoffer, *An Account of the Abipones*, I, 87-96.

into slavery for a handful of manioc meal?" the colonists
asked this Board of Conscience. And what do you suppose
the *Mesa da Consciencia* replied? [12]

Treachery was used to enslave military allies. On one occasion when the Aymores were ravaging Bahia, the Government
begged its neighbor in Pernambuco to send a force of Pita-
goares to go against them. None but a Jesuit could raise this
force: upon the oath of a leader they loved and trusted that
as soon as the skirmish was ended they should return to
Pernambuco and their families, eight hundred picked warriors
put themselves and their lives at his disposal and were turned
over by the Jesuit to the highest officials of the Portuguese
Colonial Government. By the time this force reached São
Salvador, the danger was over. Did the Colonial Government
thereupon reimburse these brave allies and permit them to
return the long journey home? They did not. They solemnly
declared them rebels, and as such attacked and reduced them
to slavery.

Pombal

The man who signed the Emancipation Proclamation of the
Brazilian Indians and finally outlawed, if he did not terminate,
all forms of chattel slavery so far as they were concerned, was
born eternally to give hope to the late starters in life. A
university man who served as a private in the Portuguese
Army before he became a notorious "Mohock" on the streets
of lawless Lisbon and won the favor of the Portuguese nobility by the unusual avenue of abducting one of their fairest,
he received his first political appointment at the age of forty,
became Prime Minister at the age of fifty, and was the Government of Portugal for the third quarter of the eighteenth
century: the man who rapped the Inquisition over the knuckles
by subjecting their courts to ordinary rules of procedure and
to publicity, secularized education in Portugal, removed the

[12] See Southey, I, 294-95.

civil disabilities of Jews and Muhammadans, converted the streets of Lisbon from the most dangerous to the safest in Europe, founded the Bank of Portugal, removed the capital of Brazil from São Salvador to Rio de Janeiro, and abolished Negro slavery in Portugal in the same year that he finally smashed the Society of Jesus—quite the most liberal European statesman of his generation, Pombal.

The Marquis of Pombal was the originator of the great Brazilian idea: to incorporate all castes and colors in one body politic on a footing of absolute equality.

Regarding the Indians, he stated truly that under pretext of those cases which the law allowed, the aborigines were still being enslaved without any other reason than the avarice and power of those who enslaved them and the weakness and ignorance of those who were enslaved; therefore he abrogated all laws which permitted Indian slavery under any pretext. This Emancipation Proclamation was published in Pará and Maranhão, I believe in 1756, and shortly after extended to the whole of Brazil. He went the whole way and declared categorically that henceforth Brazilian Indians should be exempt from any other temporal subjection than laws applying to all the subjects of the King of Portugal. There is a clause in the same decree even more remarkable: "Children of Negresses in slavery were excepted from this emancipation till further instructions," [13] it said, indicating clearly that Pombal had in mind the gradual abolition of all slavery in Brazil. This was some seventeen years before he abolished Negro slavery in Portugal, in 1773.

It is plain that Pombal aimed to reinvigorate the moribund Portuguese Empire by throwing off in one Herculean effort the internal enemies that were eating her heart out as hookworms devour the blood corpuscles of their victim; to increase the number of freemen and lessen the number of slaves who formed the rotten core of the Portuguese system; and as far as Brazil was concerned, to establish the Indians on a footing

[13] Southey, III, 513-14.

of complete social as well as political equality with the Brazilians who boasted more or less European blood in their veins. He prohibited the colonists from calling Indians "Negroes"; he insisted that the new Portuguese citizens, until then dubbed Tom, Dick, or Harry, should be given Portuguese surnames; clothes and separate houses were to replace nakedness and the communal maloca; the Portuguese language was to replace Tupi. That all the odious distinctions between Whites and Indians should be wiped out as swiftly as possible, he directed his administrators to encourage intermarriage and to make it clear to white women that Indian men were no longer inferior to Portuguese; that they were capable of rank, honors, and political place; and that they would communicate the advantages of this political status to their wives.

How wide may be the gulf between the proclamation and the realization of a policy, the generation of North Americans which is witnessing the initiation of the experiment in "prohibition" realizes full well. Pombal was engaged in war to the death with the enemies of the Throne of Portugal, the nobles and the Catholic church. The Inquisition was exercising great political power, therefore he smashed the Inquisition. The Jesuits had acquired economic power comparable to that of the Jews in the modern world of international finance, therefore he smashed the Jesuits. I use the verb "smash" advisedly: these priests, some of whose excellent qualities I have tried to portray, were taken back to Portugal packed between decks in the same brutal manner that Negro slaves were brought across the Atlantic—European politics induced Pombal to drive out of Brazil the only men who had the slightest interest in carrying out his program for the emancipation of the Indian.

The actual process of emancipation was begun by the erection of a rather sinister symbol of freedom in each of the twenty-eight settlements of the Jesuits in the north which Pombal's brother converted into towns and villages by giving them a new name and setting up in the market-place a

pelourinho, that ancient Portuguese item of civic architecture
—useful both as a whipping-post and as a place of execution
by hanging from, or strangulation or decollation against—
which conveyed to an illiterate citizenry the idea that the chief
magistrate was invested with sufficient authority to keep freedom within the bounds of decorum. There was much real
merit in the regulations, however. Directors were to be appointed for the Indian settlements whose duty it would be to
induce them to cultivate their lands and, in general, to afford
advice and assistance in their new civic responsibilities.
Newly settled Indians were exempted from taxes for the first
ten years after they came in from the bush, and received
from the director a certain quantity of food, and knives, hoes,
and axes;[14] and it was specified that local administrative
offices should be filled by Indians wherever available in preference to white men.

On the essential point of compulsory service, however, the
colonists won everything they wanted. "In order that the
Indians might acquire habits of industry and enjoy its fruits,
and that the colonists might find laborers," it was decreed
that the price of labor should be regulated by the Governor
and judicial authorities on the same system prevailing in Lisbon, where, if a laboring man could live on one *testão* (say
fifteen cents in those times) per day, the wages of common
labor were two, and of an artificer, three. All able-bodied
Indians from thirteen to sixty years of age were then regis-
tered by the director of the Indian settlement; half of these
were always to remain at home, the other half were allotted
among the inhabitants. Pombal tried to safeguard the system
by provisions regarding pay; but under the actual conditions
in Brazil, where very few people favored his revolutionary
legislation, it rapidly degenerated into peonage which in many
instances became indistinguishable from the worst forms of
chattel slavery.

[14] Spix and Martius, *Travels,* etc., II, 217 (English trans.)

Peonage

That not even legal equality was established by Pombal's decree is evidenced, for instance, by the procedure of the Boundary Commission on which the very man who put the emancipation edicts in force was engaged. The work of demarcation went on from the time of the first Treaty of Limits until both Spain and Portugal were involved in the Napoleonic Wars, and it was the Indians of Pará who were always forcibly drafted for this work—work from which the few who ever came back returned so shaken by fever that the remainder of their broken lives was a burden. Has any one heard of using up Portuguese peasants or valuable Negro slaves in such work?

That no equality before the law was established is evidenced by the testimony of Alfred Russel Wallace, who states that previous to his coming to the Amazon in 1849 it had been the custom to recruit the Brazilian Army almost wholly from the Indians of Pará, seizing them when they came down to trade in the capital.[15]

That no more equality existed in the days of the Empire than in the Colonial era is the testimony of Professor and Mrs. Louis Agassiz, who went to the Amazon in 1865.[16]

That no more actual equality exists in these days of the Republic than in the era of the Empire, is evidenced by the baby boy who used to grasp my fingers and swing up on my big mule whenever I rode past the house of a certain planter on the Rio das Contas—stolen on the feast of São João in the year 1920 from the forest Indians who still wander in southern Bahia—one of three that I know of personally who have recently been taken from their naked parents and presented to politicians in the capital of Bahia as curios, house pets, and potential cheap servants.

[15] Wallace, *Travels on the Amazon and Rio Negro* (1889 ed.), p. 32.
[16] Agassiz, *A Journey in Brazil* (Boston, 1879), pp. 193, 227, 247, 267, 269, 290, 332.

Kidnaping of children and such vestiges of slavery are growing rare in twentieth century Brazil, but one cannot say as much for the system which replaced chattel slavery as the typical contact between civilization and savagery in the nineteenth century. Peonage consists, in Brazil as in the southern United States, in getting the person working for you into your debt and keeping him there; and in lieu of other means of discharging this obligation he is forced to work for his creditor upon what are practically the latter's terms, and under varying forms of bodily restraint. Many Brazilian publicists have called attention to the evil, notably Euclydes da Cunha.

Why, then, rake over the coals of a century that is dead? Precisely because these fires are burning brightly in the twentieth century, still searing the souls of the naked brown tobacco-smokers who were swinging in their hammocks along the Amazon in the year 1500. That there be no mistake on this point, and indignant refutation by the ill informed, I call to the stand three competent witnesses. In an official report to the Peruvian Government in 1905, Jorge von Hassel, an engineer in the service of government, said: [17]

I take this opportunity of protesting before the civilized world against the abuses and unnecessary destruction of these primitive beings, whom the rapacity of civilized man has placed as mere mercantile products in the Amazon markets; for it is a fact known to every one that the native slaves are quoted there like any other merchandise. Throughout the forest region under the control of the Governments of Peru, Colombia, Bolivia, and Brazil the natives are exposed to attack without protection of the law by the whites, who hunt and persecute them like animals of the jungle, recognizing as their only value the sum represented by their sale.

Sir Roger Casement's testimony, handed to Sir Edward Grey in 1911, was: [18]

Throughout the greater part of the Amazon region, where the rubber trade flourishes, a system of dealing prevails which is not

[17] Quoted by W. E. Hardenburg, *The Putumayo*, p. 22.
[18] *Foreign Office Reports, Miscellaneous*, No. 8, 1912.

tolerated in civilized communities. In so far as it affects a labouring
man or an individual who sells his labour, it is termed peonage. . . .
The entire absence of government, which has not kept pace with
the extension of revenue-yielding communities, has left the weaker
members of those communities exposed to the ruthless greed of the
stronger. The crimes of the Putumayo, horrible as they are, have
their counterpart, I am assured, in other remote regions of the
same lawless forest—although possibly not to the same extent.

Dr. Isaiah Bowman, Director of the American Geographical
Society, as recently as 1916 wrote: [19]

In South America there has lingered from the old slave-holding
days down to the present, a labor system more insidious than
slavery, yet not less revolting in its details, and infinitely more
difficult to stamp out. In Bolivia, Peru, and Brazil it flourishes
now as it ever did in the fruitful soil of the interior provinces where
law and order are bywords and where the scarcity of workmen will
long impel men to enslave labor when they cannot employ it. . . .
Peonage has left frightful scars upon the country. In some places
the Indians are fugitives, cultivating little farms in secreted places
but visiting them only at night or after carefully reconnoitering the
spot. They change their camps frequently and make their way from
place to place by secret trails, now spending a night or two under
the shelter of a few palm leaves on a sandbar, again concealing
themselves in almost impenetrable jungle. Experience has led them
to believe that only a dead white is a good white . . . and that even
when he comes among them on peaceful errands he is likely to leave
behind him a trail of syphilis and other venereal diseases scarcely
less deadly than his bullets.

Such is the process that has ever characterized the back-of-
beyond in Brazil. There is no more sincere admirer of the
splendid work for the Indians being carried on by General
Rondon and by the Federal Government than the writer; yet,
in spite of these efforts, the dominant process in the ever
narrowing contact zone between civilization and savagery in
1926 is so little different from what it was in 1532 that there,
to this day, the only freedom for an Indian is death, and the

[19] Isaiah Bowman, *The Andes of Southern Peru* (New York, 1916), pp.
25-28.

only freedom for an Indian woman, concubinage. When the process goes on to its inevitable conclusion, when the last pure-blooded Indian is dead, this last fact—of tremendous biologic significance—will finally come to be remembered as the only fact in the relationship.

Such was the fusion of Europe and Asiatic-America. Thus was absorbed into the undying stream of Brazilian blood the fine courage, strong physique, habituation to pain, and adaptation to the environment, of the American Indian. That it should have entered so largely through the back door of bastardy has no significance from the eugenic standpoint; but that so many of the settlers who have always clung to this contact zone between civilization and savagery should have been men who were not able to live in the more populous parts, men to whom the solitude of the woods served as a protection from pursuing justice—that may give a moment's pain to a well-wisher both of the Indian who is so tragically passing and of the Brazilian from whose veins the fine blood of aboriginal America never shall pass.

The right of Brazilians to continue this process through to its logical conclusion until the last full-blooded Indian chief, a sneer curling his proud lip, is pushed over the cliff, and the last pure-blooded Indian woman enters the seraglio of some syphilitic slave-driver in the rubber country, is not to be denied. That is the meaning of Sovereignty.

But Brazil, like all the rest of the world, will probably within a century or two have to enter a much closer community of peoples in which representatives of the Human Race, gathered together in some center of a better civilization, will demand an accounting of such stewardships. When the cup is passed from hand to hand and the turn of gentle Brazil comes to speak, she will not even be able to give an intelligent account of what it was her forebears of the first five centuries destroyed—a story that posterity may appraise very differently from what we do—unless efforts are made at once to unravel and preserve for the race the true story of Indian culture in Brazil. To mankind, as well as to herself, Brazil owes it to establish an adequately financed Bureau of Ethnology manned by competent anthropologists who will continue intensive field studies until the great day comes when one hundred million Brazilians proudly gather to watch the soul of the last aboriginal American blow West.

§ 4. BRAZIL ABOUT 1700

Having escorted the Indian through the centuries to an exit from which there will be no curtain call, let us return to the seaboard and establish another point on the curve of Brazilian progress which we are plotting. Although they were beginning to cultivate cacao around Belém, and cotton in Ceará and Maranhão was making a name for itself, Sugar was King in the seventeenth century as it had been in the sixteenth. A typical large mill (*engenho*) would have seven or eight square miles of land, part pasture, part woodland, the rest under cane; from fifty to one hundred effective Negro slaves; and about as many of both horses and oxen. Each constituted an independent, patriarchal community; self-supporting, containing in the village about the manor house blacksmiths, carpenters, and what other artificers such works require.

In those days before steam, the sweep of the ocean current and the trades from southeast to northwest, during part of each year, most effectively divided the colonies of Maranhão and Pará from Pernambuco and the seaboard to the south. In Maranhão, many sugar mills were falling to ruin because of the high price of Negro slaves. Having repeated the "Parasite's Pledge," Portuguese colonists preferred to starve rather than provide themselves with food in a region where a modicum of effort means affluence. Among the many plans suggested to government for the improvement of this province, an importation of nobles was recommended; but there seems to have been no shortage either of nobles or friars.

The train of hungry dependents who accompany a Governor are perhaps more prejudicial to the community than even these convicts [wrote Vieyra in his indignation]. The sucking fish must have learnt their way of life since the Portuguese navigated the ocean, for every Viceroy and Governor who embarks for the colonies is surrounded with such hangers-on.[1]

The situation was too serious to be funny: for their services in expelling the Dutch from Cabo do Norte and São Luiz, King João IV had conferred upon Maranhão and Pará the same privileges granted the city of Porto and all the privileges of the city of Lisbon except the right to ride upon mules; the inhabitants of Maranhão and Pará were not to be put to the torture except under those circumstances applicable to fidalgos; they were not liable to be impressed for military service, nor have their beasts nor houses taken against their will. Like the *Infançoes* and *Ricos Omes* of old, they enjoyed a privileged civic status; it was good to be "noble." Now these privileges of nobility were extended to any one who held a commission in the militia, even for a few months; and in São Luiz they could celebrate the extinction of the brotherhood of the Misericordia—made up of mechanics and similar stuff, the essential skilled labor of a frontier community—because they all had at last been thus ennobled!

That there was no dearth, either, of religioners in Brazil is indicated by the fact that Belém, with a population of about five hundred toward the close of the sixteenth century, had a Mother church; a Jesuit college; a Franciscan, a Carmelite, and a Mercenario convent; two other churches; and one chapel. No wonder the fifty families brought there in 1676 from the Island of Fayal after they were blown out of home by the volcano, nearly starved. The whole coast was equally well supplied; and São Salvador, then as now, much better. It was the great Portuguese Governor, Gomes Freyre, who came out to put down insurrection in Pará and Maranhão in 1686, that reported on "the vile conduct of some of the

[1] Southey, II, 680.

clergy, who, neglecting their duties and unmindful of their profession, had upon the plea of necessity, betaken themselves to trade, and had been foremost in exciting discontent, sedition, and rebellion." The state of the people, he said, was deplorably bad; the sugar works in ruins.

Conditions were undoubtedly bad in the North, but they were better in Pernambuco and Bahia. São Salvador was then the capital of Colonial Brazil except for the two northernmost colonies with which I have just dealt. The black population there was then so numerous that travelers said one might imagine himself in Negroland; Frezier estimated the proportion of blacks to whites at twenty to one; Vieyra says that in the city of São Salvador alone twenty-five thousand Negroes were catechized and instructed in the Angolan tongue, besides a much larger number outside the city. It is safe to say that in 1700 Bahia had ten times as many Negro slaves as Virginia. Dampier says that at the end of the seventeenth century there were as many as two thousand houses in São Salvador solidly constructed, two and three stories high, and covered with pantiles. Her whale fishery about that time was the greatest in the world. And there are many other evidences of wealth and luxury.

One evidence is the pretty picture history has preserved for us of the dandies who dominated the capital of Colonial Brazil in 1700. Instead of the Fairbanks-Morse elevator we now use to get from the upper to the lower city, the cavaliers of those days, reclining upon a splendid cushion in a hammock suspended from a pole, were carried up and down the steep incline by husky Blacks. A slave walked by the side of the perfumed parasite with a parasol, but women were shielded by a curtained canopy which not only shaded them from the sun but completely shut them in from the gaze of the impertinent *"almofadinhas."*

The most superficial comparison of the course of the English with that of the Portuguese-American Colonies at this time will reveal why those north of the Equator were gaining strength day by day, while those south were already plainly showing signs of fatty degeneration at the close of the seventeenth century. In some respects they were alike: partly because of the navigation acts and partly because of overproduction of tobacco, their one money crop, the Virginia planters were as hopelessly in debt to London merchants as were those of Maranhão to Lisbon; [2] slavery had a lesser grip on the southern English colonies than on the Portuguese only because they were a century younger; and the bigotry and intolerance of Catholic priests in Brazil was no whit greater than the bigotry and intolerance of Puritan priests in New England—who in 1692, in Salem alone, executed nineteen persons for "witchcraft." When I point out that in all Brazil there was no printing-press, I do not forget that Governor Berkeley undoubtedly spoke for the Virginia gentry when he said:

I thank God there are no free schools nor printing, and I hope we shall not have any these hundred years, for learning has brought disobedience and heresy and sects into the world and printing has divulged [them] and libels against the best government. God keep us from both.

I do not believe I am maligning Brazil when I say that Governor Berkeley's philosophy was probably also the prevalent one in Brazil in 1700; in North America a better ideal was already bearing fruit. The Portuguese colonies were Catholic and were prohibited from reading the Bible; the English colonies, aside from the comparatively few Catholics in Maryland, were peopled by dissenters of one complexion or another. There were the Puritans and the devotees of the English Church in New England, the Dutch in New York, and the Swedes in Delaware; "Africa is not more full of monsters than Pennsylvania of sects," somebody charged; and the Huguenots began to arrive in Carolina after the revocation of the Edict of Nantes in 1685. The ability to read

[2] Bassett, *History of the United States,* p. 89.

the Bible was considered essential by all these Protestants.
As early as 1647 Massachusetts had passed "the mother of
all our school laws," which ordered each town of fifty families
to support an elementary school, and each of a hundred families to support a grammar school under penalty of fine. Harvard College was founded in 1636, William and Mary in 1693,
and Yale in 1701; and while none of these at the close of
the seventeenth century amounted to anything more than a
good modern preparatory school, the seeds of great things had
been sown. It is not overstating the case to say that public
education was as advanced in the English colonies in 1700
as it is in Brazil in 1926, as I shall show in a later chapter.

When England in 1689 offered the crown to William and
Mary, she waved farewell to the Stuart ideal of divine right
and asserted the supremacy of the people in Parliament;
thenceforth in her colonies, only half of which were wedded
to the slave ideal, the whole tendency is toward an increasing
popular control of their own destiny, jury trial, freedom of
conscience, and frontier democracy. In the Portuguese colonies, where the slave ideal had practically every white man,
woman, and child by the throat and every function of self-
help was becoming atrophied from disuse, the divine right
of their decadent kings and aristocracy as an ideal was un-
challenged. So we have the eloquent Antonio Vieyra, come
back to die in São Salvador where he passed his youth, grown
pessimistic in his old age and describing Brazil as presenting
a lively image of the mother country: in preparations for war,
without men or money; in full harvests of vice, without refor-
mation; in unbounded luxury without capital; and in all other
contradictions of the human mind.

Thus all is not merely going to ruin, but well-nigh ruined; this
Brazil, which is all that we have, we shall have no longer than till
any one chuse to take it; and I no longer grieve that the kingdom
should be without heirs, for if we had them, there would be nothing
to inherit. In this emergency prudent men advise us to wear cotton,
eat manioc, and take to bows and arrows for lack of other arms,

so that we shall shortly relapse into the savage state, and become Brazilians instead of Portuguese.

To such state had Brazil been reduced, when messengers brought the news for which this slaveholding nobility had been waiting for two hundred years: "GOLD HAS BEEN DISCOVERED IN BRAZIL!"

§ 5. GOLD!

The history of Brazil in the eighteenth century is the story of the dethronement of sugar and the crowning of gold and diamonds as the dominant economic motive. Somewhen between 1530 and 1540, the old wives tell us, from Santos the first Captain of São Vicente made an unsuccessful expedition southward into the interior in search of mines, from which he returned with the loss of eighty Europeans. Thenceforth, the Portuguese sensibly settled down on the coastal plain and became planters, just as the English colonists confined their early activities to the Atlantic Coastal Plain from Florida to New England. Only an occasional exploring expedition, and those flying wedges of wild men from São Paulo, the bandeirantes ("men who in useful and meritorious fellowship employed themselves in making discoveries," if you prefer), continued the search. In the last year of the sixteenth century, somebody sent to Philip III a rosary composed of Brazilian gold; just enough "color" continued to be panned and picked out of the earlobes of the Goya Indians to keep them hunting until, in the last decade of the seventeenth century, they struck it rich in Minas Geraes. Somebody jumped in a canoe and shot down the Rio Doce with the news to Victoria; somebody else ran to the Governor at Rio de Janeiro, threw the dust in his lap, and was made *Capitão Mor* of Taubaté, with orders there to establish the first smelting-house. It was a proclamation to the world that the dream of a golden Brazil had come true, and an invitation on the part of Government to the Portuguese world: "Come ye West to the garden of the Hesperides, in which grow apples of gold!"

How gallantly the indomitable spirit of man has ever answered the challenge, "Come and get rich quick, boys!" A 155 mm. shell, well placed in the center of a battalion marching in close order, would not scatter the formation over the landscape as the cry of "Gold!" splattered the colonists of the coast over the face of Brazil. The explosion hurled men and slaves from the cacao plantations of Pará to the placer washings of Matto Grosso and Cuyabá; from São Luiz and from Santos they came and from all the ports between; the cane fields of sleepy old Bahia suddenly became alive—with deserters from agriculture marching through on their way to the mines; the Governor quit his post at Rio and wouldn't return until his pockets were bulging with the yellow sand for which men sell their souls, the yellow metal which is the measure of manhood in modern civilization. If the first that was brought to the mint had been forged into a chain to hang every man who dug up any more of the damned stuff, it had been better for Brazil!

The logs in your fireplace must lie fairly close together if your fire is going to blaze. Your straight-boled, high-crowned tree, free from limbs, is produced only by the crowding and the competition for light that goes on in the forest; a tree grown in the open is always a scraggly, wide-branching affair, pleasant to sit under on a hot afternoon, but worthless as timber. So civilization requires a certain amount of social pressure for its best development. God knows human beings do not require as big a dose of it as our huge cities of the twentieth century inflict, but the gold rush in Brazil resulted in the other extreme: a scanty population which, if it could have gone on developing until it gained the strength to roll back the frontier gradually as we did in the United States, might have produced as rugged a civilization, was by this social cataclysm hurled in blobs and fragments from one end to the other of this enormous land mass. Fragments so small

that every community in interior Brazil was a frontier community; fragments with so little social solidarity that not yet,
over two hundred years later, have most of them acquired
energy enough to build a wagon road to the next equally isolated village. The whole interior of Brazil became a scraggly,
wide-branching affair.

Just at the moment when Slavery was beginning to exhibit
its pathetic fallacies in the North; just when Aristocracy was
becoming so effeminate in old Bahia that some one soon must
have taken the perfumed thing and thrown the stench into
the sea; just when Absolute Monarchy in Portugal, by its own
ineptitude shorn of the wherewithal on which to live, was
doddering along to an early and much-to-be-desired grave,
came Gold to give the degenerate triumvirate a tremendous
new lease of life.[1] The discovery, coming as it did in the
latter part of the seventeenth century, was the worst possible
calamity that could have occurred to Brazil, and the chief
reason why her development has been so different from that
of the United States.

Regarded quite apart from these major social consequences,
as an independent phenomenon exhibiting man's courage and
indomitable will, the exploration and annihilation of distance
resulting from the quest for gold was altogether extraordinary.
As soon as "foreigners" in Minas began to outnumber the
Paulistas, those restless and intolerant spirits looked about
for a less congested habitat; and one of them discovered the
mines of Cuyabá (now the capital of Matto Grosso), which
was settled about 1721. That is easy to read and looks simple
on a small-scale map. It begins to appear otherwise if you
scale it and read the distance from São Paulo to Cuyabá as
eight hundred miles in an air line, and then try to realize that
in that whole distance there was not *one* civilized settlement
when the placer mines at Cuyabá were opened; on the con-

---

[1] "Brazil, with its gold, though it made possible in general the depriva-
tion of all democratic liberties in Portugal, quite possibly on this occasion
prevented a second loss of independence." George Young, *Portugal Old
and Young* (Oxford, 1917), p. 182.

trary, there were several settlements of Indians who by this time had learned that the white man was a snake in the grass.

Goyaz was the third important gold-producing region opened up. In 1670 a Paulista known familiarly as "The Old Devil" (*Anhanguera*) had penetrated to one of the affluents of the Rio Araguaya, where, noticing that some women of the Goya Indians wore gold nuggets in their earlobes as they would any pretty pebbles from the bed of the stream, he cut off their ears to make his exhibit complete. In 1726 the Governor of São Paulo sent the son of this man, himself now well over sixty, to try to locate the spot from memories of his earliest youth; on the second try the old boy succeeded. If you add to these three extensive gold-producing regions, a diamond-bearing zone that extends from the Triangle of Minas through Diamantina and the Grão Mogul to Lençóes in Bahia, you have the whole highland heart of Brazil involved in this premature and passionate harrowing. In one year, more than fifteen hundred persons passed overland from Goyaz to Matto Grosso with great droves of cattle and horses, though twenty years before there had been neither horse, cow, nor miner in any of those regions.

We North Americans rightly consider Lewis and Clark's jaunt to the Pacific in 1805 as a classic bit of exploration. During the whole century preceding, Brazilians by the hundreds performed equally remarkable journeys: they went up the Rio Negro until they established the fact of a connection with the Orinoco by way of the Casiquiare Canal; of the whole length of the Amazon they made a trodden highway; most of its affluents from the south they followed to their sources on the Plateau; and in 1749 was made a canoe trip beside which all others seem like sculling on the Thames. A party of traders pushed from Pará to the town of Matto Grosso via the Amazon-Madeira-Guaporé. The distance, as the rivers wind, is probably not much farther than from New York to San Francisco—it is the couple of hundred miles of falls of the Madeira that count! Read the *Recollections of an Ill-fated Expedition,* by Neville Craig, the story of how the best North American railway contractors of their time went on the rocks in the first attempt to build the Madeira-Mamoré Railway, if you would visualize that stretch of white water. "From that time the navigation between Matto Grosso and Pará was frequented, notwithstanding the length, and difficulty, and danger of the way. It was found that Matto Grosso could be supplied at a cheaper rate with European goods from Pará than from the Rio, and that the voyage was far less perilous than that from São Paulo, where two such enemies as the Guaycurus and the Payaguas infested the way."

Let no man who knows these facts ever again accuse Brazilians of "inherent and spiritless inactivity."

The amount of money involved seems to us very trivial to have produced such results. Our only measure is the King's "Fifth": a fifth of all the gold minted was the share of the king, and no wife ever was more interested in the weekly pay envelope; he would slit your throat or banish you to Africa if he caught you holding out on him. An *arroba* is fifteen kilograms (231,483 grains) and would therefore make up nicely into just about ten thousand round American dollars ($9,969) each containing 23.22 grains of pure gold. In 1714, when production was just beginning, an offer of 30 arrobas in lieu of fifths made by the miners of Minas Geraes was accepted by the king, say $300,000; in 1753, the royal fifth from Minas amounted to 118 arrobas, $1,180,000, and annually for fifteen or sixteen years thereafter it exceeded 100 arrobas, $1,000,000; then, according to Southey, it began to decline.[2] Mawe estimated in 1809 that Minas Geraes yielded a fifth of not less than 150 arrobas, and he was a mineralogist on the ground who should know. Spix says that up to the year 1812 the total of the royal fifths from Minas Geraes amount to 6,895 arrobas, $68,950,000, or, say, $700,000

[2] Southey, III, 593.

a year for a century.[3] The King also received in some years
as much as 40 arrobas from Goyaz, another $400,000; I have
no figures for Matto Grosso, but at the peak of production
it must have been as large as, if not larger than, Goyaz.
So that when his health was the best, the King of Portugal
received from Brazil in gold something like two million dollars
a year.

An income of two million dollars represents five per cent
on forty millions. While that is not a large fortune measured
by twentieth century standards in North America, it was a
tremendous fortune to the pauper kings of Portugal living
the simple life in eighteenth century Lisbon. In those days
a dollar's worth of gold dust was not something to be
slipped unostentatiously into the waiter's receptive palm after
luncheon, but a quantity of powdered power over which ministers held unofficial cabinet meetings to determine how much
of it could safely be dusted into their great perukes without
their king's noticing the golden threads among the gray, in
the locks of his faithful fidalgos. It was a sufficient fortune
to enable the King to pay his bills more regularly than had
been his custom in the seventeenth century and to deny all
democratic liberties to the Portuguese peasantry, from whom
he now needed no favors; it was enough to construct such
magnificent works as the aqueduct of Lisbon and the convent
of Mafra, and in addition to contribute munificently to the
upkeep of the Papacy.

Brazilian gold was the chief source of income for Portugal,
but we must not overlook diamonds and the ordinary taxes
upon commerce. Brazilian diamonds were declared a crown
monopoly; and the rich districts, like that about Diamantina
in Minas, were fenced off as royal preserves on which there
was to be no poaching. By picking over those in excess of
seventeen carats from the package placed annually on his
desk, the King got together a collection which Mawe declared

---

[3] Spix and Martius, *Travels in Brazil in the Years* 1817 *to* 1820 (English trans.), II, 194.

unequaled by that of any other potentate in the world at the beginning of the nineteenth century. Its estimated value was only three millions sterling, however; and the crown income from those sent on to Holland to be cut and polished was comparatively insignificant when compared to the incoming gold.

It is very painful to have to state the reason why the King's "Fifth" is no measure of the amount of gold produced in Brazil—it was not a fifth. It appears that all but two or three people in Brazil were engaged in smuggling. When Antonio de Albuquerque was sent to Minas about 1711 to make the royal authority respected in those lawless mining-camps, he had instructions to eject all Religioners and Clergy who were not exercising parochial functions; for it appears there were apostate Friars and others who had taken orders to escape punishment for their crimes who could be seen exercising anything but Christlike functions in those licentious gaming hells. Between loyalty to Rome and loyalty to Revenue the King did not hesitate; indeed, Rome directed the Bishops of Rio and Bahia to assist in putting down pilfering from her favorite son. That this was difficult is indicated by the repetition of such orders in 1723.[4]

It did not stop them. When the English mineralogist, Mawe, went to Diamantina to expert the mines for the crown of Portugal in 1810, he said that from the expressions of indignation against smuggling heard on all sides he had no expectation of seeing a diamond outside the treasury chests.

A little acquaintance with the town soon convinced me that I was a novice; for, on visiting a few friends to whom I had introductions, I found that diamonds were bartered for everything, and were actually much more current than specie. Even pious indulgences were bought with them; and surely no one could have suspected that the seller of His Holiness's bulls would condescend to taste the forbidden fruits of Tejuco.

[4] Southey, III, 147.

If such was the attitude of the clergy, it may be imagined how the commonalty felt. Smugglers were thrown in prison for life, exiled to Angola, their property confiscated—without convincing any one in Brazil that the prospectors who opened up these mines at great physical cost owed a fifth of all their gold and their entire crop of diamonds to the parasites they were supporting at a court so distant that native-born Brazilians had no more affection for it than for courtiers in the moon.

At what incredible cost in human labor that mineral wealth was extracted! Mawe reported to the Prince Regent, after mining had been the key industry of Brazil for more than one hundred years, that in Minas Geraes there was not a cart nor wheelbarrow in use; that the only miners' tools in use were the iron bar and the hoe; that the "cassoon" (whatever that is) was the only hydraulic machine known. Among his recommendations for effecting an industrial revolution in Brazilian mining was the introduction of the common miner's pick and hand sieves; the substitution of "bucking-irons" for reducing the matrix instead of beating it with stones, "which is the only mode now practiced"; and the construction of pumps! They did learn to conduct water to the diggings in ditches, and there was a clumsy wheel in use for bailing out the water from deep pits, so clumsy that it required fifty or more laborers a whole day to shift it about; that, so far as I can ascertain, was the sole device in use for multiplying the productiveness of human labor by the functioning of the human brain. This was at the end of the golden century, after long practice had perfected their technique; at the beginning, in the absence of skill, knowledge, and iron tools, the earth was opened with sharpened stakes and the gravel washed in a wooden pan.

The desire of the poetic Portuguese to keep the unworthy from munching the apples of the Hesperides, led to the exclusion of all foreigners from Minas Geraes except the English and the Dutch, whom previous treaties made it difficult to exclude. By the law of 1730 these provisions and restrictions upon commerce and immigration were stiffened; not only were foreigners forbidden to enter Brazil, but

no person whatever might embark for it, unless he were appointed to an office there; he might then take with him only such number of servants as should be deemed necessary, and all these were to be Portuguese.[5]

Portuguese passports were required of every one, and wives accompanying husbands were the only women permitted to go out without the King's special permission. It was this dog-in-the-manger attitude that Alexander von Humboldt encountered when he penetrated Brazil from the Venezuelan side, and that forced him to turn back when he heard there was an order out for his arrest.

The kings of Portugal would certainly give any other string of thoroughbreds a good run for first money in a steeplechase to decide what rulers in the world's history have wielded tremendous economic power most stupidly. At the close of the seventeenth century Brazil was Europe's chief provisioner of sugar. But the *Senhores do Engenho* could not afford to pay the price for slaves that the gold miners could; so the sugar works went to decay, and the French and English took away her supremacy in that commodity, as the Dutch took away the trade of Asia at an earlier date, and as English plantation rubber was to take away the rubber trade from Brazil at a later date.

By the end of the eighteenth century the age of gold and diamonds was drawing to a pathetic close, and the miners from being the most opulent had become the most indigent. For a hundred years a people which entered the century swearing, *"I will perform no manual labor so long as I can get a single slave to work for me, so help me God and the King of Portugal!"* by a mineralogical mischance had not only been justified

[5] Southey, III, 254.

in their false philosophy, but had been enabled to indulge every madness, every lust, every gaming instinct, to the hilt. "I have tasted of the insane root, and it is sweet!" the miner said; and no one could gainsay him until he was reduced to beggary, starving in the most fertile land in the world because he had forgotten that soil will produce food-crops for a million years after the gold and diamonds have been extracted from it.

At this juncture in history (1807), Napoleon escorted the Court of Portugal to the grand European staircase leading down and out. The fleet of Sir Sidney Smith was waiting at the foot of the stairs; and under the protection of England, which was about to take over Portuguese sovereignty on the Continent, the whole parasitic pack descended upon the land on whose bounty it had battened during the Golden Century now drawn to a close.

§ 6. The Court Arrives

The arrival of the Court of Portugal is not an event of sufficient importance to merit more than mention in an outline of Brazilian history designed primarily to show how the racial stock became what it now is. George Young has adequately characterized the party of deserters as it left Europe: "The obese dullard John ('John the Goat')—the courtiers and confessors hilarious at having saved their skins—the mad Queen Maria Francisca keenly realizing the situation and loudly screaming frantic protests—the Spanish virago, Queen Carlotta, in grim disgust." [1] If we judge the school of "sucking fish" who swam in the wake of this degenerate monarchy by any modern standard of actuality, the arrival of the court brought to Brazil the least desirable crowd of degredados that ship ever dumped on her shore. Their most statesmanlike gesture, the opening of the ports of Brazil to the commerce of the world, was wholly the inspiration of England, who had taken it upon herself to save the land from which its rulers

[1] George Young, *Portugal Old and Young*, p. 209.

fled like thieves in the night when Marshal Junot was announced at Abrantes.

§ 7. SEPTEMBER 7, 1822

Brazil dates her independence from the day when a son of this King of Portugal, by previous arrangement with his corpulent sire, drew sword at Ypiranga and declared for "Independence or Death!" Actually she had been independent of Portugal from the day in 1808 when the fugitive court touched at Bahia and issued the *Carta Regia* opening the ports. However, there was then small reason to celebrate freedom—an English fleet laden with court parasites at anchor in the roadstead, and all the rest of the Portuguese leisure class that could escape about to follow. It is notorious that England urged João VI to return to his uncomfortable and tight-fitting throne long before he actually did. Rio was such a comfortable place for a fat old idler that he hesitated to forsake her bountiful board for his own lean and draughty corner of war-harried Europe, even though Napoleon had been muzzled. Nevertheless, he finally did quit Brazil, unlamented.

And no sooner was the father's back turned than the son proclaimed Brazil an independent Empire. On September 7, 1822, Brazil got an Emperor for a King; the illiterate got another century of ignorance; and the Slavery Concession was renewed for another period of sixty-six years.

The date, notwithstanding, is a good one to locate in time another point on my rough curve of Brazilian progress. It is a good date for an inventory because one great blessing that resulted from the presence of the court was a tolerance of foreign scientists; and by 1822 it is easy to picture, from accurate accounts of unbiased and trained observers, exactly what was the social status of Brazil. John Mawe, "a person devoted to mineralogical pursuits," in 1807 rode overland from Santa Catharina to São Paulo and Rio, and under royal passports journeyed through Minas Geraes to report on the diamond mines, a journey which no Englishman had ever before taken. The marriage of Leopoldina, Archduchess of Austria, with the Crown Prince, had brought many eminent Austrian and German scientists to Brazil. The King of Bavaria sent two of the members of the Munich Academy of Sciences, Spix and Martius. Their *Reise in Brasilien in den Jahren 1817 bis 1820* takes you on mule-back from Rio to São Paulo, through Minas Geraes, Goyaz, Bahia, Pernambuco, Ceará, Piauhy, and Maranhão; by sea from São Luiz to Belém; thence up the Amazon. Spix and Martius were preceded by Von Eschwege; his Serene Highness, the Prince of Neuwied, was at the time traveling along the coast from Rio de Janeiro to Bahia; Koster had already published the account of his travels; and Auguste St. Hilaire was returning to Rio from his famous trip into Goyaz as the two German academicians set out. So a picture of Brazil in 1822 may be false because of misinterpretation, but need not fail through any lack of data.

So far as territory goes, Brazil at the beginning of her independence was essentially as now, the boundaries between the Spanish and Portuguese colonies having been determined in 1777 by the second treaty of demarcation. Acre, since acquired, is the only important addition; the Banda Oriental (Uruguay) is the only important territory that Brazil ever lost.

Since 1700 noteworthy accretions to population had been received, however. During the first half of the eighteenth century, the desire jealously to monopolize the profits of the mines induced the Crown of Portugal to restrict Brazilian immigration in every way possible. The farseeing Pombal reversed this shortsighted policy: to build up the population of Brazil as a colonial buttress supporting the sagging walls of the Portuguese European edifice, he visualized as an obvious necessity. From the Islands the great minister removed a sturdy peasantry than which Brazil could have desired nothing finer, as many as twenty thousand from the Açores.[1]

[1] Ribeiro, *Historia do Brazil* (9th ed., 1920), p. 329.

When the Portuguese town of Mazagam, in Morocco, fell, Pombal removed the whole Portuguese population, about eighteen hundred, to Pará, in 1766; the town of Mazaganopolis near the mouth of the Amazon on the north shore is a monument to that move. "Gladly would the Minister have had more colonists of this description at his command; but as Portugal was not capable of supplying from its scanty population such as he would have chosen, he took those whom he could get, cleared the prisons of their inmates, paired these criminals and vagabonds with the harlots of Lisbon, and shipt them off for the Rio, thence to be forwarded to Matto Grosso, where hands were most wanted."[2] After the flight of the court, an effort was made to introduce tea into Brazil, and Chinese were imported to cultivate it; these inveterate traders soon advanced themselves from the status of agricultural laborers to independent hucksters selling cotton goods and fireworks, a wisp of oriental mist that soon was dissipated in the sunshine of the capital. Another decorative fringe of population, which has kept its identity distinct until today, was the Gypsies who had found their way into Pernambuco, where they were following the same Romany Roads as in Europe, peddling and horse-dealing. But the tidal wave of population which broke on the shores of Brazil during the eighteenth century, a dark current like that of the Rio Negro mingling with the turbid waters of the Solimões, was that which swept westward across the Middle Passage from Africa.

To describe further the population of Brazil and the most interesting experiment in racial fusion in historic times, it is necessary here to define terms.

In 1822, the term Negro meant any unmixed African type. A pure-blooded Indian was still an Indian. But a "white man" was often very different from a pure-blooded man of European descent.

For three hundred years the process of fusion between Portuguese and Dutch on the one side and the Indian on

[2] Southey, III, 589, 591.

the other had been going on; there were individuals among the darker representatives of the Mediterranean race who were more pigmented than the lighter individuals among the Indians; so that from the fusion of Portuguese and Indians no very pronounced change of skin color occurred. There was no prejudice in Portuguese minds against other races of a different complexion. So it naturally came about that all free men who were not manifestly black or jungle savages, were listed as "whites." No other interpretation can be put upon the data. A statistical report of the City of São Paulo dated 1811, for instance, and a parochial census of the whole province in 1813, list by sex and civic status "Whites, Negroes, and Mulattoes"; although nowhere in Brazil was the fusion of Mediterranean and Indian more complete than in São Paulo, the original home of the *Mamalucos*. That poetic term would not have been dropped unless consciousness of the cross which it denotes had already largely faded from men's minds.[3]

By Mulatto was meant the cross between White and Negro, still exhibiting pronounced Negroid characteristics in color and hair.

Two terms were used to describe the cross between the Indian and any white, *Mamaluco* and *Cariboca*.[4]

Finally, for the Indian-Negro cross we have the term *Cafuz*.

What was the relative strength of these six basic Brazilian types in 1822?

The "unreduced" Indians were no more to be counted than the birds. They had at that time been pushed back into three inaccessible forest regions: the Amazon forest, the coastal belt between the Rio Doce and the Rio das Contas in Bahia, and the plateau of what is now Paraná and Santa Catharina.

---

[3] "Here all men, especially free men who are not black, are white; and often a man is officially white, but naturally almost a Negro. This is directly opposed to the system of the United States, where all men who are not unmixed white are black."—Sir Richard F. Burton, *The Highlands of Brazil* (London, 1869), I, 393.

[4] As to the spelling "mamaluco," see Euclydes da Cunha, *Os Sertões* (5th ed., 1914), p. 68.

We can safely affirm, however, that the Brazilian Indian's strength was considerably less than in 1500.

Nor have we any figures for the *Cafuz*. This Negro-Indian cross was considerable only in the lawless sertões of Matto Grosso and the middle reaches of the São Francisco River, regions which had always been a refuge for fugitive slaves.

As to the other racial elements, however, we have parochial censuses which show indications of having been made with considerable care. From a study of the available data, I estimate the total population of Brazil in 1822, exclusive of wild Indians, to have been in the neighborhood of three and one-half millions. There was a Negro population of not less than one million, a Mulatto population of the same dimensions, and a "White" population of not to exceed a million and a half—always remembering that "White" included the Caribocas and the lighter-colored free Mulattoes.[5]

Of equal significance to the strength of the Negro element in Brazil at that time was its distribution, from Pernambuco to Rio Grande do Sul and from Rio de Janeiro to Matto Grosso. Pernambuco, Bahia, Rio de Janeiro, and Minas were the blackest provinces.

The only parts of civilized Brazil which had no considerable Negro element were what is now Santa Catharina and Paraná in the south, the equally backward provinces of Espirito Santo and Sergipe, and the coast from Rio Grande do Norte north to the Amazon Valley. Caribocas were probably the most numerous element in all those places.

So much for the strength and ethnic make-up of the population with which Brazil started her career as an independent nation in 1822. Its diffusion was its chief weakness. There were only two cities in Brazil with more than one hundred thousand population, Rio de Janeiro and São Salvador. Recife numbered not much over a quarter of that figure, and São

[5] In the year 1825, Alexander von Humboldt estimated the entire population of Brazil at about 4,000,000; of this number he calculated that 920,000 were whites; 1,960,000 Negroes; and 1,120,000 mixed races and native Indians.

Paulo less than ten thousand. The gold rush was not the only factor responsible for this dispersal. The pastoral industry worked toward the same end. Piauhy, for instance, was parceled out in cattle ranches of 27,000 acres each (*seismarias* of three square leagues) with another square league left between each two grants to prevent overcrowding. Ten or twelve men sufficed for the management of such an estate. At the beginning of the nineteenth century the pastoral part of Rio Grande do Sul contained only 539 landholders; their estates varied from 18,000 to 90,000 acres (two to ten square leagues, some even more).[6]

Such diffusion of population, in Brazil as in the West of the United States, led to a maximum of individual freedom and a minimum of social restraint. There was no law in the sertões but force; and men naturally grouped themselves about strong, natural leaders (*Poderosos*) in the feudal fashion, rendering loyalty unto the death in return for "protection." There are private individuals in the sertõa of Bahia today who can call out five hundred armed retainers on a moment's notice, and ten times that number in stirring emergencies, as the Federal Government found out in the gubernatorial election of 1919. This was a state of affairs much more common in 1822. Bored with the monotony of life, many of this lawless fraternity kept alive a custom once common in the towns of Portugal and Spain; they went abroad at night wrapped in long coats and with faces masked in order that they might perpetrate any cruelty or excess which instinct prompted, ripping, slashing, raping, robbing. Another set calling themselves *Valentoens* or *Bravos* ("Bullies" such as the lumber camps of North America developed) used to play king by taking station at some lonely crossroad and compelling all passers-by to dismount, take off their hats, and lead their horses until out of sight—or fight, it mattered not which. It is not easy to overdraw the barbarity of life in the sparsely populated sertoes of Brazil in 1822, but for all that life there

6 Southey, III, 864.

exhibited more soundness than did life in Minas Geraes where population was most dense. It is, however, in the nature of evil to manifest itself and of goodness to lie concealed. There has been no period of history and no place on the globe where the mass of human beings in any given community were not simple, sincere, decent men and women; more than that, were I to describe society in the rich interior centers like Diamantina, or Ouro Preto, or São Paulo, it would have to do justice to much culture, cordiality, and charm.

Upon arriving at Rio de Janeiro one encountered a great deal of culture and charm, but then as now the culture of Rio was more European than Brazilian. The Academy of Arts had already been established by the Conde da Barca, who invited several distinguished French artists and sculptors to head the new institution, foremost among them Lebreton who had been secretary to the Academy of Arts at Paris. Italian opera, however badly performed, had been heard in the capital; and one of Haydn's favorite pupils, the Chevalier Neukomm, had been imported as composer to the royal chapel. French books were greatly in demand; every educated man spoke French as well as Portuguese; and French philosophic concepts had been in vogue with the intellectuals since the days of the Encyclopedists.[7] Only none of this culture was indigenous.

How could it be otherwise when even a printing-press had been prohibited in Brazil until the arrival of the court? When Spix was there, ten years later, Brazil boasted but two newspapers, the *Gazeta do Rio de Janeiro* and in São Salvador a paper under the title *Idade de Ouro do Brazil*. Most people in the interior were quite content to get their news of the world once a year when the annual pack-train returned from the coast. There was a postal service between Rio and São Paulo which took two weeks for delivery, and another between São Paulo and Montevideo, a modern innovation introduced by the court. But even fifteen years after the time we are

[7] Spix and Martius, I, 154.

describing, according to Gardner, there was not a hotel or inn in all Brazil outside Rio, São Salvador, and one or two towns in Minas.

Now a comparison of the main trend of development in the United States of America and the Empire of Brazil in 1822 is too instructive to be forgone even at the risk of being misunderstood. The English colonies were some forty years ahead of the Portuguese in dissolving partnership with Europe; the one had to fight hard for independence; the other got it without a struggle as a by-product of the Napoleonic wars.

The United States erected upon the foundation of her hardwon liberty the most democratic form of government then existing in the world; Brazil set up an Empire with a member of a European ruling house as Emperor.

In the United States the fight against slavery had already been fought and won in all the northern states (except Delaware) and in the territory north of the Ohio River; Brazil was all slave territory.

Hookworm, introduced from Africa into both countries, was by climatic factors restricted to the southern parts of the United States; unrecognized, it was eating away at the vitals of well-nigh all Brazil.

New England was already showing talent for manufacturing; Brazil was wholly agricultural and pastoral.

In spite of Brazil's hundred years' head-start, the United States had by 1822 a population of around seven millions, just double that of Brazil (in both cases disregarding the Indians); and had developed her system of decennial censuses with results as accurate as those achieved by the Brazilian census of 1920.

The North American frontier then extended from the southern end of Lake Michigan to just west of the Mississippi River in Missouri, Arkansas, and Louisiana; the Brazilian frontier was as far-flung then as today.

The North American Republic was gradually pushing com-

pact frontier communities each year a little farther from the
old, firm settlements of the seaboard; the South American
Empire had scattered its people like pellets out of a cylinder-
bore shotgun.

The Erie Canal was within three years of completion and
the building of wagon roads had progressed further in the
settled parts of the United States in 1822 than it has in
Brazil in 1926.

The two most important differences remain to be stated.
As early as 1785 the Congress of the United States provided
for a rough survey of the western public lands and a demarcation into townships of thirty-six sections. By 1800 tracts
as small as three hundred and twenty acres might be bought
from Government at two dollars an acre on four years' credit;
in 1820 the minimum price for public land was lowered to
$1.25 an acre and land could be bought for cash in eighty-
acre lots. That meant that any penniless laborer who had
two hands and energy enough to earn and save the small
sum of one hundred dollars, could become an independent
small farmer on surveyed land whose title was guaranteed
by the Government of the United States.[8] Citizens of the
northern half of the United States were building up a nation
of small farmers. Brazil, like our South, stood for large
estates owned by a small aristocracy and worked by slaves—
and both the South and Brazil paid the same terrible price
for their preference. In 1822 it is doubtful if a Brazilian
landowner had ever taken an agricultural instrument in his
hand for any other purpose than to whack a slave over the
head; in half the United States, at least, axes, and shovels,
and plows, and picks were being handled by free and vigorous
frontiersmen who took orders from no overlord, and who
realized that every blow of their ax was struck in their own
interest. Secondly, note well that as early as 1785 each
sixteenth section of the public lands was reserved for the

[8] This legislation was but the forerunner of the Homestead Act of 1862
which provided for the free gift of small farms to actual settlers.

support of public schools in the United States; there was a
veritable passion for the rudiments of an education in the
frontier democracy of North America from the very first which
has only begun to manifest itself in Brazil in the second decade
of the twentieth century.

So in judging the progress made by Brazil during her first
century of independence, it must never be forgotten with what
handicaps she started. The Portuguese colonial régime created
almost no values of abiding social worth. Brazil in 1822 freed
herself from a parent whose history must be to her anything
but a matter of pride; burdened with disease, ignorance,
slavery, and a slave-minded aristocracy.

§ 8. IMMIGRATION FROM 1820 TO 1920

Oriented by such considerations, and frightened by Brazil's
reputation as a stronghold of yellow fever, the main current
of European immigration after the Napoleonic Wars set in
toward the northern half of America. While Brazil during
her first century of independence received 3,647,000 European
immigrants, the United States received thirty-three millions,
more coming to the northern republic during the three and
one-half years commencing in 1905 than came to Brazil during one hundred years.

The character of Brazil's overseas guests changed sharply
about 1850. Although, following Portugal's lead, Brazil in
1830 declared the slave trade to be piracy, it was precisely
during the second quarter of the nineteenth century that her
importations from Africa were heaviest, something like one
million three hundred and fifty thousand according to Sir
Harry Johnston. A committee reporting to the British House
of Commons on July 19, 1853, gave the following figures as
to the number of black recruits being landed annually on
Brazilian shores to maintain at full strength her Negro Army
of Labor: [1]

[1] Burton, *Highlands of Brazil* (London, 1869), I, 5.

```
1847  .....................  56,172
1848  .....................  60,000
1849  .....................  54,000
```

From such data, I estimate the total proportions of the African slave trade between 1821 and 1850 at a million and a half, more or less. Then an effective public opinion declared for a more democratic disposition of public lands and their colonization by freemen, and Brazil put a stop to the business within a very few years. An occasional cargo of slaves was landed, chiefly by North Americans, up to the abolition of slavery in 1888; but the numbers are negligible after 1850.

Then, and not until then, did European immigration assume significant proportions. The Brazilian Immigration Service has kept accurate records only since 1908, but in the *Diario Official* of 13 January, 1921, were published figures from 1820 to 1919 compiled from the best sources available. While the result must, in the nature of things, be far from accurate, we shall never have anything nearer the truth; and I have brought these figures together by decades in the accompanying table. The two facts which shout loudest are that fifty-nine per cent of the immigrants received by Brazil during her first century of independence were of the Mediterranean peoples who are blood brothers of the Portuguese, who learn the Portuguese language within a few months, and blend with the Brazilian population completely during the first generation; and that only seven per cent are Central and North Europeans who tend to herd by themselves and offer certain difficulties of assimilation. What are classed in the returns as "Turko-Arabians" are people from the Levant, chiefly Syrians, who as peddlers with packs penetrate to the uttermost limits of inhabited Brazil before they advance themselves to the status of settled shopkeepers and merchants. Under "Russians" are included those Poles whose picturesque covered wagons are such a feature of eastern Paraná, and many Bessarabian Jews settled in Rio Grande do Sul.

IMMIGRANTS RECEIVED BY BRAZIL DURING HER FIRST CENTURY OF INDEPENDENCE

Decade	AFRICANS	MEDITERRANEAN PEOPLES					CENTRAL EUROPEANS					ASIATICS	Miscellaneous	TOTAL
	Negroes	Italians	Portuguese	Spanish	Turko-Arabians (chiefly Syrians)	French	Germans	Russians (includes Poles)	Austrians	English	Swiss	Japanese		
1821–30	450,000						1.984						5,439	457,423
1831–40	500,000	180	467				270						1,921	502,838
1841–50	550,000	5	463	132			2,719			292	338		2,573	556,795
1851–60		24	68,918	59		141	18,920				2,395		31,290	121,747
1861–70		4,923	50,162	671		2,566	12,772		104	2,925	833		22,615	97,571
1871–80		60,029	75,282	5,177	52	4,437	17,006	8,501	7,872	3,043	1,739		35,990	219,128
1881–90		295,063	117,763	39,799	103	5,460	21,628	28,337	6,557	1,180	1,008		14,008	530,906
1891–1900		678,761	202,429	157,119	4,326	4,964	12,489	14,440	38,330	2,784	825		27,435	1,143,902
1901–10		215,891	218,173	137,613	19,704	4,795	17,533	17,221	15,990	3,818	1,126		46,295	698,159
1911–20		134,017	321,510	170,244	34,788	7,867	26,120	36,771	11,206	5,414	1,834	27,497	40,963	818,231
CENTURY	1,500,000 29%	1,388,893	1,055,167	510,814	58,973	30,503	131,441	105,270	80,059	19,456	10,098	27,497	228,529	5,146,700
	1,500,000 29%	3,044,350 59%					346,324 7%							

Buried from sight and memory in the "miscellaneous" column are four or five thousand immigrants whose history is peculiarly interesting to North Americans. As Burton started on his explorations of the Highlands of Brazil in 1867, he encountered on the road between Juiz de Fora and Barbacena a string of immigrant wagons lumbering on toward the São Francisco River as others similarly piloted by long-coated, tobacco-chewing planters were lumbering across the southern flanks of the Great Plains of the United States. They were "Southrons" disgusted with the outcome of the Civil War who had forsaken a land where slavery had just been abolished for one where their favorite economic system was still flourishing. In the first decade after the close of the Civil War parties of such unsubmitting Rebels could have been seen in Paraná near Curityba, in the Campinas district of São Paulo, on the Rio das Velhas in Minas, on the lower Rio Doce, in Bahia, Pernambuco, and even in Pará and about Santarém on the Amazon. They made small mark upon Brazil, but Brazil certainly put her stamp upon them and their descendants. They had gone to the wrong place. Slavery was nearing its end, too, in the southern empire; and even in the days of its height Brazil never had any place for such hatred of the colored man as these fugitives from Missouri, and Louisiana, and Mississippi carried in their hearts.

§ 9. THE NEGRO'S CONTRIBUTION

It has come time to speak of these colored men and women before their identity is completely merged in that larger meaning which each decade is pouring into the mold of the word "Brazilian." Slavery was the most significant single fact in sixteenth, seventeenth, eighteenth, and nineteenth century Brazil. How she finally emerged from Negro slavery without hatred is perhaps the finest tale in her whole history.

The world has fashions in great ideas no less than in hats and gowns. *Political democracy* was full of magic for men from about the time that *Liberté, égalité, et fraternité* was a shibboleth in Revolutionary France. In an effort to inject a more real and substantial meaning into such terms, the world of recent years has been devoting more and more attention to economic relations; and we have Revolutionary Russia trying to make fashionable the idea that only those who work deserve to eat. As the scroll of the twentieth century unrolls, Labor is clothed with more dignity than ever before in the history of our kind. As gravity, thanks to Galileo, has replaced the medieval notion that bodies fall because they are afraid of the vacuum above; so the medieval notion that agricultural labor is degrading, that manual toil is an attribute of slavery, has given way to the conviction that only by the sweat of one's brain and brawn is anything worth while accomplished, and that the most honorable thing in all this world is honest toil. There are by no means insignificant political parties in Europe who hold that Labor is about the most dignified thing in life; and but few of those in the forefront of progress any longer consider labor a disgrace. Honor attaches not only to the creative labor of Leonardo da Vinci or Goethals, but likewise to the drudgery of João de Providencia who hews wood and draws water. Only parasitism is deemed worthy of the contempt of modern men. Instead of rendering obeisance to a man who swears *I will perform no manual labor so long as I can get a single slave to work for me,* today the World visits upon him its utmost scorn. It sees clearly that the heaviest punishment for slavery fell not upon the slaves, but upon the class that enslaved them.

This is terribly true of the South of the United States. Negro slavery was less terrible, but the incidence of the penalty was the same in Brazil. This will become clear in the second and third books; here I will state why Negro slavery was less hideous in Brazil than in the United States.

The Portuguese are more color-blind than any other people in Europe. They are so color-blind that they will look straight at a black man and see only a man. They share this peculiar optical defect with the French, Spanish, Italians, Jews, and Syrians; but with the Portuguese it is developed to a noteworthy degree.

The Catholic Church is more catholic than any other Christian church. Although it lacked the integrity to say that if Indian slavery was wrong all slavery was wrong, in Brazil, at least, it had the integrity to say that a free Negro was a free human being and could go as far in the Catholic Church as his talents would take him.

The Mediterranean type of man is more easy-going than the Central and North European; he takes life easier, his holidays mean more to him, he plays with life instead of taking it with the melancholy seriousness of a Puritan. The Dutch and English and their colonial descendants were notoriously harder taskmasters and more cruel slave-drivers than the Spanish and Portuguese.

In slavery, the length of the working day was determined by the amount of daylight. During the principal growing season, the days are notably shorter in 15° south latitude than in 35° north. In June, in Virginia, it is daylight at three-thirty in the morning, and it is still daylight at nine at night; in Minas and Bahia, in their summer time, it is not light enough to begin field labor before six o'clock, and it is dark by seven.

This country of even days and nights, dominated by easy-going, color-blind, Catholic Portuguese, needed labor. In the dominant philosophy of the sixteenth and seventeenth centuries labor and slavery were synonymous, but good labor and poor labor were recognized: Indian labor was considered poor labor, Negro labor was good labor. Indian women and Negro women were equally desirable in the eyes of Portuguese and Cariboca males, but for money-making they preferred the black man. Good labor and black concubines being expensive, it was not until Minas Geraes revealed her wealth of gold in the early days of the eighteenth century that Brazil could indulge these expensive tastes to the full. Before that time the rules of the game had been set down on paper and had taken form in tradition and custom.

In order that the slaves might provide themselves with food, Saturday in every week was allowed them as well as Sundays and holy days, of which there were some thirty in the year. When this number was cut down in Portugal to the extent of permitting people to follow their usual occupations if so inclined, the permission was not extended to Brazil lest the slaves be deprived of time that was their own. The law (and it was not a dead letter) furthermore provided that a slave could demand his freedom whenever he could offer his owner the price originally paid for him, or what was considered a fair market value. In the seaports, where slaves were employed as boatmen and porters paying to their owners a certain sum weekly, it was easily possible for an energetic man to redeem himself in ten years. As it is traditional to banquet and make merry at a wedding feast, so it was traditional in Brazil to liberate a certain number of slaves upon the death of an owner who desired to be remembered as a liberal-handed gentleman; and there was a very pretty Catholic custom providing that if any person stepped up to the font and offered twenty *milreis*, the owner should manumit the infant there being baptized. Warm-hearted Latins not infrequently thus bestowed liberty upon the bastards of their favorite concubines. Indeed, we can say that in general the treatment of their illegitimate offspring by the Portuguese was the antithesis of the neglect and contempt heaped upon them by the British and their American descendants: they set them free more often than they kept them enslaved; they educated them as well as they educated their legitimate sons; they interposed no barriers to complete social equality.

So from the first in Brazil we have to distinguish between a black current flowing into the stinking cesspool of bondage and another current, not quite so black, trickling away to join the waters that purled down the rapids toward real freedom. Far be it from me to make light of the horrors that floated on the first, even under the best conditions. Each hardy bag of leather-covered bones that survived to reach Brazil gazed four times, on the average, upon the death of a kinsman before his own skinny body was landed in beautiful Rio de Janeiro or the Bay of All the Saints. He saw one die in the slave raid that made him captive in the forests of Africa; he saw the second drop by the wayside on the long journey down the weary trail of tribulation between his capture and the coast; disease claimed the third in the detaining pens of pestilence; and hunger and thirst claimed the fourth in the unspeakable agonies of the Middle Passage. Men have never been subjected to a more rigorous physical selection; the black slave who arrived in America proved his exceptional physical fitness by the fact that he could walk down the gangplank. It was the filthiest institution that has ever won the enthusiasm of large masses of men. Nevertheless, Negro slavery in Brazil was not so bad as in Dutch Guiana, the British West Indies, or the United States; the black Army of Labor that answered the summons of the Portuguese recruiting sergeants took up positions which were not altogether hopeless.

In the two centuries when sugar was king, the Negro shared the burdens of cultivation with the Indian. When gold came to dominate the economic life of Brazil, the Negro assumed the entire load. Every panful of earth from which the gold was washed, every clod of *cascalho* from which diamonds were gleaned, and all the millions of tons that yielded nothing at all, were moved by Negroes carrying upon their stalwart heads the loads their masters were too stupid to move in wheelbarrows. Negroes carried upon their well muscled backs the full weight of the Portuguese Empire in the eighteenth century as they alone carried the weight of the Brazilian Empire for the first half of the nineteenth century.

And these great services were rendered with such loyalty to their masters that they dared to put guns into the hands of slaves! When the French sacked Rio de Janeiro in 1711, the Governor of Minas rushed to its assistance with fifteen

hundred horsemen—and six thousand armed Negroes were
only a day or two behind.[1] In 1763, when fighting was threatened on the Rio Guaporé between the Portuguese and the
Spaniards, we read that the whole force at Conceição amounted
to two hundred and forty-four men, of whom one hundred
and fourteen were armed Negro slaves.

It is obvious that the Negro possessed capabilities of the
highest value to Brazil. Besides his fine physique and the
pigmentation which enables him to labor happily under a
broiling sun, his knowledge of cattle was such that he probably taught the Portuguese more of the herdsmen's tricks than
he learned from them. And his skill in handling metals was
revealed in every smithy of the whole mining region from
Minas to Matto Grosso, a trade that was wholly foreign to
the Indian's previous experience. Reason enough for the
other Brazilians liking the curly-haired black lads who
brought them all their gold. And because they liked them,
a plot of ground on the outskirts of the gold diggings was
always set aside where Negroes of a Sunday could go and wash
out the dust with which one day they might buy their freedom.

Now freedom, as we have demonstrated in the United States,
is not to be granted by an act of legislation when the dominant
caste in any community is determined to deny it. There was
a time when caste was pretty strong in Brazil. But Portugal
did not have sufficient population to make possible the very
expensive caste system of the Spaniard, who did everything
in his power to keep the American-born Spaniard (*Creole*)
and the Spanish-Indian half-breed, in a position of inferiority
to the Spaniard of European birth. There was very little
in Portuguese law and much less in Brazilian public opinion
to degrade either Caribocas, Mulattoes, or free Negroes. At
the beginning of the eighteenth century there were prohibitions against colored people holding positions of public trust,
but before the end of that century we encounter not only
black clergy in Brazil but even black Bishops. The position

[1] Southey, III, 123.

APPROXIMATE PROPORTIONS OF FREE AND SLAVE
EARLY 19TH CENTURY

YEAR	PROVINCE	FREE			SLAVE		
		Negroes	Mulattoes	Total	Negroes	Mulattoes	Total
1813	São Paulo	3,951	44,053	48,004	37,602	10,648	48,250
1804	Goyaz	7,963	15,645	23,608	......	......	19,889
1812	Santa Catharina	......	......	665	......	......	7,578
1812	Parahyba	8,000	28,000	36,000	......	......	17,000
				108,277			92,717

of a priest in a Catholic country is so exalted that you cannot ordain a black man without adding a certain dignity to his race.

By the beginning of the nineteenth century the numerical strength of the free colored population was fully as great as that of the slave population, and at the time of emancipation it was much greater. As to the maximum dimensions which Negro slavery attained in Brazil we have nothing but guesses and "official estimates" which are often deliberately falsified. Johnston says that in 1835 there were 2,100,000 slaves in Brazil;[2] but Adamson, who was the United States Consul at Pernambuco, placed it in 1864 at only 1,707,000.[3] In 1884 the total number of slaves was officially computed at 3,000,000; but emancipation was then writ large in the heavens, and politicians may have had motives for padding the returns.

In 1888 the Princess Isabel by Imperial decree abolished Negro slavery. It was the act of a woman whose name deserves to be enshrined in the hearts of all lovers of liberty beside those of Lincoln and Pombal. As his great qualities cost Lincoln his life, so the integrity of Isabel cost the House of Bragança the Brazilian throne; for on November 15, 1889, the Republic burst from the chrysalis of Empire, and on the bright blue wings of freedom flapped lazily off to appraise the flowers growing in the gardens of earth's earlier emancipations.

How deadly a disease was thus checked by the operation of Isabel may be gauged by contrasting it with our own. Lincoln liberated four million slaves, a number much smaller in proportion to the population of the United States than was even two million to the population of Brazil. The disease ran its course in the northern hemisphere in two hundred and forty-four years; in Brazil it was eating the heart out of a great nation for three hundred and fifty-six.

He who knows our South knows that you do not get over a disease like that in one generation or two. But convalescence

---

[2] Sir Harry Johnston, *The Negro in the New World*, p. 98.
[3] Fletcher and Kidder, *Brazil and the Brazilians*, Appendix F.

is a much sweeter thing to watch south of the equator than north. In the United States it left the patient with a hatred of the slave's descendants; in Brazil with a disinclination toward the slave's job. The Negro in the one case remains a thorn in the flesh of a people who lynch, and burn, and disfranchise, and do their uttermost to keep the wound from healing; Brazil's welcome of her Negro slaves into the ranks of freemen has in one generation become sincere, complete, and unqualified. In 1926 the only slaves remaining in Brazil are Indian peons in the sertão; and, in civilization, the still numerous slaves to the medieval fallacy that labor is degrading.

§ 10. THE RESULTANT POPULATION

Such, thus far, has been the process of the peopling of the lands. Throughout Latin America the Iberians mingled their blood freely with the Indian; whereas north of Mexico the frontier pushed the aborigines before it until they were all ultimately herded upon reservations. Except Argentina and Uruguay, which are white, the mass of the population in Spanish-America is Spanish-Indian mestizos. In Portuguese-America, the Negro forms a third equally important stock. In Brazil the fusion of Europe with Asiatic-America is a matter of four hundred years; the fusion of both with Africa is largely of the last two centuries.

The process has not gone so far in Brazil that there are not still large numbers of unmixed Portuguese, Indians, and Negroes, still some consciousness of color and even more of caste; but it has gone so far that one may expect its completion perhaps within five or six generations. The same length of time will suffice to absorb the Mediterranean peoples who so largely outnumbered the Portuguese in nineteenth century immigration that from any but a linguistic standpoint it has already become an entire misnomer to speak of Brazil as Portuguese-America. As a melting-pot Brazil develops

POPULATION IN 1920

States	Population	Area (Square Kilometers)	Density (per Sq. Kil.)
Districto Federal	1,157,873	1,164	985.9
Rio de Janeiro	1,559,371	68,982	22.6
Pernambuco	2,154,835	128,395	16.8
Alagôas	978,748	58,491	16.7
São Paulo	4,592,188	290,876	15.8
Santa Catharina	668,743	43,535	15.4
Parahyba do Norte	961,106	74,731	12.9
Ceará	1,319,228	104,250	12.7
Sergipe	477,064	39,090	12.2
Minas Geraes	5,888,174	574,855	10.2
Espirito Santo	457,328	44,839	10.2
Rio Grande do Norte	537,135	57,485	9.3
Rio Grande do Sul	2,182,713	236,553	9.2
Bahia	3,334,465	426,427	7.8
Paraná	685,711	251,940	2.7
Piauhy	609,003	301,797	2.0
Maranhão	874,337	459,884	1.9
Pará	983,507	1,149,712	0.9
Goyaz	511,919	747,311	0.7
Territorio do Acre	92,379	152,000	0.6
Amazonas	363,166	1,894,724	0.2
Matto Grosso	246,612	1,378,783	0.2
BRAZIL	30,635,605	8,485,824	3.6

even higher temperatures than the United States. The only elements which as yet do not fuse freely are Europeans who have been colonized in localities out of contact with the flame of Brazilian civilization; and the Japanese, who have arrived too recently to exhibit their racial destiny in Brazil. But numerically, as I have shown, these Central Europeans, English, and Asiatics, who may have a slightly higher melting-point, constitute only seven per cent of nineteenth century immigration and are far from being a serious menace to social solidarity. So we may bid farewell to our ethnic ingredients and hail the new "race" of Brazilians in which they blend.

Brazil has attempted four censuses of its civilized population, showing in 1872 ten millions, in 1890 fourteen, in 1900 seventeen, and in 1920 thirty. The director of the census of 1920 states that this is the first which has been carried out with any degree of accuracy, a warning which scientists will do well to accept.[1] As I write, the only published results that have come to hand are a very brief synopsis published in April, 1922, but complete demographic statistics will soon be available. It is to be hoped that decennial censuses will now be established; for until several more accurate counts have been published, sociologists can say with certainty very little about the extraordinarily interesting facts which a close study of Brazilian population is sure to reveal.

Nothing is more unequal than the distribution of population upon our earth. Brunhes figured the total population of the world in 1910 at 1,665 millions of men. Brazil's 30 million is less than 2 per cent of any such figure, whereas her land surface is 5.5 per cent of the crust that sticks above the sea. Her population density is the antithesis of that of India and China, those "masses of human beings cemented by time, against which wars, epidemics, and famines wear themselves

[1] O recenseamento de 1920 foi, não só o que obteve melhor exito, mas ainda o unico que, de facto, registrou, com a possivel exactidão, a totalidade dos habitantes existentes no vasto territorio do Brazil.—Bulhoes Carvalho, *Synopse do Recenseamento Realizado em 1 de Setembro de 1920.*

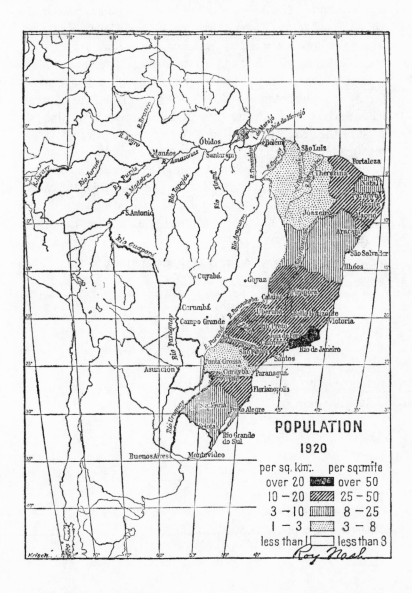

POPULATION

1920

per sq. km.   per sq. mile
over 20   over 50
10 — 20   25 — 50
3 — 10   8 — 25
1 — 3   3 — 8
less than I   less than 3

out in vain." [2]   If we eliminate the states which are practically all sertão—Matto Grosso, Amazonas, Acre, Goyaz, and Pará where the population is *less than one to the square kilometer;* and Maranhão, Piauhy, and Paraná, where it is *under three* —then civilized Brazil appears essentially as a fringe along the Atlantic seaboard.   A line drawn south from Ceará parallel with the coast and three hundred miles distant will include most of the people in Brazil, a very fair degree of compactness regained since the days of the dispersal by gold, because the nineteenth century accretions to population settled in this seaboard tier of states and in Minas.   To this zone the world looks for the training, sending forth, and sustenance of the forces which will ultimately conquer and civilize the whole sertão.

[2] Jean Brunhes, *Human Geography* (Chicago, 1920), pp. 64, 70.

CHAPTER V

ANNO DOMINI 1926

IT is still glorious to be Pope in the year of our Lord 1926 —although no one any longer considers Our World the center of the universe; although that long-whiskered brace of imaginative infidels, Darwin and Wallace, have uprooted the flowers of racial fancy that grew so luxuriantly in the Garden of Eden; although the Crusades have been labeled by history as avaricious Christian adventuring against Islam; although the Inquisition has come to be as universally execrated as any institution that ever outraged human integrity; although the Jesuits have paid the penalty for confusing spiritual and economic power; although over half the Christian world has inclined toward the position of the protesting monk, Luther; although the Cross never carried conviction to the heart of Asia.

But Kingship, in 1926, has been entirely shorn of splendor and even robbed of security. The King of Spain is one of the last of the line in Europe; although a young man, he has seen crowns removed from royal heads in Germany, Austria, Russia, Turkey, and Greece. The King of Portugal—there is no King of Portugal. Divine right the human race has put behind it forever, but the Swiss Confederation which went republican at the beginning of our story is still one of the world's unassailable strong points of democracy.

The Rape of Ethiopia has been completed. White hands, in whose clutches naked black bodies writhed powerless, grasped one hundred million Africans and then partitioned the continent among the Powers of Europe.

In 1926, the naked brown tobacco-smokers who once, unconcerned, reclined in their hammocks along the Amazon, know full well that A.D. 1500 was the Year of their Doom.

Portuguese, Negroes, and Indians, with a nineteenth century increment of Mediterranean peoples, Central Europeans, and Asiatics, have fused into a nation of Brazilians thirty million strong. Pombal's vision of a people who shall rise above race hatred, and caste, and color has come true. Except the Portuguese colonies in Africa, Brazil is the one country in the world where fusion of Europeans and Africans is going on unchecked by law or custom. More than in any other place in the world, readmixture of the most divergent types of humanity is there injecting meaning into the *"égalité"* of Revolutionary France and the "human solidarity" of philosophers and class-conscious proletarians. Destiny has erected in Brazil a social laboratory which shall reveal the significance of "race" and either confirm or give the lie for all time to the superstition that the admixture of widely different stocks spells degeneration.

If the Brazilian experiment in unconscious brotherhood fail, those who view with alarm the "rising tide of color" and see a "yellow peril" gathering in the Orient, will consider that failure an overwhelming vote of confidence in their thesis. If, on the contrary, Brazil goes on to develop the finest civilization which ever flourished in a warm climate, a civilization powerful enough to enable her to sit on the bench of equality beside the Powers of the temperate zone that now proclaim themselves Lords of Creation, an increasing conviction will, in time, lay hold of the human mind that the mating of the most diverse strains of men is no more disastrous than the mingling of the streams that form a mighty river. Brown currents, dark waters, and white unite to make the Amazon; all the rivers of the world pool their strength in the deep blue sea.

BOOK II

THE ESSENTIAL FACTS OF HUMAN GEOGRAPHY

Icó, a charming old town far in the interior of Ceará.

A very effective use of tiles as a wall-facing on a church in
Maceió Alagôas.

In the far interior of Bahia.

Blumenau, the county seat of a German colony in Santa Catharina.
(See page 183.)

The mud house. Many are not even whitewashed. (See page 173.)

The simplest form of palm-leaf hut. A temporary shelter in Matto Grosso. (See page 173.)

Santa Cruz, Espirito Santo. Grass-grown main street, path trodden by bare feet at the right, whitewashed mud houses built end to end and placed flush with the street. This is the type of thousands of hamlets in rural Brazil. (See page 184.)

Practically all buildings are of wood in the Paraná pine forests of Santa Catharina and Paraná. (See page 181.)

Typical farmhouse of the German colonies in Santa Catharina. Red brick of fine quality, timbering painted black, white sashes and door frames, and flat tiles. (See page 182.)

CHAPTER VI

THE HOUSES OF RURAL BRAZIL

WHAT are the chances that Brazilians will go on to such a conquest of themselves and their environment?

The first step is to ascertain how far they already have gone. There are standard methods of sampling coffee and cacao but no approved methods of sampling nations. If you measured ancient Greece by its artistic output it would rank exceedingly high; by the condition of the masses of men, very low. A nation may have a bathroom in nearly every house, like the United States, and yet test out lower in sweetness of soul and the fun they get out of life than some less fastidious Latins. The set of facts which Jean Brunhes singled out as the essential field of human geography gives a very fair cross-section of the more tangible evidences of conquest. I shall describe Brazil from this angle before passing on to a consideration of certain less tangible signs of civilization and criteria of human well-being.

This is how Brunhes defines the field.[1] If one rose above the earth in a balloon, what signs of man would strike the eye or impress a photographic plate? First, men themselves moving across the surface of earth like ants, swarming in the cities, scattered on the farms, disappearing within the forest. Upon men our attention was chiefly centered in Book I.

Were men themselves entirely lost to view, still would remain unmistakable man-signs. More distinctly than the men who made them, excrescences roofed with red tiles or brown thatch impinge upon the retina—their houses. From house to house run lines beaten by bare feet—paths. Double lines

---

[1] *Human Geography,* by Jean Brunhes (trans. T. C. Le Compte, ed. Isaiah Bowman and R. E. Dodge; Chicago, 1920), pp. 46-52.

worn by the feet of draft animals drawing wheeled vehicles—
roads. Double lines of parallel steel called railroads. Expanses of ocean; long stretches of navigable rivers; canals;
with the ports, and landings, and locks which make possible
the full use of the flowing roads. Houses and roads. These
are the outstanding facts of the unproductive occupation of
the soil, the sacrifice of surface which man makes to fixity
and to motility.

Along the roads and at the end of paths through the forest,
other man-signs would attract the eye or etch their images
upon the negative. In the suburbs of Rio would appear geo-
metrical patterns of truck-gardens carpeting the valleys. Upon
the plateau of São Paulo, endless lines of little trees in regular rows, snow-white with blossoms or red with berries.
Within the forest of Bahia and Pará, the gold of cacao pods
through the wine-dark sheen of the new leaves. In the valleys
of Minas, the yellow of ripe corn; upon the Atlantic plain,
the green of sugar cane; in the German colonies, the brown
of new-plowed land; on the edge of the forest, the black of
new burnings. Gardens, and plantations, and cultivated fields.
Marks of man's mastery over the vegetable world.

Elsewhere cultivated fields become subordinate to the herds,
and flocks, and droves pastured upon wide plains. Across
Minas and Goyaz and Matto Grosso move great herds of long-
horned cattle bound for the fattening pastures of São Paulo.
Upon the pampas of Rio Grande do Sul bands of brood mares,
herds of Herefords and Red Polled, white flocks of huddled
sheep. Down in the pantanal along the Paraguay barefooted
cowboys are dashing in madly to lasso the wild steers that
run before them like startled deer. Into every hamlet pour
streams of mules bearing all the produce of the field. Through
the caatingas of Ceará browse twinkle-tailed goats. Across
a flooded pasture in Marajó, an ox dragging a canoe attached
to its tail. An animal population much more numerous than
the human and as subordinate to human will as the plants
of the field. Cultivated fields and domesticated animals; facts

of plant and animal conquest. The productive occupation of the soil.

Remain the facts of destructive economy. Particularly in Minas Geraes the eye is seared by holes that gape in the hillsides, long sluices which wind with the contours, acre upon acre where soil and gravel have been turned over and over, washed and sorted, in man's greedy search for gold and diamonds. Near Itabira do Matto Dentro are many foreign engineers picking away and sampling at the mountains of iron ore. By Carangola are pits where mica is wheeled forth from the hill. In Santa Catharina other scars on the side-hill where coal is being dug. "Economic plunder," the Germans call it, *Raubwirtschaft*. Onions you may pull from the same patch week after week and year after year; coal and gold you pluck from the soil but once.

Lastly, there are certain acts which would impress themselves but slightly upon a photographic plate, yet whose aggregate and lasting effects are both visible and profound. Actions that are swift, violent, picturesque. The burning of the forest, the slashing of rubber trees, the drawing of the nets, the gathering of turtle eggs or wild honey, the shooting of egrets. Acts allied to those of plant and animal conquest, but of opposite import. Not producing and reproducing, but destroying life.

These six, Brunhes considers to be the essential facts of human geography: houses and roads, cultivated fields and domesticated animals, the exploitation of minerals and the devastation of plant and animal life. Facts of the unproductive occupation of the soil, facts of plant and animal conquest, facts of destructive economy. In their totality they will yield, perhaps, as clear a picture of the material aspects of civilization in Brazil one hundred years after she declared her independence of Portugal as any half-dozen that might easily be singled out.

The Houses of Rural Brazil [1]

Upon savage and statesman alike, upon shelterless tramps of the highways and infants in silken cradles, upon London cabby or Brazilian muleteer, the periodic tyrant, Sleep, lays his deadening hand and will not be denied. Though he may fight sleep off for a time, as do the Fangs of the Congo with kola nut or the devotees of the dance hall with black coffee, music, and roulette, yet his inability to escape has led man everywhere to seek protection from foe and weather while the tyrant has him in his grip. Wherefore, the human habitation.

Geographers use the term "house" to include all human structures; but, inasmuch as it is especially the rural house and the isolated dwelling that necessarily is built of local materials and most clearly exhibits dependence upon the geographical environment, I shall here shun the cities of Brazil. All who travel in South America know Rio de Janeiro and Bahia, Santos and São Paulo; fewer know well the interior.

Palm-Leaf Huts

Plunge into the evergreen forest at the mouth of the Amazon and enter a palm-leaf hut on the Banks of Breves. Just some piles to raise the floor above the mud, three walls of woven matting, and some thatch; yet to him who built it, it is Home. It is a shelter against the storm and driving rain. It is a place where nets, and spears, and knives, and all his beloved possessions accumulate. Hospitality it offers to the friend whose canoe passes along the flowing road. A fire it holds which boils water for his fragrant coffee and browns the fish in the pan. There his woman waits him at the close of day; there his brown-skinned boys were born and learned to laugh; there at eventide he sits and strums his violão. And the hut stands guard above him while he sleeps.

[1] First published in the *Geographical Review* (New York), July, 1923.

Such is the type that has risen in the plains of the Lower Amazon subject to annual floods—mere frameworks raised high on wooden piles and thatched with the leaves of the ubussú palm or the assai. The outer part of the stem of the latter species is hard and tough as horn. Split into narrow planks, it is used along the Tocantins for a large portion of the walls and flooring.

Up toward the headwaters of the Amazon, the forest Indians build communal dwellings large enough to house the whole village, as I pointed out in an earlier chapter. [2] These communal dwellings were originally found from Colombia to Paraguay and eastward to Rio de Janeiro.

The malocas of the Upper Amazon are the limit of the palm-leaf house in the direction of magnitude. At the other end of the scale are such temporary shelters as the one shown from Matto Grosso. Wherever men camp in the jungle for a brief sojourn, as do the *seringueiros* who gather rubber during part of each year, similar frail structures, which can be thrown together in an hour's time, are made to suffice for several months.

The palm-leaf hut in its various forms was one of the houses which existed in Brazil before the invasion of the Portuguese.

The Mud House

The vast majority of houses of rural Brazil are of mud. The gaucho who herds cattle on the pampas of Rio Grande do Sul, the matuto who plants his crops throughout the forest regions of the central plateau and along the littoral, the sertanejo who wrests a precarious livelihood from that dry region which extends from northern Minas to the coast of Maranhão and Ceará, and even those who live in the villages along the navigable rivers of the Amazon Basin, all build the same type of house. "Huts of refuge of the same dreary

---

[2] Pictures and plans of the maloca of the upper Amazon are given, for instance, in Thomas Whiffen's *The North-West Amazons*.

material as the hills" are as typical of Brazil as of Lower Egypt.

Possibly the mud house in some form or other was in use among the aborigines before the arrival of the Portuguese. It was known in parts of South America; wattle and daub, for instance, were characteristic of the Chibcha culture area. However this may be, the present prevalence of the mud-house type appears to be a result of Portuguese culture. The mud house has always been common on the Iberian Peninsula and about the Mediterranean.[3]

It may seem strange that a thing as ephemeral as the mud house should persist and keep the same general characteristics through the centuries in a country which has more standing timber than any other like area of the earth's surface. The fellah in the delta of the Nile lacks everything that is necessary to construct a solid dwelling; but the Brazilian has stone and wood and lime and fuel to burn bricks, in abundance. What is the reason for this, beyond the tremendous force of tradition?

One reason is clear. There are, even today, only two establishments in all Brazil which would be classed by North American lumbermen as thoroughly modern sawmills. The boards used by the hinterland for the most part are whipsawed by hand, as for centuries past. Whipsawed lumber is vastly expensive in labor.

On the contrary, nothing could be easier to build than the mud house of Brazil. Four corner posts and two to support the ridgepole are set into the ground, and rafters are fastened

[3] It was common, too, in medieval England: "The peasants' cabin was made of reeds or sticks plastered over with mud. His fire was chimneyless" (Draper, *Intellectual Development of Europe*, II, 230). The earliest mention of the mud house in Brazil that I can find is in a letter written by the great Jesuit, Anchieta, to Loyola, in August, 1554: "Here we are, sometimes more than twenty of us in a little hut of wicker work and mud, roofed with straw, fourteen paces long and ten wide. This is the school, this is the infirmary, dormitory, refectory, kitchen, and store-room. Yet we covet not the more spacious dwellings which our brethren inhabit in other parts, for our Lord Jesus Christ was in a straiter place when it was his pleasure to be born among beasts in a manger; and in a far straiter when he deigned to die for us upon the Cross." (Southey, I, 263-64.)

to their tops. If nails are expensive, the forest is full of flexible bark and *sipós* which make strong ties. The forest furnishes the builder with the saplings which are fixed vertically between the ground and the rafters a palm's width apart, and with the withes which are woven in horizontally until the walls are outlined as a wattlework of five- or six-inch squares. Plaster into this wattle any good heavy clay, and one has a wall which will soon dry to considerable hardness.

The covering of the house is a more delicate and difficult problem. The fellah of Luxor may get along without any roof to his dwelling; but even the sertanejo of Ceará, living in a land scourged by terrible droughts, must provide against occasional torrential rains. The thatch of palm leaves or grass, which we saw in Amazonas, is encountered on the very rudest type of mud huts in the outskirts of almost any village and on isolated dwellings in the forest everywhere; but the average Brazilian agricultural worker does better than that. He takes suitable clay from another pit, shapes it on a hollowed slab of wood, burns it in a simple kiln, and roofs his house with half-round tiles. These, like the mud of the walls, are supported on a wicker-work of saplings or on shakes split from a palm stem. The roofs of rural Brazil are usually two-sided and but slightly pitched, although four-sided roofs are not uncommon.

Trample down the earth over which this structure stands and one has an edifice which would delight a turtle: packed mud beneath, plastered mud around, burnt mud above. And no tool was necessary for its construction other than a jungle knife, the *facão* which every man owns. Occasionally one sees whole villages where the dwellings are as miserable as that and are left in exactly that rough and unfinished condition.

In its simplest form, this rough house of mud will have but one room and a single door and window. Usually, however, there are partitions dividing it into at least three rooms; and, in all but the pitiful hovels of the most wretched, the walls are smoothed while wet. That is a simple thing—a smooth, hard surface in place of a rough wall full of chinks and cracks. Yet the difference between the one and the other may be the difference between life and death, as we shall see directly.

As the wealth of the occupant increases, there come certain regular steps in attempted embellishment. The first is the application of a wash of color to the smoothed walls—frequently blue, or pink, or green, more commonly whitewash. A veranda, however narrow and however high the eaves, is always a real addition of comfort and somewhat breaks the harsh lines of the packing-box proportions; and when the owner simultaneously acquires the capital and the energy to install a floor of wood, he has almost attained the ultimate goal.

That, from the threefold standpoint of beauty, hygiene, and utility, is attained in the use of tiles as a wall surface. Just why the use of tiles should be so much more common from Maceió north to São Luiz, the region once held by the Dutch, than in other parts of Brazil, is not apparent. It is distinctly a legacy of the Moors in the Iberian Peninsula. Tiles as a wall covering and decoration have been especially used in the lands of Arab civilization, arid lands where dried mud forms an important constructional material. "Indeed it may be said that tilework is the most characteristic feature of Portuguese buildings. . . . Towards the end of the eighteenth century blue seems to have usurped the place of all other colors, and from that time, especially in or near Porto, tiles were used to mask all the exterior rubble walls of houses and churches, even spires or bulbous domes being sometimes so covered." [4] These blue tiles of Porto are the prevailing fashion in house walls along the whole northeast coast of Brazil.

The addition of gilt pineapples, colored glass balls, fantastic waterspouts, pig-tailed corners, or birds of tile and mortar, to the corners or ridgepole of a mud house piles horror upon

[4] W. C. Watson, *Portuguese Architecture* (London, 1908), pp. 22 and 28.

horror. The ephemeral character of such habitations is their chief virtue; and one cannot be sorry that such unlovely excrescences do not endure as long, for instance, as the stone houses of the Breton peasant. In the mud villages of Brazil I suppose a house fifty years old is a rarity.

But there is a kind of earth house which used to be much more common a hundred years ago than it is now, and some examples of this type have endured for upwards of two centuries. It is built on quite different principles and is altogether a more substantial structure. A form of planks, such as we use today in concrete work, is filled with earth, moistened and well tamped and gradually built up until massive structures two and three stories high have been reared. When the walls have thoroughly hardened they are pared smooth and tinted like the walls of the mud house. There are churches and monasteries in Brazil today which were constructed in this manner as long ago as the latter part of the seventeenth century.

Varying, then, between a one-room hovel with rough walls and a monastery with massive walls built up like the earthwork of a dam, enduring from two or three years to as many centuries but always reproducing itself, always remaining true to type, shaped both by tradition and by the natural environment, the mud house remains the sleep shelter of at least twenty millions of the humbler citizenship of Brazil. It is found from Amazonas to Rio Grande do Sul, and from Pernambuco to the Bolivian border.

Unhygienic Nature of the Unsurfaced Mud Hut

If the rougher forms of the mud house have been characterized in somewhat uncomplimentary terms, it is through no lack of respect for the occupants, whose simple and generous hospitality the writer has so often enjoyed. At the same time there is good reason for condemning this hut which the illiterate millions of rural Brazil call home.

For it is the home, too, of the *barbeiro*, a house-inhabiting insect living only in the little chinks of the mud walls and within the thatch of *burity*—the bearer of the scourge called "Chagas's disease," *molestia de Chagas*. In speaking of the three great endemic diseases of Brazil, Dr. Belisario Penna, the present chief of rural sanitation in the Brazilian Public Health Service, says:

The most grave of all, because it is incurable, contracted in infancy, producing a high mortality, and generally disabling its victims, is Chagas's disease, the *doença do barbeiro*, which curses the population of more than seventy counties in Minas Geraes. I calculate that 25 per cent or more of the population of the state (Minas) is profoundly afflicted or rendered useless by this scourge. It exists throughout the state of Goyaz, in vast regions of Maranhão, Piauhy, Bahia, and Matto Grosso, and in some of the counties of São Paulo. . . . Deaths by the cardiac form occur in tremendous numbers in the infected zones, individuals dying through heart failure at all ages, even in full youth. The nervous form of Chagas's disease constitutes another aspect of extraordinary social importance. It includes those humans, monstrous in mentality and physical aspect, scattered through the interior of Brazil by the tens of thousands. . . .

Curral d'el Rey, whence the disease appeared, was but a background for goiters, cripples, and idiots—a tremendous breeding ground of the terrible *barbeiro*, there in the burrows, the dens, the mud-walled houses of the old inhabitants. These destroyed and substituted by attractive and hygienic habitations, both the insect and trypanosomiasis americana disappeared in all its forms. . . .

Go to Sete Lagôas and Curvello. In the residences of the well-to-do and those who live in houses covered with tiles, with smooth, whitewashed walls, neither the barbeiro nor the disease is encountered. Both are met in the suburbs where they tolerate the *cafúas*, the houses without plaster.[5]

The world of science is chiefly indebted to Dr. Carlos Chagas, the present head of Brazil's Department of Public Health, for identifying the malady with its cause.[6]

[5] *Conferencias* (Rio de Janeiro, 1919), pp. 78-83.
[6] The disease is due to a trypanosoma—*Schizotrypanum Cruzi*—carried by *Triatoma megista* (of the family Reduviidae), locally known as the *barbeiro*. The disease appears to develop under rather special conditions, and its geographical distribution is restricted. Outside of Brazil it has

Stone Houses

What a relief it is to come upon a locality here and there where the environment has caused a departure from mud in favor of stone! Diamantina, the center of the diamond district in Minas, lies on a high range of mountains which is almost bare of building timber; and for a dozen leagues round about even such slender poles as are used in the walls of the mud houses are difficult to find. There is an abundance of excellent stone in the neighborhood, however, and all the older houses were built of this material. Many fine houses of two and three stories, constructed over a century ago in the days of prosperity, still adorn the town and grow lovelier with their increasing years. Unfortunately, since the railroad has been built, the tendency has been away from stone.

Penedo, on the São Francisco River in Alagôas, is another stone town, built of the fine-grained, yellowish sandstone on which the town stands. There must be others scattered here and there in this vast country, just as rare, isolated stone houses are seen—I encountered a temporary shelter of stone above timber line on the Serra do Caparaó on the boundary between Minas Geraes and Espirito Santo. But for the most part the Brazilian farmer, like the North American, shuns durable building materials as he would the plague.

Walls of Wattle

Now and again brush, woven into a rude wattlework, serves for the walls of dwellings like those hastily constructed at the edge of a great American construction camp in Ceará. Although it is better suited to a dry, hot country than is the mud house, in a belt of heavy rains it shelters its inmates

been reported in two localities in Venezuela, in San Salvador, and in the eastern forests of Peru bordering on Brazil. Dr. Chagas's initial discovery was made while conducting an anti-malaria campaign in construction works on the central railroad of Brazil in 1907 under orders from Dr. Oswaldo Cruz of yellow fever fame. See M. Neveu-Lemaire: "Notes de géographie médicale," section Maladie de Chagas ou schizotrypanose américaine, *La Géographie,* Vol. 35 (1921), pp. 27-35.

but indifferently. This type, wattle and thatch, is widely distributed but is not numerically important.

The Sod House

As the steppes of Russia have given birth to the *isba* built of turf, and the Great Plains of the United States to the sod house, so the pampas of Rio Grande do Sul have produced a similar hut. At rare intervals along the Uruguayan frontier, where timber is very scarce, one sees the shelter of some gaucho made by piling layer upon layer of sod from the plains whereon his cattle pasture. I have encountered this type nowhere else in Brazil, and it cannot be said to be at all common even in Rio Grande do Sul.

Houses of Wood

Just beyond Passo Fundo, traveling north through Rio Grande, one comes into the solid forest of Paraná pine (*Araucaria*) which clothes the plateau of Santa Catharina and Paraná. This is the region of the wooden house; and as there are outliers of the forest along the watercourses to the southward of this point, so has the forest projected its wooden house upon the plains of Rio Grande. The sight of the first gaucho's cabin of slabs or boards with a shingled roof is enough to make one from the Great Lakes pinery gasp with delight. Rude, unlovely, without beauty of line or color, yet it appeals more than a palace after the monotony of mud to which we have grown accustomed; for it heralds our approach toward a forest folk who are beginning to utilize the wealth of their own environment. It is but an outpost of the lumber mills we are approaching, where there are many houses built not of slabs but of boards and siding, with trim doorways and window frames, steps of wood, verandas of wood, shingles on the roof, and sometimes even a coat of paint. If we entered, our feet would surely be greeted by boards on the floor. Our enthusiasm almost leads us to praise even the "gingerbread" embellishments produced, in Brazil as in North America, by a too facile fret saw.

Surely the music of a straight log driven on its carriage against a rapidly revolving saw is one of the finest sounds a heavily forested country like Brazil can hear. If a tenth part of the timber which has been burned to make the coffee plantations of São Paulo, the cacao plantations of Bahia, the fattening pastures of Minas, and the partial clearings of shifting agriculture everywhere, had been manufactured into cheap lumber, every mud hut in Brazil could have been banished, along with the insects that infest it, and a house of wood erected in its place.

Not only in the forest region of Santa Catharina and Paraná is the house of lumber encountered, but likewise in the neighborhood of the sawmills which have been set up along the Rio Doce in Espirito Santo. Weathered walls of unpainted boards are the rule there, as in so many North American lumber towns. And not infrequently in this valley is seen a house with walls of shakes, short boards split from the log by hand and used in the wall vertically. Out in Matto Grosso round posts set side by side are used in much the same way to form the walls of more temporary shelters.

But in three years' wandering through Brazil I have never encountered a single example of that simplest type of wood house which the straight trunks of trees have suggested to forest dwellers everywhere in Europe and North America. The superposition of logs, either in the rough or squared, notched at the corners to form the walls of a log cabin, seems inherent in the physical character of the material. Yet because Brazil was settled by the Portuguese instead of by forest dwellers from the north of Europe, an obvious use for down timber never impressed itself on minds filled with other traditions. The log house can probably be found in out-of-the-way German or Polish colonies; but it must be described as an infrequent phenomenon in the forest regions of Brazil.

This infrequency is less astonishing than the general disregard of bamboo, which, by all the peoples from Yokohama to Singapore and the islands of the South Seas, is considered the God-given building material. Logs are heavy, and an isolated settler cannot place them even with the help of his wife and children; but bamboo is the lightest of all building materials. A Filipino with his *bolo* will build a house of bamboo, frame, floor, and walls, and thatch it with *nipa* quite as rapidly as the Brazilian builds his hut of mud. At the end, the Filipino has a thing of beauty, raised off the ground, cool, dry, with a floor of half-inch strips which springs under bare feet and can be polished with a banana peel; the Brazilian an ugly, unclean hovel which he shares with death-dealing insects. Bamboo will grow practically everywhere in Brazil and does grow profusely in many places now, yet it is not utilized even for fish poles.

Houses of Brick

Before we speak in praise of the brick house it is just as well to point out that there are bricks and bricks. The ordinary, soft bricks of Brazil, of the color of the clay from which they are fashioned, with rough surfaces and irregular edges, are only one degree better than the clay which is plastered into the squares of the mud house and allowed to dry in place. Like adobe, they always have to be disguised with a daub of clay or stucco or a facing of tiles; and it is easy to pass them by without distinguishing between the brick house and the better class of earth structures similarly finished.

When the traveler enters the German colonies in Santa Catharina, it is almost as if he were transported to another land. What a difference the standards of a more exacting civilization have wrought! These industrious peasants from the north of Europe started with the same materials that went into the mud hut—timber and clay; but the issue bears no faintest resemblance. In the two thriving *municipios* of Joinville and Blumenau the timber is framed in attractive patterns that reveal structure and strength and adorn the exterior; the clay has been subjected to a mold and fire, nothing more complicated. Yet in the process it has taken on a gorgeous red hue together with durability and a hardness which no barbeiro can penetrate.

The tiles which cover it are molded flat, under pressure, giving as fine a roofing as the world affords. With a chimney to carry off the smoke of the kitchen fire, dark paint on the timbering, and a bit of bright color on window and door frames —the result, when set in a well kept flower garden, is as attractive and substantial a type of farmhouse as can be found throughout Europe. I know no farming district in the United States where the houses are so uniformly pleasing as well as appropriate.

Brazil need look no further for one possible solution of its rural housing problem. The materials are found throughout the length and breadth of the land, and these hard-working Brazilians of Blumenau have shown splendidly how to use them. Indeed, the cities of Brazil might take a lesson from the farmers of Santa Catharina. The buildings which are being constructed today of soft bricks covered with stucco and a wash of color, however attractive when new, certainly will not bear comparison with the brick edifices of Blumenau half a century from now.

Such are Brazilian rural dwellings. Two types of habitations common in certain parts of the world are almost nonexistent: there is no cave-dwelling population in Brazil; and, aside from a few wandering gypsies and vaqueiros on the road with cattle, there are no tent dwellers.

The Rural Village

Lack of durability was the overwhelming impression which Spix and Martius had of the villages of rural Brazil a century ago at the end of the first extensive journey made in the interior by European scientists. Their picture of an average

village in interior Brazil is as accurate in 1926 as it was in
1822. One entirely misses the appearance of comfort and
solidity calculated for long duration which distinguishes European dwellings.

Like house, like village. If the human habitation is
frail and low, it is difficult for the village to appear anything
but ephemeral and mean. The custom of stringing one-storied
mud houses end to end along both sides of a narrow street
simply magnifies ugliness many fold. Why do we find such
crowding in the country where of all spots on the globe there
is land enough for every one and to spare? It is a characteristic of the Mediterranean type of village described by
Brunhes:

> Almost all the Mediterranean peoples, preëminently "urban,"
> have grouped themselves in settlements with houses closely crowded
> together, so closely that they have the apparance of small cities
> even when they are only simple villages. A life concentrated around
> the public square . . . , around the bastion or stronghold, the temple
> or the church, is preëminently a life of house close against house.[7]

Here again, tradition is fortified by environment. Brazil
is as yet so underpopulated, so much of life is spent in appalling solitudes, in traversing almost uninhabited campos and
caatingas for weeks on end, in pushing a canoe through watery
wastes where the sun seldom enters and men chant aloud as
they paddle to lighten the oppressive weight of the silence.
The village was built for companionship, for human warmth.

"Why set my house in the middle of a garden when I can
build so near my friend, João, that I can counsel with him
about cattle and crops without getting out of my hammock?

"Why set my house back from the street where pack trains
pass with their tinkling bells, and the chant of the cowboy precedes the rumble of hoofs of the trail herd?

"God knows there is enough of silence and loneliness in the
sertão!"

---

[7] Brunhes, *Human Geography*, p. 503.

CHAPTER VII

LANDWAYS AND WATERWAYS

SPACE is Brazil's pride. Space is equally Brazil's weakness. Social power is attained through its annihilation, not through its exaltation. Isolation and poor communications spell social stagnation, localism, death. Landways and waterways spell life. The movement of restless, inquisitive, adventurous men; intercourse within the nation; ease, and cheapness, and regularity of transport—these are the conquerors of space and the weavers of nationalism. The facility with which men and goods travel from place to place is a very accurate index of the degree of man's mastery of his environment.

§ 1. THE PORTS

In any consideration of the lines along which men and goods move in Brazil, her four thousand miles of coast and forty thousand miles of navigable streams should carry the guidon at the head of the column. How the seashore attracted our ancestors is attested by the remains of clambakes and oyster suppers still evident in their kitchen middens. In Plato's time, the philosopher saw men distributed about the Mediterranean "like frogs around a pond." And it was the greatest seafaring people of their day who first sighted the coast of Brazil in the marvelous period of the great discoveries. Inevitably the early settlements of the Portuguese sprang up along the coast, beside that shining highway without rut or grade which extends from Porto Alegre to Manáos.

Like Australia, the interior of Brazil is of such character that its states were long compelled to communicate with each other only by sea. Today it is possible to go by rail from the Uruguayan frontier to Victoria, some thirteen hundred miles to the north. But beyond Victoria for thirty-four hundred miles to Manáos, and beyond Manáos for another thousand miles to the Peruvian frontier, the sole highway uniting southern and northern Brazil remains, in 1926 as in the time of Cabral and Vasco da Gama, the ancient ocean and the mightiest of rivers.

If we recall that all of the twenty largest cities in the United States have water transportation, we shall not be surprised to find that of Brazil's six cities with a population greater than one hundred thousand, five—Porto Alegre, Rio de Janeiro, São Salvador, Recife, and Belém—are located on this main artery of commerce and travel. São Paulo alone of the great cities—and she has her port, Santos—sits on the Central Plateau and watches over herds, and forests, and coffee plantations while her sisters five gaze seaward with ears turned to catch the gossip of myriad ships. Fourteen of Brazil's twenty-one capitals lie along the highroad we are about to travel. Of these, only two—Rio de Janeiro, the peerless, and her suburb, Nictheroy, the capital of the state of Rio de Janeiro—are likely to be visited by the average traveler hurriedly making the South American tour. For as ships become ever larger and more swift, the fewer become their ports of call.

The great boats of the United States Shipping Board which have been put on the South American run since the war, like the boats of the Lamport & Holt Line of recent years, go direct from New York to Rio de Janeiro without stop, and from there to Montevideo. Only on the return do they put in at Santos for cargoes of coffee. So he who would know the many harbors of that vast extent of coast must transship at Rio to a boat of one of the two Brazilian companies which keep fleets plying up and down in the coastwise trade. (I shall describe this journey as I made it in 1921.)

Ports of the South

Wherefore, after we have had our fill of the beauties of the loveliest city that sits beside the seven seas, we take passage on one of the little boats of the *Companhia de Navegação Costeira,* southward bound. With a depth line determined by the shallow waters of Laguna dos Patos, these "Ita" boats are likely to be a rude shock to one who is accustomed to nothing more unstable than a transatlantic liner. For that essential element known as a keel is chiefly conspicuous by its absence (the better to slip over shallow bars), and the long swell of the calmest of oceans sets them rolling disgustingly. The smoothness of the channel winding up to Santos twenty-four hours later is welcome.

Santos, after Rio, is the busiest port in Brazil. In 1921 some 8,770,000 sacks of coffee came tumbling down the steep incline of the cable railway from the plateau of São Paulo, to be shot into the gaping holds of ships like water from a hydraulic ram. The port works, which the year before the war handled two million metric tons of foreign commerce in addition to the coastwise trade, are thoroughly modern in equipment. The port is a transit region serving a vast hinterland, but has little significance except as the waterfront of the greater city on the plateau, which it serves so closely that many business men make their homes in São Paulo and travel up and down night and morning.

Having more leisure than they, we take time to fortify ourselves against the ship's unfamiliar fare by luncheon at the Grand Hôtel de la Plage, at Guarujá, one of Brazil's few seaside pleasure resorts, run by the Ritz management for the returns from the Casino.

By three in the afternoon we are moving down the channel again. But with a difference. The act of landing and returning has given us the feeling of coming home. Yesterday she was just one of the "Ita" boats, highly unstable, and with a wretched odor issuing from the dining saloon. Today she is the *Itajubá,* the particular ship of all others to which we, of our own free will, have wedded our destiny—and not half bad, either! The German captain, we discover, speaks excellent English; and with a Scotch chief engineer, of course nothing can go wrong.

And those highly uninteresting people, our fellow passengers. On a second inspection made on more seaworthy legs, they begin to take on personality. Indeed, they tell a story all their own of the ports whither we are bound, and of this great melting-pot of the southern hemisphere, along whose mountain-fronted shore we are cruising. The tall gentleman in the long, black coat proves to be an Australian minister called from Melbourne via the Cape and London to preach to the Lutherans in the Catholic State of Rio Grande do Sul. There is a German bound for a managerial position in the coal mines of Santa Catharina, after having served his apprenticeship in Pittsburgh; and another of a portlier type returning to his grocery in Blumenau. Beside the omnipresent English clerk, there is a young Canadian going to Swift's packing plant; a couple of Brazilian ladies who seem resentful at the ship's movements; half a dozen noisy Portuguese traveling salesmen; a dignified Brazilian landlord, proudly escorting home to Curityba the son and heir who recently graduated in civil engineering at the University of Illinois; a couple of "guards" of the Rockefeller Commission bound for some new front in the hookworm attack; a violinist whose name once loomed large in the concert halls of Central Europe, now reduced to scraping a pittance from these little-entertained towns of Brazil; a Frenchwoman; a brace of schoolboys; and the family of an English engineer going out to police up the port works of some southern city. Truly a cosmopolitan passenger list this, characteristic of the region in which many European immigrants are settling, and very different from what we shall find in the north and on the Amazon.

At daylight next morning we enter an altogether different

Brazil from the two great ports behind. For half an hour we wind about headlands and islands as if searching for a dock. But Paranaguá has no docks. It is a sleepy little pink and white and blue village with scarcely enough movement to keep the grass down in the streets, serving Curityba on the plateau as Santos serves São Paulo. Nearly one-half of all the lumber exported from Brazil is shipped from this port, chiefly Paraná pine; but it will be linked in our memory to another drink, as Santos stands for coffee. Southern Brazil and parts of Argentina, Uruguay, and Paraguay are as addicted to maté as China is to tea; and Paranaguá exported eighty-eight million pounds of the leaf in 1921, again over half of Brazil's total.

Our departure from Paranaguá is timed to put us into Florianopolis, the capital of Santa Catharina, at an early hour next morning. The city lies on the landward side of an island in whose shelter ships of light draft find an anchorage. Unconnected to the hinterland by rail, with only thirteen feet of water, Florianopolis at present has none of the requisites of a good harbor. We weigh anchor and move out at ten o'clock without regret.

All day the rugged mountains which have been closely companioning the shore since leaving Rio continue with us, the ribbon of coastal plain between their forested flanks and the sea narrowing toward the south, a far more formidable barrier to commerce than the Coast Range between San Francisco and the Columbia River. We pass its southern extension some time late in the night, and all the following day are within plain sight of the interminable sand-dunes which fringe the low shore of Rio Grande do Sul. The second evening from Florianopolis puts us into the harbor of Rio Grande, but we are not allowed to land until morning.

Standing at the rail with vision blocked by the severe lines of Swift & Company's packing plant, we curse the unkindness of port officials; but an hour on shore reconciles us to the delay. Rio Grande do Sul is a squalid town on a sandy plain, a town which still uses the gutters as sewers, and apparently makes no effort to banish either stagnant water or dirt. Two hours are entirely insufficient to reveal any redeeming feature whatever, and we take train for Pelotas in our hurry to get away.

Ah, but Pelotas is different! Pelotas is a city with an urban population of some fifty thousand people possessed of that divine fire known in Seattle as "boost," that enthusiasm which strives to domesticate in its habitat the best and the latest of everything good on earth. Here you will be shown tramcars, just out from the United States, in which the functions of motorman and conductor have been combined by an arrangement which forces every one to enter and leave under the eye of a single autocrat. "Has New York anything better than that?" our guide asks, and we are compelled to confess that every New Yorker who boards a street car is asked to "Step lifely!" by two none too courteous gentlemen, instead of being shown every consideration by one. You will be shown a movie palace which seats a thousand people; and if you glance in at the Commercial Club (furnished by Maple, of London), you will probably see for the first and last time in Brazil that delight to a North American—a building steam-heated throughout. Our morning is all too short; but it convinces us that Pelotas abundantly deserves the appellation she has conferred upon herself in all modesty, *"A Rainha do Sul,"* Queen of the South!

We fortify the excellent impression with wild duck and light wine, and at one o'clock pull out on the last leg of this southern voyage.

Since crossing the bar at Rio Grande do Sul, the *Itajubá* has been navigating a body of shallow inland water called Lagôa dos Patos, the Lake of the Ducks; and as we move between the rice paddies that fringe the narrow channel north of Pelotas, the origin of the name appears as a V-shaped, black band traversing the eastern sky. As we chug northward, flocks of wild duck come in from their feeding grounds in the fresh-water lagoons and bed down on the broad expanse of the lake; the snowy *garça real*, which furnishes the egrets of the milliner, gazes unmoved as we steam by; a flock of rosy spoonbills takes the air; and a gray rhea, the South American ostrich, trots leisurely off across the campo. Verily, these scenes are far removed from the busy ports of Rio and Santos.

In the mud churned up by the propeller, we see the reason for the light draft of these boats and the advantage of a bottom which will slip over a shallow bar. So narrow is the tortuous channel that when fog settles down during the night, the captain lays to for three hours, and only puts us alongside dock in Porto Alegre at ten in the morning. About the only claim to distinction this port has is occasional primacy as a Brazilian exporter of lard. As a port of importance, Porto Alegre is doomed. Eight feet is the maximum draft of vessels which can enter her harbor today, and there is a hundred and fifty miles of shallow water between her and the ocean.

It has taken six days to cover eleven hundred miles, and there is still ahead of us a voyage three times as long. Let us hasten back to Rio to embark for the North and get a bird's-eye view of the whole coast before we return to certain general considerations regarding all these ports.

Atlantic Ports of the North

The return by train is only one day shorter than by boat, and we arrive in Rio somewhat travel-stained. At the office of the *Lloyd Brazileiro* we find that the next boat for the North is the *João Alfredo*.

"But she is one of the oldest and smallest of the line!" we protest.

"There is one smaller," the dignified gentleman at the wicket replies. "And because she is old, it does not follow that she is overrun by cockroaches. I myself am old—but I am not dirty!"

Against such argument there is no answer, and we buy tickets for Manáos forthwith. But before embarking, we profit by the experience of the southern trip and provide ourselves with easy deck chairs. Then the *João Alfredo* heads due east toward Cabo Frio, where the shore is laid out in a checkerboard of level plots, and beautiful piles of snow-white salt are evaporated from sea water by the benign rays of the sun.

As Rio becomes but a golden memory behind us, just a word of explanation about a Brazilian usage of place names which we shall encounter. The capitals of many of the northern states are commonly spoken of by foreigners, and by many Brazilians, too, by the name of the state. Practically every one calls São Salvador, Bahia. Recife is called Pernambuco. Fortaleza is Ceará. São Luiz and Maranhão are one and the same. And Belém—Nossa Senhora de Belém do Grão Pará on formal occasions, Our Lady of Bethlehem of the Great River—the commercial world calls Pará, the Tupi word for "river." It is like calling Boston, Massachusetts. I shall keep to the more accurate, even if less familiar, appellations.

Twenty-five hours from Rio puts us into the exquisite miniature haven of Victoria, the capital of Espirito Santo. As she glides up the exceedingly narrow channel, the ship passes within a hundred feet of sheer walls of towering granite. I look for Hartt's line whereby he determined the recent uplift of this part of the coast, but I cannot keep my eye from the monastery hovering above the topmost peak like a white gull above the masthead. At this port a few logs of rosewood from the Rio Doce are loaded for the markets of the world, and a small amount of coffee. Victoria has thirty feet of water, but the anchorage is too small ever to accommodate the larger ships of commerce. It is the last port at which the southern railway system touches the coast. He who would see the two-thirds of a continent to the north of Victoria must come with us by sea or spend many months on mule-back and in canoe. Four hours is enough to transact our business and put the *João Alfredo* on her course of five hundred and thirty miles to São Salvador, the longest reach between ports until we enter the Amazon.

It is a convenient occasion to look about the ship. The impossibility of journeying by land makes these boats on the northern run almost invariably crowded to capacity as far as São Salvador. The lower deck space allotted to second-class passengers is a web of hammocks slung at every conceivable angle and height; for we are bound for the region where every one carries this single hanging substitute for bed and bedding, and where a "furnished room" is bare save for two hammock hooks. As we have no adequate ice-box aboard, the beef for this hungry mob is carried on the hoof in close proximity to these second-class hammocks; and every other day the occupants look on with lazy interest while a steer is butchered and dressed, or they assist at removing the bristles from a protesting porker. The cages for the chickens, ducks, and turkeys destined to adorn the first-class table are forward on the upper deck, and it is altogether delightful to be awakened far out at sea by the crowing and cackling of these reassuring barnyard fowl. (If this sounds somewhat like a menagerie, it is nothing to what the return from the Amazon will be after half a hundred monkeys; a dozen egrets; two or three dozen parrots of assorted species, colors, and screeches; several jacamins and jacús; and a few cases of nonchalant turtles have been taken aboard.)

The human cargo is very different from that on the southern run, much less cosmopolitan and more typical of Brazil. In addition to whites and the brown, straight-haired types which indicate more or less Indian blood, there are numerous African blacks and mulattoes; for Negroes still make up a very considerable element in the population of Bahia and Pernambuco. Nothing measures the distance we have come from North America so vividly as this sight of all possible shades of white, and brown, and black humanity mingling on terms of absolute equality. A man's a man south of the equator, whatever the color of his skin.

If anything I have said above sounds uncomfortable or overcrowded, let me relieve apprehension here at the start of the long voyage by saying that the *João Alfredo* was kept scrupulously clean; that she was steady and well navigated by the most courteous of officers, Brazilians all; and that by augmenting with the mangos, oranges, pineapples, alligator pears, and cantaloupe to be bought for a song at ports along the way, the table, although overloaded with meat courses as are all Brazilian tables, would have satisfied the appetite of any one whose steps ever were intended to stray from the boulevards and cafés.

Now there is land ahead, and we shift attention from our boat to the bay she is about to enter, Bahia de Todos os Santos, the Bay of All the Saints. Our eyes seek in vain one friend, the mountain range that accompanied us to Rio Grande and was still with us at Victoria. Somewhere in southern Bahia it rippled out into low-lying hills and merged into the insignificant elevations of the coastal plain.

The city of São Salvador, third in size, after Rio and São Paulo, was the colonial capital and is still the religious capital where ships of war put in to be blessed before starting for adventures on the high seas. As shaped by nature, Bahia is the best harbor in South America—always excepting Rio the Incomparable. All the smaller boats come alongside modern docks inside a breakwater dredged to twenty-six feet; but the larger vessels of the European and American lines, which generally stop but a few hours, anchor outside the breakwater and load from lighters in thirty-six feet of water, or more.

As coffee gives an aroma to Santos and maté to Paranaguá, so cacao colors the commercial life of São Salvador. From six to nine hundred thousand sacks are annually exported to Europe and New York, more than that sent by any other chocolate port except Accrá, on the west coast of Africa.

The six hours' stay in São Salvador gives time for a hurried glance at the Lower City of the commercial world, at vast residential sections sprawled over the hills above, and for a leisurely stroll through one of the typical public markets of northern Brazil, a riot of color. If we be wise, we lay in a supply of a hundred or two of the finest oranges in the world, far larger and sweeter than the California navel orange which came originally from this city; and cigars for the voyage. For the best Bahia tobacco is second to none. Nothing but the fact that we are outward bound prevents us from adding a gorgeous hyacinthine macaw to our impedimenta, blue from his great yellow beak to the tip of his long tail. Truly we are getting into the tropics! Had we not set out to cover the great highway of Brazil in the briefest possible time, we should of course drop off for a fortnight at interesting cities like this, but by dusk tomorrow we are due in Maceió, and must get on.

Seaports Formed by Reefs

On dropping anchor off the capital of Alagôas, it is at once apparent that we have entered a different coastal zone. From São Salvador south the harbors exhibit the irregularity we connect with a subsiding coast. It was a sinking that carried the sea into the valleys at the base of the Serra do Mar and gave southern Brazil such deep harbors that the more recent elevation of from seven to ten feet has not been able to spoil them.[1] But from Maceió north to the mouth of the Amazon, nature has done little to facilitate shipping. We anchor a half-mile offshore in what is little better than an open roadstead. A mile or so from the shore are coral reefs extending as an irregular line for many miles to the north of Maceió, uncovered at low tide, shouldering the surf which crashes over them in foamy splendor at the flow. This

[1] J. B. Woodworth, "Geological Expedition to Brazil and Chili," *Bul.* Museum of Comparative Zoölogy, Harvard, Vol. LVI, No. 1, p. 114; Ch. Fred. Hartt, *Geology and Physical Geography of Brazil* (Boston, 1870), pp. 72, 213, 425; Branner, *Geologia Elementar,* p. 164.

reef affords some protection from the northeast winds; but when southerly storms strike this port, Maceió becomes as helpless as a baby in a bathtub. Furthermore, the harbor is constantly filling up with sand which lodges against the coral barrier.

The sun is going down behind the fringe of coconut palms as a fleet of stanch twenty-footers puts out from beneath their shadow. A provision boat laden with live pigs, ducks, chickens, beautiful fresh fish, and fruit, approaches amidst cheers from the hungry lined up along the rail. Garrulous gypsies disembark in great commotion. A boatload of the devout comes from the town to kiss the Bishop's hand. Then nightfall settles swiftly, forcing us to defer landing until the return. But it also permits us to leave Maceió convinced that we are sailing away from one of the most picturesque ports of Brazil.

The name of Pernambuco's capital, Recife, means "reef," and refers to the stone reefs which characterize the Brazilian coast from just south of the Rio Doce to Ceará. Water from the land filtering through sand beaches has precipitated enough lime to consolidate the grains of sand. To such consolidated beaches the ports of Recife, Natal, Porto Seguro, and many of minor importance, are due. The one at Recife varies in width from thirty to seventy meters. Their surfaces never rise above high-tide level, and their robbery for building stones and sidewalk pavements threatened to submerge them considerably below high tide, but that particular mode of sawing off the branch on which you sit has now been prohibited.

Pernambuco is far and away the strongest of the northern states, and in spite of a shabby deal on the part of nature, has constructed a harbor by reënforcing the reef with a break-water and dredging a channel which accommodates freighters of twenty-five-foot draft. The lightering of passengers in the open roadstead by those few large ships which do not go inside, is apt to be a memorable performance.

Three southern ports, I pointed out, contribute large quantities of three of the world's favorite beverages. Pernambuco produces the suger to sweeten them. Her foreign shipments in 1921 amounted to 110,000 metric tons. But with the superficiality of pleasure-seekers in strange lands, we shall probably give little thought to any products save the luscious pineapples which ten cents will buy, and rosy mangos which take our fancies off toward the Orient of their origin.

At Recife we embark a group of English reclamation engineers who have made their name in Egypt and India, and the talk turns to the ten enormous dams which British and American firms are building for the Federal Government in the country to the north, which is cursed with periodic drought.

Leaving Recife shortly after midnight, we are in Cabedello before noon of the same day. This is the only port of the State of Parahyba, and is connected to the capital by a miniature English railroad whose Lilliputian equipment reminds one of the coaches that carried passengers from Versailles to Paris nearly a century ago. A town on the sand with a population of but a few hundred, squalid, hot, dead! Oh, for one of the gay battles with the Dutch which centered round the old fort in the seventeenth century! Not altogether unattractive— no village that is pink, and red, and green, and blue, and set behind coconut palms can ever be quite that. But as a port, Cabedello is without importance.

Natal, the capital of Rio Grande do Norte, is, like Cabedello, a river port; with so narrow an entrance through the stone reef that it demands the nicest navigation on the part of the pilot. From the standpoint of foreign commerce, if Cabedello with twenty-three thousand tons is of no importance, Natal, with thirteen thousand, is not worth mentioning. But we are touching at the ports of a paradoxical people; and we find in this sleepy city one of the most ultramodern and useful schools for girls in the length and breadth of Brazil, the *Escola Domestica*.

On arriving at Fortaleza, the capital of Ceará, twenty-four

hours beyond Natal, a scene of extraordinary activity greets us. Here there is nothing to break the full force of the Atlantic, and we anchor in an open roadstead off an interminable stretch of glistening sand. But the anchorage is full of ships notwithstanding, and the beach in all directions littered with cranes, derricks, and locomotives; shops and warehouses; all the thousand and one items which go into a mammoth construction job. For here enters practically all the material for building the ten dams in the sertão. A breakwater is projected and may be completed in course of time. Meanwhile, as our catboat pitches like a bucking bronco in an effort to approach the landing without becoming a total wreck, we give thanks that they no longer ride in through the surf on *jangadas*, as they did when Herbert Smith landed here to investigate the terrible drought of 1877-79.

Although the foreign commerce of Ceará is unimportant with a gross tonnage of only eighty-four thousand in 1921, yet three thousand tons of that was some of the finest long-staple cotton that the world produces and represents the beginning of what can be made a great industry when the reclamation program has been achieved. And Fortaleza, in 1920, headed the list of Brazilian ports as an exporter of goatskins and *carnaúba* wax, New York absorbing the output of both these while France and Great Britain divide the cotton.

Tutóya, twenty-four hours beyond Fortaleza, the river port in Maranhão which serves as a gateway to the State of Piauhy, is the least important place we touch on the whole Atlantic seaboard—so we spend more time there than in any other. Arriving near sundown on a Sunday, we are without a pilot until too late to cross the bar; and we ride at anchor all night, getting considerable consolation out of the thought that we should be devoured by mosquitoes if nearer the shore. Although we have but an hour's business to transact with this hole in the jungle, we are forced to wait until evening to catch the tide going out again.

Fifteen hours more puts us into São Luiz, the capital of Maranhão, a city founded by the French in 1612. Like Florianopolis, it is an island capital, but so vastly more pictur-esque and colorful that even the presence of sporadic cases of bubonic plague does not deter us from wandering through its beautiful, shaded parks. This is one of the few places en-countered since leaving Rio which understands the use of trees in sun-drenched cities. It is said that vessels of any draft can enter the protected area of this port, but a large vessel would not be able to come very close in. A few tons of cottonseed and rice being the chief items in her contribu-tion to the world's commerce, we prefer to remember Maran-hão as the home of hand-woven hammocks of white cotton and linen.

This is the northernmost of the regular Atlantic ports of call. Another thirty hours will see us off the Bragança Shoal, at the broad mouth of the Bay of Marajó and the en-trance to another world.

Ports of the Lower Amazon

Belém, founded by the Portuguese in 1615, stands in the same relation to the Amazon that New Orleans does to the Mississippi, although it is not located on the Amazon at all. There is great confusion here, even in the maps put out by the best geographers. The old maps called that broad expanse of water to the west of Belém, "Bahia do Marajó"; and its continuation toward the sea, the "Rio Pará." Actually, both constitute the broad estuary mouth of the Tocantins, and the "Pará" is no more a separate river than is Delaware Bay. The latest Brazilian maps of Pará call the water—thirty miles wide—from Belém to the sea, *Bahia do Marajó*.

Under whatever name you choose, the estuaries of the Tocantins and the Amazon are connected by an intricate pattern of channels through which the tides ebb and flow; and it is entirely possible that the spill from the Amazon is larger in volume than the Tocantins. But the water discharged by both combined through the Bay of Marajó is nothing to the volume that empties north of the Island of Marajó in a torrent that discolors the sea for six hundred miles. For the Amazon, mark you, discharges more water into the ocean than the Mississippi and the Nile combined. The main mouth is about sixty miles across, but much broken by islands; so that the principal channel below Macapá is not over ten or twelve miles wide. It is badly obstructed by shifting sand bars, and from Macapá for a hundred miles to near Cabo do Norte is encountered the formidable bore of the Amazon called the *pororóca*. When two opposing forces clash head-on, one must yield. The tide of ocean is bitterly opposed by the tide of the Amazon. When the pull of the moon finally brings even the mightiest of rivers to its knees, the ocean leaps over its prostrate foe and rushes up the river in a sheer wall with a rumble like a regiment of light artillery on the stampede. At spring tide this wave attains a height of from ten to twenty feet. So it is likely that shipping will continue to enter the Amazon by way of Belém for some time.

How important is that commerce to the outside world? During the last normal year before the war, 1913, Belém imported 218,000 metric tons and exported 22,000 tons. The chief items in her contribution to the world in 1921 were 13,000 tons of lumber, 11,000 of Brazil nuts, and a paltry 7,000 tons of rubber. But neither the skinny hand of cheap coolie labor in the Orient nor the commercial chaos which has knocked the exchange value out of the milreis, can rob the streets of Belém of the glory shed by the avenues of mangos which border them, that stateliest of shade trees and most excellent of fruits.

We leave Belém at midnight. Daylight finds us traversing that expanse of open water, broader than the main Amazon, into which the Tocantins discharges. At two in the afternoon we enter the narrow channels to the west of the Island of Marajó, called the Straits of Breves. The ten hours that our steamer winds in and out between palm-fringed banks, sometimes not over two hundred yards apart, almost touching the dense forest of these tidal lowlands, afford many vistas of rare beauty and are by far the most interesting hours between Belém and Manáos. We are loath to swing into the current of the Amazon in the middle of the night.

For once in the main river we are embarked on one of the most monotonous rides in the world. A vast flowing of muddy water; the low-lying, almost uninhabited shore of the flood plain appearing on one side as a band of undifferentiated green; far on the other side the vague outline of the shore of some half-submerged island. One gets nothing of the delightful flavors of the Amazon from the deck of an ocean-going steamship, and it even robs one of the poignancy of solitude.

At midnight of the second day from Belém we drop anchor off Santarém, at the mouth of the Tapajós, where, according to the inscription on the life-sized figure of Christ he sent back from Europe, Von Martius in 1819 was "saved by Divine Pity from the Fury of the Amazonian Waves." Here, instead of going ashore, the shore comes to the boat. Women with the hand-decorated gourds for which the region should be famous, swarm out of the night and do a brisk business on deck; turtles of mammoth dimensions are offered with few buyers on this up-trip; but honeydew melons at the equivalent of two cents apiece go rapidly. A couple of steers are hoisted over the side to replenish the larder. Then the women with their hand-painted gourds and monkeys vanish into the night, as the *João Alfredo* heads once more into the west.

We cover the seventy-five miles to Óbidos by seven next morning. Here the whole Amazon flood is gathered into a channel little over a mile wide (1892 meters), but it is as deep as the English Channel. Lieutenant Herndon, who made soundings for the United States Navy in 1852, found places where the lead came up clean in two hundred and forty feet. Óbidos is the only place in the whole Lower Amazon where the two banks are within convenient shooting distance, and the Brazilian Government has set an artillery post on the hill above the town—just what it is designed to guard is difficult to conjecture.

We nose in to the shore for a few moments at Parintins on the evening of the same day, and the following morning tie up, literally, to the corner grocery store at Itaquatiára. The bank shelves so sheer that an ocean-going steamship can put her nose to the shore without danger of grounding. At all these places, as at Santarém, small boats come alongside with a wealth of monkeys, turtles, birds, and fruit. That the stops are too brief to permit landing is a fair index of their importance in the world's commerce. Were we botanizing or collecting insects, we might profitably spend eleven years in these haunts, as Bates did. But we must on to our goal.

Manáos, the capital of Amazonas, is located an hour's run up the Rio Negro, several miles from its junction with the Solimões, as the Upper Amazon is called. In the heyday of rubber, Manáos was a place of fabulous riches, leading a life that made the gold camps of the Yukon at the height of their carefree career appear like sequestered New England villages. Today it is prematurely old after the excesses of a riotous youth; there are few more restful retreats for the tired business man; little moves in Manáos but the new floating docks, which rise and subside some forty feet with the annual pulsations of the Rio Negro. In spite of the fact that she exported a trifle more of rubber and about the same quantity of nuts as Pará in 1921, I had a distinct impression, as our auto struggled over grass-grown roads which had once been boulevards, that the jungle was pressing in upon the delightful adventurers who dispatch these lessening cargoes to Liverpool and New York.

The real distinction between the two chief Amazon ports is that "at Pará it rains every day, and at Manáos it rains all day."

We have traveled a long road, although upon its surface the trace of our passing is more fugitive than the print of a camel's foot in the sands of Sahara. Had we consulted the captain's log from day to day, the distances would have read something like this:

	Miles
Porto Alegre to Rio Grande do Sul	150
Rio Grande to Florianopolis	400
Florianopolis to Paranaguá	145
Paranaguá to Santos	190
Santos to Rio de Janeiro	225
Rio de Janeiro to Victoria	300
Victoria to São Salvador	530
São Salvador to Maceió	300
Maceió to Recife	135
Recife to Cabedello	75
Cabedello to Natal	85
Natal to Fortaleza	280
Fortaleza to Tutóya	285
Tutóya to São Luiz	150
São Luiz to Belém	425
Belém to Santarém	530
Santarém to Óbidos	75
Óbidos to Parintins	100
Parintins to Itaquatiára	135
Itaquatiára to Manáos	125

Approximately ....4,640 Miles

One hundred and fifty miles on Lagôa dos Patos, thirty-five hundred miles on the Atlantic Ocean, a thousand miles on the Lower Amazon. Twenty-five is the fewest number of days that the journey can be made in the coastwise boats of 1922. If this seem long to one accustomed to transatlantic speeds, read over this by Bates written in 1859:

In the dry season, from August to December, when the trade-wind is strong and the current slack, a schooner could reach the mouth of the Rio Negro a thousand miles from Pará, in about *forty days;* but in the wet season, from January to July, when the east wind no longer blows, and the Amazon pours forth its full volume of water, it took *three months* to travel the same distance.

Which proves that distance has nothing to do with the length of the road. The little *João Alfredo,* with an engine to kick a propeller, covered it in *four days!*

The Ports of Little Cargoes

In spite of this rather formidable journey full of unfamiliar names, let no one imagine he has even glanced at all of Brazil's ports as yet. Unknown to all but the native boats with a strong homing instinct and insatiable curiosity, are the many sequestered ports which originate so much of the commerce credited to the havens of heavy freight.

Consider, for instance, the ten degrees of latitude between Maceió and Victoria. The only stop our boat made was at São Salvador. We did not dare risk the bar at Aracajú, the capital of Sergipe, which has only ten feet of water and where it sometimes happens that ships entering on the flood are imprisoned for months by the shifting sands at the mouth of the river. But smaller steamers than ours put in there regularly, and some fifty boats a year touch at Estancia. South of São Salvador are the ports of Rio das Contas, Ilhéos, Cannavieiras, Belmonte, and Porto Seguro, which originate the million sacks of cacao the capital transships to the markets of a world that cares little about origin, but a great deal about color, aroma, and break. Prado and Alcobaça are important enough to figure in the Federal records of shipping movements, and a railroad has its origin in Caravellas. How is one to get to Viçosa, São José de Porto Alegre, or Barra do São Matheus, except by sea? There is the port of Santa Cruz, just north of Victoria, on which the Farquhar Syndicate is to have a ninety-nine years' lease if the development of the iron mines at Itabira do Matto Dentro goes through. There are the river ports of the Rio Doce and the São Francisco. There are several little ports in the State of Alagôas south of Maceió. And just north of Rio das Contas, in Bahia, there is that mysterious harbor of Camamú! Perhaps one forty-foot boat a month sails past that million-dollar monument to Scotch optimism which for forty years has silently reared the smokestacks of a complete oil refinery above shales that never yielded the promised petroleum.

And between these havens of little cargoes, where curling crests break on an open beach, the lone fisherman puts to sea on his *jangada*, that characteristic Brazilian sailing-raft which will sustain life anywhere that life can cling to it.

The Havens of Heavy Freight

Obviously, we have wandered far from anything that holds much interest for the great ship which landed us in Rio de Janeiro. How does the world of commerce appraise and value the places at which we have touched? Not by Brazilian coast-wise traffic, manifestly, which by law is in the hands of Brazilian boats. The outside world is interested only in Brazil's foreign commerce. There are various ways of look-ing at it, but gross tonnage gives as good an index of the economic importance of a port as any.

A freighter of twelve thousand tons registry can actually carry about twenty-five thousand tons. In the last year of normal commerce, 1913, there were nine Brazilian ports whose gross tonnage (i.e., *total imports and exports of foreign commerce*) amounted to more than one hundred thousand metric tons, that minimum figure representing but four such shiploads.

Metric Tons

Rio de Janeiro	3,088,000
Santos	1,998,000
Recife	396,000
São Salvador	339,000
Belém	240,000
Rio Grande do Sul	240,000
Manáos	132,000
Porto Alegre	118,000
Paranaguá	116,000

If we take the returns for 1921, Porto Alegre, Rio Grande do Sul, Paranaguá, Belém, and Manáos will have to be stricken from the list. It is a fair measure of the havoc to commerce wrought by the war—havoc to Brazil's imports!

Metric Tons

Rio de Janeiro	1,958,000
Santos	1,252,000
Recife	281,000
São Salvador	154,000

The Ports of the Future

How many of these ports will continue to hold an important place in the commerce of the future? Obviously a port needs protection from wind and waves, good depth in the channels, abundant anchorage room, plenty of space for docks, level land for city buildings, a rich and populous hinterland, and easy lines of communication with the interior.

The Hydrographic Office of the United States Navy furnished the following figures which represent the maximum draft of vessels which may be taken into the protected area of the port and remain there without resting on bottom. In many cases there is less water within the inner harbor and basins and alongside the wharves:

Maximum Draft (Ft.)

Rio de Janeiro	Any draft whatever
São Salvador	36
Rio Grande do Sul	32
Victoria	30
Montevideo	30
Santos	29
Belém	29
Buenos Aires	28
Paranaguá	26
Recife	25
Lower Amazon to Manáos	20 ordinary stage.[2]

That tells the story as matters stand today. But this question of depth is not so important as some other factors, in the determination of ultimate importance. If the trade be there to justify it, channels can be dredged. The draft of steamers on the east coast of South America will always be determined by the difficulties of keeping open a channel to Buenos Aires. Her channel is twenty-eight feet now but is being deepened. Rio de Janeiro and São Salvador never will need to worry. Santos is rich enough to keep her channel deepening to any depth Buenos Aires can reach. Belém, Paranaguá, and Recife easily can meet the depth requirements of any ship that will be put on the South American run, if they develop enough foreign commerce to attract the big ones. Porto Alegre, alone of the more important ports, is doomed by this depth factor.

Victoria has the depth but can never become a great port because she lacks anchorage room. And if a channel be cut through the bar at Santa Cruz by the Farquhar interests,

[2] "At present New York is the only American seaport having a channel deep enough for great steamers drawing 40 feet. The people of Boston talk about a 45-foot channel to accommodate not only all present ships but the still larger ones that are expected in the near future. At present the Boston channel is 35 feet deep, which is practically the same as that of Philadelphia, Baltimore, Norfolk, New Orleans, and Seattle. Such important ports as San Francisco, Oakland, and Los Angeles, where the original depth of part of the harbor was only 2 feet, and Galveston, have 30-foot channels; Charleston, 28; Savannah, 27, and Tampa and Mobile, 26. No other harbors in the United States have such deep channels."— Huntington and Cushing, *Principles of Human Geography,* p. 116.

nothing but the political expedient of prohibiting its use as a port of entry will save Victoria from sinking into obscurity.

Manáos and Belém cannot rise to world prominence until the hinterland of the Amazon Basin is populated.

On the other hand, Rio Grande do Sul will take on new importance as soon as the railroad is built from Santa Anna do Livramento to Bagé, thus diverting the hides, cattle, and meat now exported through Uruguay.

Paranaguá and Santos hold their places not because of ease of communication with their hinterland, but in spite of very serious difficulties—the line connecting Santos and São Paulo is a cable incline! Nevertheless, a consideration of the wealth of the territories behind the two justifies the expectation that Santos will rapidly assume increasing importance. It can hardly be expected, however, that Paranaguá can develop a civilization behind it on the Plateau of Paraná which will yield a commerce of much interest to the world at large in less than half a century.

São Salvador, alone of the ports of Brazil, measures up in all seven respects. If the day ever come when her government does away with export duties (a 20 per cent *export duty* on cacao!), frees her capital from yellow fever and her populace from hookworm, extends her railroad system and builds a few wagon roads, Bahia should easily crowd Santos for second place.

Nothing in South America can ever wrest the primacy from Rio de Janeiro. It cannot be said that Rio's connection with the great populations on the plateau is easy, but the difficulties have been overcome by many lines of railroad and the increasing commercial prominence of the world's most beautiful seaport is assured.

§ 2. INLAND WATERWAYS

Not only is the Atlantic the only highway connecting north and south Brazil, but inland waterways still afford the sole

Photograph by Ira W. McConnell.

Left. The hammocks of the second class. (See page 193.) *Right.* A *jangada,* or fishing raft. (See page 205.)

The captain of the *João Alfredo,* on the run from Rio to Manáos. (See page 194.)

Photograph from São Paulo Geographic and Geologic Commission.

Loading bananas at the port of Santos. (See page 187.)

approach to two-thirds of Brazil's territory. Just as the Great Lakes, the Ohio, Mississippi, and Missouri opened the United States to explorers and missionaries, so the rivers of Brazil intrigued the curious, adventurous, and devout from the earliest days of Portuguese occupancy. Since the middle of the eighteenth century, when Manoel de Lima descended the Guaporé and Madeira from Matto Grosso to Pará, and João de Souza reached the Amazon via the Arinos and Tapajós, most of the navigable rivers of Brazil have been well known and annually traversed, although much land between is still absolutely unexplored. No one of the considerable streams described by articulate men for the first time in the twentieth century—the Gy-Paraná by Rondon; the Roosevelt by Rondon and Roosevelt; and the Jamauchim by Mme. Emilia Snethlage, a scientific explorer in every way worthy to stand beside the other two—can be navigated in anything but a very light canoe, except at prohibitive cost.

Rivers which are large enough for steam navigation are obviously the only ones which will retain much permanent importance in a transportation system. Of these, the Amazon is traversed by ocean-going vessels throughout its entire Brazilian length and on to Iquitos, in Peru. Manáos is usually the head of ocean-going traffic; only at the flood an occasional vessel from Liverpool goes on up for a cargo of nuts or rubber. River steamers ply up and down all of the chief affluents of the Amazon from their mouths to the fall line. (A glance at the map of physiographic regions will make this clear.) The reader should not infer from this, however, that any very frenzied commerce agitates the Liquid Confederation of the Forest. Even in the lower Amazon there may be two or three days at a time when no steamboat is sighted.

The second most important inland waterway is the Rio Paraguay. Fine river boats regularly ply between Buenos Aires and Asunción; from Asunción to Corumbá runs another fleet; above Corumbá smaller steamers carry on to Cuyabá and São Luis de Caceres; and beyond these two cities, steam launches continue on upstream for several days' journey except during the driest parts of the season. Each set of boats in the ascent is of lighter draft (and of considerably lighter luxury) to meet diminishing depths.

The Rio São Francisco ranks after the Amazon rivers and the Paraguay. Boats ascend the river from the sea to Piranhas, where goods are transferred by rail around the Falls of Paulo Affonso. Above the falls the river is navigable for steamers of light draft to Pirapora in Minas Geraes, although the two chief lines on the river do not operate below Joazeiro.

The only other river in Brazil of great importance to steam navigation is the Rio Paraná. From its junction with the Paraguay, steamers ascend to the Sete Quedas. Above those giant falls, Brazilian boats maintain a fortnightly service to Jupiá where the railroad crosses into Matto Grosso; and small boats ply as far as the falls which interrupt navigation in the Triangle of Minas.

Although the Amazon and São Francisco are the only Brazilian rivers of first rank which discharge into the Atlantic, the lower reaches of several minor streams have considerable economic importance locally. The Parahyba permits small steamers to enter and load the coffee of Campos in the State of Rio; just as the Jequitinhonha, Pardo, and Rio das Contas serve as outlets for the cacao of southern Bahia, although none of these three accommodates anything larger than a steam launch. There are a few others.[1]

Important as the steamship is, and more important as she will become, on Brazil's inland waterways, the craft which has played the great rôle in Brazilian history is the dugout canoe, made from the trunk of a single tree. On every one of a thousand small streams, as on all the great rivers of Brazil above the limit of steam navigation, there is a lively canoe traffic. Frequently on the lower reaches, too, man-

---

[1] In 1921 there were 356 steam vessels engaged in river navigation, but with a total tonnage of only 73,387 tons.—Prof. H. G. James, *Brazilian American*, July 21, 1923.

power still competes with steam. Nowhere is environmental control more manifest. Along the northern border of the United States and in southern Canada, the presence of a single tree led to the evolution of the lightest and frailest of all craft, the birchbark canoe, which one man can put over his head and portage for ten miles without superhuman effort. The high forest suggested to the Brazilian Indian, as it has to forest dwellers in most parts of the world, the dugout. Suitable trees were found everywhere, and everywhere the dugout became the typical craft of interior Brazil. Light canoes were not unknown in Brazil; Spix speaks of the Cayapó Indians on the Rio Grande making bark canoes from jatobá (*Hymenaea Courbarii*, L.) which could readily be portaged from river to river. Nevertheless, the heavier and more awkward craft has carried ninety-nine per cent of Brazil's canoe-borne commerce.

The pure and unimproved dugout varies between a craft twelve inches broad and ten feet long, popularly labeled "suicide cradle," and one sixty to seventy feet long by six broad and half as deep. It is turned up at the ends; reinforced by cross-braces amidships; the bottom of the big ones flat, four or five inches thick, and with only three or four inches of keel. The weight is terrific, and they answer the helm with great reluctance. Yet daily on the Rio das Contas I have seen such craft, loaded with carefully dried cacao until the gunwale is within three inches of the water, go charging down roaring rapids to the mad shouts of the mad rivermen—and generally to a fine finish. Two men will handle anything but the very largest dugout, loaded with the center of gravity forward, and the bowman steering. Daring and very clever feats of canoe handling can be seen on any rapid river in Brazil.

The carrying capacity of the unimproved dugout is too small for Amazon waters and the waves too high. Using it simply as the keel of a larger vessel, men fasten on sides with knees of timber and convert perhaps a third of the length into a cabin by the addition of a low, arched roof of thatch. In the days before steam, such craft with forty rowers at the sweeps could be seen on the Amazon. Today they are still the commerce carriers above the fall line on such mighty rivers as the Tocantins and Tapajós.

What prodigies of effort are expended on such streams! Within a few miles of each other on the plateau of Matto Grosso near the town of Diamantina rise navigable affluents of both the Rio Arinos and the Rio Paraguay. To descend the Rio Negro, a creek obstructed by fallen timber, into the Arinos, and thence down the Tapajós to Santarém is a voyage of over a thousand miles, interrupted by many falls and rapids; only the lower 150 miles lies in the Amazon plain. The descent must require from six weeks to two months; a heavy craft coming up loaded will consume the rest of the year—a year of poling, pulling, lifting, carrying cargo around falls, lugging the heavy craft up boiling rapids or overland on wooden rollers, sweating, swearing, slipping, singing. Yet Chandless testifies that while he was in Diamantina a canoe with a cargo of twenty-five tons (1500 arrobas) came up from Santarém, portaged over the divide, and descended the Paraguay to old Villa Maria.[2] Steamships now, of course, supply the towns of Matto Grosso from the south and make it unnecessary for canoes to descend below Itaituba. Yet even today, unless I am misinformed, the canoes from the towns of Goyaz on the upper Tocantins make but one round trip a year.

On the Rio São Francisco, and more particularly on its tributaries like the Paracatú, are still seen the *barcas* introduced from the River Douro in Portugal, in the early nineteenth century.[3] An average barca is, say, forty-five feet long by fourteen broad, drawing from three to five feet when loaded, and carrying six or seven tons. Much larger ones are known. They are flat-bottomed, with spoon-shaped prows. The cabin is sometimes forward, sometimes aft, and varies

---

[2] H. H. Smith, *Brazil, the Amazons and the Coast*, p. 251.
[3] Sir Richard Burton, *The Highlands of Brazil*, II, 207.

from a palm-thatched awning to one of finished lumber with
glass windows. Along the sides run planks upon which the
crew march up and down, heavy poles twenty feet long or
more "wearing holes in their chests," as they say. Sweeps
and sails are utilized where possible, but most of the progress
against the current is achieved by main strength and awkwardness. Six or seven miles a day is frequently all they can make.

Each river plays its variations upon these themes. Each
has its own style in streamlines and rigging. The paddle of
the Amazon has a round blade, that of southern Bahia is long
and stiff enough to serve for poling, a few are flexible like
those of the Canadian Indian. All styles, and all variations,
and all rivers are alike in requiring the application of terrific
man-power to rather crude craft.

§ 3. OLD LAND ROUTES

Brazil's present system of land transport is most easily understood by a survey of major trade routes functioning just
before the era of railroad building began, say in 1867. For
the genesis of railroads in the United States and in Brazil
was very like: [1] tapirs made trails through the forest; the
Indian followed the tapir and made the *picada;* the Portuguese
with his pack-mules followed the Indian and made the bridle-
path; occasionally a bullock cart bumped behind the Portuguese and made a double trace called a "road"; the ruts of
important roads solidified into the parallel steel of the railroad; and, in the twentieth century, the automobile gave
birth to a few real roads.

I choose 1867 as a point in time upon which to stand for
a reconnaissance of old trade routes for several reasons. In
July of that year the world was admitted to the inland naviga-

---

[1] "The buffalo trail became the Indian trail, and this became the trader's
'trace'; the trails widened into roads, and the roads into turnpikes, and
these in turn were transformed into railroads. The same origin can be
shown for the railroads of the South, the Far West, and the Dominion of
Canada."—Turner, *The Frontier in American History,* p. 14.

tion of Brazil, and the real history of Amazon conquest begins. In August, 1867, the first steamer on the Rio São Francisco left Penedo and reached Porto das Piranhas. In 1867 Sir Richard Burton began a journey through Minas and down the São Francisco to the sea, which gave us one of the best pictures ever written of interior Brazil. In 1867 the only piece of railroad in Brazil was the Mauá Railway, eleven miles in length, running from the Bay of Rio de Janeiro to the foot of the maritime mountains. But, be it not forgot, a railroad opened by Dom Pedro II with the words, *"À Barra do Rio das Velhas!"* Eighteen hundred sixty-seven was the last year in which travelers to Minas went by the lovely old coach road through Petropolis; next year the railroad was opened to Entre Rios.

From the end of the Mauá Railway, a coach-and-four with many windings climbed a 1:16 grade over a "smooth, gutter-lined, and parapetted Macadam" to the pass of Petropolis, twenty-seven hundred feet above sea-level, surely one of the fairest rides in the world. Between Petropolis and Juiz de Fóra the coach bowled along to the tune of ten miles an hour, a sufficient index of the fine quality of the road.

The sixty-three miles from Juiz de Fóra to Barbacena was another story. Bad at all times, it became impassable for a coach from November to April.[2] At Barbacena, if your destiny lay beyond, you threw your leg over a mule.

The hundred miles between Rio de Janeiro and Juiz de Fóra was then the only wagon road leading away from the imperial capital which was passable throughout the year. From São Salvador, the second city, you could not proceed ten miles in any direction in a wheeled vehicle. The approaches to São Paulo, then the third city, were about like those of Rio: a good paved road down the mountains to Santos, and another northwest to Jundiahy, where the pack trains for Minas, Goyaz, and Matto Grosso made up and fitted out. I have not informed myself in detail about the lesser cities.

[2] Burton, op. cit., I, 57-58.

Undoubtedly there were fair wagon roads in the German colony of Blumenau in 1867; short stretches out of Curityba; and some longer pieces on the pampas of Rio Grande do Sul, where Nature does most of the work of road-making. But it is probably well within the mark to say that in 1867 there did not exist in the whole Brazilian Empire five hundred miles of wagon road over which a coach-and-four could pass throughout the year.

Pack trains were the universal commerce carriers on the landways of Brazil and, beside waterways, a system of bridle paths the only fabric which bound the Empire together. They were good, bad, very bad, or horrible in exact proportion to the kindliness of nature. Man considered himself no more responsible for their condition than for the chemical composition of the atmosphere: one he breathed; the other he rode upon, waded through, or wallowed in, with equal serenity. Through the evergreen forest in a region of heavy rainfall, Brazilian trails matched in wretchedness the very worst in the world. The hoofs of the mules cut the unconsolidated surface and churned it into a puddle. More rain and the puddle became a viscous morass. Deeper and deeper worked the feet of the animals until the trail, worn lower than the soil on either side, had become a ditch. In places belly-deep, the animals, each carrying two hundred and fifty pounds or more, had to exert every ounce of energy at each step. "Ladders" formed, whose rounds were ridges of clay between the holes, one pace apart; each beast in passing a ladder must take the same-length stride and painfully raise each leg over a slippery ridge before sinking into the next hole. Outside of the forest, fortunately, there are vast regions where nothing but the scuffing of horses' hoofs is needed to form a good trail. The pampa is one, and the semi-arid northeast *during the dry season* is another. But even in arid Ceará during the worst of the wet weather, there were weeks when it was almost impossible to move a pack train across country at any price.

From an engineer's standpoint, Brazilian trails were often

as badly "located" as "constructed." Neither a horse nor a mule is a machine built to work on steep grades. Ten miles of side-hill switchbacks at a low gradient are easier on an animal than one mile so steep that he slips and struggles at every step. Yet the genius of the Portuguese, like the Spaniard, invariably seemed unable to resist shooting their trails over the crests of every elevation in their way. The only good things that can be said of them are that pavements of rubble stone were laid where it was absolutely impossible to navigate them otherwise, and that there were a few bridges— not many—across the smaller streams.

Such as they were, the pack trails led to every settlement in Brazil south of the Amazon forest; and a well-mounted man could go anywhere. From Montevideo one could ride across the Banda Oriental and Rio Grande do Sul, through the Paraná pine forest and into the evergreen hardwoods, emerging finally at São Paulo. Spix mentions meeting the magnificent caravan of the Bishop of New Cordova, driven out by political revolutions in the Spanish colonies, on his way from Montevideo to Rio de Janeiro. He had been four months on the road and still had two hundred miles to go.

The Paulista troops made up at Jundiahy, a "dry port," whence, according to Spix, a "paved road" led around to the west of the Mantiqueira to São João d'El Rey in Minas Geraes, which is not far west of Barbacena, where we left the Rio stage. From São João d'El Rey, one trail led north to Sabará and the Rio das Velhas; another northwest to Goyaz and on to Cuyabá and the other towns of Matto Grosso. Another main trail out of São Paulo led down the valley of the Parahyba carrying cattle, and live fowl, and produce to Rio de Janeiro.

North of Barbacena the busiest trail led to Ouro Preto, Marianna, Diamantina, and Minas Novas; beyond Minas Novas the territory was rather tributary to São Salvador, which was reached by a trail that entered Cachoeira through the valley of the Paraguassú. A main offshoot connected Diaman-

Pack-trains were the universal commerce carriers on the landways of Brazil. (See page 215.)

Left. The craft which has played the great rôle in Brazilian history is the dugout canoe, made from the trunk of a single tree. (See page 210.)
Right. On the main-traveled trails there are usually cable ferries across the deep rivers.

A cargo boat on the upper São Francisco. Poling such a craft against the current by main strength and awkwardness will "wear a hole in a man's chest," as the boatmen say. (See pages 212-13.)

A ferry at Joazeiro, on the Rio São Francisco.   (See page 217.)

Photograph from São Paulo Geographic and Geologic Commission.

A year of poling, pulling, lifting, carrying cargo around falls, lugging heavy craft up boiling rapids or overland on wooden rollers, sweating, swearing, slipping, singing.   (See page 212.)

PRINCIPAL
BRAZILIAN RAILROADS
1922

Roy Nash

Shaded areas have no
rail transport.

tina with Goyaz through Paracatú. " 'Nature's roads,' the vilest paths made by the foot, and never bearing the impression of the cart wheel, run down both banks of the Rio das Velhas and the São Francisco. Both are bad, but usually one is worse than the other. Even in the dry season the canoe is preferred, and during the rains these lines are inevitably closed." [3]

Cachoeira, on the western side of the Bay of All the Saints, was the terminus of the trails that radiated from old São Salvador. The trail for the west led up the valley of the Paraguassú, over the mountains, crossed the São Francisco below Bom Jesus de Lapa, and on until it met the Rio-São Paulo trails at Meiaponte, twenty-six leagues this side of Goyaz city. Another Bahia trail crossed the São Francisco at Bom Jardim and went on to Palma, in Goyaz. There was a scarcely passable route through Lençóes to the Barra do Rio Grande, but the best trail to Barra went direct from Cachoeira to Jacobina and thence west. The main road to the north led via Villa Nova da Rainha to Joazeiro; crossed the river there and continued on to Oeiras, the old capital of Piauhy; and beyond to Caxias, the head of canoe navigation on the Rio Itapicurú which connects with Atlantic transport at São Luiz. At the time of which I am writing, the ferry at Joazeiro annually carried some 10,000 head of black cattle and 1,300 horses and mules from the north for the Bahia market, according to Burton. The Ceará trail crossed the São Francisco at Cabrobó and went on to Jardim and Crato, whence several trails led down to the coast.

Thus, in 1867, there were well traveled trails without break from Ceará and São Luiz on the north coast to the Rio de la Plata twenty-five hundred miles to the south, and from Bahia and Pernambuco on the east coast to the Bolivian frontier in Matto Grosso, two thousand miles to the west.

The men who used these trails were not in a hurry. A mule carrying three hundred pounds of cotton (nine arrobas)

[3] Burton, op, cit., II, 227.

required three to four months to go from the lower reaches of the Rio das Velhas to Rio de Janeiro; and as many to return.[4] In Gardner's time (1846), the merchants of Arryas, in Goyaz, imported their goods from Rio only once in two or three years, the journey occupying from six to nine months; but the judge from Almas annually made a journey to Bahia to purchase goods, a round trip of nearly two thousand miles as the trail winds.[5] Between Rio or Bahia and Cuyabá, in Matto Grosso, a loaded troop required five months; yet when the monthly mail left Cuyabá for Rio, it contained letters which had already been two months on the road—forty days from Forte do Principe da Beira on the lower Guaporé to Matto Grosso by canoe, and twenty more by mule to Cuyabá.[6] In short, neither distance, nor time, nor the hazard of entrusting the harvest of several years to one pack train, meant much to those born in the remote corners of Brazil.

Such journeys were less wearing on men of such savage energy than on the mules they rode or drove. The caravans were well organized. An ordinary *tropa* consisted of from twenty to fifty mules, with a mounted head packer in charge. Under him were the *tropeiros*, on foot, each looking after a lot of seven animals. Along all the pack routes at reasonable intervals were rude inns in front of which was a large yard planted with posts at intervals of ten or fifteen feet, to which the mules were tied when loading. The rest of the accommodation consisted of a planted pasture into which the animals were turned for the night to forage, and sheds to cover the cargo. Failing to reach one of these, the caravan stopped wherever there was grass, hobbled the animals and turned them loose, piled cargo and packsaddles into a clever shelter very characteristic of the Brazilian hinterland, and the tropeiros made themselves comfortable wrapped in a bull's hide. While men who follow such a life are nowhere notorious for their

---

[4] John Mawe, *Travels in the Interior of Brazil* (1812), p. 340.
[5] Gardner, *Travels in the Interior of Brazil* (1846), p. 367.
[6] *Exploration of the Valley of the Amazon,* by Lieutenants Herndon and Gibbon (1854), Pt. II, p. 276.

tenderness, Brazilian tropeiros are not more cruel than their class in other parts of the world—except in one respect. It is the cruelty of ignorance and lack of skill. As a former artillery officer I know the art of packing as practiced in the army, and as a forester I have wandered for months with a pack train in central Idaho. My deliberate judgment is that the Brazilian packsaddles in common use and the run of Brazilian packers are both the worst in the world. And for this the shoulders and backs of the mules paid, and pay, an awful penalty.

§ 4. BRAZILIAN RAILROADS

With this preliminary outline of the old trade routes in mind, it is easy to see the wherefore of the railroads of 1924. Although Burton's prophecy of trains doing sixty miles an hour has not yet come to pass,[1] transportation has been vastly speeded up and cheapened since 1867. The process has been characteristically a substitution of rails for pack trains, without the wagon road as an intermediate stage. Rio de Janeiro and São Paulo are the chief railroad centers for the same reasons that they were the chief marts of the Empire.

From Rio four main trunks reach out. One runs northeast to Victoria and the Rio Doce in Espirito Santo. The second follows the ancient Minas highway up through Juiz de Fóra, Barbacena, Sabará, down the valley of the Rio das Velhas, to Pirapóra at the head of steam navigation on the Rio São Francisco. *"Á Barra do Rio das Velhas!"* cried the Emperor when the first rail was laid, back in the fifties. When I was at Pirapóra they were cutting stone for the piers of the great bridge which will span the river there, and another generation is crying, "On to Belém via the Tocantins!" The third radius

[1] "Our journey has a something of general interest; in a few years it will have its Handbook and form a section of the Nineteenth Century 'Grand Tour.' And I venture to predict that many of those now living will be whirled over the land at hurricane speed, covering sixty miles per hour, where our painful 'pede-locomotion' wasted nearly a week. Perhaps they may fly—*Quem sabe?*"

is building to Catalão in Goyaz, and is nearly there. The fourth follows the ancient pack route through the valley of the Parahyba to São Paulo. Between these four radii there is an ample network of connecting lines, which I could not show on a small-scale map.

The State of São Paulo has the best railways in Brazil and in this, as in other respects, must be ranked as a highly civilized, modern state. The great coffee region northwest of the city is a net of railways. North from Riberão Preto an arm is flung through the Triangle of Minas into Goyaz, where so many hardy Paulista bandeirantes went before. Another long arm follows the ancient canoe route down the valley of the Tieté, crosses the Paraná River at Jupiá, and continues across Matto Grosso to the Bolivian frontier—where many thousands of Paulistas preceded the rails by nearly two hundred years. Here it is a canoe route rather than a pack route which has been superseded. A third main radius recently opened runs to the Paraná River at Porto Tibyriçá. And south from São Paulo runs a line which crosses the three southern states and connects with the Uruguayan system at Santa Anna do Livramento. In five days I have covered the same ground which the fugitive Bishop of Granada rode painfully and prayerfully for nearly five months.

This north-and-south artery sends laterals down to five ports: from São Paulo to Santos; from Ponta Grosso through Curityba to Paranaguá; from União da Victoria through Santa Catharina to São Francisco; and in Rio Grande do Sul to the ports of Porto Alegre and Rio Grande. A western spur reaches the Argentine frontier at Uruguayana, where it connects with the strategic railway that parallels the Rio Uruguay. As the core of a modern transportation system, a glance at the map will show that these railroads at present cover with adequacy only the four states of Rio de Janeiro, Minas Geraes, São Paulo, and Rio Grande do Sul.

Railroad distribution outside of the southern system described above exhibits the fragmentary nature characteristic of the initial stages of railroad development everywhere. In Santa Catharina there are two isolated lines, the road bringing coal to Imbituba and the 43 miles between Blumenau and Hansa. In Bahia, a road 275 miles in length reaches in from the unimportant port of Caravellas to Ladainha. The road that brings cacao from Itabuna and Agua Preta to the port of Ilhéos is a mere 53 miles.

Four quite detached feeders land produce at as many points on the bay of All the Saints, three requiring transshipment on lighters to reach São Salvador. From Nazareth a line reaches southwest nearly to Jequié; the studied malevolence of the worst engineer in the world could not have located the salt-water terminus of a railroad in a worse place. From São Felix a line of rails displaces the old trail up the valley of the Paraguassú for 160 miles. From Cachoeira, just across the river, another 28 miles reaches north to Feira de Santa Anna. Out of São Salvador itself reaches the line which now replaces the ancient trail to Joazeiro on the Rio São Francisco; and branching off from this at Alagoinhas is the line that goes to the port of Aracajú, and beyond the sandy capital of Sergipe to the São Francisco River at Propriá.

There remains to build but the 75-mile link between Propriá and Atalaia to connect the whole northeast coast between São Salvador and Natal. Lines now unite Maceió, Recife, Cabedello, and Natal, with short feeders reaching inland.

In the State of Ceará there are two lines reaching south from salt water. South of Fortaleza there must be close to 400 miles in operation (1924) counting the branches in to the projected dams. From the little port of Camocim another 200 miles reaches in to Cratheus.

If the latest government map is correct, the railroad is now completed from São Luiz to Therezina and beyond. Until very recently, Piauhy was without railroads; and the State of Maranhão had in operation only the 50 miles between Caxias and Therezina.

Pará operates 160 miles of railroad between Belém and Bragança.

The four remaining stretches of railroad in Brazil serve to transport cargo around impassable falls in navigable rivers. Seventy miles of rail takes you from Piranhas to Jatobá, about the falls of Paulo Affonso. Twenty-five miles gets cargo past the first falls on the Tocantins between Alcobaça and Breu Branco. A line from Porto Mendes to Porto Guayra encompasses the Salto das Sete Quedas on the Paraná. And there is the 225 miles of the Madeira-Mamoré reaching from Porto Velho to Guajará-Mirim.

This last stretch of road must always have a certain interest for North Americans. Upon this bit of hard rubber, American capital seeking foreign investments cut its first tooth. The process was painful. He who wants a vivid idea of the difficulties of railroad building in the heart of the evergreen forest should read *The Recollections of an Ill-Fated Expedition*, by Neville B. Craig. It is the story of the attempt to construct the Madeira-Mamoré in 1878, when a combination of natural, political, and financial enemies utterly routed the most experienced railroad contractors in the United States and some of the best engineers of their day. A quarter of a century later the thing was put through by another generation of North Americans, but at the cost of several thousand lives. When I was in Manáos in 1920, the English manager told me he was running only one train a week, and losing money steadily on that.

Railroad construction in most parts of Brazil is a rather difficult matter. Short sections on the Atlantic Coastal Plain, the east and west lines in Rio Grande do Sul, and most of the line across Matto Grosso, have been easy railroading. Getting from the coast up to the plateau from Rio, Santos, Paranaguá, and São Francisco has been excessively laborious. The English line that connects the São Paulo network with Santos is one of the most difficult feats of railroad engineering in the world, executed with absolute perfection. And when the

Serra do Mar has been mastered, the terrain of the plateau in São Paulo, Minas, Paraná, and Santa Catharina is so eroded that construction is far from easy. Nature presented Brazil with no sinecure like the pampas of Argentina or the prairies and plains of the United States.

Brazil has been wise in laying narrow-gauge roads over the less important routes in the first instance, to be replaced by a wider gauge when traffic warrants. During the present transition stage, the necessity of unloading and transshipping from one gauge to another at certain junction points is both annoying and expensive.

Passenger accommodations on these Brazilian railroads vary within wide limits. Between Rio and São Paulo the *luxo* trains measure up to high European standards; between Rio and Bello Horizonte, the capital of Minas, they are good; and the best of the São Paulo railroads leave little to desire. The traveler who quits the main arteries, however, can expect some brand-new sensations. Wood-burning engines are all but universal because of the high cost of coal. The shower of sparks is highly decorative after nightfall; but unless you wear an outer garment which is fireproof, your clothes, before nightfall, will look as if you had taken a charge of grapeshot unto your bosom. Roadbeds have not yet attained that smoothness which comes only from much work and heavy ballast. I recall a night in an upper berth between São Salvador and Aracajú when the coach rocked like a ship in a storm and I was forced to cling to the curtain rod with all my might to prevent being thrown headlong into the aisle. Such movement does not usually result from high speed unless the train is running away. It was not much of a dog that kept alongside the "fast express" in Matto Grosso while I counted five kilometer posts go by, barking incessantly for three miles without losing breath. If you are not in a hurry (and no one should go to Brazil who is), it is rather fun having the train stop every night in some town of the back-country where you go to a hotel, sleep in a bed, and continue your journey next morning. The only disadvantage is that when the train is late you frequently reach the night stop late in the evening, and invariably pull out before daylight in the morning.[2]

§ 5. WAGON ROADS

In no respect does Brazil differ from other empires of great extent so markedly as in the matter of wagon roads. The empire of Rome and the empire of Napoleon alike were famous for highways which radiated from the capitals to the ultimate outposts. It is hardly an exaggeration to say that, except on railroad carriages, the great gift of Asia, the wheel, was spurned by Brazil until the twentieth century. Bouncing and slipping were motions preferred to rolling, south of the Amazon.

In 1924, the situation is this. Rio Grande do Sul has good natural surface roads through the drier part of the prairies, quite good enough for a cattle country. They are about like average roads in the Great Plains country of the United States. An automobile will get over them comfortably. In the wetter parts of the state during the rainy season, on the contrary, the roads are passable only for wagons drawn by four to six horses—like much of our rural South during the spring. I went east from Porto Alegre nearly to the ocean in a Ford at a bad season of the year, but not without the assistance of oxen.

In the German colonies of Santa Catharina are the finest natural surface roads in Brazil. I cannot praise them too highly. They are as good as the best of their type anywhere. And the farmers there know their value: "How would it have

[2] Total mileage of Brazilian railroads in operation in 1919 was 18,704 miles.

Property of and managed by the Union	3,956
Property of Union, operated by Lessee	5,436
State Concessions with guarantee of interest	2,280
State Concessions with special favors	4,631
State Concessions without guarantee of interest	1,303
Private Ownership	1,098
	18,704

—*Brazilian American,* Dec. 18, 1920, p. 23.

A scene at the railway station.

"I went east from Porto Alegre nearly to the ocean in a Ford at a bad season of the year, but not without the assistance of oxen." (See page 224.)

In the German colonies of Santa Catharina there are the finest natural surface roads in Brazil. (See page 224.)

São Paulo heads the list of Brazilian states as a road builder. One of her fine automobile roads, the Caminho do Mar. (See page 225.)

been possible to realize such notable progress," asks the 1919 report of the municipality of Blumenau, "without having planned, constructed, and maintained a system of roadways as vast as ours?" From the founding of the municipality in 1883 up to 1919, no less than sixty-three per cent of the total public revenues was applied to roads and bridges. The county now possesses 1,550 miles of roadways thirteen feet wide which are transitable not only for wagons and carts throughout the year, but also for automobiles, except in the extreme outlying districts during the worst of the rains. I have bowled along these roads at thirty miles an hour with perfect comfort.

Outside of the counties of Blumenau and Joinville, Santa Catharina possesses a few roads like those which connect Lages, Curitybanos, and Campos Novos with the coast; but for the most part the interior of the state is served by pack routes.

In Paraná, roads afford a passage to automobiles between most of the important towns in the eastern part of the state. A fine hard-surface road some fifty miles in length was opened between Curityba and Antonina in 1912. Fair roads with natural surface are traveled by the great covered wagons of the Poles far into the interior. And even the trip from the capital to the Falls of Iguassú in the extreme southwest corner of the state is sometimes made by automobile—the same machine, however, rarely makes the journey a second time.

São Paulo, as in most other criteria of civilization, also heads the list of Brazilian states as a road-builder, thanks largely to Washington Luis. Through the farming regions of the state you can get about in an automobile with perfect comfort; there are about 6,000 miles of automobile roads already completed and another 1,000 miles building.[1] Of those in operation the most important are from São Paulo to Santos—a hard-surface road; from São Paulo through Campinas and the best coffee district to Riberão Preto; and the road that is building

[1] *Brazilian American,* July 21, 1923.

toward Rio de Janeiro through Mogy das Cruzes and Jacarehy. This last, a twenty-six foot roadway with a maximum grade of six per cent, should have reached Bananal, the last city in the state on the Rio line, before this is published. Most of these "automobile roads" are an excellent quality of natural surface road. There is a large mileage, also, over which wagons can get about comfortably, though there are spots a bit rough for motor vehicles.

The State of Rio de Janeiro is not so well supplied. At present there is no road leading from the coastal plain to the plateau. The first effect of railroad building was the abandonment of the fine old coach road into Minas, and today it is impossible to drive a wheeled vehicle from the Federal capital to Petropolis. Once the Serra has been topped, however, there are excellent automobile roads about Petropolis and Therezopolis.

Minas Geraes is the most populous state in Brazil, but its mileage of good natural surface roads is certainly much less than that of São Paulo; I know of no hard-surface road in the state. The bullock cart is the only wheeled vehicle that moves through its less settled parts, and by no stretch of the English language can the ruts dug by that creaking equipage of the primitive Aryans be termed a "road."

Espirito Santo has one fine automobile road leading from the railroad up through the old German colonies of Santa Leopoldina and Santa Thereza; and the Federal Government has constructed a piece some thirty miles long through the forest north of the Rio Doce from a point opposite Collatina to an Indian reservation (the best chance in Brazil, by the way, for the average traveler to see fine evergreen forest without discomfort). The state as a whole is very poorly supplied with roadways.

Two other regions have some good natural surface roads, more because Nature has been kind than because man has been ambitious. Those who know that part of Brazil better than I, say there are some very good roads in the semi-arid northeast: Alagôas, Pernambuco, Parahyba, Rio Grande do Norte, and Ceará,[2] "constructed not as they are in Europe or the States, maybe, but of good material and very serviceable." In Matto Grosso, too, there are some roads which, although never "constructed," are nevertheless "serviceable." Automobiles get over the cattle trails between the Paraná River and Campo Grande, and between Campo Grande and Concepción in Paraguay. However, I find a note I jotted down while in Campo Grande which reads: "Mud to the knees during the rains from October to February, and dust well distributed by violent winds during the rest of the year." So it must not be construed that these are pleasure drives at any season.

With all due credit to the regions mentioned which have taken the problem in hand and made a good start toward its solution, notably São Paulo, it still remains true that up to date Brazil as a whole is deficient in good wagon roads. Aside from oxcart trails, the only road in Bahia that I could learn about—a state over three times the size of England, with a population of three and a half millions—is one stretch of thirty miles leading out of São Salvador. Sergipe, Piauhy, Maranhão, Goyaz, and most of Matto Grosso are little, if any, better. To the best of my knowledge the only pieces of road in the whole Amazon Basin (outside of the immediate environs of the towns) are the sixty or seventy miles between Macapá and the Rio Araguary; the one that cuts off the oxbow on the Xingú between the head of steamboat navigation and Altamira; and the road in from Lago Salgado, north of Óbidos.

Before quitting the subject, just a word about the Brazilian oxcart and the trail it makes. It is a two-wheeled vehicle with solid wooden wheels and a solid wooden axle, drawn by from six to ten oxen. It is in no respect an improvement upon the wagons of the primitive Aryan hordes that moved

[2] C. J. P. Lucas, of the Reo Motor Car Co., "The Good Roads Movement in Brazil," *The Brazilian American*, Oct. 21, 1922.

through the forests of Europe before the Christian era. Its sole merit is strength. Over boulders and through rocky fords it bumps undismayed, the shrill whine of the friction of wood on wood resounding for miles through the sertões as it creeps along. Having a narrow tread, it cuts a deep rut. The road is better the first time it passes than it will ever be again. When it has made one track impassable, it cuts another one alongside. But being neither graded, surfaced, nor bridged, it is inflicting considerable violence upon the English language to call these tracks "roads."

§ 6. Footpaths and Bridle Paths

Beyond the railroads and wagon roads of today? Precisely the same pack routes which existed in 1867, or, for that matter, in 1767. The old bridle paths have not changed; the character of the trails has not bettered; the form of pack-saddle is identical. There are new trails, too, to be sure, but the ancient system of landways breeds true to type. A week's ride from São Salvador to Ilhéos which I have often taken exhibits precisely the degree in which railroads have modified the system of pack transport.

When I was last over the route, the railroad led to within thirty miles of the old cattle town of Jequié. At railhead, without any transition of animal-drawn vehicle between railroad train and pack train, one took to the Jequié trail. Now I suppose an average of a hundred loaded pack mules have passed over that trail daily for two hundred years. In 1920 as in 1820, it was full of holes and "ladders" where the mules wallowed belly-deep; over many streams there were no bridges so that much cacao and tobacco coming to market this way got splashed and mildewed as a consequence; one long stretch was so steep and slippery that it was a horror to watch the struggles of the beasts. Although I am a light rider and owned the best saddle mules that money could buy, I rarely got over that trail during the rainy season without my mount going down. Straight up the side of the highest mountain the trail went, straight down the other side, although the railroad has no particular difficulty in finding an easy grade by which to enter the town. Moreover, this trail does not lie within the evergreen forest, but on its inner margin where the rainfall is so much lighter that the high forest gives way to deciduous woodlands. It is better than the forest trails.

At Jequié I used to turn east and make for the coast by the trail that follows the bank of the Rio das Contas, the highway into the evergreen forest. At the crest of the floods the river trail was entirely impassable. At moderate high water, in crossing the mouths of tributary creeks I was obliged perhaps half a dozen times a day to unsaddle, swim my animals across, and get myself and duffel over on a foot-log or in a dugout canoe. In the dry season I could follow the water's edge and get along comfortably, except where the trail entered deep forest; there at all seasons I was sure to encounter bog holes, bad ones.

Three days of this river trail brings one into the heart of a great cacao producing district. Chocolate is the chief money crop of the state; cacao also is a bean which must be carefully dried and which mildews if damp. Leaving the Rio das Contas anywhere between the mouth of the Gongogy and Pancada and striking off through the evergreen forest toward the Ilhéos Railroad, one met troop after troop strug-gling with their precious cargoes through mud that ate the very heart out of the beasts and through water that ate much cash value out of the beans. Two days to the railroad, two days back, two weeks for the animals to recuperate!

If these pack trains came to the railroad between stations, they mounted the track, the sharp hoofs of the mules dis-lodging ballast faster than section gangs could put it in place. Rarely have I ridden over that railroad when the train did not have to stop more than once to let loaded pack trains get out of the way. And the English owners did not dare to end this outrage for fear they should find rails torn up and stations burned down the next morning if they did. These two railroads have shortened the trails without modifying the connections between railheads a particle. The railroad is the twentieth century penetrating, under protest, the sixteenth.

In the interior of the great Amazon wilderness, not only railroads and roads are lacking, but even bridle paths are almost unknown. Away from water, the only passage is that afforded by tapir trails and the footpaths of the Indians. Almost every man nowadays owns a facão, a long, heavy jungle knife. With this the forest dweller or the rubber gatherer slashes the thorny vines and creepers which impede his way. Any impediment that he cannot sever at a stroke he courteously walks around. Neither timber work nor shovel work is wasted; the picada there is the expression of the repeated impact of bare feet plus an occasional slash with a facão. For that reason it is better than a forest trail over which pack animals travel.

Such are the worst of the landways at the back of beyond. Not all Brazilian trails are so bad. Yet when the country is viewed as a whole, the footpaths and bridle paths of twentieth century Brazil will not stand comparison with those of the Inca at the time of the Conquest.

CHAPTER VIII

CULTIVATED FIELDS

Good people, things will never go well in England so long as goods be not in common, and so long as there be villeins and gentlemen. By what right are they whom we call lords greater folk than we? On what grounds have they deserved it? Why do they hold us in serfage? If we all came of the same father and mother, of Adam and Eve, how can they say or prove that they are better than we, if it be not that they make us gain for them by our toil what they spend in their pride? They are clothed in velvet and warm in their furs and their ermines, while we are covered with rags. They have wine and spices and fair bread; and we oat-cake and straw, and water to drink. They have leisure and fine houses; we have pain and labour, the rain and the wind in the fields. And yet it is of us and of our toil that these men hold their state.

— JOHN BALL (14th Century).

Sowing seed upon the soil, waiting a period, reaping the harvest. This is at once the simplest and the most important of man's relations to the earth upon which he dwells. Brazil is so preponderantly an agricultural and pastoral country that no other facts can have quite such importance as the facts of the productive occupation of her soil.

Agriculture is a game that is played with many degrees of intensity and skill according to the temperament of and the pressure upon the players. In the lowest stage of hand agriculture, man expends little energy and less thought. He avails himself of such natural sites as will sprout seed, makes a hole with a stick, drops a seed, and leaves the rest to nature. A more laborious process, but one which goes with about the same sort of mentality, is the game of shifting agriculture practiced in the evergreen forest throughout the tropical regions of the world. Chop down the trees that can easily be felled, girdle the rest, set fire in the dry season, plant one or two crops, abandon the clearing to the weeds, and move on to another piece of virgin forest. It is the same in the Philippines, the Malay Peninsula, India, Africa, and Brazil.

When men settle down to the task of growing crops upon the same piece of soil year after year, they generally pass through a period of error when everything is sacrificed to one chief money crop, with the result that the land is drained of the elements utilized by this particular crop and finally refuses to produce. Diversified agriculture follows monoculture as an attempt to adjust the load to the permanent possibilities of the soil. Ultimately he learns to return to the soil, in the way of fertilizers, the constituents taken from it by his crops. In the highest type of agriculture in the world, that of China and Japan, fertilization, and tillage, and irrigation have become such perfected arts that you find fields there which have been cropped continuously for more than four thousand years showing less deterioration than the soils of the eastern half of the United States, which have been under the plow for a mere two centuries.[1]

The standing and stature of Brazil amongst the farmers of the world can best be appraised by a historical approach. I pointed out in the second chapter how great landholdings came to be given lavishly during the wars of the Portuguese against the Moors. At the time of the discovery of Brazil the prevailing type of agriculture south of the Tagus and in the Islands was great estates worked by slave labor. This feudal system was transplanted bodily to Brazil. Land there was such a drug on the market that Brazil was parceled out to court favorites in grants of unprecedented generosity. The result is that the census of 1920 finds only 648,153 landholdings in Brazil with a population of thirty millions. (In Portugal in 1908 for 5,423,132 inhabitants the number of holdings was 11,430,740!)[2]

No more accurate index of the distribution of wealth and political power in Brazil could possibly be devised than the picture of private landownership given in the reports of the last census.

[1] See Prof. F. H. King, *Farmers of Forty Centuries.*
[2] Aubrey F. G. Bell, *Portugal of the Portuguese* (1916), p. 30.

Sixty-four thousand of the big landowners own 338,000,000 acres.

Six hundred thousand small proprietors (how large they would loom in Europe!) own 100,000,000 acres.

Twenty-nine and a half millions of Brazilians own—no land at all.

PRIVATE LAND OWNERSHIP IN BRAZIL

Census of 1920

Size of Estate Acres	Number of Rural Estates	Average Area of Estate Acres	Total Area Acres	Percentage of total number estates	of total area of private land holdings
Small Holdings					
Under 100	317,785	48	15,000,000	49.0	3.5
100 to 250	146,094	165	24,000,000	22.5	5.5
250 to 500	71,377	365	26,000,000	11.0	6.0
500 to 1,000	48,877	720	35,000,000	7.6	8.0
Total	584,133		100,000,000	90.1	23.0
Large Holdings					
1,000 to 2,500	37,705	1,600	60,000,000	5.8	13.6
2,500 to 5,000	13,186	3,600	47,000,000	2.0	10.8
5,000 to 12,500	8,963	8,000	72,000,000	1.4	16.4
12,500 to 25,000	2,498	18,000	45,000,000	0.4	10.2
25,000 to 62,500	1,207	38,000	46,000,000	0.2	10.4
62,500 and over	461	148,000	68,000,000	0.1	15.6
Total	64,020		338,000,000	9.9	77.0

Note. *Synopse do Censo da Agriculture*, p. iv. In converting hectares into acres I have used the approximation 1 hectare equals 2.5 acres (actually 2.47104 acres).

Rumor has it that Costa Ferreira & Company, of Pará, a firm operating boats on the Amazon, owned largely by two men, have an Amazon estate larger than England, Scotland, and Ireland. Another man in Pará owns a private estate larger than Portugal.[3]

Brazil, then, is the land of large estates with a vengeance.

[3] I have this from Mr. Henry G. W. Romer, of Waterlow & Sons, London.

Nevertheless, there is still plenty of public land. Brazil totals 2,100 million acres (8,511,189 square kilometers). The total private holdings amount to 438 million acres, and of this some twenty-eight per cent is forest, leaving 315 million acres as the agricultural and pasture lands privately owned. Of course the pasture lands are many times the acreage of the farm lands, but just how much is cultivated the census does not show. This 315 million acres is the essential Brazil of the present. Most of the rest is forest which as yet has not begun to assume an economic rôle in the nation's life; a potentiality and a vast promise, but not a more intimate Brazilian actuality than moonlight or the recent distress of Europe.

If there are only 650,000 landowners in Brazil, how does an agricultural population of twenty-five millions function? The majority of those who till the soil work on shares. I stressed the fact that both Negroes and Indians in their native habitats were communists in their concept of land-ownership. They have never accepted the Portuguese concept of private property in land, although forced to recognize the superior power of the landowners. Inarticulate rebels against the institution of private property have carried the agricultural frontier of Brazil in every advance it has made. Adventurous freemen and fugitives always formed, and still form, a thin fringe just beyond the habitual reach of the law, about every agricultural community. The law calls them squatters; they call themselves *moradores*, settlers. Shifting agriculture is their mode of life.

When squatters in the free lands had established the values which only labor can create, the legal owner stepped in with the law behind him. He was not foolish enough to persecute these geese that laid the golden eggs. "Stay on as long as you like," said the *fazendeiro*; "only, since I own the land, you must pay me in labor or in part of your crops for the privilege of squatting on my property." He established a little store and became the squatters' banker. He stood at the baptismal font and became godfather of their children, their host at the feasts, the patron who stood between the outlawed and that "law" which to the illiterate is ever a menace, a vindictive, incomprehensible thing designed as the undoing of their dream. He bound them to him by all the ties of feudal fealty. Their sorrows he genuinely shared; their joys he made his own—also a goodly share of their crops. One generation become settled serfs on land to their liking, a new generation of the restless moved farther into the bush and carried the conquest a step further.

This process can be witnessed on any frontier of Brazil today. Long since, it has won legal recognition. Brazilian law protects the squatter in the right to the buildings and crops which his initiative has created, and he cannot be driven from the land without remuneration. Woe to the foreign corporation that does not respect this ancient social institution! The whole community will be up in arms, and rightly so.

If this is the process by which land has been won from the wilderness in Brazil, the institution which has consolidated the winnings is the *fazenda*. "Fazenda" in Brazil means any landed property, agricultural, pastoral, or forested. Looking at the nation as a whole, I should say that the fazenda rather than the family is the fundamental social unit. Let us look at two or three, as I saw them in this third decade of the twentieth century.

You will look the length and breadth of Brazil without seeing anything finer than Fazenda São Martinho, in the Comarca de Sertãosinho, in São Paulo. As we drive up in our Ford, a Rolls-Royce speeds in from the plantations and the manager, Colonel Ribeiro, steps out, a Brazilian gentleman in immaculate and well tailored riding-gear. He leads us to the manor house, a large, two-storied, brick mansion with deep verandas, polished hardwood floors, luxurious baths, and a wine cellar which proves the colonel a man of discriminating taste. After coffee, our host points to a map of the estate, which conveys this idea:

	Acres
Virgin hardwood forest	14,100
Inferior woodland	3,700
Forested "islands"	1,700
Second-growth forest	2,000
Coffee plantations	9,500
Cultivated crops	900
Assigned to the colonists	2,100
Prairie, pasture, and meadow	35,000
	70,000

Seventy thousand acres of *terra roxa,* the finest coffee land in the world.

With that outline in mind we inspect the plantations by automobile: three and a half million coffee trees in one solid plantation; coffee in straight rows to the far horizon; green foliage, white blossoms, red berries; beautiful as any culture in the whole wide world. The industrial plant that prepares this crop for market is on an equal scale—concrete flumes for washing the berries as they come from the field; several acres of brick and concrete floors for drying in the sun; a mill equipped with efficient machinery where the husks are separated from the beans, the coffee graded, and sacked for the Santos market. A picture not easily forgot is the shed where twoscore black-eyed Italian girls turn out a daily stint of two hundred and fifty baskets each of *jequitabá*. After our ride through that sea of fragrant stimulant, the colonel shows us his playthings and pets: a herd of three or four hundred Herefords, a couple of pens of a fine type of lard hog, an imported Arabian stallion.

I suppose there are five hundred hands working on this estate, mostly Italian "colonists." Each colonist gets a mud house, pasture, wood, and a garden patch. For each thousand trees he cultivates, he receives 200$000 (200 milreis) a year; for picking the crop when ripe he gets 1$400 (1.4 milreis) per sack; when straight wages are paid, he gets 3$000 per day. There is a pharmacy on the estate which dispenses free medical service. There is a school for his children and a chapel for his soul, if my memory serves me. It is feudalism at its best, with the serfs free to migrate if they can better themselves, after their contract has been fulfilled. Many indeed do ultimately become peasant proprietors.

Jump ten degrees nearer the equator to a cacao fazenda in the State of Bahia, where the Rio Gongogy joins the Rio das Contas. Here we cannot make our entry by automobile. From Ilhéos we can wallow on mule-back through the forest for two days, or follow the water route. We choose the latter. For two days we ride the beaches and the trail beside the sea, then go by canoe for another two days up the Rio das Contas. Colonel Vasconcellos is down at the landing to greet us, a dignified frontiersman in *chinelas* and a clean cotton suit. His manor house is a one-story, rambling, mud structure, whitewashed, and with floors in all but the main living-room. His hospitality is as real and as cordial as that of our São Paulo host. In the drawing-room we erect our own cots. A barefooted maid brings us a basin of hot water. She is one of Sr. Vasconcellos's godchildren, one of several orphans he has taken into his elastic household, a beautiful, brown girl. We go in to the evening meal. The colonel presides at the head of a very long table, his guests near him. Beyond them, the Negro carpenter, the canoe-maker whose breast only last year received an Indian's arrow (deservedly), the clerk from the store which adjoins the dining-room, a neighbor who has stopped for the night, the white child left as a souvenir by a foreign engineer who spent some weeks here four years ago, and half a dozen or so of the colonel's own fine boys and girls. His wife is in and out, up and down, attending to our material wants. She has almost forgot that trip to Paris when she was a girl in her teens.

I remark on the goodly number gathered about his generous board. "There were sixty here during the revolution last month," the colonel replies.

This being a special occasion, he takes the bottle of cognac down from the shelf. Beef, pork, chicken, beans, manioc meal, and sweets adorn the board in abundance.

It is not so easy to obtain accurate information as to this fazenda. Who knows how large it is? Perhaps ten thousand acres. Cacao? "Two hundred thousand trees, *mais ou menos.*" (When later I come to appraise this estate, I find half that figure nearer the truth.) Over our coffee, the colonel tells us how he came here twenty years ago and with rifles and barricades defended Pontal against those who disputed his claim. His title is still not altogether clear, but he has made terms with those who claim all this part of the world as the legal heirs of a sixteenth century Governor-General of Brazil.

Our inspection of the estate must be on mule-back. Two hundred yards from the manor house the trails plunge into the evergreen forest. At intervals along the trail, a clearing planted with cacao. There are fifty or more such separate holes in the forest. No straight rows here, no selection of seed, no experimenting with new varieties. It is done as it has always been done; yet the thing works. This Bahia region as regards quantity is the second cacao producing region of the world, after the Gold Coast.

Near each plantation dwells the man who made it. He lives in a mud hut of the utmost simplicity. He has never wrapped a blanket about him in his life. His food is the meal of manioc raised by himself, black beans, and dried beef. The tragic part of it is that the beef was born a thousand miles away on the pampas of Rio Grande do Sul; and the beans grown in Minas Geraes, almost as far by the routes of trade. Both could be raised upon the fazenda if the tradition of monoculture did not have the whole cacao region by the throat. The morador is Vasconcellos's man, body and soul. No retainer of medieval Europe ever belonged to plumed and mail-clad knight more completely. The colonel is the political chief of the river, a *poderoso;* his word is law. His "protection" is the most valuable asset a serf can possess. Without it, life here would be as cheap as it is twenty miles up the Gongogy, beyond the colonel's reach.

This is the type of frontier fazenda which for four hundred years has been consolidating the winnings from the wilderness.

At the third fazenda we shall stop only for a cup of coffee. It is in Ceará, within five degrees of the Line. Fifty acres will cover the holdings of João de Providencia. A manioc patch, some prodigious cotton plants which produce year after year and yield a little ready money, a herd of twenty goats. He is not very certain about his title and probably will be evicted if the great irrigation dam is built and the land becomes valuable. If not, drought most certainly will drive him out once every ten years. The independence of the small proprietor in Brazil yields some freedom but small comfort. His culture as a rule is scarcely an improvement upon that of the aborigines or Africans whose lineal heir he is. He wrests a precarious living from the soil, but he cannot be said to live.

The first two, the large fazendas, must be considered the essential Brazilian types. Viewed as a whole, it cannot be said that large-scale agriculture has yielded any better results in Brazil than in Russia or the south of the United States. Everywhere it is essentially a process of skimming the cream from virgin soil. Even coffee, the finest culture in Brazil, has meant that. It is appalling to a forester to contemplate how much virgin forest has been felled for coffee plantations which have since been abandoned. Even today fertilization and permanence receive but scant attention; there is yet too much virgin forest in São Paulo; the pressure of population upon resources is too slight to develop intensive agriculture.

What Brazil as a whole produces is indicated with some accuracy for the first time by the yield for 1919-20 published by the recent Census.

PRINCIPAL PRODUCTS FOR THE AGRICULTURAL YEAR

1919-1920

Products	Unit		Quantity	Value Milreis
Coffee	Metric Tons		788,488	1,025,034:530$
Corn	"	"	4,999,697	999,939:540$
Cotton	"	"	332,338	664,676:400$
Rice	"	"	831,495	415,747:550$
Sugar *	"	"	455,522	273,313:740$
Beans	"	"	725,069	253,774:290$
Manioc Meal	"	"	658,114	164,528:725$
Tobacco	"	"	73,647	110,470:800$
Cacao	"	"	66,883	80,259:200$
Rum	Hectoliters		1,463,759	43,912:770$
Potatoes	Metric Tons		145,985	43,795:590$
Wheat	"	"	87,180	43,590:350$
Starch (?) (Polvilho)	"	"	66,527	26,611:080$
Wine of the grape	Hectoliters		480,139	24,006:950$
Castor beans (mamona)	Metric Tons		42,957	12,887:340$
Tapioca	"	"	24,397	12,442:623$
Alcohol	Hectoliters		43,005	2,709:315$
Syrup (mel de canna)	"		504,081	2,520:405$
Maniçoba	Metric Tons		1,330	2,262:530$
Wines of other qualities	Hectoliters		5,084	305:040$
TOTAL				4,202,788:768$

* This represents only the sugar made in the rural establishments, *engenhos;* another 239,739 metric tons is made in the refineries, *usinas.*

Many of these chief agricultural products give character to the life and culture of distinct regions; others grow everywhere. The geography of agricultural production in Brazil is also illuminating as to the geography of political power. São Paulo and Minas Geraes together constitute the greatest coffee producing region of the world, with Rio de Janeiro and Espirito Santo in third and fourth place among Brazilian states.

Minas, São Paulo, and Rio Grande do Sul produce three-fourths of the corn crop.

São Paulo likewise produced nearly one-third of the cotton crop in the census year, with the states of the semi-arid northeast producing most of the balance.

São Paulo, Minas Geraes, and Rio Grande do Sul are the chief producers of rice.

A young mango tree in fruit. No mangos in the western hemisphere are equal to those in the Orient, but Brazilians are rapidly improving theirs. (See page 245.)

Papaya, a fruit that grows everywhere in the tropics.

Upper Left. A Guzerat bull at seven months. It is obvious that a sire of this shape will produce something very different from the standard beef breeds. The humped cattle of India have thus far been the most popular blood imported into Brazil. (See page 265.) *Upper Right.* Range cattle coming from the sertões to the Bahia market, on the old Jequié trail. Note the longhorn in the lead, and several of the little short-horned *curraleiras* just behind. No Zebu blood is evident in this herd. (Photo by Hugh M. Curran.) *Lower Left.* Showing the rank growth attained by jaraguá grass the first year, if not pastured, and the necessity of burning. (See page 263.) *Lower Right.* A planted pasture of jaraguá grass. Lean cattle will fatten here in two to six months. (See page 263.)

Pernambuco, Minas, and Rio de Janeiro grow more than half of Brazil's sugar.

São Paulo, Minas Geraes, and Rio Grande do Sul produce more than two-thirds of the crop of beans.

Bahia, Rio Grande do Sul, and Pará are the ranking states in the production of manioc meal.

Bahia alone produces two-fifths of Brazil's tobacco, with Rio Grande do Sul and Minas Geraes trailing behind.

Bahia—indeed, a small zone in Bahia—produces nine-tenths of Brazil's cacao, with Pará and Amazonas a poor second and third.

Wheat is practically synonymous with Rio Grande do Sul.

São Paulo, Minas, and Pernambuco produce the castor oil.

Wine of the grape, like wheat, is largely a monopoly of Rio Grande do Sul.

If the chief centers of production are thus indicated, it should equally be noted that several of these staple products are grown in considerable quantity in every state of the union: notably rice, corn, beans, tobacco, cotton, and manioc.

In world production, Brazil takes first rank in coffee, producing far more than all the rest of the world combined. In cacao it ranks second to the Gold Coast; and in corn, second to the United States. The United States and Russia are the only countries which surpass Brazil in the growing of tobacco. In sugar production Brazil also ranks third, after Cuba and British India.

It is important to place Brazil from another angle, that of the tools and machinery used in tillage. The most highly developed agriculture is like the most primitive in being largely hand work. In the one case, the savage in the forest uses his muscles as little as may be; in the other, Asiatics and market gardeners work over every particle of soil as lovingly as a sculptor molds his materials. Between these extremes is such tillage with draft animals and plow as most European peasants and North American farmers practice; and beyond draft animals, the gang-plows, harvesters, threshers, tractors, and the other adjuncts of big-scale farming by machinery on the prairies of the United States and Canada.

It is astounding how little draft animals are used in Brazil. Until the twentieth century plows were almost unknown. The first furrow in many a piece of ground has been made with a tractor and gang-plow within the last ten years. In my fairly extensive travels through the country, the only places where I have ever seen manure spread on the land and plowed in with draft animals are the German and Polish colonies of the south. Historically, it is accurate to say that the bulk of agricultural labor in Brazil has been hand work with the crudest of tools. In 1926 most of the corn, manioc, cotton, tobacco, potatoes, beans, and much of the sugar represent culture with nothing but an ax and hoe. Coffee and cacao of course are put in without stumping the land.

A new day, however, is dawning. One of the most hopeful things about Brazilian agriculture is the amount of farm machinery sold in the last ten years. The idea is taking hold. This is the sort of revolution which in Brazil may happen almost overnight. I recall a Rio firm with the agency for an American broad-tire wagon. For a year it had not sold one. A North American salesman persuaded the manager to send one up to a great sugar fazenda in the Campos region and give a demonstration on the ground. A two-wheeled solid wooden cart was loaded with as much cane as six oxen could handle. When it was demonstrated that two animals could easily walk off with the same load on the four-wheeled wagon, the fazendeiro on the spot bought every wagon the company had in stock.

It is interesting to note how much of modern Brazilian agriculture is based on indigenous plants and how much on importations from other parts of the world. In the order of their value, the principal agricultural productions are coffee, corn, cotton, rice, sugar, beans, manioc meal, tobacco, cacao, potatoes, and wheat. Of these, corn, manioc, tobacco, cacao, and potatoes were cultivated by the Indian before the coming of the white man; the rest are importations. Sugar was a chief crop in Madeira at the time of the discovery of Brazil and was brought over in the second quarter of the sixteenth century. Spix says the various kinds of red, black, and speckled beans and the *mundubi* bean were brought from the African colonies, and that the two commonest beans cultivated in Brazil also are cultivated by the Kafirs and the Hottentots.[4] Brazil is indebted to the early Portuguese trade with India and the East Indies for a whole lot of nice things, including the pigeon pea, ginger root, several kinds of watermelons, and the fruits of the jack and mango. Breadfruit is another link to the South Seas.

When the Court of Portugal arrived and the Rio botanic garden was founded, some attempt at systematic plant introductions was made. Tea was brought from China and Chinese coolies to work it, but tea never was much of a commercial success in Brazil. Cinnamon, the tamarind, and the date palm were set out there, none of them destined to become important. There will come a day, however, when some of these plants and a great many more will assume an important rôle in Brazilian agriculture. There is no reason why Brazil should not be an important coconut producer, for instance. It could easily produce a thousand times more than Costa Rica or the Philippines—only it does not. There are probably not five million coconut trees in all Brazil![5]

For the benefit of my friends who have to live in New York and the Bahianos who ought to be profiting by that misfortune, I must mention a crop which Brazil produces but does not sell outside her own markets. I have never tasted any oranges grown in the United States which can compare with the best

[4] Spix and Martius, op. cit., I, 175.
[5] C. S. Bontecou, "The Cultivation of Coconuts in Brazil," *The Brazilian American*, July 17, 1920. This author says: "When I say 'cultivation' I use the word because the trees do not grow wild, but as far as cultivation actually carried out is concerned, it does not exist, as understood in India, Porto Rico, the Philippines, Costa Rica, etc. There is no idea of symmetry exercised in laying out the plants, no common sense used in the selection of the seed, the handling of these, or the most rudimentary care in forming the nurseries."

Bahia oranges—the original of the California navel orange. They ripen when California and Florida oranges are out of season, yet they cut no figure whatever in the New York market.[6]

While it would be inaccurate to picture Brazilian agriculture as a whole as either intensive, scientific, or farseeing, that is not all the picture. Intensive agriculture can be seen in the market gardens near the large cities, and, I have no doubt, in the rice paddies of the Japanese in São Paulo. Some irrigation seems on the point of being introduced in Ceará. There is promise on the horizon. At the present moment, a large section of the agricultural population of Brazil is just making the transition from the traditions of the slaveholding days to those of modernity.

This is the opinion, too, of Dr. P. H. Rolfs, organizer and director of the agricultural college at Viçosa, Minas Geraes:[7]

There is no more misinformation and superstition among the rural people of Minas Geraes today than there was among the rural people of the southern states thirty or thirty-five years ago. I came to Florida in 1891, and worked there almost continuously until 1921, so I know what pioneering in agricultural education means. In 1891 practically all that was known in an agricultural way was what was handed down from one generation to another, frequently as much misinformation as information was passed along. In the early days every one knew (?) that pure-bred live stock simply could not endure the climate. Within the last three years pure-bred animals from Florida and Georgia have taken Grand Championships at the Chicago Stock Show. It was also well known (?) that cotton was the only crop that could be produced profitably in the South. It took lots of work and infinite patience to displace these erroneous conceptions.

Within the last six years, Minas Geraes has made great progress in developing from a one-crop system to a general and diversified agriculture. No country in the world, not even the southeastern United States, has been permanently prosperous on a one crop system. During prosperous years "cotton was king" and ruled with

[6] See "Turning Oranges into Gold," by P. H. Rolfs, *Brazilian American*, Jan. 6, 1923.

[7] From a personal letter to the author, March 22, 1922.

a lavish hand. During years of low prices the great mass of the population suffered indescribable hardships. These unfavorable conditions were remedied only when a diversified agriculture was adopted. Similarly, Minas Geraes is finding herself more prosperous and the population generally in better circumstances since she has taken up the extensive cultivation of rice, corn, and hogs. While she made coffee and cane her only crops, a few prospered and the masses suffered, especially during the years of low prices. There are at least a score of other crops that Minas can well afford to accentuate strongly. An unlimited quantity of fresh fruits can be produced, especially oranges, mangos, and alligator pears. Cotton can be grown to a much greater extent than at present. There are several species of oil-producing palms that might be employed on an extensive scale to great financial advantage.

In no direction does Minas Geraes show up to better advantage than in the large production of crop from the small amount of labor employed. There are tens of thousands of acres of excellent corn grown without the employment of any other instrument or implement than the ax and the hoe. What is true of the production of corn is equally true of the production of sugar cane. In spite of employing these primitive methods in crop production, the farmers of Minas are able to compete successfully with those of countries like Cuba and Java, where the most improved implements and machinery are being employed. The superior excellence of her climate and soil makes it possible.

Modern farming implements are being imported and distributed by the thousands. In the course of ten years, at the present rate of improvement, the change will be nothing short of a revolution in agricultural production.

CHAPTER IX

HERDS, FLOCKS, AND DROVES

A wide outlook upon the World's supplies of meat and its steadily expanding requirements would seem to indicate that demand is tending to overtake supply, largely as the result of a steady growth in the white populations of the world, and an improving standard of living, but partly as a direct consequence of the Great War. It is estimated that whereas fifty years ago there were 300 million potential meat-eaters in the World, there are today 587 million.

The increased consumption of frozen meat in this country [England] and on the Continent is also due in a large measure to the troops having acquired a taste for it when on active service, and asking for it after demobilization, in preference to home-killed. The war destroyed the last remnants of prejudice against frozen meat in this country; and, on the Continent, it did the work of twenty years of peaceful penetration.

Statistics, incomplete as they are, go to show that the flocks and herds of the world have not expanded since the beginning of the century. Several countries appear to have reached their limit of capacity for export, such as the United States, Canada, and in a less definite degree, Australia. The new sources of supply in South America (other than the Argentine Republic), South Africa and elsewhere, do not amount to very much as counter-weights to these other obsolete or inexpensive sources.[1]

REVOLUTIONS are not always violent. What North American in the decade 1895-1904, when the United States contributed three-fifths of the beef exported by the nine surplus-producing nations, imagined that by 1912 Argentina would be supplying four-fifths of the world's exports of chilled and frozen beef? or that before the beginning of the Great War, the United States would have ceased to count as an exporter and have

[1] *Thirty-third Annual Review of the Frozen Meat Trade,* 1920, by W. Weddel & Co., Ltd., of London—the most authoritative voice in the packing world.

learned the taste of meat pastured on the pampas? Among the new sources of supply in South America, that of greatest *potential* importance is Brazil. She has thirty-four million cattle to Argentina's twenty-seven. Are we about to see another dark horse break from the bunch and take the lead away from Argentina, as Argentina took it away from the United States? Why did Brazil export a mere 62,000 tons of refrigerated meats in 1921 against some 436,000 tons by her little sister to the south?

The answer will lead us into what is far and away the most picturesque industry in Brazil.

BRAZILIAN HERDS, FLOCKS, AND DROVES

Census of 1920

Species	Number of Animals	Average Value per Animal	Value of the Herd
		milreis	milreis
Cattle	34,271,324	113$	3,872,512 :993$
Swine	16,168,549	65$	1,055,864 :320$
Horses	5,253,699	131$	686,237 :289$
Asses and Mules	1,865,259	199$	370,359 :987$
Sheep	7,933,437	16$	123,076 :549$
Goats	5,086,655	15$	75,694 :318$
			6,183,745 :456$

§ 1. CATTLE

It is easy for a North American to envisage the Brazilian cattle industry if he has in mind the history of cattle in the United States. In the eighteenth century the "cowpens" were among the pea-vine pastures of the South, whence drovers took their scrub herds to Charleston, Philadelphia, and New York. As soon as we cut loose from England we began to import Shorthorn cattle, and some Shorthorn blood was turned into the bluegrass pastures of Kentucky before the close of the eighteenth century. In 1817, one hundred head of prime fat Shorthorn steers went over the Alleghenies to Philadelphia;

and the next year the first western cattle were driven through from Kentucky to New York, an eight-hundred-mile route

THE INTERNATIONAL STANDING OF BRAZILIAN HERDS

About 1920 *

Country	Number of Animals	Country	Number of Animals
Cattle		*Goats*	
1—India	129,591,00c	1—India	33,165,000 †
2—United States	66,811,000	2—Turkey (Europe and	
3—Soviet Russia	50,000,000	Asia)	20,269,000
4—Brazil	34,271,000	3—Union of South	
		Africa	8,019,000
		4—Brazil	5,087,000
Swine		*Sheep*	
1—United States	59,368,000	1—Soviet Russia	95,000,000
2—Soviet Russia	19,000,000	2—Australia	75,554,000
3—Brazil	16,169,000	3—United States	48,615,000
		4—Argentina	45,767,000
		5—Union of South	
Horses		Africa	29,305,000
		6—Turkey (Europe and	
1—Soviet Russia	33,000,000	Asia)	27,095,000
2—United States	20,142,000	7—United Kingdom	24,161,000
3—Argentina	8,324,000	8—New Zealand	23,285,000
4—Brazil	5,254,000	9—India	21,984,000
		10—Spain	20,522,000
		11—Uruguay	12,000,000
Asses and Mules		12—Italy	11,754,000
		13—Jugo-Slavia	9,772,000
1—United States (mules		14—France	9,372,000
only)	5,451,000	15—Bulgaria	8,600,000
2—Spain	1,967,000	16—Brazil	7,933,000
3—Brazil	1,865,000		

* For Brazil I have used the totals of the 1920 Census; for the United States, the live stock *on the farms* in 1920. Figures on cattle, sheep, and swine from the surplus meat-producing countries are from *Review of the Frozen Meat Trade*, 1921, by W. Weddel & Co., Ltd., London; the rest from the *World Almanac* (New York, 1923), p. 755. Horses and goats are from the *Annuaire International de Statistique Agricole* (Rome, 1917-18). The figures thus range from 1917 to 1922, and vary in accuracy. Soviet Russia includes both European and Asiatic.
† This does not include the goats of the native states.

which required ten weeks to cover.[1] Another cattle drive led from Lexington to Charleston, South Carolina, nearly six hundred miles long. Later, cattle were driven to the eastern sea-

[1] Alvin H. Sanders, *Short-Horn Cattle* (Chicago, 1918), p. 184.

board from as far west as Iowa; and there is even a record
of a herd of several hundred Texas cattle being driven through
to New York, nearly five months on the road.[2] The majority
of these cattle were anything but beef breeds, as the term is
now understood.

Then we annexed Texas, and with it several million Longhorns descended from the earliest Spanish importations into
old Mexico. There was so little market for them that they
were killed for their hides and tallow, and the carcasses left
rotting on the plains. But even as early as the late fifties,
men with the long view were bringing Shorthorn bulls from
the Kentucky and Missouri herds and putting them in charge
of Longhorn cows. The Mormons took Shorthorn cattle with
them to Utah, and many a beast of Devon or Shorthorn ex-
traction traveled the Oregon and Santa Fe trails with the
gold-seekers.[3]

It was not until after the Civil War, however, that the
great western range opened up, and North America there began to raise cattle *in quantity*. The foundation herds of the
western ranches were the Longhorns, which by the million began drifting up from Texas to the pastures north of Thirty-
six.[4] Raising cattle was then neither an art nor a business—
it was a gamble. When a trail herd started, no man could
say how long it would take to reach railhead nor how many
cattle would reach their destination; no man could prophesy
what the freight charges would be or how promptly the in-
efficient railroads would handle the stock; no man could say
what price the animals would bring. There was so much
luck and guesswork about the game that men thought little
about breeds or conditioning cattle for market. About 1870
this began to change. By 1870 the packing-houses furnished
a cash market for range cattle. By 1870 the beef breeds had

[2] H. W. Vaughan, *Types and Market Classes of Live Stock* (5th ed.),
p. 74.
[3] Alvin H. Sanders, *The Story of the Herefords*, chap. xvi.
[4] See *Fifty Years on the Old Frontier*, by J. H. Cook (New Haven,
1923), and Emerson Hough, *North of 36*.

proved themselves in the East. About 1870 the first Hereford bulls were turned loose upon the Colorado range.

Now that, as I see it, is precisely the point in cattle history which Brazil has reached today.

The first cattle in Brazil were brought to São Vicente by Martim Affonso de Souza very shortly after 1530.[5] When the capital was established at São Salvador, the crown sent over cattle, brood mares, sheep, and goats both from the Cape Verde Islands and from Portugal. So the live-stock industry is as old as Brazil. It is older than that of Paraguay, Uruguay, or Argentina.

There must have been both a longhorn and a shorthorn type among the early Portuguese importations. The Longhorns were identical with the Spanish cattle introduced into Mexico. The type has never been distinguished as a flesh-maker, but it had compensating qualities. It must not be forgotten that the pampas, prairies, and marshes of South America, like the open range of Mexico and Texas, were right rough places in those early days. The cougars licked their chops when they saw the first cow bid farewell to the conquistadores and break for the tall grass. A pair of long horns was as much prized by a cow as a six-shooter later came to be by a cowboy, and for the same reason. These animals were of fair size, and some reached heroic proportions and legendary fame. As draft animals they are hard to beat. The qualities which stood them in best stead in their new environment—qualities which took on an edge in America—were their cow sense, their weather wisdom, their ability to rustle for themselves, to find grass and water whether it was there or not. They would fight for their get to the death. And in later years, when the blood of the beef breeds became mingled on the plains, it was always the skinny Longhorns that led the herds in their migrations, with enough élan and esprit de corps to stampede at the end of a thousand-mile trail. Let us give the devil his due and say frankly that it was due more to the hardihood

[5] Southey, I, 35.

of the breed than to the intelligence of man that both Brazil and the United States found millions of wild cattle to work on when they got around to the idea of really breeding beef cattle. Longhorns were the bandeirantes of the cattle world.

I argue the early importation of a shorthorn type from Portugal because of the present wide distribution of what Brazilians call the *curraleira* (corral cattle). The curraleira is a light cow, well proportioned, with small horns and bones. Thomas Canty thought them survivals of even worse treatment than the Longhorns can stand—perhaps they found life in Brazil so hard that they couldn't even support the luxury of long horns.

With the bandeirantes these Portuguese cattle went pretty much everywhere. The discovery of gold carried large numbers of men into Minas, Goyaz, and Matto Grosso; and with them went horned herds to furnish food. From the sugar plantations of Bahia and Pernambuco the sertões of the São Francisco and Piauhy became stocked. So that early in the eighteenth century all the great ranges of Brazil were pasturing wild and half-wild Portuguese cattle.

These four-footed invaders asked but three things of their new environment: water, grass, and salt. In their quest for these they got little assistance from man. Indeed, by selecting the best males for beef steers, man artificially bred his herds down rather than up. But grass and water were pretty much everywhere in southern Brazil, except in the evergreen forest, and Nature was entirely competent to breed good cattle except in one respect—she did not always furnish the salt. For this element the bulls and cows prospected frantically while their masters dug for gold. Where it was lacking, the herds paid heavily.[6]

[6] "Cows in milk and sheep show the greatest need of salt; fattening cattle, horses, dry cows, and stock cattle require less salt; and pigs but little. However, western stockmen estimate that as a rule a cow should consume ten pounds of salt per year, a horse about six, and a sheep two or three. These figures will vary considerably depending upon the nature of the range. In the summer in the higher altitudes on green feed and fresh water, more salt is needed than at other times."—H. W. Vaughan, Professor of Animal Husbandry in the University of Minnesota, in a personal letter.

There are many places in Brazil where, as in the Salt River valley in Arizona and along the Rio Grande in New Mexico, the alkali or salt in the water satisfies the cravings of the animals, and they will pay no attention to salt when it is placed where they can reach it. Throughout the arid zone along the São Francisco River and in the basin of the Rio Salitre and elsewhere in interior Bahia, salt deposits are encountered, formed by the evaporation of lakes. Elsewhere the leaching of chlorides of sodium and magnesium from limestone forms what the Brazilians call *barreiros*. These are clay beds where a layer of hardpan has caused the deposition of enough alkali to form a "lick," about which tapirs, deer, wild pig, armadillos, and jaguars rendezvous, just as the buffalo and the lesser life of the Great Plains forgathered about our salt licks. General Rondon says:

In the region bounded by the Rivers Taquary, Negro, and Paraguay, there are plains in which salt lakes are found, riches still more precious than the simple barreiros. There the animals develop unrestrained according to natural law, without human intervention even to supply the salt, which becomes so necessary on the plateaus.

The truth is, however, that on all the larger breeding ranges of Brazil (as distinguished from the fattening pastures) the cattle grew up "without human intervention even to supply the salt," whether there was enough supplied by nature or not. I have seen barreiros that looked as though a steam shovel had been at work, where there is so little salt in the clay that a critter must eat perhaps a ton of clay to get a pound of salt, with holes where they fairly bury their heads in their frantic efforts to get enough of the stuff their systems crave. This clay-eating in quantity does cattle no good. Inflammation of the stomach and intestines is set up, the animals lose appetite, and their calves show the result of malnutrition. Salt-starved cattle have often attacked perspiring men in Brazil, and not all got off as easily as Colonel Roosevelt that night a Matto Grosso steer tiptoed into his tent and ate his underclothes. Even today, many breeders of the far interior think that salt twice a year is ample, one dose at the beginning of the rainy season and another a few months later. But salting at such rare intervals simply acts on an animal as a purgative and does little good.

The bulk of Brazilian salt has always been produced by the evaporation of sea water at Cabo Frio, Sergipe, Ceará, and Rio Grande do Norte. The imposition of an interior customs duty upon a commodity so necessary for the well-being of the herds was folly of the first magnitude; yet salt, a hundred years ago, was encumbered with a heavier duty than any other article of import, iron alone excepted.[7]

Other things that prevented Brazil from being an unqualified cattle paradise were the presence of certain insect pests, and, in the northeast, drought. There is a fly which lays its eggs in the drying end of the umbilical cord; the larvae hatch in a few hours and cause ulceration and the death of the calf if not attended to. Ticks (ask the Texans) are pretty much everywhere that the pastures are brushy, and in places account for heavy losses. The berne fly is far worse. Maggots as large as the segment of a man's finger develop under the skin and fester out, leaving a round hole which is long in healing.[8] It is common to see hides that look as though they had been used as targets for prolonged rifle practice. Regions which are free from these pests enjoy a tremendous natural advantage over the pastures where they abound. Dr. Moraes Barros states that the plateau south of Campo Grande in Matto Grosso is free from berne; General Rondon avers it does not occur in the plains of the Paraguay; and I have seen perfectly clean cattle in Ceará and some in eastern Bahia. The droughts of

[7] John Mawe, op. cit., p. 307.
[8] The "berne" (*Dermatobia cyaniventris*) has an interesting life-history which was discovered by Dr. Adolpho Lutz. It catches small sweat-licking diptera and clasps them in an embrace while it deposits its eggs on them. These diptera fly around with the eggs on them while they visit animals to lick their sweat. When the eggs are ripe, the heat of the animal visited induces the maggots to open the lids of the eggs and to come out and burrow into the skin of the vertebrate, where they develop till pupation time, then fall out to make pupæ in the ground.

the northeast periodically accounted for frightful decimations in all the herds.[9]

The estimate of the Brazilian Geologic Service [10] placed the campos, pantanaes, caatingas, and other formations outside the forest as originally 41 per cent of Brazil's land surface, some 872 million acres. Practically all of this has been made to serve as pasture land of some sort. Whatever the original area was in 1500, it is larger rather than less at present, because agriculture in Brazil has made its gains almost exclusively at the expense of the forest, rather than in the campos. A considerable area of forest land, too, has been converted into planted pastures for fattening cattle. It is pertinent to inquire the carrying capacity of these native pastures, and as a standard of comparison it will be convenient to have in mind the capacity of the western range in the United States.

The carrying capacity can be told only by experience [says Hitchcock]. A range must be exceptionally good to average for a season one cow to every five acres, and such ranges would be found only in the less arid portion of the Great Plains where the grass is abundant.[11]

That veteran cattleman, Murdo Mackenzie, who is as well known in Brazil as in the United States, says of such "breaks" of the plains and rough country as the Matador ranches in Texas:

In order that the Herefords do well during the year round they should have at least fifteen acres to every head with a plentiful supply of water at distances not greater than four miles between watering places.[12]

The following figures regarding Brazil should be considered

[9] The *secca* of 1915 was far from being one of the worst, yet Baron Studart, British Consul in Fortaleza, gives the losses in Ceará alone as 680,000 cattle, 2,441,000 sheep and goats, 211,000 horses, 112,000 asses and mules, 243,000 swine. This is only an estimate and appears to me high.

[10] See page 70.

[11] A. S. Hitchcock, *A Textbook of Grasses* (New York, 1914), p. 25.

[12] Sanders, *The Story of the Herefords,* p. 776.

the roughest kind of approximations for two reasons. Cattle-men everywhere talk confidently of these matters without making them subjects of scientific study, and in Brazil there is so much land that cattlemen habitually talk in terms of "square leagues." Now a square league in one part of Brazil is not a square league in certain other parts. In Rio Grande do Sul a square league measures 6,660 meters on a side and therefore contains 10,954 acres. In other regions cattlemen have defined a square league for me as six kilometers on a side, which would contain only 8,892 acres. But such parsi-mony is unworthy a nation with estates the size of those in Brazil; and in converting into acres I have in all cases used the long league, the large league, the old league, the league that existed before the meter was born.[13]

On the best cattle lands in Rio Grande do Sul they figure 50 to 60 head per quadra of 215 acres, which is only four acres to the cow and represents exceedingly fine pasture. Their *"campo da serra"* will carry only from 25 to 40 head throughout the year, that is, from five to nine acres to the cow.[14]

In Matto Grosso, at Capão Bonito and in similar country on the plateau south of Campo Grande, they figure 800 animals to the square league, which is 14 acres to the cow.[15] The best pastures in the Plains of the Paraguay, on the other hand, will carry as many as 2,100 to the square league, or a cow to each five acres.

In Minas Geraes, they allow six acres to the cow in the campos about Barbacena.[16] But as you get toward the semi-

[13] It is interesting to note how the ancient Portuguese land measures still prevail over the metric system. The braça is 2.2 meters. Instead of the unequivocal hectare, in Minas Geraes they use the alqueire, 100 braças on the side, containing 4.84 hectares. The alqueire in São Paulo, Paraná, and Rio Grande do Sul is exactly half this size.

Besides this, in Rio Grande do Sul, they use the quadra, containing 87.12 hectares, the square league containing 50 quadras, and the seismaria containing three square leagues.

[14] Mr. S. T. Lee, U.S. Consul at Porto Alegre.

[15] Dr. P. de Moraes Barros, President, *Sociedade Rural Brazileira, the Brazilian American*, June 10, 1922.

[16] Sir Richard Burton, op. cit., I, 93.

arid northeast, the carrying capacity drops off. The region about the Rio Paracatú will probably not carry more than 400 head to the square league, or 27 acres to the cow.

North and east of this you get into dry regions where it is largely a matter of water holes and the distance between them. From the numbers that die in every drought, he would be a bold man who would say that the Northeast can carry more than it now does carry.

All these figures indicate what the land can do simply with the grasses that God planted there. On this basis, the ranges of Rio Grande do Sul can be considered fully stocked; but there still remains so much unused cattle land in Minas, Goyaz, Matto Grosso, and Amazonas, that I think it probable the native pastures of Brazil can support a herd of seventy-five million cattle easily. What she might do beyond that on planted pastures intensively handled—*quem sabe?* No other nation in the world has the potentialities of Brazil as a cattle country.

The technique of handling these native pastures consists in the periodic application of fire. Once a vigorous grass crop has gotten away from cattle, the stems become so coarse and so high that they will not touch it. When this is burned over, it is again ready to graze in two or three weeks. Then another tract is burned, and so on in rotation until the whole range has been fired in the course of the year. Of course this can be done only when the grass is dry, and it becomes a very nice problem to keep the herds supplied with succulent and nutritious grass that they will eat. Few men will affirm that this burning does the soil any good; its physical make-up seems bound to suffer from the humus destroyed. Yet there appears to be no other way of economically getting rid of this manifestation of a superabundant nature.

The technique of handling the herds themselves brings us to more interesting things, human beings, vaqueiros, cowboys. First and last, I find the gaucho the most interesting man in Brazil. He is a vital chap and he still eats his beef with the

The vaqueiro of the south, gauchos of Rio Grande do Sul. They wear *bombachas*, baggy trousers of light material, with an apron of leather to keep the lasso from cutting. The man on extreme left has his bolas around his waist. (See page 256.)

The vaqueiro of the Northeast, dressed in leather from hat to shoes, as a protection from the thorns of the caatingas. (See page 259.)

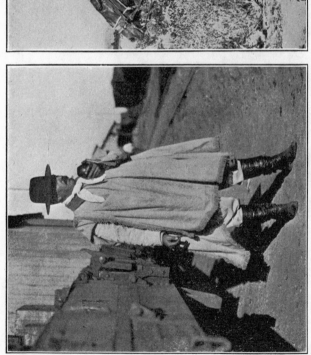

Photograph by Dr. L. W. Hackett.

Gaucho cattle buyer drinking maté. Meat and maté are often the sole fare of the cowboys on the range. (See page 257.)

hair on.[17] He has brothers in Uruguay, and on the pampas of Argentina, but as far as Brazil is concerned the gaucho is confined to Rio Grande do Sul.

Before the coming of the white man there were guanaco hunters on these plains confounding the swiftness of the guanaco and rhea with the entangling alliance of their bolas. There was a marriage on the pampas, and the gaucho is as proud of the Indian blood in his veins as of the Portuguese. There was likewise a marriage of cultures. As soon as the white man appeared with his horse, the gaucho quit walking; but he kept the bolas. Never has there been a more intimate union of man and mount. The gaucho fished on horseback; he fetched water from the well on horseback; his drinking bouts were in the saddle; when there was mortar to mix he rode his horse back and forth through the mess; mass he listened to lounging in the saddle at the door of the church. Gambling and sleep were the only things that ever made him dismount.

His adoption of cattle was as whole-hearted. In his hut, a cow's horn served for drinking cup. Frequently enough a cow's horn was the only thing in which beef broth could be boiled for the ailing woman—meat and water in a horn with embers around it. For seats, the blanched skulls of cattle and horses. As an ornamental fence about his hut, he erected neat piles of the same, with horns forming a decorative motif rhythmically repeated. A bull's hide stretched on four sticks or spread on the ground was his bed. The gaucho tasted beef, and he liked it. Thenceforth he became carnivorous. He ridiculed as effeminate any one who ate vegetables or drank milk. Meat and maté, year in, year out.

As a small boy, the gaucho was presented by his father with a long, thin knife. He went out and tried its edge on a calf. He cut a chunk of meat, stuck it on a spit, and broiled it at the fire. In eating, he grasped a hunk in his teeth and sliced off the remainder, if possible without slitting his own

[17] *Carne com couro,* it should be on Chicago menus.

nose. Having eaten, he wiped his mouth with the back of the blade, like his elders before him. In his teens, he learned to slit the jugular of a steer at one coup. Somebody about the fazenda had to kill a steer or a heifer almost every day—meat does not keep long, and gauchos disdained all but the choicest cuts. Besides, killing was fun. What else was there for a man to do but kill and skin? He became very clever with his long, thin knife. He could castrate with the skill of a surgeon. Sometimes he became a bit excited and slit a comrade's throat. But he never stayed awake nights over it. A man's blood is no redder than the blood of a steer, nor does the stench of his rotting carcass pollute the pampa so far.

The priests who came with the conquerors told the gaucho he was naked, if not ashamed. So he wrapped a poncho about his waist, pulled one corner between his legs—and lo, *bombachas!* (The seams are a modern innovation.) Add a poncho of fine wool, a black hat with a chin strap, leather to the knees, a broad belt, and silver spurs, and you have the gaucho dressed for today.

His gear for handling cattle is simple. For throwing, he uses a forty-foot rawhide lasso. (The bolas break so many legs that, since horses have become valuable, most cattle owners discourage their use. The vaqueiros still keep them to play with when out of sight of the *capataz*.) His saddle has no horn on which to snub. Instead, he uses a second cinch that ordinarily passes over the seat of the saddle. The rendering ring lies under his thigh, and in this ring he hitches his lasso when snubbing a steer. Over one thigh he wears a leather apron to keep the lasso from cutting when he uses his leg as a fulcrum for the rope. Should he be without a rope, the gaucho is quite competent to throw a bull by the tail.

I have spoken of him in two tenses. That expresses the fact. The gaucho is yet of the present, but he is passing; he is more of the past. He still sits by his fire and sings of the faithlessness of woman and the fleetness of a horse, but his song today is likely to be broken into by the screech of a locomotive or the burr of an automobile. I shall hate to see him go.

The caatingas of the north have bred another vaqueiro altogether: the *sertanejo*, par excellence. His cattle feed in brush so dense that when they break he must ride on their heels or lose sight of them completely. The bush is full of thorns, and low trees grab at him with gnarled limbs as he flies past. So the sertanejo dresses in leather from head to foot: a wide hat of heavy, plaited leather, with a strap; a jacket; a bib; and breeches of buckskin or goat's hide. He uses a short lasso, but his distinctive tool is a lance (*ferrão*) ten or twelve feet long with a sharp iron in the end. The iron is leathered to within half an inch of the point so that it cannot penetrate the animal too deeply. This he can use where the going is too thick to swing a lasso. He rides full tilt at his steer with a quartering charge, catches him in the haunch with his lance, and with it topples him as neatly as with a lasso. His lore is that of the desert: watering holes, and weather signs, and the digging of wells. At times of drought he is called upon to cut fodder for his starving cattle from the trees, the leaves of the evergreen joazeiro. Like the gaucho, he is a knife-fighter. Like the gaucho, he has many rugged, upstanding qualities.

Also he is a fanatic, in a way that the gaucho is not. The sertanejo has been the backbone of the most ghastly mob madnesses in the history of Brazil. Twice during the nineteenth century—the last time but thirty years ago—there has been a great slitting of throats in his sertão over the return of that King Sebastian who died in a mad crusade against the Moors back in 1578. Leather hats covered many a loosely connected head when the Federal troops finally finished with Canudos, in Bahia.[18] His Mecca today is Bom Jesus de Lapa. There is no danger of the sertanejo passing soon from

[18] For the remarkable history of Antonio Conselheiro and his cowboy followers, see R. B. Cunninghame Graham, *A Brazilian Mystic* (New York, 1920).

the scene, and the nation would be poorer were the leanness of his hardy virtues to disappear. But Brazil well could get along without the conditions which breed his fanaticism—the sire is Illiteracy and the dam, Isolation.

In the Plains of the Paraguay, in addition to vaqueiros of all the mixed breeds of Brazil, one can see pure-blooded Indians handling cattle, and Paraguayans who are nearly pure bloods. The Paraguayan has the reputation of being the cleverest man in South America with the lasso, and I have heard North American cowboys say he has no equal. Out on a two-million-acre ranch called Descalvados, on the Bolivian frontier (one of the old Farquhar properties, still managed by North American cattlemen), is a good place to see them work.

It is Monday morning. They leave the ranch headquarters, thirty vaqueiros with a string of cow-ponies and one cart carrying manioc meal and salt. No tents, no blankets. They are barefooted, riding with the great toe alone in the stirrup. Each man has a sixty-foot rawhide lasso, and it takes a man to throw a sixty-foot rope. They drive before them three or four tame steers as a herd nucleus. Upon sighting a bunch of wild cattle, the vaqueiro dashes in, hurls his lasso, and trips from the cinch. Another vaqueiro ropes the hind legs and straightens the critter out. Leaving the horses to hold the prostrate animal, they saw off the horns, leaving bloody stubs three or four inches long; if it is a bull and very *bravo*, they castrate. Then they turn him into the herd. Before night the ponies will be all dappled with little, round, red spots where the stubs of charging steers have hit them.

That is the easy end of it. But if a vaqueiro has to follow his animal two or three kilometers from the herd and finds himself alone when he finally ropes him, then it is a different game. He cannot dehorn the beast alone. He cannot drive him alone. Herd instinct he cannot bring into play until he gets to the herd. So he lassoes the bull by the horns and teases until it charges. Before the charging bull, horse and rider run toward the herd, until tauro stops and sulks. Then he coils his rope and reels in until the pony confronts the long, sharp horns at the range of a few feet. The vaqueiro takes off his hat and fans the bull's face. He makes insulting remarks about the bull's courage. When these insults are resented it is a leap for life, with everything wagered on the quickness of your pony. It takes a real cowboy to play the game.

At night they build a fire, kill a steer, and feast; while a watch rides herd and croons the melodies that cattle love the world over, songs, some without words, which all cows and cowboys understand.

> E cou mansão . . .
> E cou . . . é caõ! . . .

For bed they have the sheepskin and the leather *manta* of their saddles. For diversion, the snarl of a cougar. At the end of a week they drive into the home corrals from three to five hundred cattle. At the end of a month they get their wage of fifty milreis (twelve dollars at normal exchange).

"Why, that's old Texas of the sixties!"

Exactly. South of San Antonio, just half a century ago. And the trail herds of Brazil today repeat all the sensations of the trail herds of the sixties and seventies between Texas and Nebraska, except Indian fighting.

For there was, and is, a long journey between the breeding beds and the markets. (I speak now of the central ranges; Rio Grande do Sul is a world apart.) Up to the beginning of the World War, Brazil did not figure in the returns of the refrigerated meat industry. Her market was entirely within her own borders. Each Brazilian city kills every morning the meat it will eat next day. Refrigeration is still a novelty; I never saw a butcher shop with an ice box. Rio de Janeiro requires about seven hundred head of cattle daily, São Paulo two hundred and fifty, and other towns in proportion. It is a nation of tremendous meat-eaters. In addition to quantities of fresh meat, Brazilians consume enormous amount of *xarque,* "meat of the wind" and "meat of the sun." It is prepared on every fazenda in Brazil as well as in slaughterhouses. Kill a steer, cut the meat into blankets an inch thick and as large as possible, rub in a handful of salt, and hang in the sun and wind. Manioc meal, beans, and xarque are the triumvirate that head the Brazilian menu.

To meet these demands the great cattle trails developed. From each city they radiated, and into every hamlet one led. São Paulo drew unto itself cattle from Paraná, Matto Grosso, Minas, and Goyaz. One of the busiest crossings of the Rio Paraná is Porto da Taboada, where both Matto Grosso and Goyaz herds converge. From farther east in Goyaz the herds have to swim both the Paranahyba and the Rio Grande as well as countless lesser streams. The São Paulo market draws from as far north in Minas as Paracatú. Most of the cattle for the Rio market come from Minas. Old São Salvador draws cattle from a tremendous radius: from northern Minas they go north by Conquista and Jequié; all central Goyaz sends cattle due east over a seven-hundred-mile trail; and Piauhy ferries her cattle at Joazeiro and sends them south to the Bahia markets. All the old trade routes were mainly cattle trails. All the major routes are comparable in length to those from Kentucky to Philadelphia and New York; and, in difficulty of crossing, to those that cut across the Red River, the Canadian, and the Arkansas. Cattle have been driven from Matto Grosso to the eastern markets which have been over a year on the road; most of these drives, however, can be covered in from sixty to ninety days. Three leagues a day—twelve miles—is considered a good steady pace for cattle in Brazil.

At the end of their long peregrinations the cattle are generally in poor flesh, sometimes mere skin and bones. They must be put in fattening pastures for from three to six months before they are ready to kill. The fattening pastures have to be at the end of the walking: in the old days that meant near the cities, now it means at the shipping points on the railroad. The planted pastures are always located in land good enough to support forest, if available. The forest is burned and grass seed sown. Two grasses compete for favor in the planted pastures of Brazil, *jaraguá* and *gordura,* the "grass of fatness." Their respective merits are thus appraised by Mr. Murdo Mackenzie: [19]

As jaraguá grass is not injured by burning, it is more economical to plant that grass and burn the undergrowth off each year for three years, when there will be well-established, permanent pastures. The jaraguá grows best on low, damp land and is an excellent fattening grass. I do not agree with the statement that gordura does not produce a hard fat. My experience has led me to believe that beef produced on gordura is superior to any other grass beef in that country. The fat is not only hard but is of good color. We had cattle fattened on gordura killing out 61 per cent, which is excellent. I have no wish to belittle the excellent qualities of jaraguá, but fat of the beef produced on jaraguá has a yellow tinge and for export purposes the color would play an important part, as it does in this country.

The gordura, however, grows on high ground and will not withstand heavy frost as will the jaraguá. Consequently it is necessary, on a large area of pasture, to have pastures of both grasses. In the Barretos district there is never frost enough to kill the roots of the gordura and the topography of the country is well suited for gordura pastures. Along the river bottoms and low lands jaraguá thrives best.

Another good point about gordura is that it can be allowed to grow fifteen or eighteen inches high and accumulate forage in the bank, whereas jaraguá that high is inedible. Of the great fattening pastures of the present, those about Porto Real, Curvello, and Cordisburgo in Minas Geraes are chiefly jaraguá; those of Tres Corações, Passos, and Santa Rita de Cassia, in Minas, and the most important of all—those of

[19] From a personal letter, Dec. 12, 1923.

Rio Preto and Barretos, in São Paulo—are gordura. The new pastures opening in the forest along the Noroeste Railroad in western São Paulo, destined for great things when the bridge is built across the Rio Paraná, are all jaraguá. The origin of gordura grass is in doubt, but it has certainly been in Brazil for two hundred years. It is one of those grasses that seem to follow man everywhere, creeping along his roads and trails, and taking possession of fallow fields. If jaraguá be not a native grass, at least there are great areas in southern Goyaz where the natives believe it has always existed. An interesting outcome of this fact will develop in a moment.

With almost illimitable breeding ranges and fat conditioning pastures near the local markets, the stage is set for the production of prime beef—but for one thing! What of the breed?

Although the idea of artificial selection hardly reached Brazil until the twentieth century, there did develop spontaneously something surprisingly like a beef type of animal. Brazilians call it the *Caracú*. Thomas Canty had an explanation of the origin of this breed that sounds entirely plausible. The eighteenth century gold rush carried curraleira cattle to the headwaters of the Paracatú and on into Goyaz. The miners cut down the forest, grew a couple of crops, and then planted gordura. The placers exhausted and the miners decamped, the fences soon ran to decay and the cattle roamed at will; while the ambitious *gordura roxa* took charge of more and more pasture land. The cattle waxed fat and heavy, and beef having no longer value, the best bulls were not killed but remained to take charge of the herds. So there evolved spontaneously from the little curraleira a breed with a large plump body, short legs, and short horns with a characteristic incurving at the tip. This explanation of their origin may be right and may be wrong; but at any rate men rediscovered them late in the nineteenth century with considerable amazement, took them down to civilization, and many breeders are now trying to make of the Caracú a genuine Brazilian beef breed. An association for the purpose was formed and the Caracú Herd Book now contains over two thousand cows and a couple of hundred bulls.

Up to the twentieth century there was small reason for any one in Brazil to worry much about breeds and types. It was simply a question of how many animals, costing nothing to raise, could be sold in the local markets at any price. But British taste for beef during the nineteenth century brought to a point of great perfection what all the world now recognizes as the six standard breeds of beef cattle, the Shorthorn, Polled Shorthorn, Hereford, Polled Hereford, Aberdeen-Angus, and Galloway. The United States and Argentina, when they got to the point of grading up their herds of wild and scrub cattle, imported from England and Scotland, and within half a century came to be the two greatest factors in the meat markets of the world. The North Americans led in the development of the packing industry, and as soon as they became strong in their art at home, moved to the Rio de la Plata and established themselves on the edge of the pampas. In both Uruguay and Argentina they could get in quantity the very finest types of beef cattle.

But Brazil went a road of her own. In the last decade of the nineteenth century, breeders from around Uberaba, in the Triangle of Minas, began importing from India Zebus and Guzerats, white cattle with a hump (*Bos gaurus,* a different species from *Bos taurus*), and crossing these sires on the longhorns, crioulas, caracús, curraleiras, junqueiras, and the rest of the range stuff. Many, many words have passed— some of them heated—about the wisdom of the move.[20] Be

[20] The Zebu mestiço has undoubted merits, thus summarized by Mr. Tippet, manager of the Brazilian Meat Company: "Now sixty per cent of the cattle of central Brazil are Zebu mestiço, comparable to our longhorns, or to Colorado cattle. All of the cattle have long ears and a big hump on their withers, are hardy and long-legged, and can outrun a horse; have very cross dispositions but are practically immune to all of the many diseases of cattle; are great rustlers and really are an admirable animal for any new country, though the beef cannot compete in price on account of quality in the European market with beef from other countries where they use the known beef breeds of cattle."

that as it may, at the beginning of the World War the Brazilian herd was preponderantly Zebu mestiço.

The only place where the beef breeds were beginning to gain a foothold was in Rio Grande do Sul. Isolated from the civilization of central Brazil by the Paraná pine forest, Rio Grande has always been much influenced by the civilization of the Rio de la Plata. The gauchos saw the herds of blooded beef cattle which were bringing such high prices in Buenos Aires and Montevideo. Herefords appealed particularly to Rio Grande; and shortly thereafter the white faces, with some Red Polled and Shorthorns, began to appear on the southern pastures.

If the Brazilian herd at the beginning of the World War was low in quality, it was numerically strong. The census of 1920 showed thirty-four million cattle. India and Russia have greater herds, but each consumes its meat at home. The United States herd of sixty-seven million was, at the beginning of the war, just about sufficient to meet our home demands. Brazil with only thirty million population should have possessed a greater exportable surplus than any other nation in the world.

However, between cattle on the range and quarters hanging in the hold of a refrigerator ship in this modern world, there must ensue a packing-house operation which is refined, and elaborate, and intensive. Brazil did not have one modern packing-plant and had never shipped a cargo of chilled beef. The houses in Rio Grande and the Brazilian companies were equipped to handle low-grade products exclusively, canned, dried, and salt meats. She entered the war period unknown and inconsequent in the meat markets of the world.

She emerged from the mêlée with nine freezing works with a combined capacity of about six thousand cattle per day, three plants in Rio Grande do Sul, one in Rio de Janeiro, and five in São Paulo. As a result of building operations begun during the war, Brazil now has modern packing-plants owned and operated by some of the strongest packers in the world:

Armour and Company, Wilson and Company, and Swift and Company; and Vestey Brothers of England. Armour put ten million dollars into the greatest plant in South America with a daily capacity of fifteen hundred cattle, five thousand hogs, and two thousand sheep.[21]

For Brazil it was an industrial revolution. She saw her exports of chilled and frozen meats leap from about six tons in 1916 to 66,000 tons in 1917, and remain not far from this upper figure until the close of 1921. Ranchers out there in the sertões of Matto Grosso and Goyaz could not believe it—the world was crying for and paying cash for their old, half-breed steers. The dust never got a chance to settle on the cattle trails during the glorious years when the young men were dying in France. It was a wonderful war—if you happened to have ten thousand fat steers on your range.

Disillusionment was as swift. Once the young men ceased to eat at the expense of their governments, beef had to meet the demands of a more fastidious market. Nobody but the Italians wanted Zebu beef, and the Italians could not pay for all that they wanted. The Weddel report for 1921 says, "The quality of Brazilian beef is still considerably below the standard required on the British market." Armour and Company opened their giant plant in January, 1921, and closed before

[21] APPROXIMATE CAPACITY OF CHIEF PACKING-PLANTS

COMPANIES	DAILY CAPACITY	
	Cattle	Hogs
Armour & Co., São Paulo......................	1,500	5,000
Swift & Co., Rio Grande do Sul..................	1,000	.....
Wilson & Co., São Paulo.......................	800	.....
Brazilian Meat Co. (Vestey Bros.), Rio	600	100
Rio Grande Meat Co. (Vestey Bros.), Pelotas......	400	.....
Cia. Mechanica, Barretos, São Paulo.............	200	100

the end of the year without ever having run a single day at capacity, closed a ten-million-dollar plant and withdrew every man but a vice president and a night watchman. "We doubt if in the whole State of São Paulo we could buy enough exporting cattle today to run our plant for a week," they stated in closing. Rinderpest had broken out in São Paulo to challenge the illusion that the Zebu is disease-proof, and drought had done a lot of damage.

But the basic reason for the complete collapse of Brazil's refrigerated meat trade in 1922 was that Brazil does not produce the highest qualities, and consequently is the first to be stricken from the buyer's list when the European market slumps. Her position is somewhat analogous to that of South Africa.[22]

The moral is obvious. Brazil does not need to worry about her product being put on the market in unattractive shape— the packers know their end of the business—but she does need to increase by the million her number of first-class animals, if she wants to compete for the frozen-meat trade of the world. Today England dominates the export market. Before the middle of the twentieth century, Brazil will also have a chance to cater to the United States. What these two nations demand is well known: "Sufficient finish and quality are not often found in carcasses weighing less than 800 pounds. The greatest demand is for carcasses from 1,200- to 1,400-pound steers."[23]

It is a legitimate ambition for Brazil to become, not only a factor in the world's refrigerated meat trade, but *the dominant factor* in that trade. She possesses the physical plant, as I pointed out in the third chapter.

Rio Grande do Sul is larger than Uruguay; conditions are

[22] See 34th *Annual Review of the Frozen Meat Trade*, 1921, by W. Weddel & Co., Ltd., London, p. 17.
[23] Vaughan, *Types and Market Classes of Live Stock* (5th ed.) chap. ii. The average weight of the 3,790,000 cattle received at the Union Stock Yards in Chicago in 1918 was 941 pounds; this includes everything from fancy stuff for hotel trade to what Chicago calls Dairy Maids, Nellies, Hat Racks, Skins, Dogs, Sea Horses, and Bologna Bulls.

identical. The southernmost Brazilian state should not rest
a minute until she overtakes, in the production of high-grade
beef cattle, the lost province of Banda Oriental. The gauchos
are on the way; with four and a half million Durhams, Herefords, Angus, Devons, and Red Polled, her herds will soon
grade up. Nobody need fear for the future of that state.

The only question, then, is whether central Brazil can
breed beef cattle. On this point the North American cattlemen in Brazil, among them several whose names carry great
authority in the packing world, •are of one voice. The acceptance of their experimental point of view by Brazilian cattle
breeders is a matter of such great importance that, at the
risk of becoming tedious, I am going to set forth their
opinions.

The Land, Cattle, and Packing Company imported over
three thousand head of Shorthorns and Herefords. Of this
move, Mr. Murdo Mackenzie writes:

I am very enthusiastic on the subject of improving the cattle of
Brazil by introducing Hereford blood into the native herds. When
I became manager of the Brazil Land, Cattle & Packing Company
in 1912, my first move was to import a shipment of over 900 Hereford and Shorthorn cattle. When it became known among the
cattlemen of the country that I was bringing down these cattle, they
hooted at the idea and declared that I could not get fifty per cent
of them to Brazil alive and that if I did succeed in accomplishing that
feat not fifty per cent of those arriving would survive the tick fever
and climatic conditions. The arguments were so strong against me
that I began to feel nervous, although I had taken the Texas longhorn in the early days and by crossing with Hereford bulls, produced,
to my way of thinking, the best range cattle in the world.

When the first boatload of cattle reached the port of Paranaguá,
I was on hand with a group of incredulous Brazilian friends, to meet
it. After inquiring of the man in charge as to the health of the
men on board I screwed up courage enough to ask how many head
of cattle he had lost.

"Five head, including one washed overboard!"

We only suffered a loss of seven per cent on the 400 cattle in the
last shipment from the time they left the States until the first year

expired. To make a long story short, the importation of these Hereford cattle was a success, in spite of the fact that we were pioneers in the work; and the cattle were eventually sent from the ranch in Paraná to our ranches at Arapuá and Capão Bonito in the State of Matto Grosso.

The calves from Zebu cows by Hereford bulls are wonderful, with white faces and the conformation, and generally the coloring, of the sire. They are hardy and are rustlers, and in my opinion have proven the future success of the cattle industry in Brazil.

Armour and Company imported pedigreed Hereford cattle both from England and from Uruguay:

The Herefords from Uruguay have come from the tick zone and in every instance have proved their immunity to ticks in this section of Brazil (São Paulo). Due to the very similar conditions found for cattle raising all through this south-central part of Brazil, the Armour Company especially recommend the importation of Herefords from Uruguay, for reproduction purposes here. At our Fazenda Anastacio, we have mestiços Hereford-Zebu and Hereford-Creoulo calves six months old which carry the Hereford type and color markings perfectly and demonstrate their superior beef qualities over the native calves at the same age. Our pure-bred Hereford calves born here in Brazil show good growth and rapid development on the catingueiro and jaraguá pastures.

Within the last two years (1921), several hundred mestiço steers carrying Hereford and Shorthorn blood have been marketed in São Paulo and the results show the increased financial gain which is derived by the breeder in producing this class of beef cattle. These steers averaged over twenty-one *arrobas* of dressed meat as four-year-olds, i.e., 693 pounds.

Mr. Tippet, the North American manager of the largest English packing concern in Brazil, is as unequivocal:

There are a few English and American companies that have introduced Hereford and Shorthorn bulls and crossed them with these cross-bred cows with most wonderful results. The calves from such a cross take practically all the color markings as well as the conformation of the sire, and on the splendid grass we have here such animals will attain a weight of from 600 to 750 pounds of dressed beef at three years old.

Let me conclude this account of the cattle industry with the judgment of a man who carries even more weight in Brazil, Dr. Paulo de Moraes Barros, president of the *Sociedade Rural Brazileira:*

The present crisis in the price of meat is world-wide. Nevertheless, Brazil has a lesson to learn from the failure of the packing plants and the refusal of the world to buy Zebu beef. It has been a humiliating lesson to us, but it is one which can be made profitable if we take advantage of what we have learned. If the Zebu has been the cause of the failure of the Brazilian meat exportations, and if the pests which are endangering the health of the national herds [i.e., rinderpest], prefer this animal, let us substitute foreign, blooded stock. There is a wonderful opportunity to do this today, for cattle are cheap the world over, in Argentina, Uruguay, and in foreign countries. The cattle industry can be built up on a big scale in Brazil within twenty years.[24]

DISTRIBUTION OF CATTLE IN BRAZIL
Census of 1920

STATE	NUMBER OF CATTLE
1. Rio Grande do Sul	8,489,496
2. Minas Geraes	7,333,104
3. Goyaz	3,020,769
4. Matto Grosso	2,831,667
5. Bahia	2,698,106
6. São Paulo	2,441,989
7. Piauhy	1,044,734
8. Maranhão	834,596
9. Pernambuco	745,217
10. Pará	615,482
11. Santa Catharina	614,202
12. Rio de Janeiro	581,203
13. Ceará	580,028
14. Paraná	539,765
15. Parahyba	444,928
16. Alagôas	388,371
17. Rio Grande do Norte	318,274
18. Sergipe	311,239
19. Amazonas	238,449
20. Espirito Santo	161,160
21. Districto Federal	23,367
22. Territorio do Acre	15,178
TOTAL	34,271,324

[24] From an address translated in the *Brazilian American,* June 10, 1922.

§ 2. HORSES

The horses which are in the world today seem to derive from at least three wild sources, a short and shaggy forest type of northern Europe, a coarse Asiatic type resembling the tarpan of the steppes, and the desert type of northern Africa. Whatever is fair and fast in horseflesh in Brazil, as in most parts of the world, is due to the little Libyan, the "drinker of the wind." How early the blood of the fleet and docile sons of the sand began to cross into the Iberian Peninsula we cannot say; but Hannibal, whose cavalry was largely recruited from the Algerian nomads, certainly injected a large dose in 219 B.C.[1] Horse traders trickled it across Gibraltar for a thousand years more. Then the Moorish Conquest fairly flooded the Peninsula with the blood of what were far and away the finest horses in the world, the Barb and his noble kinsman, the Arab.

Far more of this desert blood soaked into the south of the Peninsula than into the north. Andalusia and Estremadura in Spain, and Portugal from the valley of the Tagus south, became saturated, exalted, blest by the blood of the Barb. All the horses in the Peninsula were modified by the cross. The result in the south was an almost pure-bred desert type, with bay as the dominant color and the famous Jennets as the kingly caste. That the desert breed extended into Portugal at least as far as Lisbon and the Tagus is evident from Pliny's yarn of the mares in that region bearing offspring to the West Wind—which was the fastest fable the ancients could invent.

In the rugged northwest, where the infusion of desert blood was less in quantity, we have as a result of crossing the African horse on a coarser, smaller northern type, the ponies of Asturias, Galicia, Minho, and Tras os Montes. They are not

---

[1] On the early history of the horse I follow Sir Wm. Ridgeway, *The Origin and Influence of the Thoroughbred Horse* (Cambridge Biological Series, 1905), pp. 254-61.

The gaucho rides a good cow pony and rides him well. He has a couple of sheepskins and a leather mantle over his saddle which are his bed at night.

The remounts of the Brazilian cavalry are excellent saddle animals. The best of them are bred in Rio Grande do Sul. (See page 277.)

The strange and wonderful pack-saddle seen in Rio Grande do Norte, essentially a mattress covering the animal from haunch to ears with a half-inch rope cutting the beast about the girth. (See page 278.)

so large as Andalusian horses, nor so fast, nor so fine; but they are hardy and active mountain ponies. A great many wear gray coats.

Both these strains made their way to Brazil early in the sixteenth century. Among the mares and stallions brought to Brazil by the first Captains and sent over by the Crown a few years later, we may be sure there were representatives of the best blood of Portugal, as well as horses from the Cape Verde Islands and from the north of Portugal. The blood of the fine Andalusian horses also entered unbidden by the back door.

When Don Pedro de Mendoza was given the piece of ground from La Plata to the Straits of Magellan, he undertook to deliver there at his own expense a thousand men and a hundred horses and mares. There was a misunderstanding among the delegation delivered in 1534, and some of the men ate some of the horses; whereupon several of the high-spirited Andalusians struck out for themselves and founded the wild bands which soon pastured on the pampas by the thousand. The mutual interaction of horses, grass, and Indian carried the four-footed friend of man into the Plains of the Paraguay ahead of the white man; so that the first gold hunters in Matto Grosso were met by great tribes of equestrian Indians mounted on the descendants of the feral Andalusian steeds.[2]

Most of the horses in Brazil today are descendants of these two strains, modified very little by man. Artificial selection and breeding for type has played small part in the Brazilian horse industry. Castration of the undesirable is not the rule. The result is that the majority of horses in Brazil today stand under fourteen hands. And my impression is that there are far more grays in Brazil than horses of any other color.

Throughout her history, Brazil has used horses for two purposes, primarily, as saddle animals and as the mothers

[2] General Rondon says that since the old capital of Matto Grosso was abandoned, feral horses have again appeared in the marshes of the Rio Guaporé, escaped from the national fazenda of Casalvasco.

of mules. Now wherever men have used saddle animals to cover long distances, as distinguished from mere exercise, they have seemed partial to the easy gaits and very reluctant to rise to the trot. Major General Carter assures us that during the Roman occupation of England and for a thousand years after, the favorite saddle gait was the slow pace, then more commonly called the amble.[3] A sixteenth century writer says of the Irish Hobby: "For the most part they be amblers, and therefore verie meete for the saddle, and to travell by the way." The Jennet was an ambler and the little horses of Asturias (*asturiones*) were famous for their pace. Long after the pace became unfashionable in England, pacers continued to be imported into the North American colonies; and from a cross on this stock originated the many-gaited American Saddle Horse, whose rack has been the delight of Kentucky for nearly a hundred years.

The easy saddle gaits were as popular in Brazil as in Virginia and Kentucky, and so far as I can ascertain, this was the only direction in which breeders previous to the twentieth century exercised any selection. What Dobrizhoffer said of the horses in Paraguay is equally true of Brazil:

Much attention is paid to their paces. There are the Amblers, which are sometimes called *Asturiones*, because the Asturians used to be famous for breaking horses to this pace. If not born to the step, they are taught it by having the fore and hind feet linked together by straps of the length of the step desired, or by tying a muffled stone on the fort part of the hind feet, so that it shall hit the fore legs if the animal moves at any other rate. At this easy pace, which will not spill water from a full cup in the rider's hand, they will perform eight miles an hour; but it is not safe out of a beaten track. The *Trotones*, or trotters, are safer; and the *Passitrotes* or *Marchadores* who may be called Shufflers, their pace being between the walk and the trot, are preferred to either for a journey.

What the good priest meant by the Shufflers is obviously what we in the United States call the running walk; and the gait at

---

[3] "The Story of the Horse," *Natl. Geog. Mag.*, Nov., 1923, p. 539.

which a small horse will do eight miles an hour without spilling water from a full cup in the rider's hand is not the fast pace, which is rough and uncomfortable, but the rack.

Such are the horses which have been the constant companions of men in Brazil for four hundred years. It is difficult to exaggerate the importance of the rôle they have played in Brazilian history. In a country of immense distances, whose sole system of landways until recently was a network of bridle paths, life could hardly have been sustained without saddle and pack animals; nor could the cattle industry have been developed on the unfenced range without fleet cow-ponies. It will be gathered that the best saddle animals, collectively if not in any single individual, possess and have always possessed all the gaits of the American Saddle Horse. Brazil will probably use vast numbers of saddle animals longer than any other part of the western hemisphere. Having in mind the asses presented to George Washington by the King of Spain and by La Fayette and what their descendants have done for the United States, I venture to suggest that one of the handsomest presents the United States could make to her sister Republic—one whose ultimate benefits would perhaps rank with those of a Naval Mission—would be a select stud of the peerless descendants of Denmark for which Kentucky is so justly famed. American Saddle Horse sires crossed on their best gaited mares would soon give Brazil a breed of saddlers that would make the heart of the fazendeiro leap with joy. Which reminds me that when gaited mares are found in Brazil, it represents inheritance and not training as a rule; for mares are never ridden or worked if a Brazilian can get a stallion or a gelding, a prejudice inherited from warriors of old.

The bits used for handling this very mild mannered horse in Brazil are nothing short of atrocities. Blunt says that "the Bedouin never uses a bit or bridle of any sort, but instead a halter with a fine chain passing round the nose. With this he controls the mare easily and effectually." The Spaniard, on the contrary, has always had a predilection for curb bits that are the most vicious varieties of jaw-breakers, bits with a high, and sometimes sharp, port and long bars. Vigorously applied, they will cause an animal's mouth to bleed profusely. In addition to such curb bits, the Brazilian regularly uses a metal noseband with a sharp serrate edge. In the south this nosepiece is so rigged as to come into play whenever the curb is applied; in the northeast (Ceará at least) it is used with a double bridle as we use bit and bridoon, the snaffle reins in this case being fastened directly to the metal nosepiece. Such needlessly severe gear is not the mark of the highest type of horsemanship.

In another respect Brazil's horsemanship has lagged behind the rest of the world. In many parts of the interior horses are shod with a type of shoe which was common in the early centuries of the Christian era, a shoe entirely closed at the heel and with a very high heel-calk in addition so that the frog of the horse's foot has no bearing and degenerates.[4] The Brazilian cavalry and civilian riders in the larger cities use shoes which are open at the heel, however, and it cannot now be many decades before the better way will gain acceptance in the sertões, too.

Brazilian saddles are moderately heavy, padded affairs, with a pommel as wide as the cantle, frequently "ornamented" with silver or white metal. Next the animal's back they use felt or cotton pads, leather, or the skin of the wild pig with the bristles on. Over the seat, fastened by a surcingle, is spread a sheepskin (sometimes two) and a leather mantle. With this gear the rider is able to make a comfortable bed if night catches him on the road. Side-saddles, with a back like an armchair, are still used in the interior by Brazilian women, although over bad trails they are a positive menace to the rider as well as an abomination to the horse.

Only one unusual disease affecting horses in Brazil has come to my attention. The lowlands of Matto Grosso are afflicted with the *peste de cadeiras,* a disease whose nature has

[4] Ridgeway, op. cit., pictures similar ancient shoes, p. 503.

not yet been worked out, which deprives the animal of its ability to stand on the hind quarters.

It must be understood that while the foregoing describes the majority of Brazilian horses, it by no means describes them all—the traveler who visits only the cities would see neither such horses nor such gear. Rio Grande do Sul again has in this respect marched along with the civilization of Argentina and Uruguay, both of which breed as fine horses as any in the world; and Rio Grande owns a million and a half of Brazil's five million horses. She has several fine studs of Thoroughbreds; she breeds a fair type of heavy carriage horse; and her saddle animals are beginning to show more height and breeding than those in the rest of Brazil. Most of the best remounts in the Brazilian cavalry now come from Rio Grande do Sul, whereas formerly they were imported from Argentina. Racing is so popular in Rio de Janeiro that the Thoroughbred seems likely to play the same high rôle in Brazil that it has played in other lands. One breeder at least in São Paulo is making a beginning with Hackneys.

But aside from the studs of Thoroughbreds maintained for the race-track, one can count on the fingers of two hands the Brazilians who are maintaining notable studs of any of the other standard breeds. Heavy horses are unknown: in three years' travel I never saw one Suffolk, Clydesdale, Shire, Belgian, or Percheron. The Hunter is as rare as the giraffe. Nor has Brazil developed any breed of saddle, driving, or draft horse herself. The entire labor of traction and packing falls so nearly exclusively upon the mule that I shall speak of wheeled transport in connection with that animal "without pride of ancestry nor hope of posterity."

§ 3. Asses and Mules

When the day comes that the burden bearers of the world take rank beside parasites and politicians, the Mule should be handed a bunch of roses and an address from the throne.

Most of the functions which in the United States are insepa-
rably associated with carts and wagons, in Brazil are performed
by pack animals, as in medieval Europe. Pack trains are
an expensive form of transportation and one which strictly
limits the character of goods, but they have the advantage
of being able to go most anywhere. The pith and core of
Brazil's pack trains has been the mule. The United States
and Spain are the only countries which use more.

All the Brazilian mules that I have seen would be classed
on the St. Louis market as "Cotton Mules," that is, animals
standing from thirteen and a half to fifteen and a half hands
and weighing from 750 to 1100 pounds; most of them well
toward the lower range of the class. This follows from the
diminutive size of the mares as well as from the jacks used.
Many splendid jacks have been imported into Brazil from
Italy, Spain, and France; but I doubt if in the whole country
there is a single representative of the so-called American Jack,
some of which stand sixteen hands or over and weigh as much
as 1150 pounds; nor of the best class of North American mules,
which stand from 16-3 to 17-2 hands and weigh 1600 to 1700
pounds.[1]

A century and more ago the breeding center was Rio Grande
do Sul, and great bands of mules were driven from the southern
frontier to markets even north of the São Francisco River.
Today the center of production has shifted to Minas, São
Paulo, and Bahia which together breed over half the mules in
Brazil.

Inasmuch as packing plays so prominent a part in the
transportation system of the country, I cannot forbear a plea
for the patient mule. I stated above that I considered Brazilian pack saddles and packers the worst in the world. Let me
specify. Keeping an animal under a dead weight of 250
pounds or more day after day without lacerating his back is
one of the fine arts. It consists essentially in fitting a pro-
tective cover to the pack animal, in nicely balancing the two

[1] Vaughan, *Types and Market Classes of Live Stock*, p. 468.

sides of the load, and in throwing a hitch which will keep the load in place. Every one knows at least that the commonest hitch is the diamond. And every expert packer knows that the *aparejo* is the best device for keeping an animal's back in condition that has ever been invented. I have critically observed many hundreds of pack animals in Minas, Bahia, Rio Grande do Norte, and Ceará. *I never saw one aparejo nor any standard hitch!* Instead, such pack saddles as the primitive type pictured. And to lash a load, a half-inch rope thrown once around the mule and twisted with a stick until it nearly cuts the beast in two. It is the most extraordinary instance of utter degeneration of standard in a daily practiced art. I say degeneration, because the aparejo is an ancient Spanish rig, and good packers are found in Spain and Portugal and elsewhere in Latin America. (Needless to say, these strictures do not apply to the Brazilian Army.)

The mule has done not only the packing for Brazil, but most of the work in harness, too. That consists chiefly in hauling carts on the city streets and in dragging wagons through such country districts as Paraná and Rio Grande do Sul. Nowadays, to be sure, horses are displacing him in the last two regions, but the change is fairly recent; not infrequently one sees mixed teams. Now a team in those southern states means something different from anything I have seen elsewhere: a common hitch is a wheel pair with a postilion riding the near animal, and a lead team of five animals hitched side by side. These outfits of the Poles in Paraná and the seven-horse teams of Rio Grande are strongly reminiscent of the Conestoga wagons which before the days of railroads toted freight from Philadelphia across the Alleghenies to the Ohio Valley.

§ 4. Hogs

I compared the cattle industry in Brazil to the state of the industry in the United States in 1870. Her hogs are just

about where ours were in 1860. Before that time hogs were
self-starting and moved under their own power. Droves
ambled hundreds of miles to market. It took an athletic,
mirthful animal to go the pace, a hog with a flapper's temperament. A lard type could no more have entered those Mara-
thons than the crowd that ride around in wheeled chairs at
Atlantic City. By 1860 we no longer drove hogs any considerable distance, although we did not then, as we do now, escort
them to the railroad station in an automobile. From that
point we began to grow corn by machinery and to develop the
lard types, as well as the bacon.

In Brazil today, as with us then, a hog is a hog without
much palaver about breeds. But since the packing companies have established themselves, they, as well as the Federal Government, have been introducing new blood. Armour
and Company imported and raised at their fazendas over a
thousand head of pedigreed Poland China, Duroc-Jersey, and
Berkshire hogs which they sold at cost to Brazilian farmers
in order to improve the type. This process has hardly had
time to show its full effect, but already you see in São Paulo
and Paraná small droves of good hogs.

The future is very bright—if an animal destined to adorn
the table can be said to have a bright future. Brazil is
such a magnificent corn country that when they learn to grow
corn by machinery it should be a porcine paradise.

§ 5. SHEEP AND GOATS

Why Brazil ranks so low as a sheep herder I cannot say.
In the interior, there is so strong a prejudice against mutton
that many ignorant people cannot be induced to touch it.
There is nothing in the climate of much of Brazil that is
against sheep—the best wool in the world now comes from
the hot parts of Australia. Brazil is cursed with the screw
worm, to be sure; the slightest wound becomes infected and

the mortality is high; but that does not account for the prevailing prejudice against the animal and its meat.

Considerably over half the sheep in Brazil are in the southernmost state of Rio Grande do Sul. There they may be seen grazing in the same pastures with cattle, a practice that has nothing to commend it.

Most of the sheep north of Rio Grande, in Bahia and Pernambuco principally, have degenerated until they actually dress out fifteen to eighteen pounds, and the wool is simply a coarse hair.

Goats, on the other hand, do exceedingly well in the semiarid region from Bahia to Piauhy and Ceará, where they are plentiful enough to place Brazil fourth, after India, Turkey, and South Africa. This industry is capable of great expansion.

§ 6. The Camels of Ceará

I cannot conclude this account of Brazilian herds without mention of an abortive attempt at the introduction of the camel. Back in 1801, Dr. Camara, a botanist of distinguished talents, suggested that the semi-arid Northeast should prove as congenial a home for the camel and dromedary as Arabia and North Africa.[1] In 1859, ministers of the Imperial Government made a bid for the honor of introducing the animal. Fourteen dromedaries were imported from Argelia and set ashore at Fortaleza, although one died as soon as he looked upon his future home. The thirteen were kept in the capital as long as they gave the fashionable world an excuse for a *passeio elegante,* and then banished to the interior.

It will be remembered how Cyrus the Persian, when the cavalry of Croesus seemed about to overwhelm him, stampeded the horses of the Lydians by the simple expedient of putting his camels out front. Similar was the consternation in the

[1] Southey, *History of Brazil,* III, 790.

sertão. Pack trains and pacers were scattered promiscuously all the way from Fortaleza to Quixeramobim.

It is related that the dromedaries produced several little ones. Each time this happened, a new governor was inaugurated with more than oriental splendor, to furnish an occasion for exhibiting the sisters of the sand. But the formalism of Fortaleza saddened them, and the drinking they witnessed in the sertão shocked them, and at the end of seven years only four were left.

CHAPTER X

MINERAL EXPLOITATION

THE whimsical forces which reveal a nugget here and a vein there, have shown Brazil to be possessed of her full share of mineral wealth. In iron, Brazil is second to none. Branner says the high-grade iron ores of Minas Geraes are the most important in the world.[1] The coal to smelt it, chiefly in Santa Catharina, is of somewhat low grade and far away; however, recent investigations indicate that Brazilian coal by special methods can be utilized for a good quality of metallurgical coke. Oil-bearing shales have long been known. Brazil possesses the largest deposite of manganese in South America, Bahia and Minas being particularly rich. Good mica is scattered all over central Brazil. The monazite sands concentrated by the sea on the beaches of Bahia and Espirito Santo constitute the world's chief source of thorium salts and zirconium. The Bahia chrome-bearing district is the only one of importance known in South America.[2] Mineralogists have claimed that the porcelain clay near Ouro Preto, in Minas, is equal to that of Sèvres. There are many such riches in the Archean rocks of Brazil which have not yet been developed commercially.

The exploitation of this wealth, however, has not yet assumed dimensions of much importance to the Brazilian people. Transportation difficulties have thus far prevented the utilization of Brazil's reserves of iron. The first small all-electric plant making steel from iron ore by the Swedish type of electric pig-iron furnace, began producing at Riberão Preto,

[1] Branner, *Geologia Elementar*, p. 293.
[2] J. E. Spurr, *Political and Commercial Geology* and *The World's Mineral Resources*, see index under Brazil.

in São Paulo, in 1923.[3] This may mark the beginning of great things, but as yet the only mineral wealth that has profoundly affected the life of Brazil is gold and diamonds. With these I dealt in Chapter IV.

[3] See *Bulletin* of the Pan-American Union, Nov., 1923.

CHAPTER XI

THE DENIAL OF LIFE

WHILE man undoubtedly possesses the power to visit irreparable injury upon the human race by a shortsighted exploitation of the world's mineral wealth, he has it easily within his power to make the world utterly unhabitable for himself and the higher forms by the mishandling of life.

Life is a unit upon this globe. It is a fabric of interwoven forces—forces of primal power comparable to light, gravity, the surge of the tide. Among them is a very even balance. Many are the forces in life capable of overwhelming, dominating, devastating the earth through the very plethora of their fecundity, were they not kept in check by the counterpoise of their natural antagonists. While it seems at first glance but a mad game of dog eat dog, the participants have been selected by a process that has been going on for millions of years, and which has resulted in a structure of complexity unparalleled by anything within the cognizance of man.

Into this mechanism, incomparably more delicate than any machine, man has not the slightest hesitancy in throwing a monkey wrench for the sheer joy of hearing the crash. It may be said that man is as much a part of Nature as the monkey, and that any act of his, no matter how subversive of his ultimate interest, is as much a part of the scheme of things as the unthinking foraging and reproducing of the lesser life. From another point of view, however, man has made himself little less than a god and has to a large degree substituted his fiat for the evolutionary process which produced him.

I suppose since the World War there remain few people who think it is as easy to get ten million men back into the social complex as it is to pull them out and set them at each other's throats. But in the world at large, how many are there who ever think how much harder it is to grow a forest than to destroy it? how many who deem the extermination of a species a catastrophe? How many realize that man is decreeing what forms of life shall continue to live in the ocean and walk beside him on the land without giving the slightest heed to the consequences five hundred years from now? Who, besides German foresters, ever laid concrete plans five hundred years ahead? And yet that represents but four generations of a northern forest, and but seventeen generations of man.

We should distinguish sharply between two modes of making a levy upon the world's raw materials without thought of restitution. Where Nature provides for the indefinite reproduction of any form of life, we cannot speak of devastation, no matter how violent man's attack. But when his attack ends in want for himself or in extinction for other forms of life, then we have cause for grave social concern and can look forward confidently to catastrophe after catastrophe.

While primitive peoples must share with civilized man responsibility in this respect, it is the latter, with the splendor of his industrial technique, who is incomparably more "efficient." We consider ourselves highly civilized in the United States, yet Professor Giddings hardly exaggerated when he wrote apropos of this matter: "For three hundred years we have been a herd of wild asses in the wilderness." So it will surprise no one to learn that Brazilians, in their way, have at times acted like wild asses, too.

§ 1. Plant Devastation

Aside from the devastation of an agriculture which permanently attacks the fertility of the soil, the chief mode of plant devastation evident in Brazil is the ravaging of the forests by fire. Three-tenths of the forests existent in 1500 have disappeared, according to the Brazilian Geological Survey.

Those of Rio Grande do Sul have been reduced by one-half. It is certain that half the primitive forests of São Paulo are gone. In so far as that means a conversion to agriculture and planted pastures it is a great social gain; the large areas which today are covered with a worthless second growth are a total loss. The coastal forest that once margined the sea from Cape São Roque to the Rio São Francisco is no more. Gone are the green mantles from the mountain tops of Ceará and the dry Northeast. Fifty-eight per cent of Brazil was forested in 1500; forty per cent only in 1910. Not utilized, burnt at the stake! For the timber which has been used by man in Brazil is not a ten-thousandth part of that burned. So it is pertinent to inquire into the manner of the burning.

Forest fires may occur as natural cataclysms without the agency of man in certain rather narrow zones. In Paraná pine interspersed with clumps of bamboo, where the ground is littered with resinous knots, it is conceivable that after an unusually dry season a forest fire might start from a flash of lightning; and the same is true of the dry caatingas. In Matto Grosso the years from 1744 to 1749 are said to have been so dry that the forests about Cuyabá took fire.[1] As a matter of fact, however, outside of the caatingas, fires which are not man-made occur so rarely that they may be entirely disregarded. In the evergreen hardwood forest they never occur.

Yet if one could hover over Brazil in a balloon and get a bird's-eye view of forest after forest as each comes to the end of its dry season, he would see myriad smokes curl heavenward year after year, and century after century. Farming by fire—shifting agriculture—is as much the mode of life of the nomads of the Brazilian forests as of the Fangs of the Congo. It was pointed out in a previous chapter how the people always have considered the forests as a communal possession which they felt free to hack, burn, and abandon at will. It takes but an easy act of sympathetic imagination to

[1] Southey, *History of Brazil*, III, 360.

understand how this interminable green monster that shuts out the sun of heaven should appear to unthinking folk as a veritable enemy, a trap ever ready to snap its jaws and entomb them, an insidious thing that creeps up in the night and overruns his garden while he sleeps. Destroy it!

And with a certain amount of truth we can say that the reproductive capacity of the evergreen forest is so intense that it is not within the power of such puny enemies to destroy. That needs some qualification, however, even in the Amazon, as the devastated forest region between the Rio Gaumá and the coast proves.[2] If the hole in the jungle is small, as most of the plantations of shifting agriculture are, two years generally suffices to produce a growth which will drive the nomad to the labor of felling another patch of timber. Return in ten years and look down upon the old clearing from a height. It will look like a forest, but the different color of the foliage easily identifies the spot. The species are not the same. Descend and try to enter, and you still encounter on the ground the prostrate trunks of the former forest giants, rotting to be sure, yet able to block your passage. Above them is growing the nastiest tangle of weeds and vines imaginable, with trees reaching above them. Very few of these new trees will be of the economic species destroyed. Just as in the region of the Great Lakes in the United States, cherries, birches, and other worthless species follow fire, so in Brazil. It easily will require a hundred years before the damage done by man to obtain two meager crops of manioc and corn can be repaired by Nature and the old clearing reclaimed by the forest. Sometimes, as we shall see, the damage is permanent. Not infrequently the abandoned clearing is taken possession of, not by any type of forest growth, but by a fern (*samambaia*) which is tremendously difficult to eradicate—a veritable pest.

It is only when you consider the sum total of this hacking away at the forest that the problem assumes serious importance. Mr. Hugh Curran, who for many years managed a

---

[2] *Mappa Florestal*, Brazilian Geological Survey, pp. 76-77.

The burden bearers of Brazil.   (See page 277.)

The bull carts in the sertão are generally drawn by from six to ten oxen.
(See page 227.)

Good lard-type hogs are beginning to be seen in central Brazil. (See page 280.)

The little asses, burros, are used in Brazil as water carriers and more rarely for wheeled transport.

70,000-acre forest property in Bahia in which there were
several hundred nomadic squatters, believes that shifting
agriculture destroys one acre per year for each inhabitant
who gains his living that way.   Perhaps between two and
three million is a fair figure for the number of these forest
nomads in Brazil.   At 5,000 board feet per acre, which is a
low average for the class of forest they operate in, that
represents an annual burning of ten billion board feet—nearly
as much hardwood as the United States uses.

Now and again these fires started by man do not stop where
he wishes.

Beyond [says Gardner], a higher chain of mountains exists called
Itacolumi [in Minas Geraes]. . . . This range was once covered
by forests, which about forty years ago [i.e., in 1800] were acci-
dentally destroyed by fire.[3]

If I am rightly informed, that forest on Itacolumi has not
returned yet.

Where Brazil is heading in this matter can best be seen
in the State of Minas Geraes.   Its seven million people make
it the most populous state in the Union.   Although most of
the prospecting was in the campo region, the miners of the
eighteenth century gold rush quickly made cinders of the
considerable bodies of timber which originally grew northwest of the Mantiqueira.

Timber [in Diamantina] was brought ten or twelve leagues and
fuel, in the year 1799, was as dear as at Lisbon, where it used to
be cheaper to consume pit-coal from England, than the wood which
grew within sight of the city, in the pine-forests of Alem-Tejo.
This inconvenience began to be felt in all the most populous part
of Minas Geraes; it was occasioned by the wanton manner in
which the woods had been destroyed: a farmer made no scruple of
setting fire to them and laying waste a track of ten or twelve miles
round his miserable plantation.[4]

[3] *Travels in the Interior of Brazil*, p. 484.
[4] Southey, *History of Brazil*, III, 825.

As early as 1735, the evil was so crying that Gomes Freyre de Andrada, a great governor, saw the permanent prosperity of the mines threatened and did his best to put a stop to it. His efforts were in vain. When I was in the capital of Minas in 1920, one could buy Austrian fir and spruce from Norway in the lumber yards, but one could hardly find a stick of Brazilian timber. Unless he were a millionaire, however, he would not buy much of either.

Lumber is one commodity that should be so cheap in Brazil that no individual would have difficulty in supplying his needs. That presupposes a forest near the market. It does Brazil small good to know that she has untold reserves of timber in the Amazon, if that near her centers of population is gone. It might as well be in the moon. As a matter of fact, Louisiana, Norway, and Austria are today economically nearer to Bello Horizonte, the capital of Minas Geraes, than the superb forests of the Rio Doce—in Minas Geraes. And instead of lumber being a cheap commodity which all may enjoy, Brazilians, living in the most heavily forested country on the globe, pay more for their lumber than do sheep men in the deserts of Australia.

I can not get excited about the devastation due to hacking away at rubber trees, or an Indian's cutting down a forest giant to obtain a gourdful of honey, or even the felling of a tree a hundred and fifty feet high to get a few bushels of paradise nuts for the New York market. But in shifting agriculture Brazil has a problem with which, in self-protection, she has got to deal.

§ 2. ANIMAL DESTRUCTION

Hunting is not easy in the Brazilian forests. Where the going is so thick that you have to get within forty or fifty yards to see your game, or where birds perch on the roof of a tree from a hundred to a hundred and fifty feet above your head, neither mammals nor birds are in serious danger of extinction. To my knowledge, the only Brazilian bird whose numbers have been seriously diminished by man is the delicate, snowy egret—thank the ladies! I recall but a single Brazilian mammal remotely threatened with extinction. It is chiefly among the inhabitants of the waters that man's attack upon the animal world has been somewhat ill advised.

Brazilian waters, both fresh and salt, are very rich in turtles. Deposition of eggs is with them a herd phenomenon; the great fresh-water turtles of the Amazon make of it an annual social function. In the shallow waters near their favorite sand bar, the turtles for twenty miles about forgather like Baptists at a camp meeting. When the constellations are auspicious, forth they creep from the murky waters in countless swarms. Bates says several turtles will deposit in the same hole, each laying from one hundred to one hundred and fifty eggs, so that in one nest there may be four or five hundred eggs. And at the end of a fortnight, the sand bar is dotted with these nests, easily located by a man prodding with a stick. For weeks before this occurs, the villages have had their sentinels watching. When it is over, whole villages descend upon the bar and make a holiday and a feast, while converting the eggs into turtle butter. Add to this the great numbers of mature turtles caught and shot in shallow pools when the Amazon floods abate, and those killed to obtain the much prized ovarian eggs, and it will readily be seen that this constitutes an attack so violent in method as to threaten the species. There has been a notable diminution in the number of Amazon turtles in the last fifty years. If the very meager population of Amazonas has accomplished this, it takes no prophet to foretell the passing of turtle meat as a staple article of food on the Amazon menu if the day ever comes when a moderately dense population takes up residence there.[1]

The same entire disregard of the elementary truth that

[1] For descriptions of the modes of turtle destruction, see Bates, *The Naturalist on the Amazons* (1884 ed.), 285-87; and on marine turtles, Hartt, *Geology and Physical Geography of Brazil* (Boston, 1870), pp. 107-112.

society is a continuing concern and that our descendants will have to depend upon the same sources for the raw materials of life a thousand years hence, may be seen in every fish-market in Brazil. I refer to the destruction of young fishes. Extreme youth is as critical a time in the life of a fish as in the life of a mammalian biped. As a rule, all animals put on weight very rapidly from birth to adolescence; then comes a time when it no longer is economic to prolong the life of an animal destined for human consumption. Tropical conditions the world over tend to the utilization of small fish which have not yet passed the period of rapid growth. Fish is fish to some tastes, and it is a matter of indifference if the pound be made up of one adult or of fifty small fry seined in shallow water.

On this point we have some very expert testimony, that of Prof. G. W. Field, who was called by the Brazilian Government in 1920 to advise in the matter of fish policy. No contemporary name carries more weight among men who go down to the sea in ships to gather the harvest of the waters.

It requires but a little fair thinking and economic honesty on the part of the fishermen and of the public [writes Prof. Field] to realize the destructive effect of killing both the young and the breeding adults of any species. Yet this is being done to practically every species of fish in Brazil which is of any food value to man. This practice is comparable to using week-old chickens for market, thus requiring an excessive number of individuals to secure the required weight. Such practices added to the destruction of mature fishes are an excessive burden upon the species, and if extended persistently will result in serious upsets of the balance of nature, and increased scarcity and cost of the most desirable species for market.[2]

Another mode of animal destruction in Brazil is the excessive netting of the herring family, sardines, anchovies, and the like. In Brazilian waters, unlike those of our Atlantic coast, the surface feeders are economically more important than the

[2] From a letter to the Almirante Inspector de Portos e Costas, Rio de Janeiro, October 1, 1920.

"ground fish." Surface feeders like the mackerel—a family large and important in Brazil—bluefish, and others particuarly prized, are just as fond of the little herring tribe as is man. The big fish follow the food on which they prey, and it is obviously to nobody's interest to drive them away from the big markets by destroying the only thing that makes such localities attractive to a handsome fish.

While items like turtle and fish that menace to some degree the future menu of Brazil are the modes of animal destruction which really matter, a sentimental scientist might here point out that the killing of Indian males in the institution of slavery went far toward the extinction of one characteristic Brazilian mammal, and that there are a few localities where the closed season on this kind of game is not yet rigorously enforced.

Book III
SOME ESSENTIALS OF HUMAN HAPPINESS

CHAPTER XII

FREEDOM IN TRADE

THE round world spins upon its axis toward the east; and trade winds brush against our faces, going west. And whatsoever bark, nautilus or seven-master, signals by spreading sail, the trade winds sweep along. Messengers of mercy are they, bearing cool drink to sun-parched lands. Watchmen of the night warning mosquitoes from fever-stricken coast, bestowing the priceless boon of sleep upon men tossing on a torrid couch. Bearers of greetings from the black folk of West Africa unto the brown folk of America, from Incas and Aztecs unto the yellow folk of Asia, from the spicery of the Indies unto Africa looking east. A beneficent breath is the trade wind.

No less beneficent are the winds and currents of trade. Long lines of camels laden with silk brought the wisdom of ancient Asia through the Tarim Basin and Samarkand unto Damascus and imperial Rome. Caravans freighted with ivory carried the greetings of Negroland to the brunet folk of the Mediterranean and returned proudly bearing Christ and Muhammad. Caravels of commerce swarmed back and forth across the oceans until Lima became a suburb of Madrid, and Manila the neighbor of Panama. An empty Standard Oil can is a bond uniting rice growers of Malay paddies with cacao growers of Bahia and men gleaning fruit from the oil palms of darkest Africa. What a tremendous fertilizing influence is the contact of peoples who differ, each of which in the fullness of time has worked out a different way of molding the same material! Each scorns the other and deems his own way best, yet from the shock of contact inevitably each absorbs from the other, and in the long run there is born a single better. The patriot with all his passion desires to see his own country strong and rich and all the world else weak and poor; but the trader desires that all men shall be rich, for from international riches flow his wealth and well being. A beneficent breath is the wind of trade.

Neither the one nor the other was intended to serve the selfish schemes of monopoly. Trade serves its largest function as a current free-flowing like the trade wind. Where man has laid his hand upon it with least violence, as in the British Empire, trade has worked its worthiest results. The States from Maine to California are *United*, because over that whole sweep of land surface there is no economic frontier; no one of the forty-eight is permitted to erect a trade barrier between itself and any other. The states between Cork and Constantinople are disunited and at one another's throats, because within that area there are a dozen economic frontiers. Each nation "protects" itself against the beneficent breath as assiduously as a Dakota farmer protects himself against optimum health by shutting tight every window that might admit fresh air into his sleeping quarters. Protectionism is a chief obstacle to terrestrial unity, a spur upon the heels of hard-riding statesmen which ever goads the nags called nations from the easy gaits that get over the ground of life comfortably into that mad steeplechase named war.

To the governing class of the Portuguese-speaking world, trade has always been a fat cow pastured without permit by a neatherd who must milk her for their benefit every time she steps over the bars of a corral. In their view, a statesman's concern with trade should be: Into how many corrals can one drive the beast without drying up her udder? The early kings of Portugal told the Jews they might trade with their blessing so long as they supplied the court with pocket money and enabled it to deal high-handedly with the landed nobility. When Portugal became a vast colonial empire, an absolute trade monopoly was their slogan, their ideal, and the thing for which they fought.

The hampering of Brazilian commerce began with Manoel's sixteenth century order that all the spice plants in Brazil should be rooted up, lest the trade with India be injured. Although tropical nature makes such an order meaningless, it sufficiently illustrates the economic temper of the sixteenth century. In the seventeenth, the Dutch smashed the Portuguese monopoly by force and by the peace of 1661 insisted upon their right to continue trading with Brazil. The English won similar privileges by the marriage treaty of Charles the Second. Both suffered their rights to fall into disuse. The considerable trade which developed spontaneously between the Rio de la Plata and Rio de Janeiro was by common consent of the kings of Spain and Portugal throttled, in 1693. And the moment gold production assumed proportions in the early eighteenth century, the gates were shut against all foreigners just as tightly as the power of Portugal permitted; in direct breach of treaty, the Portuguese denied the Dutch their right to trade with Brazil and confiscated their ships if they tried.

Governmental trade monopoly bred, as a protest, that splendid brood of buccaneers who made piracy as honorable a profession in the century of Drake as banking is in the century of Morgan and Stillman. Scenting the perfume of yellow gold as humming-birds scent the fragrance of flowers, the brotherhood of the black flag infested Brazilian waters so thickly that Portugal, in the first decade of the eighteenth century, imposed a ten-per-cent duty upon all imports into Brazil to defray operations against the freebooting fraternity; but history does not record that Portuguese prophylaxis against piracy ever took effect. The necessity for annual fleets continued until Mazagam, the last Portuguese stronghold in North Africa, fell to the Moors of Morocco in 1765. With the termination of the long war against the Moors, Pombal felt that the Barbary cruisers would now follow the Pirates and the Buccaneers into retirement; and decreed that as soon as the fleets from Rio and Bahia returned, trade with those ports might be carried on by single ships.[1] Provided they were Portuguese ships. For even the enlightened Pombal, according to a British diplomat of his day, held, "Trade in order to be prosperous should not be free."

The Carta Regia of 18 February, 1808, which opened the ports of Brazil to foreigners and admitted Brazil to planetary society, should not be credited to the Portuguese ruling caste. It was an English inspiration pure and simple, forced down Portuguese throats at a moment when the destiny of Portugal lay in the hollow of England's hand; and the commercial treaty negotiated in Rio by Lord Strangford in February, 1810, actually gave the English flag greater privileges in the ports of Portugal and her possessions than the Portuguese flag itself.[2]

If foreign commerce was shackled in colonial Brazil, internal trade wore hobbles no less galling. In a vain effort to limit smuggling to gentlemanly proportions, the gold-producing regions were fenced round with every restriction known to government. One could go from Minas to Bahia to buy cattle, but if he wanted to return with a piano or a slave he was obliged to make a journey of a thousand miles or so and come in by way of Rio de Janeiro.

A drover from Rio Grande do Sul who sold mules in the north had about as comfortable a time as a man who tries to get into a war cantonment after midnight. At every provincial frontier he was met by the challenge:

"Halt! who goes there?"

"A man with a mule."

"Advance, man, and pay for the mule," was the economic formula.

A century ago one could buy a good mule in Rio Grande do Sul for from one to two milreis. A tax of one milreis was

---

[1] Southey, III, 589.
[2] Spix and Martius, I, 180.

paid at a registry in that province; three and one-half were paid at Sorocaba, in São Paulo; and Minas clapped on a third equal to the other two. So a mule destined for Matto Grosso or Goyaz had paid about eight times its purchase price in internal taxes before it reached the frontiers of its destination.[3]

That system has come down without change into the twentieth century. Brazil is no more an economic unit in 1926 than it was two hundred years ago. Each state has the right to help itself out of every bag of manioc and cut a steak from every steer that enters from another state, and the right is exercised with formidable ferocity. I cannot forget that it cost me fifteen milreis to "import" from Espirito Santo into Minas Geraes a gunny-sack containing a saddle used two years in the army, a pair of ancient boots, and my old, gray riding breeches. God pity the interstate junk dealers in Brazil![4]

Another medieval economic fallacy which Brazil still defends is high *export duties* levied by the individual states and therefore differing on the same commodity in different parts of the Republic. Take cacao, for instance, a forest plantation product I happen to have studied in some detail. There are many indications that the natural factors are so favorable in the State of Bahia for cacao production that she can produce chocolate more cheaply than the Gold Coast, Ceylon, Java, or the Caribbean chocolate centers. Instead of using this God-given vantage to advance Bahia to the same rank in the cacao market that São Paulo has won in coffee, her politicians,

---

[3] Southey, III, 854.
[4] Compare the wail of Alfred Russel Wallace in the days of the Empire: "Though in a small boat, and going up a river in the same province, we were not allowed to leave Pará without passports and clearances from the custom-house, and as much difficulty and delay as if we had been taking a two-hundred-ton ship into a foreign country. But such is the rule here even the internal trade of the province, carried on by Brazilian subjects, not being exempt from it. The forms to be filled up, the signing and countersigning at different offices, the applications to be made and formalities to be observed, are so numerous and complicated, that it is quite impossible for a stranger to go through them; and had not Mr. Leavens managed all this part of the business, we should probably have been obliged, from this cause alone, to have given up our projected journey." *Travels on the Amazon and Rio Negro* (New York, 1889), p. 36.

municipal and state, clap on export taxes which total more than twenty per cent of the São Salvador export price—and hand over primacy in quantity production to Accrá, on the Gold Coast. Many of the superb advantages which Nature has conferred upon Brazil are thrown away by her politicians; and much foreign capital which would otherwise seek investment there is deterred by the too well justified fear that the moment a new industry becomes flourishing, it will be taxed out of existence by statesmen who seem determined that their country shall not become a great producer.

It is unbelievable to what absurdities a thoroughgoing theory of trade restriction can lead. Rubber is perhaps the most typical of all Brazilian products: *Hevea Braziliensis,* but little over half a century ago, was unknown outside of the Amazon evergreen forest. An English collector took out some seeds which were coddled by the Kew Gardens, transplanted to Calcutta, cultivated and guarded until the plants became mature trees and in turn produced seeds which enabled the British to build up their rubber plantations in the Orient and wreck the Amazon wild rubber industry. The only way to combat such competition that occurred to Pará was to forbid the export of rubber seeds—locking the door after the horse had been stolen—a prohibition as absurd and as impossible of enforcement as Manoel's order to extirpate all the spice plants in Brazil. Three years ago a North American forester wanted to experiment with rubber in Bahia, and tried to obtain some seeds from Pará. There he was met by the old governmental prohibition and actually had to smuggle rubber seeds with the connivance of a friendly scientist, in order to get them from one Brazilian state to another.

If plantation rubber is cheaper than wild rubber, obviously the only way for Brazil to combat the cultivated product of the Orient is to establish plantations in the original habitat of *Hevea.* At present, the only practicable way to accomplish this is to set conditions sufficiently inviting to attract the foreign capitalists who dominate the crude rubber industry, chiefly British, Dutch, and North American. There is a classic case which throws light on one reason why the old home of rubber does not possess a single commercial plantation of any size, while the South Sea Islands and Malay Peninsula are reducing Brazil's wild rubber industry to insignificance. The "Guimaraes Claim" was the subject of negotiations between the State Department of the United States and the Government of Brazil for so many years that the outstanding facts are not questioned by either government. Briefly, they are these:

In 1905, while Barros was president of Matto Grosso, a North American company which has since become a dominant factor in the plantations of Sumatra and the Malay Peninsula, the General Rubber Company (working through a citizen of the United States named Guimaraes and the American Commerce Company), obtained a twenty-year concession to work the native rubber and exploit generally the forests "situated on the right bank of the Juruena River, tributary to the Tapajós River, and also on the banks of the tributaries of the said bank of the Juruena River, from its principal source down to its junction with the Arinos River." Both of these main branches of the Tapajós have been known to Brazilian explorers and geographers since the days of gold in Matto Grosso, nearly two hundred years. Something like 33,000 square miles of howling wilderness was involved, and the company had the option of purchase. (I am not here concerned with the wisdom of a government which would grant a concession of such dimensions, nor with the wisdom of a company which would expect such a government to keep any kind of contract.) The fact of chief interest to Brazilian industry was that one of the greatest of the North American rubber companies, amply able to finance and put through operations of tremendous scope, decided to embark upon large-scale production in Brazil. Success in the venture of exploiting wild rubber would, very probably, have led them to locate their plantations in the same country.

The year after their concession was granted, one Colonel Ponce headed a successful revolution and "elected" himself president of the State of Matto Grosso by methods which unfortunately are still fashionable in the more backward Brazilian states. Barros was assassinated in July, 1906. Within a month thereafter, applications were filed by Colonel Ponce and Americo Vieira for the purchase of two extensive tracts of public lands on the banks of the Cravary River, a stream which was within the concession of the General Rubber Company. Pending the assumption of presidential privileges by Ponce, his partner, Vieira, proceeded to drive out the crews and cattle of the company. It was a not unusual frontier affair of Winchesters, threats of death, beatings with the flat of a facão, the doing to death of a foreman in a foul prison, and an amusing injunction issued by a local court, enjoining *"perpetual silence"* concerning the whole affair.

What was a trifle unusual was the rewriting of the geography of Matto Grosso by Ponce as soon as he became president. By the simple device of interchanging the names "Juruena" and "Sangue" on the map, he lopped off three-fourths of the General Rubber concession. The effect will be at once apparent to North American readers by transferring the case to more familiar territory: suppose a concession included all that part of Iowa between the Mississippi and the Des Moines River; if a governor of Iowa came along and proclaimed officially that the Cedar River is the Des Moines, it will be evident that the concessionaire would lose a very handsome portion of prairie. Ponce has long been dead, and the Federal Government long since returned the old names to the old rivers—but it is also long since the vast capital the General Rubber Company devotes to producing rubber was invested in the Orient instead of in Brazil.

Import duties are levied by the Federal Government and at least have the merit of uniformity throughout Brazil. She is committed to a policy of high tariffs. Her petty officials are committed to a policy of fines, part of which they receive

Acres of brick and concrete floors where the coffee berries are dried in the sun. (See page 236.)

The flumes of concrete where berries are washed when the coffee comes from the field. (See page 236.)

This primitive sugar press is characteristic of the tools and machinery found on the poorer farms of Brazil. (See page 242.)

Opening cacao pods. Cacao is the great crop of the state of Bahia. (See page 238.)

to help out their small salaries; and foreigners, at least, complain bitterly of custom-house abuses.

In fine, to a foreign observer it looks as though officialdom were pulling too hard and too often at the teats of trade; the old cow's udder is in danger of drying up. Free-flowing the currents of trade in Brazil are not and of large dimensions they never will be, until government learns to keep meddling hands off and comes to a realization that a small tax upon enormous volume yields vastly greater revenue than heavy imposts upon an insignificant commerce.

CHAPTER XIII

DOMESTIC RELATIONS

The androcentric theory is the view that the male sex is primary and the female secondary in the organic scheme, that all things center about the male, and that the female, though necessary in carrying out the scheme, is only the means of continuing the life of the globe, but is otherwise an unimportant accessory, an incidental factor in the general result. . . .
LESTER F. WARD, *Pure Sociology.*

WITH that, I feel sure, few Brazilian men can find it in their hearts to disagree. Although Professor Ward devoted the next fifty or sixty pages to demolishing the androcentric theory, in one of the most brilliant and profound appreciations ever penned of the position of the female in the biologic scheme, Brazilians apparently never read beyond the paragraph quoted above. For there is no social soil in the world where that efflorescence of the masculine mind produces sprouts of more imposing dimensions, exhibits gaudier petals, or exhales a ranker perfume.

The Brazilian variety is a botanical specimen worth dissecting. For of factors which contribute to that fugitive commodity, human happiness, right relations between the sexes claim consideration second to none. One cannot consecrate his pen to a discussion of a more solemn or fundamental theme. The continuance and quality of the race is involved. The dignity of half of humanity and the renunciation of despotism by the other half is implicit. The relations between the sexes which prevail in Brazil in this third decade of the twentieth century are more easily understood if their origins are recognized. Modern Brazilians have contributed less to the actual practice of marital relations than the Moors. Except for that numerically insignificant fringe of ultramoderns saturated with European culture, most phases of family life in Brazil are survivals of ancient folkways. To these I shall devote attention first.

As with most Brazilian institutions, all three of the chief ethnic elements contributed mutually modifying ideals. Most Indians placed small value upon virginity and abhorred celibacy; both sexes regularly discarded the first upon attaining maturity and avoided the second by marriage within a year or two thereafter. In certain tribes the medicine men upheld a tradition of virgin brides, because the *jus primae noctis* pertained to the *pajé*. But the prevalence of the practice of lending a wife to a guest indicates scant respect for theories embodied in the Christian code. Polygyny was a perquisite of chiefs, medicine men, and the upper classes generally; and was often welcomed by the women as partial relief from intolerable burdens of manual labor. Neither birth control nor the destruction of infants was unknown. Marriage by service, marriage by consideration, marriage by exchange, and in some tribes an actual commerce in young women does not indicate that romantic love had dawned in Brazil previous to the year 1500.[1]

Negroes, drawn from widely distant parts of Africa, brought with them the whole gamut of primitive domestic arrangements, from full liberty before marriage to the strictest kind of monogamy. Polygyny was as common with the Negroes as with the Brazilian Indians.

Neither Negroes nor Indians had injected much idealism into natural love. Neither regarded marriage as indissoluble. Both lived under androcentric systems, treating woman as a beast of burden with no rights over her own person, her progeny, or the product of her labor.

The Portuguese brought to Brazil a modified Roman Catholic code of domestic relations and superimposed it upon the savage systems of the other two. In some ways it was an advance. Until the Church became the dominant power in

---

[1] Westermarck, *The History of Human Marriage* (5th ed.; New York, 1922), I, 193, 225, 535; II, 230, 360, 367, 378; III, 87.

Europe, the position of woman there was little better than in Africa or aboriginal Brazil; her status was but slightly more dignified than that of a chattel slave. Clearly foreseeing the tremendous accretion of power which would accrue by assuming cognizance of marriage and determining the numberless questions pertaining thereto, the Church decreed that man should content himself with one wife and bind himself to her and their issue by an indissoluble bond; and was rewarded by an intense devotion from the class whose status she thus dignified. At the same time, by excluding women from the priesthood and all except the imperial post in government, the Church fixed a domestic régime of unrestricted childbearing or the avowal of perpetual chastity and life in a convent as the horns of the feminine dilemma. To the latter condition a fictitious value was affixed which it had never before possessed. "I praise the married state," said St. Jerome, "but chiefly for this, that it provides virgins." Even the clergy finally found it advantageous to impose upon themselves a formal celibacy.

The three great Roman Catholic ideals, then, which were squarely opposed to the African and Indian codes of sex relations were monogamy, the indissolubility of marriage, and a celibate priesthood.

I said the Portuguese brought to Brazil a *modified* Roman Catholic code. What were the modifications which the Portuguese brought to Brazil? The first was the example set by many of those solemnly consecrated to its defense. There was a long period of European history when it was the rule, rather than the exception, for the Catholic clergy to live with "subintroduced" women who passed as sisters of the priests and by whom they had natural children without creating any extraordinary scandal.

The second modification was the inevitable coloring of the Catholic concept of marriage in Spain and Portugal by the five hundred years of Moorish occupation. Muhammad categorically denied the superlative value of chastity. Instead of glorifying asceticism and virginity, he sang the praises of polygyny, enjoining its practice upon the Faithful in this life and promising unlimited means for its enjoyment in the next. In the confused mind of many a Portuguese Catholic, the Christian concept of Paradise became blended with the Muhammadan—to arise from the dead, naked and unashamed, and find a winged white camel with a saddle of gold awaiting; to pass unscathed over the swordlike bridge of Al-Sirat, and drink of happiness at the waters of Al-Cawthor; to sink on the soil of musk beside a river flowing over pebbles of rubies and emeralds, there to await the Houris of unfading youth who from their tents of hollow pearls will come forth to greet you, bearing in their own lovely persons the seductive sweetness of eternal felicity. For five hundred years the Portuguese forebears of modern Brazilians were ruled by swarthy princes who lived in the hope of such a colorful hereafter and who basked in the luxurious voluptuousness of an equally colorful present, in whose seraglios many a Christian maid found a delightful retreat. Is it strange that the austerities of the Catholic concept of indissoluble monogamy suffered certain practical modifications from which it has never quite recovered in Spanish- and Portuguese-speaking countries?

A third powerful force making for practical modification of the Catholic code was the public example of the most illustrious kings and fidalgos of Portugal. For one who knows Portuguese history, it is enough to call the roll of her most noble dead. The beautiful and talented mother of that first King of Portugal, whom time has magnified to almost godlike proportions, was Theresa, the illegitimate daughter of Alfonso VI. The treaty of Windsor ratified by Henry IV in 1403 was sealed by the marriage of the illegitimate daughter of João I of Portugal by Ines Pires. Turn over a century or two and read on:

To the surprise of Philip, another competitor for the crown—Dom Antonio, the Prior of Crato—declared himself king at Santarem. . . . This Dom Antonio was the son of Dom Luis, Duke of Beja, the second son of Emmanuel "The Fortunate," by Violante de

Gomes, surnamed "the Pelican," one of the most beautiful women of her time.   Dom Antonio alleged that his father was secretly married to his mother, and reminded the people, in a proclamation, that, even if the marriage were not legal, one of the greatest of all the kings of Portugal, the victor of Aljubarrota, was a bastard also.[2]

And the lovely lady whose story has been sung in a thousand songs, Ines de Castro: she was the lady-in-waiting to Pedro's bride before she became Pedro's mistress—that Pedro who sired one king of Portugal by his legal wife, who sired another king of Portugal by Theresa Lourenço, and who, after he ascended the throne, disinterred the bones of his murdered mistress and had them solemnly crowned Queen of Portugal in the Convent of Alcobaça.   Whoever knows his Portuguese history can fill pages with the names of illustrious Portuguese bastards, mistresses, and supernumerary wives—not to mention Portuguese patriarchs, metropolitans, archbishops, and bishops who have also been great lovers.   Weighty precedents, these, for domestic irregularities in twentieth century Brazil.

Whoever knows Portugal knows that there are still corners of that sleepy little country where linger vestiges of the viewpoint that woman is not a citizen of the State but the subject of a Sovereign Spouse; knows that throughout history the number of crimes of passion that have gone unpunished are appalling, that apparently they have the sanction of the communities in which they occur.

Such were some of the traditions which the Portuguese imposed upon domestic relations in Brazil.   Inevitably the Catholic code underwent further warping when subjected to the equatorial sun in tropical America.   Whatever the relationship was in law, in fact the type relationship of Portuguese-Brazilians to Indian and Negro women during the sixteenth, seventeenth, eighteenth, and most of the nineteenth century, was plain, unadulterated polygyny.   Until the abolition of slavery in 1888, there were few slaveholders who did not keep colored concubines in addition to the one legal wife.   Nor did

[2] Stephens, *Portugal,* p. 281.

the devotees of the system regard themselves as living in hopeless sin, as an incident in Maranhão about 1700 proves. When
Fr. Timotheo do Sacramento was appointed to the diocese, he
began throwing men right and left into prison for living in a
state of concubinage; in the fight that followed we see the
Bishop nailed up in his own house by the unrepentant sinners.[3]

If any reader at this point were to press me for the relationship of all this ancient history to twentieth century Brazil,
I should fall back upon that tremendous generalization of the
biologist:

"Ontogeny is the recapitulation of phylogeny."

I repeat, there is no social soil in the world where the androcentric theory produces sprouts of more imposing dimensions,
exhibits gaudier petals, or exhales a ranker perfume. Of passion there is plenty in Brazil, but of equality and real companionship between the sexes, very little. Despite a fringe on
the margin of progress of women who have revolted and won
for themselves all the privileges of the most advanced Europeans, women as a whole in Brazil still occupy a status of decided inferiority. The position of an intellectual woman
caught in the soul-crushing gears and rollers of such a system is not enviable.

But if the social environment in Brazil is not one in which
intellectual women function to maximum advantage, it does
furnish optimum conditions for the functioning of the prosti-
tute. Ubiquitous, she occupies a status which is unique. The
courtesy of the Brazilian gentleman does not fail him when
dealing with this lowly class. There is a decorum in the
music halls and gambling palaces of Brazilian cities, a delicacy
of demeanor toward the courtesan, which can scarcely
be equaled in Paris itself. I have made many voyages in
Brazilian coastwise steamers, and always there have been
prostitutes on board; yet never has Brazilian man, woman,
or child been rude or uncharitable enough to refuse to sit at
table or enter into conversation with the unfortunate members

[3] Southey, III, 35.

of this ancient sisterhood. In small country towns, during the morning hours, it is not uncommon to see these women making social calls upon their more hard-working, respectably married neighbors. In the cities of Brazil, prostitution is almost always segregated and "regulated." [4] Streets devoted entirely to orderly brothels lead off from Rio's most famous and fashionable seaside boulevard; and the whole institution enjoys the dignity which comes from a definite, recognized social status to which, in Brazil, but slight stigma is attached. Few are the Brazilian youths of the upper classes who quit their teens without having been initiated into the mysteries of sex by women of this class.

Turning now from the actual to the legal aspect of domestic relations, we find the age at which it is permissible to marry fixed at sixteen years for men and fourteen for women, as in Texas and North Carolina. Brazil has advanced to the concept of a prenuptial contract which permits a married woman to retain control of her own property; but should she marry without such a contract, she retains no property right except that of contributing as freely as she may.

As yet, however, the current of liberalism which has so altered the status of woman in Europe and North America during the last half-century, and given France, republican Portugal, Uruguay, and Yucatan as liberal divorce laws as those of Protestant countries, has not impinged effectively upon the intellectual shores of Brazil. Marriage there, in 1926, is still indissoluble. Two children of an age at which they would be required to attend school in most states of the United States may contract a legal marriage. The man may be syphilitic, insane, he may offend her person with a club or her spirit by daily adulteries, he may fail to provide or squander his substance upon cachaça and the lottery, leaving her to stop the belly-pains of an annually increasing progeny as best she may. Or the woman may develop all the slatternly vices of

---

[4] On the inwardness of regulation and its relation to disease, see *Prostitution in Europe*, by Abraham Flexner (New York, 1919).

a sex which is equally liable to originate conditions which make of marriage an antisocial horror whose continuance is a sacrifice of every individual or social value. Neither may divorce the other until Death, the Deliverer, lays the infamous relationship upon the lap of God as the worthiest offering which a Catholic Christian may bring from Earth to Eternity.

If, notwithstanding, domestic relations with the mass of the Brazilian people are much what they are anywhere else, it is because, the world over, there are a whole lot of people better than the institutions under which they live. There seems to me to be fully as much happiness in the Brazilian homes I have been privileged to enter as in average North American homes; a feeling of family solidarity which includes the most distant relations; a kindliness toward the illegitimate child and its mother which is truly Christlike; an atmosphere where children are very, very seldom abused or coerced; a parental reverence which is beautiful, even if sometimes undeserved.

When all is said and done, the Spirit of the Law is more important than the Law. And the spirit of Brazil in domestic relations is gentle, tolerant, easy-going, charitable. I recall a scene which for me takes the sting out of much that I abhor in the Catholic theory of marriage. I had been spending some months on a large fazenda far in the interior of Brazil. The parish to which it pertained was so enormous that the priest visited its outlying parts never more than once a year, and sometimes only once in two years. There came a day in July when preparations were made for a great festival, and I was informed that the good padre was to make one of these rare appearances. The image of the local saint was got out and dusted, a vast quantity of food prepared, an altar extemporized in the new drying shed, and a canoe sent down river to fetch the priest and his son. For ten leagues round about his parishioners assembled. Baptisms, marriages, and prayers for the dead became the order of the day for a whole rural community. Then appeared a ceremony which struck me, a foreigner, as perhaps the quaintest and most charming of the unusual ceremonies that ever came under my observation in strange lands. Many a couple, as soon as their marriage had been solemnized, brought forward a baby, and sometimes two, to be baptized! It appears that life in the sertão had continued serenely on the way determined long ago by Nature, even though the priest should be too far away punctually to perform his functions. And many marriages, not destined to endure, I learned, had been consummated and terminated between the visits of the priest, without blessing and without censure from a Church which is very wise in the ways of erring men.

CHAPTER XIV

EDUCATION

Upon any country, more than by the progress of industry, more than by the prosperity of commerce, more than by the abundance of private wealth, more than by the excellence of state finance, the degree of development is stamped by the status of its educational system. The percentage of illiteracy is the most just and reasonable standard by which to measure and appraise the forces that make for life, and the degree of progress. For each nation, preëminence of the body politic varies inversely with the number of illiterates,—not as the square, as in the cosmic phenomenon of gravitation, but according to a power very much higher.

—FLORIANO BRITO.

IN Arabia, they speak of the age before Islam as "The Ignorance." Unto Brazil—the Prophet has not yet been born. Diffusion of knowledge is not the outstanding characteristic of the Portuguese-speaking world. In Portugal, seven hundred and fifty in the thousand are illiterate;[1] three out of every four Brazilians cannot tell a book in their own language from one in Sanskrit, and sign their names with a cross.[2] So a study of education in Brazil must be primarily an appraisal of the significance of illiteracy in a twentieth century republic, and an estimate of the efficacy of an ignorant peasantry as the foundation of a rugged social fabric.

As our forebears stumbled down the long corridor of time, some half-wit was forever scratching pictures in the moist sand of the seashore when he should have been scooping minnows out of a mudhole. The scratches conveyed an idea to his more intelligent son, who saw them as symbols. Written speech was born, making it possible to preserve hard-won ex-

[1] Census of 1911, quoted by A. F. G. Bell, *Portugal of the Portuguese* (New York, 1916), p. 67.
[2] *Annuario Estatistico do Brazil* (Rio, 1916), p. xxix; *Diario Official* (Rio, 21 Feb., 1922), pp. 3887-3890. The 1920 Census figures on Brazilian illiteracy have not been published as I write.

perience for posterity, making it unnecessary that every anthropoid to whom it comes natural to walk erect should endlessly repeat each trial and error of the foretime. Wipe out man's ability to profit by recorded racial experience and his superiority to other mammalia is not markedly manifest. He can talk, but savages do not say much that is more significant than the chatter of the monkeys above their heads. I prefer the companionship of my dog to that of a Dyak. I am certain my saddle mare has more sense than some Hottentots, and horse sense is not high.

Written speech could do the masses of men but little good until the invention of printing. All instruction was through the pulpit. Information passed from mouth to mouth, not from eye to eye. It was a great day for oratory, but rather too chilly an atmosphere for knowledge to prosper. All the ancient governments except China found they could get along excellently well without a numerous reading class. For rank is a relative matter, and the presence of a thousand illiterates made the one man who could read almost a god. He might be no better educated than a high-school boy, still they would take off their hats and call him *"Doutor"* as though he were a doctor of philosophy. Their humility, their feeling of inferiority before one who possessed the magic power to read, made possible on his part an ostentation of learning which was a sham. The ignorance of the many made possible such lines of social cleavage as those between landlords and landless, between the possessing and the dispossessed, between freemen and slaves. They even defined slavery in terms of knowledge.

It was so defined by the Supreme Court of North Carolina in 1829: "The end of slavery is the profit of the master, his security, and the public safety. The subject is one doomed in his own person and his posterity to live without knowledge and without the capacity to make anything his own, and to toil that another may reap the fruits." They were honest in Carolina back in those days of darkness. There are four words in that definition from which all the rest follows: *to live without knowledge.*

The ignorance of the many emboldened their masters to proclaim publicly what has always been the secret social faith of aristocracy: a monopoly of learning; cheap labor; an inarticulate mass that is easy to manipulate. "I thank God there are no free schools nor printing, and I hope we shall not have any these hundred years," said Governor Berkeley of Virginia, undoubtedly speaking for the landed aristocracy of his day.

Came printing to confound this philosophy of the ancient world. Cheap books made it possible for whoever could read to know; made possible the democratic ideal of a world wherein the ordinary citizen is an informed, as well as consulted, unit in a society whose destiny he may help intelligently to shape.

Now let me try to fit Brazil into the picture. The truth about education there is not one of the first to impress itself upon the foreign traveler. I am sure that when Mr. Elihu Root, then Secretary of State of the United States, walked down the gangplank at São Salvador to meet thousands of politicians in top hats and faultless morning garb, he had no idea that he was setting foot in a state eighty-seven per cent of whose children of primary school age have no schools to which they may go. How could a diplomat have gazed upon the splendor of that assemblage of statesmen and imagined that two years' pay—pitifully small pay—was owing the school-teachers of Bahia somewhen in that period of the world's history? But if you settle down and study Brazil, as I have done, you come to realize that a top hat and the title *"Doutor"* are merely the external marks distinguishing the literate from the illiterate. Floriano Brito is right: it is the fundamental classification.

The distance to the democratic goal in Brazil is still very great, and the reasons seem very plain. During the eighteenth century the Church had such a strangle-hold on Portugal that no intellectual movement could exist in the open; a charitable foundation for the blind had a monopoly of all publications.[3] No press was suffered in Brazil until after the removal of the court; at the beginning of the nineteenth century Brazil was in the same state as if printing had never been invented. Ignorance formed the bulk of the social heritage bequeathed to the Republic by the Empire in 1889; the tradition of the Empire was an educated ten per cent running the country for the private profit of an educated ten per cent, and keeping the rest in absolute ignorance.

To be quite frank, the illiteracy of Brazil appears to me as a survival of the philosophy of slavery, the sincere belief that lots of land and cheap labor is a profitable economic system. It is not an original Brazilian idea. An illiterate peasantry was the dominant European ideal up to the French Revolution. The South of the United States defended the ideal far more vigorously than Brazil ever defended it. In 1834, South Carolina imposed fifty lashes for imparting instruction, or the keeping of school, or teaching any slave or free person of color to read or write. Mississippi used to cut off the right thumbs of slaves who had learnt to write. In the South today, the dominant group publicly defend the thesis as applying to their colored citizens. Whatever he thinks in private, no Brazilian politician would dare voice such sentiments upon the rostrum. Yet the result is the same. Brazil is even more illiterate than our rural South.

Now I am not a sentimentalist who thinks that men act against what they consider their immediate interest. Mainsprings of human action are economic to a delightful degree. To those who still cling to such ideas, I would reply that an illiterate peasantry is not economically profitable. The great fortunes of the United States are not in the South, where labor is cheap; they are in the North, where common labor commands two dollars and a half a day or better—and where practically every laborer has at least a primary school educa-

[3] George Young, *Portugal Old and Young*, p. 186.

tion. It is no longer a secret of modern capitalism that willing intelligence is far more profitable than sullen ignorance. Mr. Henry Ford, paying a minimum wage of six dollars a day to men who are worth it—more than many a Brazilian member of the top-hatted bureaucracy receives—has rolled up more wealth than any fifty Brazilian landlords with their millions of acres and their illiterate, fifty-cent labor. But industry and agriculture are not comparable quantities? The literate peasantry of small landholders in pre-war France and Germany is comparable to the illiterate peasantry on the great estates of Brazil. In the one case you have a social structure whose solidity is unequaled elsewhere in the world; in the other, a social fabric diseased, of low productivity, of degrading standards of comfort, lending itself readily to the chicanery of scheming politicians, lacking ambition and without hope, hostile to the manifold applications of science knocking at the door, crying, "Give us entrance and we will rebuild a better world!"

There have been countries where a small rich and ruling class, living on the toil of inferiors, has cultivated art and letters with brilliant success, but we find nothing of the sort here. The ignorant mass has depressed the whole, as a glacier chills the air of its valley.[4]

Or, as Lord Bacon put it:

The learning of the few is despotism; the learning of the many is liberty.

Approach the quantity aspect of Brazilian education from what angle you like, it must be stamped "I & C," as we used to say in the army, "Inspected and Condemned." What of the quality? Let it be said at once with all emphasis and appreciation that the best schools of the cities of Rio de Janeiro and São Paulo measure up to high European stand-

[4] Lord Bryce, *South America* (New York, 1920), p. 476.

ards; that the country schools in the German colonies are excellent; that the schools in cities like Bello Horizonte, Curityba, and several in Rio Grande do Sul are good; and that there are isolated instances, like the *Escola Domestica* in Natal, that one cannot praise too highly, measuring them by the most advanced standards. But when you ride through the sertão and at intervals of stupendous distance hear the voices of children droning over in monotonous chorus the platitudes of medieval pedagogy, *memorizing verbatim* whole pages of erroneous history and problems in mathematics, led by a half-trained and underpaid teacher, you glance up expecting to see Peter the Hermit coming over the crest of the hill—or imagine yourself plunged back into the appalling darkness of our own rural South.

The women who teach in these rural schools are devoted souls with splendid spirit. They are paid as a rule about 200$000 a month (fifty dollars at normal exchange). Out of that they often have to provide a schoolroom and the whole equipment of the plant. The schools are so overcrowded that they frequently hold two sessions daily for different sets of pupils, so that one teacher will try to instruct a hundred pupils in a day; so overcrowded that even the rich state of São Paulo, in an effort to expand the capacities rapidly enough to wipe out illiteracy before the Centenary Celebration, reduced the prescribed course of primary instruction from three to two years. They held a conference on Primary Education in November, 1921, at which Professors J. M. Mello e Souza and Orestes Guimarães were delegated to report on school facilities throughout Brazil.[5] These scholars were competent and worked with every facility afforded by governmental prestige. They found that in all Brazil, seventy-one per cent of the children of school age are unprovided with school facilities of any description; and that in Amazonas, Pará, Maranhão, Piauhy, Ceará, Rio Grande do Norte,

---

[5] "Conferencia Internacional do Ensino Primario," *Diario Official*, 21 February, 1922, pp. 3887-90.

The Escola Domestica, Natal, Rio Grande do Norte.
(See page 320.)

The University of Paraná. (See page 321.)

Brazilian school building of the better type. São Luiz,
Maranhão.

Illiteracy and hookworm.

Alagôas, Sergipe, Bahia, Goyaz, and (strangely enough) the state of Rio de Janeiro, from eighty-three to ninety-five per cent of the children have no schools.

A stream can rise no higher than its source, and as yet the fountainhead of education in Brazil is not high. There are three universities in the Portuguese-speaking world: Coimbra, founded by Diniz in 1300; Lisbon; and the University of Rio de Janeiro. From Coimbra sprang almost everything that was fine in Portugal, from Camões and Pombal to the leaders of the Revolution of 1910. Immediately after the arrival of the court in 1808 it was intended to give a university

PERCENTAGE OF BRAZILIAN CHILDREN OF SCHOOL AGE WHO ARE UNPROVIDED WITH SCHOOL FACILITIES

An Official Investigation published in the *Diario Official*, 21 de Fevereiro de 1922.

Goyaz	95	Espirito Santo	78
Piauhy	95	Pernambuco	75
Alagôas	94	Paraná	74
Maranhão	92.4	Parahyba do Norte	74
Amazonas	91	Matto Grosso	71
Ceará	89	Minas Geraes	64
Bahia	87	São Paulo	56
Rio Grande do Norte	85	Rio Grande do Sul	44
Pará	85	Santa Catharina	43
Rio de Janeiro	84	Districto Federal	41
Sergipe	83	BRAZIL	71

to the new monarchy; plans were formulated; and there was much discussion as to whether it should be located in Rio de Janeiro or up on the plateau of São Paulo.[6] The University of Rio de Janeiro actually was founded 7 September, 1920, by the reunion on paper of the Escola Polytechnica, the Rio Faculty of Medicine, and the Rio Faculty of Law, with Dr. Ramiz Galvão as the first Rector. This is the only university in Brazil if one is speaking of actualities. The so-called "University of Paraná," for instance, has not the equipment of a second-rate high school. Nor does the Superior Council of Education make any pretenses in the matter.

[6] Spix and Martius, *Travels*, etc., I, 152.

THE NUMBER OF PUPILS IN THE PRIMARY SCHOOLS OF BRAZIL

From the Census of 1920

	Total population	No. attending primary schools	Total population	
		Brazil	U.S.	
São Paulo................	4.592.188	271.600	652,476	4,663,228	Texas
Minas Geraes..............	5.888.174	248.815	703,560	5,759,394	Ohio
Rio Grande do Sul..........	2.182.713	136.599	344,699	2,348,174	Alabama
Districto Federal...........	1.157.873	112.955	178,910	1,296,372	Nebraska
Rio de Janeiro.............	1.559.371	58.286	182,147	1,449,661	Maryland
Bahia....................	3.334.465	52.194	404,928	3,155,900	New Jersey
Pernambuco..............	2.154.835	47.959	304,665	2,028,283	Oklahoma
Santa Catharina...........	668.743	37.854	102,876	646,872	N. Dakota
Ceará....................	1.319.228	28.978	162,750	1,356,621	Washington
Pará.....................	983.507	27.884	126,189	968,470	Florida
Paraná...................	685.711	26.140	91,322	636,547	S. Dakota
Maranhão.................	874.337	21.033	94,312	783,389	Oregon
Parahyba do Norte........	961.106	19.816	121,353	939,629	Colorado
Rio Grande do Norte.......	537.135	16.328	71,513	548,889	Montana
Espirito Santo.............	457.328	16.032	71,611	449,396	Utah
Alagôas..................	978.748	13.183	93,615	768,014	Maine
Sergipe..................	477.064	11.535	51,544	443,083	N. H.
Matto Grosso.............	246.612	8.845	27,336	223,003	Delaware
Goyaz....................	511.919	8.571	38,962	437,571	D. C.
Amazonas................	363.166	7.513	52,829	360,350	N. Mexico
Piauhy...................	609.003	7.442	74,872	604,397	R. I.
Territorio do Acre.........	92.379	1.280	65,102	431,866	Idaho
	30.635.605	1.180.842	4,017,571	30,299,109	

Brazil is abundantly supplied with faculties of engineering, medicine, and law, no one of which approaches European or North American standards. She is just making a beginning in organizing agricultural schools, destined some day to become a great fountainhead of wealth for this agricultural colossus. But, for obvious reasons, this is not the point where emphasis should be placed at the moment. In the United States, the attendance at agricultural colleges was very slight until the public schools had given at least a primary education to practically the whole surrounding rural population; and agricultural extension was not practicable until we had agricultural college graduates by the tens of thousands. Emphasis today belongs on primary education; on normal schools to train teachers for primary instruction; and on a university which is a university, to serve as a focus, a background, a fountainhead, an inspiration, for a campaign which will be long and hard and must be carried on by unrelenting idealists who can envisage the distant goal.

Deep-rooted traditions do not die in a day. Youth must speed the parting guests. The idealism of the generation which has been born since slavery and the Empire passed away must take them by the throat and kick them downstairs. Let one who has dedicated herself to that splendid work close this chapter; the brilliant author of *Renovation,* Maria Lacerda de Moura:

And what are we to do about all this?

What is necessary for tomorrow's happiness?

But little, senhores. Popular education, there is the key to all the mysteries. The school is the religion, the influence irresistible of the forerunners. It is the solution of the darkest enigmas.

Not the school as we now know it, not the inflexible dogmatism of the masters ex cathedra, not the school of antiquity, but the new school reborn from the ancient principles, the school idealized by the dreamers of another day, the school of Ferrer, la Ruche, Montessori —where the sentiment of fraternity exists, wherein liberty is sung in the hymn of life, where equality is a natural law.

CHAPTER XV

CO-OPERATION

In this stage of society, to "work for others" stultifies a man exceedingly, and the real Portuguese of the old school would rather want than do anything incidentally likely to supply the wants of his neighbours. Every school in the Empire should put up the motto of the Free Cantons—
"Each for all, and all for each."
—Sir Richard Burton.[1]

Comte has somewhere said that the most fundamental attribute of the human species is the tendency to make sociability prevail over personality. In Brazil I have sometimes felt as though the opposite were true. What I mean by that best can be made plain to North Americans by recalling some facts in their own history.

When individuals emigrated from Europe to North America and entered a wilderness, a complex society, developed under conditions of relatively dense population, dissolved into exceedingly simple, primitive social groupings. It is hardly an exaggeration to say that the family group became the outer boundary of consciousness of kind for many an isolated frontiersman in the United States. The frontier and limitless free land made for the most intense individualism. It bred a type of men as impatient of social control as a wild mustang is of bit and saddle, men who liked to define liberty as the absence of all government and who regarded all taxes as a foretaste of tyranny. The tendency of frontier conditions was toward the production and the nourishment of a large *nonsocial class*.[2] And the frontier was the dominant fact in the history of the United States for three hundred years.[3]

---

[1] *The Highlands of Brazil* (London, 1869), I, 58.
[2] For a fuller definition of social classes, see Giddings, *Principles of Sociology* (3d ed.; New York, 1896), pp. 126, 127.
[3] See *The Frontier in American History*, by Frederick J. Turner (New York, 1921).

Also, the frontier in the United States was a happy hunting-ground for *antisocial classes,* as well as the matrix in which the nonsocial crystallized and became firmly embedded. (Upstanding, independent individualists to whom it comes more natural to settle a dispute with fists, or bowie knife, or six-shooter than to go to court, should not be confounded with the criminals—the difference between Andrew Jackson and Jesse James.) There the "bad man" found a congenial habitat. There the card sharp, the cattle "rustler," and the desperado flourished. There horse-thief and hold-up man alternately stood treat at the bar of the "wide-open" saloon and agreed that life was simple and sweet. When such high-spirited elements became too obnoxious or united in gangs, they were opposed by equally lawless associations like the regulators of the Carolinas, the vigilantes of California, and lynching parties in the cow country.

Precisely the same thing happened in Brazil. Similar conditions produced similar results. In spite of all efforts to restrict settlement to the coast, the presence of limitless land calling to an adventurous race of men served as a solvent for social restraints of European manufacture, drew men forever away from the settlements, and set the patriarchal family group of the large fazenda as the boundary of consciousness of kind in much of interior Brazil. A self-reliant, aggressive individualism became the very price of existence in the placer washings of Minas and Matto Grosso, as in the isolated cattle ranges of Piauhy, Goyaz, or Rio Grande do Sul. Broad human sympathies were quoted below par, if not entirely erased from the slate. The lowly serf of Minho or Tras-os-Montes became a swaggering citizen of the sertão with a pistol on his hip, a knife in his bootleg, and a chip on his shoulder. The sons of Portuguese governors became the Strong Men of the interior, with four or five hundred armed personal retainers at their call. The more civilized centers of the coast could exercise but slight collective regulation over either of them.

Interior Brazil was as nonsocial as the frontier of the United States.

Likewise the sertão of Brazil has always been an unfenced range of pastures rare for those criminal classes which live by aggression upon the social. I do not find the antisocial class south of the equator as attractive as the "bad men" of the Wild West. This is probably a mere matter of racial tradition—the ways of Robin Hood and Dick Turpin have been handed down to us in more delightful guise than those of brigandage in the Iberian Peninsula. Nevertheless, I should prefer yielding my purse to a chap who strode into a crowded barroom, set up the drinks, and then proceeded to collect the wallets and loot the till in manly fashion, to being knifed in the back as I rode along some lonely road, which too frequently is the way of criminal Brazil. With the exception of this difference in technique, banditry and brigandage on the Brazilian frontier exhibit the same phenomena as they did on the frontier of the United States.

In one case we are speaking of the past, in the other of the present. The same lawless elements flourish today in Brazil as flourished in the Wild West in the decade 1850-60. In my own limited experience within three years, I witnessed the operations of a highwayman enjoying the picturesque name of *"Bigode de Ouro,"* ("Gold Mustache") who was running off cattle, robbing pack trains, and playing a game of raid, rape, and run which the rural police of Bahia for a long time were powerless to break up. I have been forced to make long detours to avoid a gang of "bad men" two hundred strong who were operating about railhead in the cacao zone behind Ilhéos, riding into towns of three or four thousand inhabitants with Winchesters across their saddles, and laying a whole rich agricultural district under tribute. My trip down the São Francisco River in 1920 had to be abandoned because that whole region was up in arms at the bidding of a *"Poderoso"* of the sertão strong enough to successfully dispute an election with all the troops of a great state and prevent a line of government steamships from operating. I have witnessed a shooting at a dance in the cattle country and a knifing on a railroad train. Within the same period, hired gunmen (*ca-pangas*) under the leadership of one political chief fired upon troops under his brother, the Governor, in the state capital of Espirito Santo. None of these things are anything more than the high spirits of the frontier. Parts of Matto Grosso and much of the Amazon are today as lawless as was any cattle or gold camp in the Wild West in the middle of the nineteenth century. The six-shooter and the .44 Winchester are still either sovereign arbiters or the rough regulators of judicial process. Many of the same men who find the diminishing cow country of our fenced plains too cramped for operations, in Matto Grosso find free scope for the activities of a day that with the United States, alas, is dead.

The parallel between frontier conditions in Brazil and in the United States could be carried much further. The Indian considered as a common enemy, for instance, was a unifying factor tending to break down individualism and making for coöperation in both continents. Brazilian gold hunters were no more able to make their way from São Paulo to Matto Grosso, except as strong bands held together by the bond of a common danger, than were the wagon trains of the North American gold seekers able to cross the Great Plains or the Santa Fe Trail a century later.

It is the differences, however, rather than the agreements that are most revealing of Brazil. Foremost among them, the fundamental difference between the frontier in the United States and in Brazil which I mentioned when discussing gold. The United States frontier was *primarily* a skirmish line of humanity advancing from areas of permanent settlement in an east-to-west direction over a period of three hundred years. In our census reports it was treated as the limit of settlement having a population density of two or more to the square mile, and was declared officially nonexistent in 1890. It showed a fairly orderly westerly advance decade by decade with no bad breaks until 1849, when the gold rush to California carried the margin of humanity in one great leap to the rim of the Western Ocean long before the frontier had been annihilated in the Great Plains and Rocky Mountains. But in Brazil, as early as 1700, gold broke the frontier into a thousand fragments and scattered humanity over the boundless face of nature like bombs dropped from a careless, wide-cruising airplane. By the same standard of population density, two per square mile, Brazil is still mostly frontier. But even in those regions where population long ago passed that figure, frontier conditions continued to prevail. Until the dawn of the twentieth century Brazil might fairly have been described as exhibiting frontier conditions throughout all of her vast domain, except for a very thin fringe of civilization along the coast.

The second difference exhibits something far more basic than a geographic accident. It may be that I have not looked far enough or deep enough, but thus far in my travels in Brazil it has been in vain that I have kept my eye open for equivalents to the social side of frontier life in North America which was as important as it was delightful. The individualism of the frontiersman in the United States and Canada was not so accentuated that he fell over backward in his effort to stand erect and alone: he also developed a great capacity for voluntary association and mutual aid. When a clearing has been made in the forest, the down timber is obviously too much for any man to handle unaided. In the United States this situation gave birth to the "log-rolling," at which the whole neighborhood for miles around assembled for mutual aid in rolling the logs off the clearing and for the festivity that should be the handmaiden of all heavy work; in Brazil the logs just stay on the ground. The house-raising, the husking bee, the flax pulling, the maple-sugar boiling, the apple paring, the squatters' associations of the North American frontier exhibit a social tendency which, unless I am entirely mistaken, is very much weaker in Brazil. A pioneer writing back from the Middle West to friends in the East in the middle of the nineteenth century, ended with this significant sentence which expressed the situation in the United States: [4]

"It is a universal rule here to help one another, each one keeping an eye single to his own business."

In Brazil, an equally truthful writer would have written from the sertão:

"It is a universal rule here for each one to keep an eye single to his own business."

I have so often observed an attitude of, "Why should I repair that piece of trail or the bridge in front of my house even if it is on my own property, when others besides myself use it?" that I cannot but feel there is a vast difference between Brazil and the United States in the degree of development of coöperation and mutual aid. It is difficult to exaggerate the importance of the social functions which, in the United States, are carried on by entirely voluntary associations. Organized groups of coöperating citizens lead every substantial advance, government trailing reluctantly along. In Brazil, the absorption of all social functions by the state, the habit of looking to government for everything that concerns more than two people, has developed an unregenerate individualism. It is significant that Dr. Warbasse, in his recent world-wide survey of the organized coöperative movement,[5] makes no mention whatever of Brazil.

Inability to coöperate was observed as a Portuguese trait by Antonio Vieyra, when he wrote in the middle of the seventeenth century:

Finally, the Dutch have their industry, their diligence, their desire of gain, their unanimity, and their love of the common weal; we have our disunion, our envy, our presumption, our negligence, and our perpetual attention to individual interests.[6]

In short, it appears to me that the nonsocial class embraces an appalling percentage of the Brazilian population;

[4] Turner, *The Frontier in American History*, p. 248.
[5] J. P. Warbasse, *Coöperative Democracy* (New York, 1923).
[6] Southey, II, 226.

that the antisocial elements dominate too much of the sertão; that the pseudosocial class of congenital and habitual paupers is disgustingly large about the doors of every church in the land; and the social class of men in whom the consciousness of kind is highly developed, is pitifully small considering the jobs in Brazil which can be successfully put through by no other weapon than intelligent coöperative effort. How could it be otherwise? A broad consciousness of kind and social vision is not habitually born in the brain of illiteracy.

Great things have been accomplished now and again in Brazil by great individuals. But the day which will send a thrill throughout the uttermost sertões and a chill down the spine of medievalism, the day when Brazil will take its first great stride toward Power, will be the day the intelligence, youth, and idealism of the land learn to march shoulder to shoulder, learn to present a united front to the forces of re-action, to fraternize as well as to criticize, to *coöperate* for large social ends.

CHAPTER XVI

HEALTH

DISEASE is one of the most democratic and truly international forces in the world. Unconscious of caste, disdaining to notice color, preferring the genial company of the masses but by no means spurning the classes, attendant upon life before birth, hovering in the background at supreme moments like war and famine, ministrant indefatigable unto the dying, disease is eloquent in proclaiming the unity of mankind. Until all men deny disease, no man may. If Africa continue to breed malignant germs, carriers will be forthcoming to convey them to Asia. If Bahia is permitted to harbor Yellow Jack, the ships of Boston trade with her at their peril. Spanish influenza, the wanton, within the selfsame week is overintimate with a comrade in the trenches of France, a citizen in San Francisco, a coolie in India, and a capital in Brazil—and leaves them all with a nasty temperature.

Here we come to grips with the core of this matter of the conquest of the tropics. My thesis is one which the Regional Director for Brazil of the International Health Board, Dr. L. W. Hackett, made plain during the several weeks I accompanied him on an inspection of Brazilian hookworm posts: All but three or four so-called "tropical diseases" are by no means peculiar to the tropics; they are *essentially* those of a backward social environment.

Leprosy in the fourteenth century was more common in England than it is now in Palestine. What ravages smallpox caused in Asia and northern Europe during the Middle Ages! Have we already forgotten that as an epidemic disease, yellow fever appeared during the last century in Quebec, in Wales, in

Italy, in Montevideo, in Valparaiso—far outside the tropics? and that over thirteen thousand lost their lives in the Mississippi Valley as recently as the epidemic of 1878? Malaria is as much at home in the coastal plain of the Atlantic and Gulf states as it is in the flood plain of the Amazon, and the inhabitants of the Sacramento Valley in California would be particularly indignant if any one claimed malaria as a "tropical disease." No part of the United States is tropical, yet hookworm is endemic all through our rural South just as it is in Brazil and Africa. History does not record that any epidemic in the tropics ever caused a greater proportionate loss of life than the epidemic of plague in the fourteenth century known as the Black Death, which carried off twenty-five million Europeans and thirteen million Chinese, according to Hecker. The late World War was a life extension institute compared to that.

Nor, with the characteristic contempt of parvenus for the class out of which they have recently arisen, should we feel hopeless about the redemption of those regions of the earth which are less swift to avail themselves of new sanitary knowledge. The best of our knowledge is so very, very new! Major General Gorgas says:

The army [of the United States] which went to Santiago suffered as severely from yellow fever and other tropical diseases as any military expedition into the tropics had suffered before that time, and its death rate, had it remained, would have been just as high as was that of the French army of similar size which was exterminated in the island of Haiti just one hundred years before.[1]

That was in the year of our Lord 1898. The picture, drawn by the greatest health officer the world has so far produced, of North American officers and men breaking down and weeping because they could not go back on the next ship is very different from the picture of contentment of the same class of soldiers three years later in Havana, "the healthiest and

[1] Gorgas, *Sanitation in Panama* (New York, 1918), p. 4.

cleanest city in the world." In that interval the Reed Board
had, by one of the finest feats of intelligent courage ever
performed by man, established beyond question the thesis of
old Dr. Finley, of Havana, that the female of the stegomyia
mosquito (now labeled by science *Aëdes Aegyptus*, Linn.) was
the sole carrier of yellow fever. It was as recently as 1895
that science related malaria to the anopheles mosquito. Hookworm never attracted much attention until the terrible out-
break of "tunnel disease" in 1882, when Italian workmen were
excavating the St. Gotthard tunnel; the technique of eliminat-
ing it from large populations is a twentieth century invention. It was 1908 when Simond fastened responsibility for
bubonic plague upon the rat. Dr. Carlos Chagas described the
disease named after him about the same time, when the Central do Brazil Railway was under construction in Minas Geraes.
These dates are not yesterday in racial history; they are today; and their results cannot be reaped before tomorrow.

As the Indian, the Negro, and the European all contributed
to the culture of Brazil, so each contributed his quota of
disease. Each in his own environment had developed special-
ties. Each had lived with his special diseases so long as to
develop an immunity which the other two lacked: syphilis,
which the crew of Columbus brought to Europe from the
West Indies, spread over the whole world with incredible
rapidity; [2] the hookworm of the African bored into the blood
corpuscles of Europeans and Indians with indiscriminate im-
partiality; the white man's contribution of smallpox was particularly devastating to American aborigines.

Sir Harry Johnston holds that

Africa is the chief stronghold of the real Devil. . . . Here Beelzebub,
King of the Flies, marshals his vermiform and arthropod hosts—
insects, ticks, and nematode worms—which more than in any other
continent convey to the skin, veins, intestines, or spinal marrow of

---

[2] Draper, *Intellectual Development of Europe* (New York, 1875), II, 231,
232; Rosenau, *Preventive Medicine and Hygiene* (1920); *Jour. Amer.
Med. Assoc.*, June 12, 1915, LXIV, 24, p. 1962.

men and other vertebrates the microörganisms which cause deadly, disfiguring, or debilitating diseases.[3]

He believes the Negro conveyed to Brazil the "sleeping sickness," blackwater fever (Haemoglobinuria), elephantiasis, the guinea worm, and hookworm.

The white man, of course, cannot lay claim to much originality in disease; he got all his from the cradle of the race, in Asia. It is as a carrier that the mobile white man shines; and we must credit him with carrying to Brazil malaria, tuberculosis, smallpox, bubonic plague, cholera, dysentery, typhoid, and yellow fever.

There is considerable difference of opinion as to whether or not yellow fever plagued the Indian before the coming of the white man, but General Gorgas located the original focus of the disease somewhere about Vera Cruz in Mexico,[4] and this position is ably supported by the more recent evidence from pre-Columbian Maya writings brought to light by Dr. Herbert Spinden.[5] The geography of Chagas's disease argues its American origin; and possibly malaria is an older American tradition than Columbus or Cabral,[6] although this is an old-world disease as intimately related to the downfall of Greece and Rome as yellow fever probably was to the Maya tragedy.[7]

After all, whence is not the important question, but whither. And we cannot think intelligently about the future until we get clearly in mind what are the outstanding health problems of Brazil.

No man can obtain a grasp of this matter unless he can

---

[3] Johnston, *The Negro in the New World*, Preface.
[4] Gorgas, *Sanitation in Panama*, chap. viii.
[5] Spinden, "Yellow Fever—First and Last," *World's Work*, Dec., 1921.
[6] Dr. L. O. Howard, "Economic Loss to the People of the U.S. Through Insects That Carry Disease," *Natl. Geog. Mag.*, August, 1909, p. 737.
[7] "Dr. Henry Carter [of the International Health Board] is writing a history of yellow fever and this has put into his hands a mass of early Spanish, Portuguese, and English records of the early expeditions, and their experience with disease in this hemisphere. He is convinced that yellow fever came from Africa; malaria was brought by the white man to the New World; but syphilis was an American disease, unknown in Europe before the voyage of Columbus."—Dr. L. W. Hackett, in a personal letter to the author.

divest himself of preconceptions which filled the minds of
even the best informed right up to the beginning of the
twentieth century. "For several successive evenings before
the fever broke out the atmosphere was thick, and a body
of murky vapour, accompanied by a strong stench, travelled
from street to street." That was the "mother of yellow fever,"
not in the mind of some superstitious priest of the Middle
Ages but in the heads of nineteenth century scientists. Man
fears what he does not understand, and under the inspiration
of fear of frightful epidemics which he was powerless to control, the educated accepted the fantasies of the ignorant.
When yellow fever appeared in Pará in 1850, the government
fired cannon at the corners of the street to purify the air.
A colleague in the Philippine Forest Service once saw a priest
stand all night in the public square leading the village band
in music designed to frighten away the cholera, preaching
between numbers against the measures the Americans were
taking to stamp it out—the auditory poison was worse than
the intestinal.

A world where such things could happen said, "The tropics
are a pesthole."

What it should have said is, "Man's ignorance is the only
fundamental disease."

Yet how could a rational mind arrive at any other conclusion than that the tropics are a pesthole, previous to the
twentieth century? From the moment that population became
sufficiently concentrated at points along the coast of Brazil to
feed an epidemic, certainly since the early seventeenth century, wave after wave of smallpox, cholera, and bubonic plague
moved up and down that coast from Santos to Pará with the
foul and devastating breath of a vindictive god. It was the
middle of the nineteenth century before Yellow Jack leered
at beautiful Brazil out of his jaundiced eye and took unto his
full embrace Belém, Bahia, Rio, and Santos. It was the second
decade of the twentieth century before his pestilential grip
was finally broken in most of those ports: the capital of

Bahia he still claims for his bride. The twentieth century dawned with bubonic plague in São Paulo, Santos, and Rio de Janeiro. No wonder man looked upon the tropics as a place accursed.

It is as bewildering as it is inspiring how the "facts" have changed in less than twenty years. And the greatest change of all is in the point of view. Medicine for untold centuries has been curative; in our generation for the first time it is becoming preventive. In addition to doctors of medicine, Harvard, Johns Hopkins, and Yale are now turning out doctors of public health. The new facts and the new point of view necessitate an estimate of the possibility of tropical conquest entirely different from anything man had the right to expect even a quarter-century ago.

If we carefully distinguish the factors that are inherent and fixed in a tropical environment from those that are flexible and already under man's control, the horrors of the tropics begin quietly to fold their tents and slip away. Heat and high humidity are the outstanding facts in the climate of the Amazon Basin; in much of the Brazilian plateau region, one or the other of those factors is absent a large part of the year, giving climatic conditions like those of southern California, where men of every color function to advantage. It is doubtful if at any point in the Amazon Basin maximum temperatures will reach the figure attained in New York City every summer. I have never heard of a case of sunstroke or thermic fever there. Certainly safeguarding against heat in the tropics is much less of a problem than safeguarding against cold in the misnamed "temperate" zones.

The Life Extension Institute, of New York, has said something on this matter of heat which is very much to the point. Calling attention to the fact that in the United States Registration Area in 1920 the death rate for February was 14.6 per thousand, and for August 6.8, Dr. Fisk went on to say:[8]

[8] *How to Live,* August, 1923.

Hot weather has an altogether undeservedly bad name. It is the season of lowest mortality. The death rate is much lower and the sickness rate lower in the months of July, August, and September, than during the other months of the year. It is up to us to pat hot weather on the back and acclaim it as a friend of man. This may be extremely irritating to some who feel discomfort during sweltering heat. Nevertheless we must tell the truth about this hot weather bugaboo. The fact that there are more deaths from lightning stroke than heat stroke annually may be a surprise to some people. The comparative bill against lightning would be still heavier if heat strokes were properly recorded. A great many so-called deaths from heat stroke are from heart disease, kidney trouble, or some other serious organic disease that was awaiting the final push from either heat or cold or some other passing accident or strain. It is not to be denied that in tropical and semi-tropical regions the death rate is higher, but it is not due to the heat. It is due to the overabundance of life in these regions. A good deal of this life is harmful to man—pest-bearing insects, for example.

It may well be that the death rate from diarrheal diseases reaches excessive proportions where high humidity and high temperature coincide.[9] Certainly the external insect world flourishes magnificently. This is the first valid charge against high temperature and humidity which we must admit: insect pests multiply beyond the rational interpretation of the biblical injunction. Fleas bore into bare feet and leave festering sores; ants, mosquitoes, flies of myriad species and in myriad swarms; insects that bite, and sting, and burrow, and devour, all proclaim the wonderful fecundity of nature. The actual number of insects, however, is always greatly reduced whenever the jungle is cleared.

A second valid charge against heat and humidity is that profuse perspiration and frequent bathing lead to a thinning and increase in vulnerability of the human epidermis.[10] Small wounds and insect bites become infected more readily than

[9] Frederick L. Hoffman, "Climate and Health in the South American Tropics," *Monthly Weather Review*, Jan., 1922.
[10] Councilman and Lambert, *The Medical Report of the Rice Expedition to Brazil*.

in northern climes and are longer in healing, as any one who has lived in both places can testify. This factor affects practically every one and for that reason is of considerable importance.

We can never do away with insects, and we cannot avoid profuse perspiration. Nevertheless, most of the factors that make for disease in the tropics are capable of modification by man equipped with the New Knowledge, and probably of ultimate control. Let us test the truth of this by a consideration of the most important diseases encountered in Brazil.

So far as *gravity* of the public health problem goes, venereal disease easily heads the list. If we consider only the *number of people affected*, rural endemic diseases would rank something like this: hookworm, malaria, trachoma, tropical ulcers, Chagas's disease, and leprosy. The important epidemic diseases are typhoid, paratyphoid, and the dysenteries; yellow fever, smallpox, and bubonic plague, in about the order named. These, like tuberculosis, are primarily city diseases, because they require a relatively dense population in order to develop epidemic proportions. The hospitals of Brazil are filled with venereal, tuberculosis, Leishmaniasis, malaria, and the dysenteries.

About hookworm we have very precise information. When the International Health Board began its work in 1917, from Bahia north a full 100 per cent of the rural population was infected; this zone of complete infection extended south through the low-lying littoral of Espirito Santo, Rio de Janeiro, São Paulo, Paraná, and Santa Catharina. The rate dropped to 85 per cent of the rural population in the lagoon region of Rio Grande do Sul, well outside the tropics; faded out entirely in the highlands of the extreme south, and generally diminished both in area and in intensity as one left the tropics on the southern plateau. The International Health Board has never yet examined an agricultural laborer in the State of São Paulo (where it made its most detailed studies) who was free from hookworm.

That has been the case since the sixteenth century when Negroes first introduced the disease from Africa. Piso, writing about health conditions in Brazil in 1582, says:

A liver complaint was endemic among the lower classes and as peculiarly their disease, as gout is that of the rich. It was particularly frequent during the wet months; the sufferers were tormented with a craving for food, and their countenances were meagre and death-like.[11]

That is enough for the initiated.

The very geographic distribution outlined above seems to contradict the thesis that tropical disease is essentially a function of a backward social environment. Hookworm loves warmth and moisture, and perishes in the cold, to be sure; but that does not invalidate the generalization. Here I must speak of something that is not pleasant, but the well-being of twenty-five million lives in Brazil alone is involved. Hookworm is spread through the barefooted tropics by the habit of defecating indiscriminately on the ground, the parasite later entering its human host through the pores of the skin.

It is rare in any uncivilized African center of population to find places deliberately set apart for the deposit of exuviae [writes Johnston]. Consequently the outskirts of African towns are noisome to a degree.[12]

That describes rural Brazil sufficiently. It also describes the filth habits of at least two million whites in the South of the United States, and, according to the same writer,

at least ten millions of British landlords and peasantry who disdain to supply or to use earth closets.

If further evidence is needed to clinch the argument, it will be found in the surprising ease with which hookworm can be

[11] Southey, II, 327.
[12] Johnston, *The Negro in the New World*, p. 18.

eradicated—two doses of chenopodium and latrine construction—and the way Brazil is grappling with that problem since the International Health Board showed the way is an inspiring tale which I have told elsewhere.[13] Such a disease is an attribute of illiteracy and ignorance pure and simple. Tropical labor in general and the Negro in particular have gained the reputation of being lazy and shiftless. God knows they are! But—there is no man of any race that ever rambled over this sphere, from Neanderthal to Nordic, that can harbor three hundred hookworms for ten years and not grow anemic, lazy, and shiftless.

Something like 40 per cent of the population of Minas Geraes, the Brazilian state with the largest population, is afflicted with permanent or periodic attacks of malaria, according to Penna, the Federal Chief of Rural Sanitation; and most of Minas is mountainous or hilly. In the riverine flood plains the incidence would be much higher. This disease is more difficult; but its control is not impossible, as Panama proves.[14] It is impossible to control malaria over any such areas as are involved in the mosquito breeding zones of Brazil, but it is not impossible to control mosquitoes in an area equal to their comparatively short flight about any given habitation or town. In many places in the world the agricultural population lives in villages and goes out each morning to work in the fields. This is done, for instance, in the island of Majorca,[15] and in many regions in China, Japan, and the Philippines. The malarial mosquito is a night flyer. Develop a population intelligent enough to see the need of residing in immunized villages instead of scattered all over the face of nature and the crux of the malaria problem is solved: a problem in popular education. And as Gorgas has somewhere said, it is no more expensive for a tropical farmer to keep out malaria than

---

[13] Nash, "Conquering the Hookworm in Brazil," *Current History*, March 1923, p. 1021.

[14] See Gorgas, *Sanitation in Panama;* and Le Prince and Orenstein, *Mosquito Control in Panama.*

[15] Brunhes, *Human Geography,* p. 503.

for a North Dakota farmer to keep out cold. This is not theory; it was done in Panama, and no greater stronghold of the mosquito-borne diseases ever existed upon the face of the earth.

As to the distance that even the educated classes have yet to go in this matter of denying themselves to insects, the condition of many Brazilian hospitals shows. I have personally visited hospitals, not in poverty-stricken county seats, but in cities like São Paulo, Santos, and Curityba, which were unprovided with screens. Two nurses are regularly required to serve the food, one carving the meat while the other stands by with a fan—against flies! those ubiquitous carriers of typhoid fever.[16]

Every intelligent man now knows that yellow fever is another mosquito-borne disease, although the fact is no part of the mental equipment of the illiterate millions of the tropics. When America was discovered, if General Gorgas is right, the "black vomit" was confined to the Caribbean and the southern shores of the Gulf of Mexico. The fever crept down the coast of Brazil and up the Amazon rather slowly. It was not until 1849 that it became endemic in Belém, Rio, and Santos; and some thirty or forty years more before it took up permanent residence in Manáos. São Salvador, of course, was quicker to grasp such an opportunity. It was rough riding in all these ports. Many a time in Santos, as in Havana, ships lay at anchor and could not move—all hands dead.

That day is behind us. Reed and Gorgas showed how the disease could be mastered in Havana, in 1901. Dr. Adolpho Lutz was the first Brazilian to profit by the New Knowledge; he cleaned up São Paulo. Dr. Oswaldo Cruz made his name forever glorious by performing the same service for Rio de Janeiro; and when neither 1909 nor 1910 showed a single case

[16] See L. O. Howard, "A Contribution to the Study of the Insect Fauna of Human Excrement (with special reference to the spread of typhoid fever by flies)," *Proceedings* of the Washington Academy of Sciences, II, 541-604.

in Rio, that distinguished Brazilian sanitarian felt free to go north and clean up Belém.

The latest great victory of this sort was the most spectacular. Guayaquil, in Ecuador, was probably the worst stronghold of yellow fever in the world. In 1918 the city authorities invited the International Health Board to coöperate with the government health service and clean them up. Just six months after Dr. M. E. Connor (now in Mexico serving as acting director of the special commission against yellow fever of the Mexican department of health) appeared in Guayaquil, the last case of yellow fever disappeared, at a cost which was altogether insignificant.

It is interesting to note how the Great War aided this campaign. A person who has once had yellow fever is immune; and practically every one who has lived ten years in an endemic centre has contracted the disease, whether he was aware of it or not. (Such, at least, is the working theory of the sanitarians.) The mosquito is short-lived. If a continuous supply of non-immunes fail, yellow fever is eliminated through the failure of its human host. That actually happened with a lot of small ports, including some in Cuba, La Guayra and Maracaibo in Venezuela, Cartagena in Colombia, and Corinto in Nicaragua, where commerce and immigration practically came to a standstill while the ships of the world were diverted to the purposes of war. This temporary dropping out of the world sweetened several of the minor ports of Brazil which were too lazy to clean up voluntarily, and seems to have swept Yellow Jack from the entire Amazon.

That situation at the close of the war made it possible for the International Health Board to propose a sublime proposition of the sort that some day a League of Nations will handle —to make a simultaneous attack upon every one of the comparatively few remaining foci of yellow fever in Central and South America and the West Coast of Africa, and rid the world of this pest for good. It was and is perfectly feasible. It exemplifies the sort of statesmanship which is music and poetry to the international-minded. One city in Brazil demurred, São Salvador. More recently, however, Bahia has seen the light and now seems determined to rid herself of the stigma of being the last stronghold of yellow fever in the Western Hemisphere.

Of the other epidemic diseases, Brazil has smallpox pretty well in hand through compulsory vaccination, notwithstanding that in 1919 there were some five thousand cases in the city of São Salvador. Although bubonic plague is endemic, and occasional cases appear in São Luiz, Ceará, Pernambuco, and more rarely in Porto Alegre; the days of epidemics of the *peste* seem to be behind. How Rio reduced the mortality from plague from 360 in 1903 to nothing in 1912 is another fine story in the history of Brazilian sanitation. There is no harbor on the Atlantic seaboard of the United States whose port works are as rat-proof as those of Rio de Janeiro and Santos. Typhoid is common in Porto Alegre, but throughout Brazil epidemics do not assume dimensions of serious importance because of the mild nature of this disease in the tropics. Furthermore, the water supply of cities like Rio and Santos is excellent. The dysenteries are still a big problem in Brazil. Cholera is a thing of the past.

Trachoma is extensively encountered in São Paulo and Pernambuco. Tropical ulcers are fairly common everywhere: Baurú, in western São Paulo, is considered Brazilian headquarters for cutaneous Leishmaniasis; but it also occurs in Bahia, and to some extent all through the North. With that terrible by-product of the mud house, Chagas's disease, I have dealt in the chapter on rural houses.

It may interest those who live in the United States to learn the tropical fate of some of their familiar friends. Scarlet fever does not exist anywhere in the tropics; diphtheria is common but benign; whooping-cough and other infantile diseases are about the same as in the United States; there is very little infantile paralysis. Neither do the deficiency diseases offer any particular problem: beriberi exists in Matto Grosso and from Bahia north, and rickets is sometimes encountered in cities; but pellagra and scurvy are practically nonexistent.

Certain little matters of diet and daily habit are vastly more important from the standpoint of public health than any disease mentioned in the last paragraph. Expectoration is one. As Sir Richard Burton observed:

Expectoration is a popular habit in the Brazil as in the United States. Most men do it instinctively: some, as they whistle, for want of thought; others, because they consider it sanitary, think thereby to preserve a spare habit of body, or hold it to promote appetite or drinketite. My conclusion is that spitting is natural, so to speak, and refraining from it is artificial, a habit bred by waxed parquets and pretty carpets.

The learned doctors of the Harvard School of Tropical Medicine saw more in this matter than did the genial translator of the *Arabian Nights* and the *Lusiads* of Camões.

Catarrhal conditions of the respiratory mucous membranes as evidenced in coughing, hawking, and spitting, seem to be common, although severe infections of the parts are rare. On the steamers it is not uncommon to see a pool of expectoration beneath the hammock. How much this unpleasant feature is merely a habit or how much due to conditions induced by constantly smoking the irritating tobacco of the country is uncertain. That it is not seen among the foreigners is in favor of its being merely a habit.[17]

These two distinguished observers should be heard upon another subject, very attentively. Although they saw only the Amazon country, their remark has meaning for the rest of cachaça-drinking Brazil:

It has seemed to us if we selected the one disease of the region to which the greatest degree of physical degeneration is due and which indirectly furnishes the underlying cause of many infections, it is alcoholism.

[17] Councilman and Lambert, *The Medical Report of the Rice Expedition to Brazil* (Cambridge, Mass., 1918), 105, 106.

That remark applies even more to white men living in the tropics than to native elements. Men of the highest grade do not always gravitate to the most isolated posts; social restraint is less, salaries and leisure generally more than at home. The result is that Europeans and Americans become—well, cocktails gradually take the place of exercise. Until this factor is eliminated, it is not wise to generalize too glibly about the impossibility of the white man ever getting along there.

Personally, and as men go in this world, I do not consider Brazil a hard-drinking country. Gardner said he saw more drunks the Sunday he arrived home in Liverpool than in all the five years he wandered through the sertão of Brazil. A drunken man is a rare phenomenon on the streets of Brazilian cities. In the country I have seen more. And I can say that all the bad temper, shooting, and knifing that I have seen or heard of in Brazil has been invariably connected with alcohol.

Unless modern dietitians are all wrong in regard to the value of a low protein diet, there would seem to be more of a health problem connected with Brazil's food than with her drink. For man upon this planet never became more nearly carnivorous than in many extensive sections of Brazil. In my travels, I do not recall sitting down to a Brazilian dinner where fewer than three or four meat dishes were served, and at the heavy meal in the middle of the day black beans—likewise heavy in protein—are added, or, with the poorer classes, form the main dish. Dr. Hackett inclines toward the position that high protein and the dysenteries go hand in hand.

Now any such set of facts, withdrawn from their background, gives an unduly gloomy impression. I do not by any manner of means intend to suggest, as did a Brazilian doctor in a public address that reverberated throughout the realm in 1916, that, "Brazil is one vast hospital!" And yet the health problem is so grave that Brazil's Chief of Rural Sanitation, Dr. Belisario Penna, was moved to write this:

As to the laboring class of Brazil, its productive capacity is reduced by more than two-thirds. Vigorous persons with normal physical efficiency are in number pitifully few; we calculate that 50 per cent are no more than half efficient; that 20 per cent have lost two-thirds of their normal efficiency. And 25 per cent are entirely unfitted by Chagas's disease, ulcers, leprosy, syphilis, anemia, etc. . . . When I think that, with the exception of Rio Grande do Sul in large part and São Paulo up to a certain point, that is the sorrowful condition of all Brazil—still worse in several regions—I have the sensation of having been born in a land accursed.[18]

Such a situation is a challenge to action. What has Brazil done about it?

The stamping out of epidemics was obviously the first duty of Brazilian medicine, and to what an admirable degree that has already been accomplished is indicated above.

Establishing General Headquarters for the Brazilian War upon Disease seemed the second. With the erection of the *Instituto Oswaldo Cruz,* Brazil organized a center of medical research which furnishes inspiration and leadership to the whole profession, one of the best equipped medical research laboratories anywhere. Its publications command scientific attention throughout the civilized world, the most important appearing in four languages. In the *Memorias* of the Institute appear the contributions to knowledge of that prolific and indefatigable veteran of Brazilian science, Dr. Adolpho Lutz. The *Report on the Journey down the River Paraná to Asunción* made by Drs. Lutz, Souza Araujo, and O. Da Fonseca in 1918, and the important *Studies on Schistosomiasis* made in the north by Drs. Lutz and Oswino Penna, are but two of many important works by this savant which are available in English. Dr. Figueiredo Rodrigues's *Experimental Beriberi and Beriberi in Man,* and Dr. J. P. Fontenelle's contributions in the field of hygiene are both admirable. Of the studies made in the dry sertão by Arthur Neiva and Belisario Penna, Frederick Hoffman says, "There has never been a better leprosy survey for any section of the United States, but particularly for the southern portion of Louisiana, where unquestionably the dis-

---

[18] Belisario Penna, *Conferencias* (Rio, 1919), p. 68.

ease is endemic." The list of fine researches by the Rio group could be enlarged indefinitely. And research is only one function of the Institute: it furnishes all Brazil with serums against plague, diphtheria, tetanus, and meningitis.

São Paulo is no less distinguished. The Instituto Butantan is the world's headquarters for information and serums against snake-bite, and Dr. Vital Brazil's beautifully got out publications are available in the French. Of the report on epidemic influenza, with particular reference to the State of São Paulo, by Drs. Meyer and Teixeira, Hoffman further says, "There is not extant for any portion of the United States a more thorough inquiry into the facts of this supremely important disease." [19]

The fountainhead, then, of medical knowledge in Brazil is pure and flowing. But it cannot be said without flattery that the medical schools of Brazil as yet come up to modern standards, or that the medical profession in rural districts is at all adequate. Many, however, receive their medical education or do postgraduate work in Europe and the United States, and under the leadership of such men the situation is rapidly improving. The disappearance of the epidemics noted above has been the work of Brazilian doctors. And that hookworm is in a very fair way toward ultimate extinction is due to the enthusiastic backing of the International Health Board by the medical profession. Now many Brazilian states are rapidly taking over that work themselves.

The nursing profession has until recently been a monopoly of Catholic sisterhoods whose members lacked high professional standards and who were without anything approaching modern training. The first training-school for nurses on modern lines was organized in Rio de Janeiro in 1922.

In general, we can say that the public health work entrusted to the Federal Government, such as inspection of incoming

[19] "Health Conservation and Vital Statistics of the American Republics South of Mexico," by Frederick L. Hoffman, Vice-Pres. and Statistician, Prudential Insurance Company of America, *Bul.* of Pan-American Union, Oct., 1921.

vessels and the establishing of quarantines against infectious diseases for both men and animals, is efficiently carried out.

MORTALITY RATES OF BRAZILIAN CITIES IN 1920

(Data furnished by the *Inspectoria de Estatistica Demographo-Sanitaria,* of the Brazilian National Department of Public Health)

BRAZILIAN CAPITALS	DEATHS PER THOUSAND OF POPULATION	FOR COMPARISON	
		Bombay	46.7
		Madras	41.2
		Cairo	39.84
		Calcutta	38.81
Fortaleza	36.27	20 registration cities of Central and South America and West Indies, 1917	24.0
Recife	32.52		
Maceió	28.21		
Nictheroy	27.48		
Natal	25.99	20 registration States of Central and South America and the West Indies, 1916	22.0
Victoria	24.92		
Aracajú	24.06		
Porto Alegre	23.12		
São Salvador	22.24		
São Luiz	21.95		
RIO DE JANEIRO	18.92		
São Paulo	18.24	Trieste	18.4
Manáos	16.80		
Belém	16.51		
Florianopolis	15.45	Vienna	15.14
Curytiba	15.03		
		Paris	14.43
		Copenhagen	13.5
		New York	12.93
		Chicago	12.70
		Dresden	12.45
		Hamburg	12.13
		Christiania	11.5
		Stockholm	11.07
		Antwerp	10.5
		Amsterdam	10.34
		GERMANY	16.3
		UNITED STATES REGISTRATION AREA	13.1
		White	12.8
		Colored	18.4
		ENGLAND AND WALES	12.4

The public health functions devolving upon the states vary

greatly, being very satisfactory in São Paulo and very wretched in some of the northern states. Municipal functions like water supply, sewage disposal, inspection of markets, and street cleaning are but indifferently performed in any but the best of Brazilian cities; the best—Rio, for instance—is as clean and fine as anything in the world, far cleaner than most North American cities of comparable size.

I should like to close on that optimistic note and leave the impression that the death rate is about to drop ten points, but candor will not permit. For the field of medicine in Brazil is disputed by the *curandeiro,* and as yet he occupies tco extensive a portion of the field. The intellectual habitat of the curandeiro will be understood by any one who knows the back country of North Carolina. There diagnosis of disease is easy because there can be but two things the matter with a child: "hives" and "thrash." There can be the bold hives, the inward hives, or the plain hives; bold hives is always fatal; inward hives are where no rash appears. "Thrash" is any disease of the throat or mouth and includes what "them fool doctors" would call diphtheria, tonsilitis, thrush, bronchitis, and peritonsillar abscess. The treatment for thrash is to pass the child backward through a white mule's collar. In backward Carolina, the chief cause of death is "perishing to death."

The curandeiro is a social institution that has come down through the centuries of Brazilian history, accumulating traditions if not knowledge, and with as rigid professional ethics as his scientific rivals. Half the fun in life will for me be gone if ever he should disappear. I love to contemplate him as he sat at the church door on Sunday mornings a hundred years ago, making urinalyses long before we had laboratories for the purpose. An anxious husband or father galloped in from a weary ride of perhaps a hundred miles and handed the curandeiro the cow's horn containing the liquid he had so carefully guarded all that way. The curandeiro took the sample without asking any questions about the patient, poured a little into the palm of his hand, looked at it toward the

light, and tossed it into the air. Painstakingly he repeated
the experiment in the interest of absolute accuracy. He
watched it minutely to see whether it fell in large drops or
small. From this he was able to tell if the disease were hot
or cold and to prescribe accordingly.

Although history has not preserved all his prescriptions,
contemporary practice enables us to fill in the picture. An
infallible cure for snake-bite, for instance, is the following
"magical words":

```
S A T O R
A R E P O
T E N E T
O P E R A
R O T A S
```

Each line is to be written separately on a slip of paper, and
then rolled into the form of a pill, the whole five to be administered as soon as possible after the person or animal has
been bitten. He has an infallible means of prognostication in
cases of severe cough: catch the fish called the *mayú*, have
the patient spit in the fish's mouth, replace the fish in the
stream—if the mayú swims upstream the patient will live,
if down he will die. The curandeiro has an unwritten manual
which might be entitled "Birth Made Easy," which doth
affirm:

If a woman in labor will change shirts with her husband, each
wearing the other's inside out, she sitting with his hat on in the
center of a twenty liter tub, she "gives the child to the light" much
more successfully. To extract the placenta, cut the cord and apply
to the inside of the right leg. Place a slipper, sole outwards, over
the cord and tie with a red ribbon.

Alcoholism offers no problem to the curandeiro. Place a piece
of bread in the armpits of a dying man; the smallest portion
administered without his knowledge to one addicted to intem-
perance will produce a perfect cure.

Following the subject further would lead us into obscenities compounded of Roman Catholicism, the technique of the Indian pagé, and Darkest Africa; the three elements are perfectly easy to trace back to their sources, and beyond to the dark traditions of the childhood of the race. It is not all balderdash, and the curandeiro fills a pathetic public need. There is a county only twenty miles from São Paulo where a rural population of ten thousand has not a single doctor. If one started at Manáos and went toward Bogotá, say twelve hundred miles, one would not encounter a doctor in the whole distance; yet he would pass many people who are diseased and frightened. These curandeiros are the fine flower of a backward social environment; they bloom only in a rich soil of illiteracy and ignorance. Their power is so real that many times the free consulting rooms of the International Health Board have been emptied by them. They flourish in the highly civilized cities of Rio and São Paulo and are patronized by wealthy people, as well as in the sertão where their fee is a young pig, a Standard Oil can full of beans, or a brace of pullets. You first hear about them with roars of laughter; as you think about them and really learn what they mean to Brazil, you are inclined to weep.

A catch comes in my throat, too, when I pick up a beautiful pamphlet put out by the *Liga Pró-Saneamento do Brazil* telling how to guard against malaria, or hookworm, or Chagas's disease. On the cover it says, *"Folheto para ser distribuido gratuitamente ao povo"* (Leaflet to be distributed gratuitously to the people). But the people of rural Brazil cannot read! If seventy-five per cent or more of the entire population is illiterate, and the educated are chiefly in the cities, it means just that.

Now Brazil's public health problem can be stated. Nay, more than Brazil's problem—it is everywhere the basic problem of the tropics. The problem is simply to educate a population so ignorant that it does not know it is diseased, to the point where the mass of men and women can appreciate and apply elementary modern sanitation.

What of the white man in the tropics? Until 1900 the

richest food-producing regions of the earth were closed to the dominant breed of food-consuming bipeds. It was disease, not climate, that shut the door. Since Panama we know that the white man can live, and work, and thrive even in the hot, moist, tropical lowlands. In a recent article reviewing what he calls "anthropological researches into the unsentimental history of mankind," Dr. Herbert J. Spinden brilliantly punctures the bubbles of illusion that Nordics have blown about the superstition that only a disagreeable, bleak, intemperate climate produces an agreeable, sunny, and civilized man.[20] There is space here to mention but one of his conclusions: "That Nordic blondness does little damage and no good—except in a social way—and the whole world is the field of competition for all the great races of the world." The same question is handled from the standpoint of practical statesmanship in the "Report of the Subcommittee on the Question of the Possibility of the Permanent Occupation of Tropical Australia by a Healthy Indigenous White Race."[21] The report goes into the data furnished by the recent war draft, actuarial statistics, and school examinations in northern Australia; makes constructive suggestions regarding the prohibition of alcohol, housing, clothing, diet, and hygienic education; and concludes that they are now in a position to bury the superstition that the white Australian cannot develop his tropical country by the sweat of his own brain and brawn. If the white man, how much more easily the colored races may live and work and thrive even in hot, moist, tropical lowlands.

The thing that makes it possible for black, and white, and brown, and yellow men to dream of a real conquest of the tropics with a prospect of the dream coming true, is that Science today knows how to handle every one of the worst health problems that cripple Brazil. In the understanding of the New Knowledge, yellow fever is carried by *Aëdes*

---

[20] Spinden, "Civilization and the Wet Tropics," *World's Work*, Feb., 1923.
[21] *Tropical Diseases Bul.*, Vol. XVII, No. 3, April 5, 1921, p. 223.

Instituto Butantan, São Paulo's splendid laboratory where serums against poisonous snakes are prepared, and fine research work in medicine carried on. (See page 347.)

The type of hospital seen in the smaller cities of Brazil; they have not yet learned the value of screens. (See page 341.)

The heart of the tropics. *Left.* A street of small shops in São Luiz, under the Equator. *Right.* *O Teatro Municipal*, Manáos, a relic of the days when rubber was rolling and every one drank champagne for breakfast. Not bad for the heart of the jungle? (See page 202.)

Aegyptus and prevented by mosquito control. Malaria is carried by *Anopheles* and prevented by mosquito control. Chagas's disease is carried by the barbeiro and prevented by building a house with a smooth wall. Bubonic plague is carried by a flea and prevented by catching a rat. Hookworm is the penalty of a filth habit and is cured by chenopodium and a latrine. Typhoid and paratyphoid can be eliminated by inoculations and watching the water supply. They were thus controlled during the World War, whereas in previous gatherings of great masses of men they accounted for far more than battle losses. Dysentery and cholera are avoided by boiling drinking water. Venereal diseases are controlled by prophylaxis, as all the armies of the world proved. In the understanding of the New Knowledge, spitting all over the premises is not the way to stamp out tuberculosis.

Any man armed with the New Knowledge can travel the length and breadth of Brazil and remain in perfect health even today when infections and contagions menace him on every side. If one man can do it, the problem of all men doing it becomes a question of human intelligence. The difficulties are not climatic; they are questions of food, clothing, housing, and habits. They are matters that are amenable to control by populations of the comparatively low average intelligence of Germany, France, or the United States. Nothing in the tropics that now menaces man is fixed and unalterable. The game is his if he will play it, and the stakes are unimaginably high. The tropics are not a pesthole if their sanitation be considered as a problem in public education. But the New Knowledge cannot be sucked into a sterilized needle and injected into the brain of illiteracy. Ignorance is the fundamental tropical disease.

CHAPTER XVII

THE DRAWING OF THE NET

The Latin world in all its aspects, political, social, literary, scientific, moral, and economic, is governed, unhappily, by the norms and dictates of an antiquated society, in which the most immoderate aspiration of inequality and privilege constitutes the dominant principle of national life.
—MARIO PINTO SERVA.

BRAZIL—immense, fantastic, green and brown and sear; forests of deadly silence, prairies and pack trains, and the sound of a guitar; dugouts gliding down sluggish rivers and coffee in straight rows to the far horizon; gold in the gravels, gold on the cacao stems, the golden crown of the *ipé;* mud, and melancholy, and the march of human hosts against the embattled forces of nature.

"The march of tin soldiers against an environment that is too much for them!" sneers the Scoffer. "Don't talk of that people sitting on the bench of equality beside the Powers of the temperate zone. If a people is illiterate seven hundred and fifty in the thousand, shot through and through with endemic disease, unable to coöperate for large social ends, the female half of the race still fettered with the inferiority of the Middle Ages, their trade fettered with all the hobbles and hamperings known to petty government, living in mud houses because they are too lazy to saw the timber lying in their front yard, content to travel over trails and cart tracks that would have disgraced medieval Europe, still cultivating with the hoe as though the plow had never been invented, herding humped cattle that world markets won't buy, guarding their natural resources as would a herd of wild asses in the wilderness—what more is there to say? What now of your 'universal brotherhood amidst the stars'? 'Not what men are but what they do, constitutes their claim to deference.' Mill

said it. They stand condemned out of your own mouth."
No, senhor!

There is an inarticulate mass in Brazil which I will call
"The People." They are wholly unlettered. Because they
are unlettered they have no standards in agriculture, or animal
husbandry, or architecture. They have never seen a fine,
hard, graded road with bridges over the streams. They have
never seen a field manured and plowed. They do not know
that any breeds of cattle exist except those they see in their
pastures. They have never stood before an open fireplace
with a chimney to lead away the smoke. They have little
consciousness of the great outside world, which some of them
call "Paris." They have no part in government. For the
most part landless, their only stake in the country is vicarious,
through their *patrão* and their *chefe politico*.

There is a highly articulate class in Brazil which I will call
"The Betrayers of the People." They are lettered, apt at
phrase-making, eloquent in oratory. Because they are lettered
and have gone to Europe, they are familiar with the best
standards in agriculture, animal husbandry, and architecture.
They have built a few fine, hard, graded roads out of their
capitals, with bridges over the streams, in order that their
automobiles may have a place to play. In their European
travels they have seen thousands of fields fertilized, and irri-
gated, and plowed. At the Palermo show in Buenos Aires
they have seen the finest cattle in the world. They know the
comforts of a ventilated house. They know far more about
the great outside world than they do about Brazil, for they
have gone to Paris. Government is the job for which they
consider themselves born. They own the land and everything
in it, for they are the patrões, the doutores, and the politicos.

Of the People we need say but two things here. "These
people are good, simple folk, and can be molded to any form
we elect." And that sober judgment of an American who
knew men, Theodore Roosevelt:[1]

[1] *Through the Brazilian Wilderness,* p. 254.

Looking at the way the work was done, at the good-will, the endurance, and the bull-like strength of the camaradas, and the intelligence and the unwearied efforts of their commanders, one could but wonder at the ignorance of those who do not realize the energy and power that are so often possessed by, and that may be so readily developed in, the men of the tropics.

If the People are ignorant, diseased, landless, and without standards, whose fault is it? There is but one answer. It is the fault of the Betrayers of the People who misgovern Brazil, who have misgoverned Brazil from the day they set foot in America. It is the fault of the system of chattel slavery which they fastened upon Brazil from 1530 to 1888. It is the fault of the glorification of governmental place-holding which has come down undimmed from the days of Golden Gôa into the present. It is the fault of the system of great landed properties which goes back to the days of the conquest of Alemtejo from the Moors. It is the fault of that most false article in the entire Spanish-Portuguese creed, the indignity of manual labor. It is the fault of the glorification of faith and the denial of science.

When a narrow class successfully takes unto itself all power, all knowledge, all wealth, it can rightly claim that the laurels of national glory should deck its brow alone. Unto it by right pertains all praise and all blame. If there be no glory, it still must bear the blame.

Does Brazil's four hundred years of history yet prove that the admixture of widely different stocks spells degeneration? that the "child of the future" is stillborn, and had better be buried? By no manner of means. The indictment of a ruling class, of an economic system, of a false philosophy, is not the indictment of a people. Classes pass. The *ancien régime* is but a dim memory in France. The inbred type of homo-with-a-crown is passing. One great nation has thrown overboard the capitalist system. Who can imagine that the ideals of a day that is so dead can endure in Brazil more than another generation? Already within the shell of this medieval actuality which I have portrayed there is growing the hard, clear-visioned idealism which shall rend the veil and carry the conquest of themselves and their environment to a conclusion acceptable to an integrating world-civilization.

Many are the Brazilians who know better than I that Brazil during four hundred years sought unsuccessfully to construct an enduring civilization with the soft adobe blocks of slavery, disease, and ignorance; who know that of the hard-burnt bricks of freely coöperating labor, public health, and popular education must be built the Brazil of the Future.

Let one of them here be heard.[2]

For a century we have been living in a dream. . . . The great democratic movement of the French Revolution, the English parliamentary agitations, the liberal spirit of the institutions which rule the American republic, all this has exercised and exercises over our governing classes, politicians, statesmen, legislators, publicists, a magnetic fascination which completely befuddles their vision of our own national problems. Under the ineluctable fascination, they lose their objective sense of the real Brazil and create in its place a Brazil altogether artificial and extraordinary, a Brazil bearing the custom-house manifest, *made in Europe*—a sort of extravagant cosmorama wherein, above forests and campos yet to be discovered and civilized, pass and repass scenes and figures typically European.

Furthermore, the ingeniously dithyrambic mode in which we caress our honeyed patriotism has woven for us a radiant web of presumptions about our capacities and greatness, very capricious and beautiful with its woof of silver and gold, no doubt—for that the poets strove!—but which the hard realities, which we shall have to confront in the near future, will rend with impiety and brutality if we do not have the foresight to divest ourselves of it sooner, in a very honest desire to see clearly what is going on among us and about us, for the greater security of our collective existence.

Because that which the most superficial observation of international affairs reveals is the absorbing preponderance of those peoples who organize themselves under objective criteria; of the races nourished on a sense of the realities; of the men who pay nothing to theories nor fictions, and who know how to face, with serenity and coolness, life as it is in its ugliness and egotism, in its instincts and

[2] F. J. Oliveira Vianna, *Populações Meridionaes do Brazil* (São Paulo, 1920), Preface, pp. ix-xii.

passions—because they believe in their power to transform it voluntarily, when they apply themselves with tenacity, continuity, energy, to the work of self-salvation. The sentimental and imaginative peoples, the idealistic races, who do not believe in the force of this incalculable power which, like faith, moveth mountains, these shut their eyes to reality in order not to see, when their weakness, their incapacity, their insufficiency, their misery, is mentioned:—prefer to remain like the fallen sepulchers of Scripture.

These peoples, who thus consciously and systematically practice the cult of self-illusion, are doomed to perish. Those who will eliminate them are those lusty manipulators of fact and reality, those practical and experimental peoples whose splendid objective sense of the facts of life shields them against the insidious suggestions of an optimism which, instead of accepting the cruel and sad truth in order to correct or eliminate it, prefer to dissimulate, to cover it with the flowered embroidery of amiable fictions.

Sonorous, showy, brilliant withal, these optimists are so only in appearance. Sound them well in the depths of their soul, and what you will encounter beneath the pleasing aspect of confidence, of enthusiasm, and of faith in the destinies of the country, is the empty hand of the most discouraged pessimism. They are afraid to point out a defect of their people or to mention an incapacity of their race, because they do not believe that man can remold life by the action of his own will. They are fatalists in their way, unsubmitting fatalists, who do not resign themselves, like the Mussulman, to fatality, but elude it, deny it, color it with ideals and with hopes. Like opium smokers, they enjoy the voluptuousness of artificial paradises and encounter in their induced illusion the euphoric sensation of force, of greatness, and of triumph.

For a century we have been like smokers of opium, in the midst of races who are active, audacious, and progressive. For a century we have been living upon dreams and fictions, in the midst of practical and objective peoples. For a century we have been cultivating the politics of delirium and illusion before men of action and prey, who, on all sides, into all regions of the globe, go planting, by peace or by force, the standards of their sovereignty.

In this ever-narrowing contact our destiny is traced. It is that of the earthen pots of the fable, which whirled and gyrated in the same quiet spot beside the pots of iron, against which, with a crash, they broke in pieces.

From this destiny, from such fatality, we may escape by but one road: by seriously taking a courageous resolution to change methods —methods of education, methods of politics, methods of legislation, methods of government. The problem of our salvation must be solved by other standards than those now dominant. Above all, we must deal with facts and not hypotheses, with realities and not fictions, and, by the force of heroic resolution, renovate our ideas, remake our culture, reëducate our character.

Book IV

LOOKING AHEAD

Gather yourselves together, that I may tell you that which shall befall you in the last days.

CHAPTER XVIII

HIGHWAYS

In this Empire, about to be so mighty and magnificent, communication signifies civilization, prosperity, progress—everything. It is more important to national welfare even than the school or the newspaper, for these will follow where that precedes. And travellers who wish well to the land must ever harp, even to surfeit, upon this one string.—SIR RICHARD BURTON, *The Highlands of the Brazil* (1869).

As a traveler who wishes well to a land which has given him much, I reiterate the obvious wisdom of her Majesty's onetime Consul at Santos. Men mingle in exact ratio as migration is facile, and only by mingling can there be woven a strong fabric of nationality.

I recall an island in the Philippines scarce thirty miles across. On both coasts were villages, but through the center was a barrier of mountain and forest. With good porters one could walk across the almost impassable trail, but when he got to the other side his porters could not talk with the people on the other shore. A totally different language, hatred, misunderstanding, border feuds. When the Americans drove a macadam road through from one side to the other, one could see the old isolations breaking down day by day. Natural surface roads and graded trails are matters of the first importance if Brazil is to break down the isolations, ignorance, superstition, and medievalism of her hinterland.

That good graded trails are a simple matter was demonstrated on a forest in the rainiest part of southern Bahia. The characteristic of many existing trails, as I pointed out, is the concavity of the cross-section. They are ditches. But by inexpensive shovel work, ditching the sides and raising the center, instead of forcing the pack animals to wallow in a trough worn by their own feet, the mules can be pulled up out of the mud. British, French, Dutch, and American foresters in tropical forests have constructed thousands of miles of good pack trails in regions as difficult as the worst of the evergreen forest of Brazil.

By a natural surface road I mean one whose surface is the soil in which the road is built, or a mixture of sand and clay that can be had cheaply almost everywhere. It is an inexpensive type of construction. It is the type of more than nine-tenths of the roads in the United States. They are intermediate between the road with a hard surface such as gravel, broken stone, concrete, brick, or asphalt, and the ruts of oxcarts, which are no roads at all. Metaled surfaces are expensive. They are likewise unnecessary except for trunk lines which must stand up under a heavy automobile traffic: witness the fact that only about six per cent of the roads in the United States have a hard surface, and that the United States Office of Public Roads estimated that eighty-five per cent of the roads of North America would remain indefinitely with natural surfaces only.

Brazilians sometimes complain of their heavy rainfall as though it presented an insuperable difficulty to the building and maintenance of good roads. That this factor offers less of a problem than the annual freezing and thawing experienced by more than half the United States is the judgment of highway engineers familiar with both countries.

The thing that seems difficult for agricultural communities everywhere in the western hemisphere to learn is that the initial construction of a road is the least of it. Maintenance is the secret of good roads. Like a woman's love, roads are to be held only by unfaltering devotion. Twelve months in the year the repair squad must be on the job in a wet region, if the complexion of the highways is to remain fresh and blooming.

CHAPTER XIX

FOREST POLICY [1]

WHAT magnificent whiskers men grew when the world was young! What luxuriant beards adorned the blond heads of the Barbarians, impenetrable jungles of hair that swept their chests as they chatted and caught the crumbs as they fell. We can only faintly imagine their luxuriance from the few examples that have come down into modern times. Then man looked in the mirror. And he shaved. And he trimmed his long locks. But his eyebrows and the hair of his head he did not shave. And the problem confronting the unresting bipeds who are spinning the world on its axis just now is: Shall man continue the devastation and destroy the hair of his head and eyebrows? or shall he keep a certain portion of his globe permanently producing pelage as a contrast to the smoothness of his face?

I think I am the first scientist to point out that this problem hinges entirely upon the subsidiary and seemingly unimportant question of what man decides to do with the forests. For it is easily demonstrable that the hairiness of the whisker-growing branch of the human race is lessening *pari passu* with the deforestation of the globe. So even for men who never have been within a forest in their lives—and that is probably true of over half the race—a discussion of forest policy has an intimate, fireside interest.

When the world was young—and not so much younger either —the forests were as luxuriant as the whiskers of the Barbarians. Softwood forests of conifers balked the bitterness of the north wind from Alaska to Labrador. Towering Douglas fir and the ancient redwoods extended down the Pacific

[1] First published in the *Bulletin* of the Pan-American Union, July, 1924.

coast to below San Francisco, linking the crucifixion of 1914 to the crucifixion of Christ in memories already stored with the events of 2,000 years when Jesus walked in the flesh. Various pines formed a loin-clout of richest fabrication about the buttocks of the Sierras and Rockies. East of the Great Plains the conifers reappeared in the white-pine forests of our northern boundary from the Great Lakes to New England as a monument marking the last stand of the continental glaciers. And a wreath of conifers, too, garlanded the continent from Texas to New Jersey. Across the Atlantic the coniferous forests swept with scarcely a break from the Scandinavian Peninsula through Finland, European Russia, and Siberia to the shores of the Pacific, arguing ever with Nordic and Mongol and the migrants between that the East and the West are one.

Marching with the conifers on the south, the temperate hardwoods occupied a better class of soils, but were nowhere so extensive; light-hearted, temperamental, feminine forests which changed their raiment three times in the day of their year. When spring called them from their winter's sleep, they decked themselves in all the delicacies of green and blossom that an indulgent mother could contrive. Their midday gown, a full, easy leafage for the shade and sunshine of the idle summer. But as the dinner hour of fall approached, what a riot of color, what slim bare arms against the harvest moon, how surpassingly beautiful they made themselves! Gay forests that laughed at the stern solemnity of their northern brother with his one frugal suit of green.

Tropical hardwoods formed the third great belt, a sacrament of silence that revealed the inward and spiritual grace of Asia from the foothills of the Himalayas to the point of the Malay Peninsula and on into Sumatra, Borneo, and the Philippines. Richer, in the intricate variegations of ten thousand species, than the costliest canopy of oriental prince, the hardwoods of the low latitudes shaded a large part of the peninsula of India. In Africa, sorrowful as the stunted spruce of the Arctic and weeping the tears denied Sahara, the evergreens of the Tropics reached dejectedly from the Great Lakes to the Atlantic in Angola, writhed above the wickedness of the Belgian Congo, and reaching thence through French Equatorial Africa and along the Guinea coast to the Gambia, shrouded in oblivion deeds too dark to bear the light of day. But the greatest extent of tropical hardwoods was, and is, in South America, particularly in Brazil. The Amazon forest, with the contiguous timber in the Guianas and Venezuela, covers not less than fifteen hundred million acres and carries at the minimum five thousand billion board feet of timber.[2]

"Incredible, inexhaustible, illimitable" were the forests which clothed our bearded earth when the world was young.

It is hoped that the world will wag along some years more. Neither does human society seem about to perish; an organism with such superabundant energy that it can squirt thirty million men into a carnival of slaughter is surely going strong. Yet none but a fool would nowadays speak of the world's forest wealth as inexhaustible, illimitable. Only four countries of Europe any longer possess more than enough timber to supply their own present needs: Norway, Sweden, Finland, and Soviet Russia. Most of China has been trimmed as bare as a newborn babe. Spain, Italy, and Greece have shaved their eyebrows with no marked improvement in looks. What happened about the Mediterranean is aptly summed up in an interview with Prof. Patrick Geddes:[3]

"I have been specially interested in the history of the Mediterranean lands and peoples—e.g. in the association of the decline of ancient Rome and of modern Spain and Turkey with the gradual deterioration of their soil."

"In what way?"

"Chiefly by the cutting down of trees, which has altered not only the soil, but even the climate, of the countries bordering on the Mediterranean. It is everybody's obvious interest to cut down trees, so for the sake of immediate gain the interest of the future is sac-

[2] H. N. Whitford, *The Forests of Brazil* (in preparation).
[3] *British Weekly,* July 8, 1897.

rificed. Under the great maritime civilizations, from the Phoenician to the Venetian, the country was recklessly stripped of its forests. The peasant, too, did it to make a clearing, the shepherd to find grass. Then came the torrential rains of every autumn and spring, the soil was washed away, and the slopes were completely denuded, so that now we find barren rock where once was fertile soil."

At this point the Professor showed me a number of very curious photographs of Cyprus, showing how by the destruction of forests the rocks have gradually been laid bare. The work of afforestation in Cyprus or the East generally will be, of course, a slow affair, but, so he says, a holy war, a war lasting over centuries, but one which, as it goes on, will bring back wealth, health, and happiness to the impoverished and degenerate Eastern races.

The forest maps of Canada and Siberia look limitless in their splash of green; but when one realizes that all those far northern stands in the interior of the continent are very light and that it takes three or four hundred years to grow a decent tree up there, the deep green pales to a greenish gray. The delusion that the United States can lean indefinitely upon her northern neighbor is a dream from which the wood-pulp industry is already awaking.

In short, the two northern forest belts have been so reduced that today the combined acreage of conifers and temperate hardwoods scarce equals that of the tropical hardwoods, which are still fairly intact.[4] The world situation is such that in the western hemisphere within half a century the center of hardwood production will pass inevitably from the United States to Brazil. Brazil has the goods. She has more timber which can easily be dumped on the deck of an ocean-going steamship than any other region in the world. She may be sure the lumbermen of North America, like wolves on the flank of the caribou herd, will be after it the minute they have cleaned the carcasses of the remaining redwoods, Douglas fir, and southern pine. What then will Brazil do? The time to draw up battle orders is before men go over the top.

There are two ways of playing this game. One way is to

[4] Zon and Sparhawk, *Forest Resources of the World,* I, 14.

Left. What is called "a good burn" in Brazil. *Right.* The original type of forest in which practically every coffee and cacao plantation and planted pasture has been located. Western São Paulo. (See pages 286 ff.)

The covered wagons used by the Poles in the State of Paraná. Reminiscent of the Conestoga wagons that used to tote freight from Philadelphia over the Alleghenies. Paraná pine in the background. (See page 279.)

play it according to the rules of her great sister of the North, the United States of America. Treat the forest as a mine and not as a continuing crop. Accept the frontiersman's hatred of forests as a national philosophy. Regard the forest simply as an enemy of farmers, herdsmen, and cities; a thing to be destroyed by fire if it cannot be hacked down with an ax. Deny that society as a continuing concern has any rights or interests which conflict with those of profits from private property. Grant a timber concession in the public lands to every politician who hops on the winning band wagon. Alienate the nation's title to a basic source of raw material until all the heavy stands of desirable saw-timber are in the hands of the lumber barons. Then set aside the bare tops of Rocky Mountains and the rocky ranges where the sheep pasture as "National Forests." When you finally find yourself with your remaining timber supply from 1000 to 3000 miles from the great markets, and lumber getting so costly that housebuilding is seriously curtailed, begin buying back the burned-over, abandoned lands of the lumbermen and at colossal cost to the community undertake the century-long task of bringing back a forest cover upon lands that never should have been stripped.

Then will you be able to make such proud report as that of the Chief Forester of the United States: [5] that having shaved off two-thirds of the forest growth which covered the United States when Columbus dropped anchor, and standing on the brink of a timber famine, we are eating into our forest capital for three-fourths of our annual cut; that 52,000 forest fires in 1922 swept over 8,000,000 acres of forest land; that for every private owner of timber land who has attempted reforestation, hundreds butcher and burn in the good old ways of their forebears; that while government in the last few years has bought back some 4,000,000 acres of land which had been skinned and abandoned by lumbermen in the East, 75,000,000

[5] W. B. Greeley, Chief, U.S. Forest Service, "Balancing the Forest Ledger," *American Forestry*, Dec., 1923.

acres of virgin forest in the South and West have been reduced by said lumbermen to the same worthless condition.

"Wild asses in the wilderness."

The second way of playing the game is based upon altogether different assumptions. It assumes that the teams which will be frolicking on the gridiron a hundred years from now will have the right to find a field in good condition despite the fact that we, in our heavy boots, are kicking the ball about, this particular fine fall day. It assumes that human beings 10,000 years from now—our descendants—will have to depend upon exactly the same sources for the raw materials of life as we—soil that can produce food or forage crops, mines, waters, and forests.

"Why not put all possible land to producing food or forage?" puts in the Scoffer with an ax to grind. "Your descendants can't eat hardwood, or conifers either!"

Even that is no certainty in the light of recent experiments on hydrolized sawdust for dairy cows. But it cannot be done; because there is much land in the world so poor that it is of small use to agriculture, which nevertheless will produce fine forests. There is much land which lies so steep that if deforested the devil is to pay. There are watersheds which must be kept permanently under forest or the waters will run away with the soil and in ungovernable floods sweep the very foundation of life from beneath man's feet and carry it out to sea. In the days before man thought of planting crops, he demonstrated that he could live on a densely forested earth; but the agriculturist has not yet been born who could very long feed a densely populated earth shaved clean of forests.

So the first forest act of an intelligent nation mildly interested in the future, will be to delimit the "absolute forest soils"; those areas which, in so far as we can see into the future, will always serve society better as forest land than as farming, grazing, or denuded land. If private titles exist within such *protection forests,* they will be quashed, extinguished, wiped equitably out! Items upon which the very existence of the collectivity depends cannot be permitted to drift into (or remain in) the category of private property.

A further assumption of the social forest code is that for some time to come it will be desirable to have a steady, abundant, and cheap supply of lumber; wood for industrial uses; and fuel. Pleasant, also, to have a bit of shade in which to sit on a hot afternoon, a solitude into which one may retire when folks become too formidable. Now forests, to serve well these everyday functions, cannot be far away from the places where people live. Small forests located close to cities and scattered through farming communities are far more desirable than vast expanses of forest on the moon—and at the present moment in history, most of the Amazon forest enters no more into the life of our globe than would forests on the silvery satellite. The delimitation of such *production forests* involves an appraisal of social needs for, say, a hundred years ahead; just as a prudent housewife provides for Sunday dinner before the shops close Saturday night. Mistakes in judgment will be made, and there should be a revaluation of the whole matter at least every half-century by the light of the wisdom of more mature times. Production forests should be worked in accord with those simple forestry principles which look to the reproduction, as well as to the harvesting, of the crop.

The word "reproduction" spells the essential difference between the forester and the lumberman. At the touch of the one, profit-guided, forests wither and melt away. A certain amount of social passion and love of the medium wherein he works, plus trained intelligence, enables the forester to use and reproduce endlessly what the lumberman rapes but once.

These two categories of protection and production forests handled on forestry principles represent a permanent feature of any sound national organization. As to what proportion of productive soils should be thus kept under forest cover, we can speak only in generalities. France and Germany have the best managed forests in the world. In France the forests occupy 18 per cent of the total land area, and in Germany 24 per cent.[6] Neither produces enough wood for its own use; both have to import heavily. For a nation like Brazil to contemplate keeping less than one-third of its productive land surface permanently under forest, would be sheer folly. That would leave 60 per cent for crops and pastures, and 7 per cent for the unproductive occupation of the soil.

With these permanent production forests, as with protection forests, the first question to decide is, What shall own them? My answer to that is as unhesitating in the second case as in the first: The nation, the states, the cities, the towns. There is no possible common ground upon which to compose the diametrically opposed interest of private property in forests and social interest. If I owned a private forest (and I hope to get a concession in Brazil before she adopts these suggestions), I should be converting it into round American dollars just as fast as it could be shoved through the mill, like every other sensible American lumberman. What interest have I, an individual, in growing a second crop that I am not going to live to see harvested? If the history of the United States proves anything, it proves that for government to alienate its title to forest lands is *to sign the death warrant of the forests.* Brazil can much better afford to take Canada as a model in this respect.

In Brazil, after setting aside these two categories of permanent forests, there will still remain a great area of forest on land which ultimately will come under the plow and produce food. Here, if anywhere, is the place for the politician to locate his concessions and treat his friends to something soft on the inside; this is the land to sell to the North American lumberman; here let the nomads of shifting agriculture hack and burn at pleasure during the two or three generations it will take to lull the nefarious institution into a deep, deep sleep. But Brazil should be very sure the forests she wants to hold

[6] Zon and Sparhawk, *Forest Resources of the World,* I, 4.

for the community are well staked down before the high wind
of capitalistic exploitation strikes her.

So much for the forester's faith. What steps has Brazil
already taken? Where is she to look for further light and
leading? What is the next move in the game?

Brazil has taken three tottering steps in the direction of a
sound forest policy. The first was in 1735 when Gomes Freyre
de Andrada tried to guarantee a continuing source of timber
for the placer mines of Minas Geraes against the wishes of
the complacent miners who were working havoc with the
forests west of the Mantiqueira.[7] The miners won, and the
forests went. The second step was taken in 1911 when the
Geologic Survey published a forest map which tries to dis-
criminate the land which was originally forested from that
which appears never to have been. The last step was the
passage, in December, 1921, of a Federal forest law looking
to the establishment of a Brazilian Forest Service and outlining
its job. My information is (1923) that this law is still "but
a scrap of paper." The Brazilian Government has not yet
done anything that would bring a forester and the forests face
to face. Brazil then, at the moment, stands exactly where
British India stood sixty years ago when the Governor-General
in Council called Dietrich Brandis to organize the Indian
Forest Service.

And it is toward India that I would direct Brazil's opening
eyes for light and leading. No other country holds such pertinent lessons for Brazilian forestry.

In 1805 the King's Navy waked up to the fact that oak in
England would soon exist only in the ancient ballads. The
King asked India if he might depend upon the Malabar Coast
for a permanent supply of teak. As a result, a captain of the
police was appointed the first Conservator of Forests in India,
and within a couple of years he had quashed all private rights
of the natives in the forests of Malabar-Travancore by assum-

[7] Southey, *History of Brazil*, III, 825.

ing their nonexistence.[8] Then began a half-century dominated by the idea that society can attain its ends through money-making lumbermen. If, without going through the experience, Brazil can learn what England learned by that half-century of exploitation *à la* Police, she will save herself 200 years of grief. What England learned in that era has been confessed by a British official of large experience in India: [9]

Followed the period of leasing forests and allowing them to be worked by private enterprise, a plan which failed both in Madras, Burma, and the Central Provinces in the case of teak, in the accessible sâl forests of the Northwestern Provinces, and in the Himalayan forests with deodar. Areas of forest of enormous value were cut out by timber traders, who cared nothing for the future of the forest, while the government did not receive adequate value for the produce extracted. Instances of this nature had been plentiful in the history of many forests in Europe, but India failed to profit by these examples, and for many years Government authorities pinned their faith to the ruinous method of leasing out forests to capitalists in the hope that the latter would so work the areas as to insure a future crop of young trees taking the place of the mature, and often immature, ones felled. The hope proved as elusive in India as it has elsewhere in the world. *The method meant, and will always mean, reckless waste and inevitable ruin.*

In 1852 Pegu was annexed. Teak had always been a royal monopoly in Lower Burma and a principal export from Rangoon; so it was easy to declare all forests public property as soon as the British took over. Annexation meant a kill for capital. Public property was synonymous with meat for all the carnivora. Immediately the timber wolves began to harry the flanks of the herd. Capitalistic exploitation soon littered the road to Mandalay with so many stinking carcasses of butchered forests that Lord Dalhousie was forced to define a forest policy which would protect public interests.

So it was not because hard-headed old England had a leaning toward communism and was given to indulging the Em-

---

[8] B. Ribbentrop, Inspector-General of Forests to the Government of India, *Forestry in British India* (Calcutta, 1900), p. 65.
[9] E. P. Stebbing, *The Forests of India* (London, 1920), II, 511.

pire in Utopian philosophies that she came to the conclusion
that private ownership, or private exploitation, of forests spells
death to the forests. She arrived at that conclusion only after
the trials and errors of over half a century during which she
tried to reconcile her faith in *laissez faire* with the continuity
of Imperial raw materials.

When she did put her hand to the job of setting her house
in order, she did it in thoroughgoing, hard-headed English
fashion. The dispatch of the Governor-General in Council to
the Secretary of State, dated November 1, 1862, is good reading for Brazil—and, in my judgment, has even more meaning
for the United States:

In the first place, we may express our belief that under no conceivable circumstances is it possible that personal interests can be
made compatible with public interests in the working of forests,
otherwise than under a system of such stringent supervision as would,
in fact, reduce those working under it to the position of mere agents
of the administration. . . . We think that the idea of giving a
proprietary right in forest to any individual should be abandoned,
as the possession of such a right is almost certain to lead to the
destruction of the forest; personal interests, in short, under existing
conditions and in this respect, are not only incompatible with public
interests, but they are absolutely antagonistic.

We consider also that all Government forests should be strictly
set apart, and made unalienable; of course, where private rights
already exist, or where in the case of the forests of Burma certain
rights have been conferred on private parties for a limited time,
they must be respected, though it might be good policy to extinguish
such rights on equitable terms whenever it be found possible to
do so. . . .

Of course it can not be said that any forest which is now thought
to be necessary, or worth preserving, will be held to be so for all
time, but the facilities for the destruction of forest are so great, the
difficulty of reproducing it so insurmountable, and the general tendency in this country to accept as truth the fallacy that the clearance
of forest is of itself necessarily an improvement so common, that it
will be important to record forest boundaries and so set forest land
apart in a very strict and formal manner. . . .

Having thus secured, as far as possible, that the boundaries of
those forests which it is intended to preserve shall be respected, and

having obtained maps and surveys of the whole of them, a solid basis would be got on which to establish an efficient forest administration, the great end of which should be to obtain the largest possible quantity of produce from the forests, consistent with their permanent usefulness. . . . The forests, when set aside as such, should be made to assume a distinct plan of their own in the departments producing revenue, and the success or failure of the administration should be made at once apparent from the state of the balance on the forest budget.

After some obvious remarks on the necessity of a trained personnel, the dispatch concludes:

Organization to be of real and permanent value must not be essentially, or even mainly, dependent on extraordinary personal acquirements or activity; the machinery should be such as will work with average men under the direction of the best of their class. And this is peculiarly the case as regards the administration of forests. Results will be so long in coming, and ruin is so easily and so immediately brought about by the neglect of first principles by a single individual, that as little as possible should be left open to the local executive authorities in this respect.

O wise old England, with the long look ahead! Sitting at the desk of the Secretary of State in London town was a statesman who not only could see the cogency of such argument, but could see more clearly than they in India that at the beginning of forest management there would be expenditures which would not always be covered by returns in the same year, land purchases, plantations to make, roads to build and streams to improve, which should be looked upon as just as sound a capital investment as the building of a great irrigation dam.

In reply to the above proposal to found the Indian Forest Service, the Secretary of State said:

It requires the stability of a settled administration to prevent the present destruction of forests, and hand them down in such quantity and conditions as to leave a due supply for future generations. A permanent government only can be expected to wait long enough to reap the profit obtainable from an article which it takes eighty or a hundred years to bring to maturity. Permanency, as far as it

can be obtained, is, therefore, of the highest importance in any
arrangement for the due administration of forests. And Her
Majesty's Government, therefore, entirely approve of your proposal
to make a separate department at Calcutta.

Nor did England balk at a complete reversal of her economic
policy and a denial of the dominant economic thought of the
nineteenth century.

It is very satisfactory to me to learn that you have come to the
same conclusion as Her Majesty's Government, that individuals can
not be relied upon for due care in the management of forests, inasmuch as private interests must be opposed, in this instance, to the
public interests. . . .
While alluding to financial considerations, I will observe that,
although it is of course to be hoped, and although I firmly believe
that a considerable profit will be derived from the forests, when
permanently placed under experienced and careful management;
still, profit is not the only object to be kept in view, and in the
state in which many of the forests now are it may not be possible
at once to obtain a revenue from them. An outlay, even, may
now be necessary in many instances, and, when necessary, should,
I think, be incurred. And it is another advantage of a permanent
administration that it will look forward with certainty to the repay-
ment of such an outlay in future years. I may add, too, that the
superintendents should be supplied with a sufficient staff, or it will
be impossible for them, and particularly at first, to enforce the
rules and give efficient protection to the forests under their charge.[10]

Thus England bestowed her blessing upon forestry and government ownership of forests in India. That there was no
cause to worry about the ability to make it pay will become
evident directly.

The first concern was for men to breathe life into this radical
determination of policy. When Lord Dalhousie tried to halt
the spoliation of Pegu, he cast about for some one who knew
forests and how to manage them scientifically. At that time
there was not one forester in the whole British Empire. England was deterred by no false pride. Without hesitation she

[10] Stebbing, *The Forests of India*, I, 526-30.

turned to Germany for help, and in 1856 sent out Dietrich Brandis, a highly trained German forester, to be the first superintendent of forests in Pegu, Tenasserim, and Martaban. His eight years' work in Lower Burma revealed him a scientist, forester, and administrator rolled into one; and Brandis was summoned to Calcutta to become first inspector-general of forests. His immediate problem was a staff and how to create it, the question Brazil faces at the present moment. Brandis went back to Europe and sent out two young foresters trained for the German forest service, Schlich and Ribbentrop, both of whom later filled the post of inspector-general. At the same time, before he made his initial move in the field, Brandis provided for a constant, if small, stream of technical foresters by sending selected probationers from British universities to the forest schools in France and Germany. A man without a technical education is no more able to formulate a working plan for a forest—one that will work—than a policeman to calculate the stresses for a Brooklyn Bridge. On the other hand, a forest properly handled will, with each rotation, show fewer weeds and a higher percentage of valuable species, and will put on wood faster than in a state of nature. He is a poor forester who cannot beat the methods of a virgin forest. Tropical forests, in particular, are so complex that if managed by persons ignorant of their profession, ruin would be almost as inevitable as if left to the mercies of the lumbermen. England saw it. For many years she trained her foresters at Nancy, in France. Then Schlich was called from the inspector-generalship to organize the forest school in the Royal Indian Civil Engineering College at Cooper's Hill, now transferred to Oxford University.

With a supply of brains thus provided for, the next question was to get some eyes and ears and arms, men for the subordinate executive positions. After some floundering about, trying to work with untrained men, the Imperial Forest School for native rangers was opened at Dehra in the Dun in 1878. For deputy rangers a two years' course was given in Hindustani at

Dehra Dun, a similar course in Burmese at Tharrawaddy, and a one year's course at the Madras school in English. For the last twenty years it has been an accepted dictum of the Indian Forest Service that even the forest guard cannot remain an untutored man of the woods if he is to be of any real use. Every grade between him and the inspector-general now receives a forestry training suited to his needs and intelligence.

The Indian Forest Service so organized has proved itself from every point of view. If it had not proved itself financially it would have been scrapped long ago in all probability. During the first five years of its organization, when no revenue at all should have been expected, Brandis made it pay an annual net surplus of £90,000. When Schlich succeeded to the inspector-generalship, the net surplus in 1884-85 was £207,000. When Ribbentrop, the last of the German inspectors-general, retired in 1900, he had brought the annual net surplus up to £600,000. And by 1920 the British foresters who have guided the Indian Forest Service in the twentieth century could show an annual net surplus of £1,584,000.[11]

The system of government-owned and government-worked forests adopted by the Indian Forest Service has proved itself by the total failure of the opposite system of private exploita-

[11] At the present juncture attention may be drawn to one point which this history demonstrates beyond possibility of dispute. Each reorganization and each increase of the staff, coupled with enhanced budget grants, made for the development of the forests, was quickly followed by a considerable increase in the gross and net revenues. Had more liberality been exhibited in these matters at an earlier date there seems to be little doubt that the present revenue could have reached a higher figure. For instance, for the quinquennial period 1864-69 the gross revenue amounted (annually) to Rs. 37,40,000; expenditure to Rs. 23,80,000, net surplus to Rs. 13,60,000; for the period 1884-89 the gross revenue was Rs. 116,70,000, expenditure Rs. 74,30,000, net surplus Rs. 42,40,000; for the period 1894-99 the gross revenue was Rs. 172,00,000, expenditure Rs. 98,00,000, net surplus Rs. 79,20,000. By 1919-20 this latter revenue had trebled.—Stebbing, *The Forests of India*, preface to Vol. II, p. vi.

In notifying the retirement of Mr. B. Ribbentrop, the Governor-General in Council pointed out that: "During his term of office the gross revenues of the forests have risen from 102 lacs of rupees in 1884-5 to 190 lacs in 1898-9, and the net surplus from 31 lacs to 90 lacs of rupees."—*Idem*, II, 615.

The lac is 100,000 rupees; and by the law of 1897 the rupee was given a fixed ratio of 15 to the English pound sterling.

tion. Brandis in the early days was so violently attacked by the predatory interests that the Pegu forests were again thrown open to lessees. The Tharrawaddy forests alongside remained subject to government control and were worked by departmental contractors. Result: in the Pegu forests the State incurred heavy financial losses, whereas the Tharrawaddy forests have always turned in a large and regular income.[12]

The Indian Forest Service has proved its ability to keep the markets stocked with timber. And while thus functioning at a profit, the foresters of India have reproduced the areas lumbered and can show a forest property, today, in every way more productive and serviceable to man than it was when Brandis took the helm in 1864.

A clever metamorphosis of evil into good was his handling of shifting agriculture. By persuading many of these hereditary vandals to sow teak seed along with their rice, he made a system which had been destroying forest since the childhood of the race produce pure plantations of teak at a cost far below that of the regular plantations.

So well has the Indian Forest Service proved itself that its officers have been called upon to initiate forest management in every forest in which England is interested from Siam to South Africa. They have solved every one of the major problems Brazil has to face, under conditions entirely similar. That their solutions were to the satisfaction of unsentimental England was made evident when she knighted Dietrich Brandis.

The next step for Brazil would seem obvious. Do ye likewise! Before she can set aside national forests, she must have a thorough reconnaissance of the existing public domain, state and national. That can be done only by trained and experienced tropical foresters. There is today no Brazilian with the training and experience which would qualify him to organize a forest service; she must look abroad in the first

[12] Ribbentrop, *Forestry in British India*, p. 74.

instance, as England did. The Indian, French, Dutch, and Philippine services offer plenty of competent men to draw from.

To assist in the preliminary reconnaissance by experts, there should be appointed young men of good education and physique from all the Brazilian forest states. Those who make good in the field and show a real love for a rough life that is the antithesis of that of the average Brazilian bureaucrat, should be sent to Nancy or Oxford or Yale to be trained as tropical foresters. When these first probationers have brought back to Brazil the forest lore of Europe and North America, if not before, a forest school should be founded in the University of Rio de Janeiro. There should be at least five schools for rangers—in the Paraná pine forest, in the hardwoods of São Paulo, in the maritime forests of the Rio Doce or southern Bahia, in the semi-arid northeast, and in the Amazon. With these schools functioning, the states can organize their individual services, with the Federal Forest Service to direct policy and carry on research throughout the Republic.

The place for forestry to sink its first roots into Brazilian soil is not in the Amazon, but in the forests near the centers of civilization—in São Paulo, Paraná, Santa Catharina, in the forests of the Rio Doce, and southern Bahia. Minas has already destroyed far too much forest for her own ultimate good. In another quarter-century, as things are now going, São Paulo will not be able to set aside state production forests; and there will be scarcely a stick of saw-timber standing between Santos and Bolivia.

The fact that most of the public domain has been turned over to the individual states complicates the problem in Brazil. If, however, the forest states once realize that forestry has been made to pay in dollars and cents, to yield an assured revenue in India, in Java, in the Philippines; if they realize that only by developing their forest resources can they approach a parity of economic power with the great agricultural states; if in forestry they can see the most promising weapon for winning the lowlands of the Amazon, a decision should be no more difficult for Pará and Amazonas and Matto Grosso than for São Paulo.

The stadium is packed with the élite of the western world. The event, a foot race, one of those dual international matches so popular in North Amercia since Zev ran away from the Derby winner and Dempsey knocked out the Argentine. This one, to determine relative intelligence in utilizing the wealth of forests. The distance, two miles, each mile a century; with the take-off at the 1800 post. The odds are 10 to 1 on that fine-muscled white chap with "U.S." across his breast. Few believe the brown runner, Brazil, has a chance.

At the crack of the gun they are off, though with such unequal speed that the brown man seems tied to the post. The hyphenated Anglo-Saxon does the first hundred in ten flat, sprints through the back stretch of the nineteenth century with the speed of a frightened doe. At the 1900 post the Northerner is so far ahead that the gamblers are making for the booking office to collect. But wait! A catch in the breath of the crowd. There is no runner, born of the wealth of the most prodigal environment, who can carry that pace for the distance. At the 1950 post he is staggering. Then the crash, the last stick of sound native timber in his overstrained frame exhausted. A shiver runs through the stadium.

"What if the Latin-American should have the intelligence to husband his resources and walk through to a winning?"

Brazil has as easy a proposition as that, if she has the intelligence to run the race as a distance event and not as a sprint.

The milk in the coconut is this:

The coniferous forests and the temperate hardwoods cannot much longer supply the world with the timber it wants. The day of the tropical hardwoods is at hand.

India, China, the Mediterranean, the United States should demonstrate to a blind man that there is no bench long enough for capitalistic exploitation and continuity of forest production to sit down together without crowding. Forestry is a function of the collectivity. Lumbering for profit on lands which should be kept permanently under forest is plain economic plunder, for which society in the end pays a terrible price. If you want three weeks of high life, take lumbering for profit and go on a debauch; if you want a marriage that shall endure, pick the other woman. Polygamy will ruin the temper of both.

If the choice be for out-and-out government ownership and for forestry, protection and production forests, of a total area not less than one-third of Brazil's land surface, should be definitely demarked and entrusted to the management of a trained personnel.

How to develop a trained personnel and handle tropical forests at a profit can be learned from the Indian Forest Service.

Every consideration that makes forestry sound in temperate regions makes it doubly and trebly sound in the Tropics. Whatever the uniform heat and moisture of the wet Tropics may do to man, it certainly offers optimum conditions for forest growth. It is just as easy to grow three crops of mahogany in a century as one crop of oak. Not otherwise shall the conquest of Brazil attain its possible significance for man.

CHAPTER XX

CAN THE AMAZON BE CONQUERED?

How many human settlers will perish in new countries simply for not having understood the necessity of combining their efforts!
—Prince Kropotkin, *Mutual Aid.*

There are few situations more intriguing to the traveler than to be lying at midnight off Nossa Senhora de Belém do Grão Pará. The mouth of the mighty river in whose warm heart the bitter snows of bleak Andes have become gentle. Lights of the channel buoys, and the contentment of happy ships riding at anchor.

Blackness toward the west, and silence. How it calls to the heart of a wanderer! Naked Indians on the shores of the Xingú. Alligators basking in the mud. Birds of gorgeous plumage and strange fruits. The black current of the Negro between the yellow and the shore. Pastures, and pestilence, and poetry. Green mansions where dwell the fancies of a Hudson. The endless reaches that La Condamine first charted. Secluded glades where sunshine seldom enters but where the ghosts of Bates, and Wallace, and Agassiz still love to roam. It pulls with the force of a primal passion.

Yet somewhat about the Amazon repels like the hand of Death. On the map of water it is so black; on the map of men, so white! As white as the sands of Sahara or Gobi; or the Australian bush. As white as the tundras of Siberia.

Why is it that where Alexander von Humboldt a century and a quarter ago visioned thriving cities and a great civilization, there is a population of less than one to the square mile in an area as large as fifteen of our Mississippi Valley states?

Why is it that the forest which once, in the mind of man,

was linked to rubber as roundness is linked to a ball, a forest which would cover the whole plain between the Rockies and the Appalachians, in 1926 produces less than a few plantations in Sumatra?

Why is it that Belém, with half the continent of South America as a hinterland, is less important in the world's commerce than the port of Providence, with Rhode Island for a background?

Why has every optimistic prophet from Humboldt down ruined his reputation when he wrote of the Amazon?

Why does the jungle still grow serenely over the graves of the puny men who have been trying to dominate it for four hundred years? The fact is undeniable. Not without reason has a Brazilian author called the Amazon forest *O Inferno Verde*, the Green Inferno.

Before we descend into the bowels of this infernal enigma, let be build a portal to mark the place where we went down— many better men who have ventured into the labyrinth of Amazonian speculation have not returned. Let me set two substantial pillars: on the left I shall nail placards bearing in large letters the best things that can be said about the Amazon; on the right, the worst. Peering skeptically between them, perhaps we may discern a light moving distantly among the trees.

Alfred Russel Wallace, after his four years in the Amazon, came out as enthusiastic as Humboldt. I shall nail some of his dicta to the Pillar of Optimism:

It is a vulgar error that in the tropics the luxuriance of the vegetation overpowers the efforts of man. Just the reverse is the case; nature and the climate are nowhere so favorable to the laborer.

What advantages there are in a country where there is no stoppage of agricultural operations during winter, . . . where the least possible amount of clothing is the most comfortable, and where a hundred little necessities of a cold region are altogether superfluous. With regard to the climate, I repeat, that a man can work as well here as in the hot summer months in England, and that if he will only work three hours in the morning and three in the evening, he will produce more of the necessities and comforts of life than by twelve hours' daily labor at home.

I fearlessly assert that here the primeval forest can be converted into rich pasture and meadow land, into cultivated fields, gardens, and orchards, containing every variety of produce, with half the labor, and, what is of more importance, in less than half the time that would be required at home, even though there we had clear instead of forest ground to commence upon.

. . . . . .

Now, I unhesitatingly affirm, that two or three families, containing half a dozen working and industrious men and boys, and being able to bring a capital in goods of fifty pounds, might, in three years, be in possession of all I have mentioned.[1]

Wallace wrote in 1853. Misled by such overoptimistic reports, some two hundred disgruntled Southerners emigrated after our Civil War and located a colony about Santarém, near the mouth of the Tapajós, to put Mr. Wallace's theories to the test. Many of them were irresponsible adventurers from Mobile, but this riffraff was soon eliminated. The families that Herbert Smith visited in 1874 fulfilled all the conditions that Wallace postulated. The American colony had then dwindled to about fifty souls; but these were people from Tennessee, Mississippi, and Alabama who knew how the frontier game should be played; lean, hard men with their wives and children, men who had come to stay. Their experience will have to be nailed to the Pillar of Pessimism. Smith found them, after seven years of hard struggle, burdened with debts, living in squalor, with broken-down bodies and discouraged hearts.[2] Our commercial attaché at Rio de Janeiro, who has just visited the region as chief of the crude rubber survey in Brazil, informs me that today (1926) there are not more than twelve or fifteen left, including the second generation! The only North American in that Santarém colony who can be said to have made a success was a man who started with a very considerable capital.

[1] *Travels on the Amazon and Rio Negro* (London, 1853).
[2] H. H. Smith, *Brazil, the Amazons and the Coast*, p. 141.

On the right-hand pillar, too, must be posted the long list of insect pests which torment man and devour his crops.[3]

And on the gloomy side of the gate belong two very telling statements by Colonel G. E. Church, who probably knew South America as a whole as well as any American who has ever lived:

It has been argued that the tribes of Amazonia lacked the mental qualities necessary to enable them to emerge from their savage state; but the question may be asked, What has civilized man been able to accomplish during the four centuries he has occupied the valley? Does he also lack the attributes or fitness to combat the forces of nature, develop and utilize the resources of the valley, and make it the home of one or more great peoples? *In reality, with all his advantages, he is worse fed there than were his aboriginal predecessors.*[4]

The second is even more startling, and, I think, equally true:

. . . there are probably not 25 square miles of its [the Amazon] basin under cultivation, excluding the limited and rudely cultivated areas among the mountains at its extreme headwaters, which are inaccessible to commerce. The extensive exports of the mighty valley are almost entirely derived from the products of the forest.[5]

To complete my portal of descent, let a beam be thrown across to connect the solid post of optimism with the pillar of well grounded pessimism. Upon it let there be chiseled in bold letters one word—RAIN. For whatever man can and may do, the Amazon will remain as wet as the Sahara is dry. Damp, steaming, muggy in the "dry" season. During the "rainy" season, slippery, soft mud; roaring, flooded streams; soaked, drowned, disheartened inhabitants. Such a mountain of a fact is this that I am inclined to say the basic problem of the conquest of the Amazon is: Can man be happy in the rain?

Were there ten times twenty-five square miles under culti-

[3] See Chap. III, § 6.
[4] *Aborigines of South America* (London, 1912), pp. 13-14.
[5] *Ency. Brit.*, article "Amazon," by G. E. Church.

vation in an empire as extensive as the Amazon Basin, yet should we have to say there is no agriculture whatever. Such meager results are below my limit of vision. If the present generation of Brazilians in the Amazon is worse fed and no better housed than the naked Indians in the malocas of primitive communism (and I, for one, believe it); if the Madeira-Mamoré Railway, which was to send a thrill all up and down the spine of the great inland waterway, is scarce able to get one train a week over a roadbed which seems determined to revert to jungle, we must say that the first four hundred years of Portuguese-Brazilian nibbling has not even made a hole in the rind of this mammoth green cheese. On one side of the ledger, four hundred years of paddling up and down the river; on the other side of the account, the destruction of most of the aboriginal population and the mutilation of a few rubber trees.

Here, then, is a hard nut to crack. But it should never be forgot that some things which are hard for one generation become easy for another. When confronting a naked Zulu armed with an assegai, the lion appears as a rather formidable beast; but before an Englishman with a high-power rifle, it more often appears as a somewhat cowardly cat. How many generations of men stood on the brink of Niagara awed by the force of such prodigies of falling water that they felt utterly insignificant in its presence! Modern hydro-electric engineers, however, have harnessed that "unconquerable" cataract in the service of man. In the heat and moisture of the Amazon inheres a fertility, a fecundity of life, which is to the forces men harness in the plowed fields of the temperate zone as Niagara is to the Hudson. So great a force that thus far—in Brazil—men have not been able to make the slightest impression on the evergreen hardwood forest. But I am unable to look at the plantations and populations of Java, Sumatra, and the Philippines, and doubt that the world will see a generation of men who will harness the prodigies of fertility and power which indubitably inhere in the Amazon Basin; just as

Niagara has been bent to the will of man. And in full view
of the wreckage of prophecy strewn around the reputations of
my illustrious predecessors, I venture to prophesy the way
Amazon conquest will come about.

Let us enter the portal I have built and adorned with the
words of wise men.

In the third chapter I discriminated the flat Amazonian
trough from the highland above the fall line. Here it is necessary to make a sharp distinction between two regions in the
trough itself, the flood plain and the dry land (*terra firme*).
The flood plain varies from fifteen to more than one hundred
miles in width, and extends along the Amazon proper from its
mouth almost to the Andes. There are flood plains likewise
along the lower reaches of the lateral affluents. This is land
recently built by the rivers, nowhere more than a few inches
above the highest flood and much of it inundated annually.
As the equator rocks back and forth beneath the sun, a pul-
sation in the rainfall is set up which gives rise to great rhythmic
floods. In the Lower Amazon below Óbidos, high water will
not be more than thirty-five feet above low water. Up at
Teffé, on the Upper Amazon, there are two annual pulsations,
the one in November and December amounting to only fifteen
or twenty feet, the June freshet attaining forty-five. The dark
veins on the brow of the Purús region stand out to sixty feet
when that river gets excited.

The flood plain of the Lower Amazon shows vast extensions of grassy meadow, alternately flooded and baked, in
patches sewn together by deceptive seams of forest. The
flood plain of the Upper Amazon is mostly forested. On the
flood one may canoe through the forest for hundreds of miles
along the river, ducking branches which, at low water, would
be thirty feet above one's head.

The dry land lies back of the flood plain and is high enough
so that it never is affected by the highest flood. There are
islands and hills of this solid ground scattered here and there
through the flood plain, too.

Now it is evident that the flood plain is precisely the most difficult, unhealthy, and mosquito-infested part of the whole proposition. Cattle pastured on the meadows there have luxuriant grass when the floods subside but starve by the thousands when the water comes up. It is alternate feast and famine for the people as well. Yet it is precisely on the margins of the rivers, *and nowhere else,* that man has made his attack. The whole present white population of the Amazon is perched on the little islands of dry land which pop up here and there in the flood plain. I doubt if man will make much more progress here in a thousand years than he has made in four hundred.

But as you go back from the great rivers things begin to look up. The solid ground in the Amazon trough is infinitely better as a human habitation than the swamps of the flood plain; the highland above the fall line is infinitely better as a human habitation than the solid ground of the trough.

If that be more than the vaporings of a winter-bound New Englander longing to be back between Cancer and Capricorn, then the place to attack the Amazon Basin is from the high plateau of Central Brazil and not from the stagnant sloughs where malarial mosquitoes breed. Leave the mud flats to the alligators. Conquer from the south!

And the weapon with which to attack the Amazon is not frontier individualism, but modern collectivism armed with the keen-cutting weapons of science.

For North Americans, there is a close analogy in the winning of the West. When our frontier democracy reached the arid lands and the Rockies, no conquest was possible without governmental aid, coöperative action, and a large capital. "In a word, the physiographic province itself decreed that this new frontier should be social rather than individual," [6] precisely as the character of the Amazon itself decrees that this frontier shall be social rather than individual.

Primitive communism was the weapon which enabled the

[6] Frederick Turner, *The Frontier in American History,* p. 257.

Indian to cope with Nature in the forests of the Liquid Confederation. He watched the peccary metamorphose itself into
a formidable foe when attacked by the jaguar—by a simple
manifestation of group solidarity. He studied that most social
of birds, the parrot. He learned the meaning of mutual aid
from the gregarious monkey. And I would ask, in what way,
pray, is the rank individualism of the Brazilian pioneer an improvement upon the primitive communism of the Indian if, as
Colonel Church maintains, he is worse fed there than were his
aboriginal predecessors?

Likewise, and by the same token, modern collectivism is
the only weapon that will enable the Brazilian to beat the
savage in the Amazonian environment. Here we have our
finger on the chief difference between the civilization of the
Anglo-Saxon and that of the South American Latins.[7] And
Brazil will need to avail herself of the power of collective
action in all its forms: extralegal, voluntary associations; the
full force of governmental aid; the social force of the great
corporation wielding large masses of capital; and better devices as yet unborn.

I envisage the conquest of the Amazon as a continuation,
in time and in space, of the conquest of Goyaz and Matto
Grosso. When a dense and intelligently coöperating civilization has developed on the high plateau where the southern
affluents of the Amazon have their sources, the frontier will
roll northward decade by decade—century by century, perhaps—but it will roll! It will not be a process of throwing
a degredado into the bush in the hope that he may escape the
teeth of his enemies. It will be battle. Each advance will be
planned with infinite care and detail. The determined engineers and sanitarians of a farsighted government will make
their reconnaissance of the terrain ahead of the shock troops,
whose battle losses will be heavy enough in any case. Every
inch gained will be consolidated by an army of agriculturists,
herdsmen, and mechanics. Their produce will not have to

[7] See Lester F. Ward, *Pure Sociology*, p. 567.

gallop madly down over the thousand rapids and crawl through the malarial flats of the great rivers, but will come south to market over the railroads that shall bind the Amazon to the civilization of Minas and São Paulo as intimately as a porcupine is bound to its quills.

Whether or not this attack will ever go through until the outposts look down upon the world's mightiest river, pulsating in the swamps of its flood plain like a gorged anaconda, is of no moment. When the highlands and Amazonian *terra firme* have been conquered, it will be time enough to talk about the winning of the swamp. For the next hundred years, at least, the Amazon lowlands which are accessible by steamboat will yield most if they are regarded as a purely forest property. By all means let us have as many people as possible there producing food and herding cattle. But until the day comes when the railroads of the Plateau run down to the landings of the river steamer, let the forester, rather than the agriculturist, be the right-hand man and chief adviser of the lowland statesman.

Porto Alegre, the capital of Rio Grande do Sul. (See page 191.)

The docks at Santos. No North American harbor has port works which are as rat-proof. (See page 343.)

Many vistas of rare beauty open in the narrow channels in the Straits of Breves, Lower Amazon, west of the island of Marajó, when the steamer winds in and out between palm-fringed banks. (See page 201.)

The port of Paranaguá, the outlet for the wealth of Paraná. The Serra do Mar can be seen dimly in the background. (See page 189.)

Botafogo Bay, an arm of the great Bay of Guanabára, which extends far to the left.

Rio de Janeiro, the loveliest city that sits beside the seven seas.

A rocky island in the Archipelago dos Alcatrazes, off the São Paulo shore, typical of this bold coast.

CHAPTER XXI

POPULATION POSSIBILITIES

No theorem was ever more warmly debated than was Malthus's proposition that population tends to multiply beyond the limits of subsistence. . . . In the discussions of half a century ago, it was assumed by the disputants on both sides that over-population is an evil, and an evil only. We know now that it is only the overmultiplying population that makes progress. Wealth, art, learning, and refinement, presuppose a certain density of population and active competition. Where these co-exist the struggle for existence has been known in full severity. Social sympathies and powers of abstract thought have not appeared until men have had to stand by one another and have learned to live by their wits, and these beginnings of wisdom have come to birth only when numbers have pressed hard upon subsistence,—not upon resources, not upon potential subsistence, but upon that actual subsistence obtained by the industrial methods at the time in vogue.

—GIDDINGS, *Democracy and Empire.*

ON the Map of Man,[1] certain areas are shown in white—less than three human beings to the square mile. Australia, all but the eastern fringe, and New Guinea are white. White the deserts of Mongolia and the steppes of Siberia, Arabia, and the Sahara, and southwest Africa. In North America, Lower California, much of the Great Plains, and practically everything north of the fiftieth parallel. In South America, southern Argentina, the Chaco of northern Argentina and western Paraguay, the deserts of Chili and Bolivia. And then a great white splash that covers fully three-fourths of Brazil, including the entire Amazon Basin.

This distribution of mankind is by no means final. In Asia and Europe there has been a dense enough population for sufficient time to have proved out the regions which can support masses of humanity. But that is not yet true in North America. And South America has never felt the slightest pressure of population upon natural resources. Present dis-

[1] See, for instance, Brunhes, *Human Geography,* p. 72; also map of Brazilian population, p. 163.

tribution there represents nothing but the road of least resistance.

If my ideas about the possibility of ultimately conquering most of the Amazon prove correct, there is less land in Brazil which—when subjected to the pressure of a great population equipped with the commonplaces of the applied science of Europe and the United States—the human race will find unfit to serve basic wants of man, than in any like extent of territory upon the face of the earth.

We live in an economically integrating world; so rapidly integrating that sovereignty is becoming meaningless. South American sovereignties which are still debating the ancient issue of Church and State will do well to wake up to the fact that certain powers of the temperate zone have arrived at a far more intimate union of Business and State. A crowded, seething, unsentimental globe.

Now, however good the process of crowding and struggle may be for cultural results, the men caught in the meshes of the machine always feel pinched. Boys playing baseball on the city streets can never be convinced that they should not occupy the vacant lot. Men whose numbers begin to press hard upon subsistence are ever eager to migrate to the free lands.

Since the last descent of the Barbarians upon western Europe, the bulk of the population of the earth, the millions of Asia, has been bottled up. The "St. Bartholomew's Day" which Spaniards perpetrated in the Philippines, served notice on the Chinaman that those lovely islands were closed to migrations from the Asiatic mainland. As soon as the Japanese showed appreciation of the Hawaiian Islands, the United States evinced a rather discouraging fondness for the same territory. Since we built the Union Pacific Railroad with Chinese coolies, most of the mainland of North America has been tabu. A Hindu is about as welcome in Canada as the ex-Kaiser at Buckingham Palace. Australia is psychologically as white as the North Pole. South Africa is not notoriously pro-Asiatic. Asia is fermenting liquor, bottled up; 900 million men caught in the meshes of the machine feel pinched.

During the nineteenth century, men who felt the pinch of Europe freely migrated to the United States. Except Asiatics, she welcomed all comers and gave them homesteads of 160 acres of land out of the public domain. From the immigration restrictions imposed since the World War, it is evident that the United States has reached the conclusion that she can develop her domain with the natural increase of her own great population. The sign, "Standing Room Only," has been hung outside the ticket window. In any case, her population will reach the two hundred million mark during the present century. As soon as there are two hundred million people in the United States, some men are going to feel a pressure of population upon the actual subsistence. Men whose numbers begin to press hard upon subsistence are ever eager to migrate to the free lands. These will be a hard crowd to bottle up if they ever take a notion to go.

The European today who desires to strike new roots where there is room to swagger and strut a bit, still has the choice— outside of the tropics—among New Zealand, Australia, Canada, South Africa, Chili, Argentina, Paraguay, Uruguay, and southern Brazil. The capacity for absorption of all these together is less than was that of the United States in the nineteenth century. Australia is mostly very dry. New Zealand is not large, nor is Africa south of Capricorn. Most of Canada lies north of the isotherm of crops and comfort. South America below the fortieth parallel will not accommodate a large population. But it should be evident to a blind man that—government and present social conditions aside—as far as the natural factors of climate, soil, and resources go, South America between the twentieth and fortieth parallels has more to offer migrant mankind than has any of the dominions of the British Empire.

I have stated my faith that the only possible way to conquer the Amazon is to build up a dense population on the plateau to the south. But leaving tropical Brazil entirely out of the question, it is evident that the most densely populated states are still underpopulated. Much of the strictly temperate states of São Paula, Paraná, and Santa Catharina is as virgin today as in 1500. Beautiful country, rich, cool, high, delightful, well watered. It should be filled up.

From every point of view it would seem highly desirable for Brazil to add to her body politic by a large immigration, and that immediately. Today she can pick and choose her immigrants from all Europe and Asia. But if she fill up no faster than during the first four centuries, it is conceivable that by the year 2000 she might have to welcome those who choose to come. Why not? There are nations in the world today as much more powerful than Brazil, as Portugal was more powerful than the Brazilians of 1500. Monroe Doctrine? What if the good old shepherd dog that has kept the Americas from the wolves this hundred years should itself turn predatory, as did sixteenth century Portugal? Who can view the madness that recently possessed Germany? who can view the tendency of the United States increasingly to concern herself with the affairs of Mexico and the republics of the Caribbean? and prophesy what a nation two hundred million strong, in the year 2000, may do if economic power continue to gravitate into her hands?

Brazil is the only Latin-American nation with the physical plant to make parity of power with the United States a possibility. I, for one, should like to see that potentiality developed to the full.

As to ways and means, Brazil wisely has kept the door open to Asiatics, the best agriculturists in the world. It is likely, however, that she will continue to draw chiefly upon the easily assimilated Mediterranean peoples, and make an effort to obtain an increasing proportion of literate immigrants. But numbers Brazil must have if the conquest is to continue toward a conclusion.

How is Brazil to get numbers? In considering what bait

is most attractive to the immigrant, the query inevitably presents itself, Why have the great tides of European immigration hitherto sought the temperate English-speaking dominions and relatively shunned equally blessed *temperate* Latin territory? Greater freedom in trade. Greater freedom in religion. Better public schools. State universities. But the greatest drawing-card ever dangled before the eyes of a population beginning to press upon subsistence was that parcel of 160 acres of land which Uncle Sam during the nineteenth century presented to every European peasant with backbone enough to go after it. A homestead for the homeless. Land for the landless.

Were I a responsible Brazilian statesman, I should agitate unceasingly for a survey of all remaining public lands; and for homestead laws that, without fuss or formality, would give any capable, hard-working immigrant as real a stake in the country as the landlords now possess. Having located him on lands connected to civilization by roads, I should try to keep him in health, and to give his children a better education than their father's. Then, as I ambled about on my gaited saddle stallion viewing the swift increase of national strength and soundness, I should gaze off toward the bottled-up hordes of the Orient and the darkening northern horizon with entire unconcern, knowing that equality is one quality which every man respects.

ABOUT BOOKS ON BRAZIL

North American friends in Brazil who had no access to the older works, many of them procurable now only by diligent search of the secondhand markets, showed great interest in my collection of books on Brazil and often requested that I list those most worth reading. The following is a select bibliography of books in English that seem to me valuable and interesting to the general reader, with the date of publication. An equally interesting list could be made of books in German, French, or Portuguese. And a volume could be devoted to listing works on Brazil in all languages which are worse than worthless.

1809 ANDREW GRANT, M.D., *History of Brazil* (London).
1810 ROBERT SOUTHEY, *History of Brazil,* Part I (London).
   This is a tremendous work based on original Portuguese documents. Part II was published in 1817; Part III in 1819.
1812 JOHN MAWE, *Travels in the Interior of Brazil* (London).
   Mawe was a mineralogist with long experience in South America who was sent to Diamantina to report on the diamond mines by the Crown of Portugal, the first English writer to journey in Minas Geraes.
1820 JOHN LUCCOCK, *Notes on Rio de Janeiro and the Southern Parts of Brazil.*
1820 PRINCE MAXIMILIAN OF WIED-NEUWIED, *Travels in Brazil in the Years* 1815, 1816, 1817 (London).
1821 JAMES HENDERSON, *A History of the Brazil* (London).
   Based entirely on a Portuguese work, but interesting.
1822 MARTIN DOBRIZHOFFER, *An Account of the Abipones, an Equestrian People of Paraguay;* translated from the Latin by Sara Coleridge (London); 3 vols.
   Dobrizhoffer was a Jesuit priest who spent his life among the Indians. His fascinating work is the best account extant on the equestrian Indians of Argentina, Paraguay, and southern Brazil.
1824 SPIX and MARTIUS, *Travels in Brazil in the Years* 1817-1820 (London). 2 vols.
   A classic of early exploration. These two famous scientists rode from São Paulo to Maranhão and then went up the Amazon; unfortunately, the English translation follows them only as far as Bahia.
1830 REV. R. WALSH, *Notices of Brazil in* 1828 *and* 1829 (London). 2 vols.
1836 W. SMYTH and F. LOWE, *From Lima to Pará* (London).
   British officers so busy getting through alive that they did not see as much as they might.
1845 DANIEL P. KIDDER, *Sketches of Residence and Travels in Brazil* (Philadelphia). 2 vols.
1846 GEORGE GARDNER, *Travels in the Interior of Brazil* (London).

A botanist who spent four years collecting in Ceará, Piauhy, Goyaz, and Minas Geraes.

1849 H.R.H. PRINCE ADALBERT OF PRUSSIA, *Travels in Brazil;* translated by Sir Robert H. Schomburgk and John Edward Taylor (London). 2 vols.

The narrative of an adventuring junket up the Xingú by Adalbert and Prince Bismarck, when both were young men.

1853 ALFRED RUSSEL WALLACE, *A Narrative of Travels on the Amazon and Rio Negro* (London).

An invaluable picture of the two rivers and of the inhabitants, flora, and fauna of the Amazon.

1854 LIEUTS. WM. HERNDON and LARDNER GIBBON, U.S.N., *Exploration of the Valley of the Amazon* (Washington). 2 vols.

How these two young naval officers put through two expeditions by separate routes, from the Pacific to Atlantic, on an appropriation of $5,000, is one of the fine tales in the history of American exploration. Their books are rich in information.

1856 THOMAS EWBANK, *Life in Brazil* (New York).

HENRY WALTER BATES, *The Naturalist on the River Amazons* (London).

A classic record of eleven years collecting in the evergreen hardwood forest.

1865 W. D. CHRISTIE, Late H.M. Envoy Extraordinary and Minister Plenipotentiary in Brazil, *Notes on Brazilian Questions* (London).

Relates to slavery and the contraband trade.

1866 REV. JAMES C. FLETCHER and REV. D. P. KIDDER, *Brazil and the Brazilians* (Boston).

What these two missionaries did not know about the Brazil of their day was not worth knowing.

1867 PROF. and MRS. LOUIS AGASSIZ, *A Journey in Brazil* (Boston).

A lively narrative of a great scientific mission by the wife of the great Harvard professor. It is amusing now to see how far from the facts Agassiz permitted his enthusiasm for glaciation to carry him.

1869 SIR RICHARD BURTON, *The Highlands of Brazil* (London). 2 vols.

This is another classic, an account of a mule-back journey through Minas Geraes and the descent of the Rio São Francisco, by one of the greatest travelers and explorers that ever lived.

1870 JAMES ORTON, *The Andes and the Amazon* (New York).

1870 CH. FRED HARTT, *Geology and Physical Geography of Brazil* (Boston).

Mostly non-technical and very readable. Poor Hartt died down there.

1875 FRANZ KELLER, *The Amazon and Madeira Rivers* (Philadelphia).

1878 THOMAS P. BIGG-WITHER, *Pioneering in South Brazil.*

1878 C. B. BROWN and WM. LIDSTONE, *Fifteen Thousand Miles on the Amazon and Its Tributaries.*

1879 HERBERT H. SMITH, *Brazil, the Amazons and the Coast* (New York).

Smith, later professor of geology in Cornell, knew the Lower Amazon as few men. *Scribner's* sent him into Ceará during the terrible drought of the late seventies. His style is delightful.

1887 JAMES W. WELLS, *Three Thousand Miles Through Brazil* (London). 2 vols.

Wells was an engineer whose work made him thoroughly familiar with the Northeast.

1887 C. C. ANDREWS, ex-Consul General to Brazil, *Brazil, Its Conditions and Prospects.*

1901 BARON DE SANTA-ANNA NERY, *The Land of the Amazons;* trans. from the French by George Humphrey, F.R.G.S. (London).

1907 NEVILLE B. CRAIG, *Recollections of an Ill-Fated Expedition* (Philadelphia and London).
The story of the first attempt to build the Madeira-Mamoré Railway, by one of the engineers; an enthralling story of daring and disaster.

1908 RICHARD SPRUCE, *Notes of a Botanist on the Amazon and Andes* (London). 2 vols.

1910 NEVIN O. WINTER, *Brazil and Her People of Today.*

1911 HENRY C. PEARSON, *The Rubber Country of the Amazon* (New York).

1911 PIERRE DENIS, *Brazil;* translated from the French by Bernard Miall (London).
M. Denis is a trained geographer, and his book is perhaps the best of all the recent works on Brazil.

1912 COL. GEORGE EARL CHURCH, *Aborigines of South America* (London).
Col. Church, the original promoter of the Madeira-Mamoré Railway, was an American Civil War veteran who knew South America backwards and forwards. He at one time was vice-president of the Royal Geographical Society. Indians are but one of many interests. It is not the work of an anthropologist.

1912 W. E. HARDENBURG, *The Putumayo, the Devil's Paradise* (London).
Narrative of atrocities committed by Peruvians in the rubber country.

1912 J. B. WOODWORTH, *Geological Expedition to Brazil and Chili, 1908-1909* (Harvard).
Chiefly technical.

G. J. BRUCE, *Brazil and the Brazilians.*

1914 FRANK BENNETT, *Forty Years in Brazil.*

1914 THEODORE ROOSEVELT, *Through the Brazilian Wilderness* (New York).
The narrative of the descent of the Rio Roosevelt by the Rondon-Roosevelt Expedition.

1915 THOMAS WHIFFEN, F.R.G.S., *The Northwest Amazons* (New York).
Notes of some months spent among cannibal tribes.

1919 CLAYTON SEDGWICK COOPER, *The Brazilians and Their Country* (London).

1920 E. C. BULEY, *South Brazil* (New York).

1921 E. C. BULEY, *North Brazil* (New York).

1925 HERMAN GERLACH JAMES, *Brazil After a Century of Independence* (New York).

The North American who expended most study on Brazil was the geologist, the late John C. Branner, one-time president of Leland Stanford University. His writings on Brazil are voluminous, but mostly on scientific subjects. Whoever travels in Brazil, however, should know his *Brief Grammar of the Portuguese Language.*

INDEX

403

INDEX